THE HISTORY OF

Magic

AND THE OCCULT

THE HISTORY OF

Magic

AND THE
OCCULT

KURT SELIGMANN

Harmony Books/New York

Copyright, 1948 by Pantheon Books, renewed © 1975 by
Arlette Seligmann

All rights reserved. No part of this book may be
reproduced or transmitted in any form or by any means,
electronic or mechanical, including photocopying,
recording, or by any information storage and retrieval
system, without permission in writing from the
publisher.

Published by Harmony Books, a division of Crown
Publishers, Inc., One Park Avenue, New York, New York
10016 and simultaneously in Canada by General
Publishing Company Limited by arrangement with
Pantheon Books.

HARMONY and colophon are trademarks of Crown
Publishers, Inc.

Manufactured in the United States of America

Library of Congress Cataloging in Publication Data

Seligmann, Kurt, 1900–1962.
    The history of magic and the occult.

    Bibliography: p.
    Includes index.
    1. Magic—History.   2. Occult sciences—History.
I. Title.
BF1589.S4   1983   133.4′09   83-12570
ISBN 0-517-55008-3
ISBN 0-517-55129-2 (pbk.)

10 9 8 7 6 5 4 3 2 1

First Harmony Edition

To Arlette

Contents

CONTENTS

List of Illustrations

The fairest thing we can experience is the mysterious.
Albert Einstein

Acknowledgements

Grateful acknowledgement is herewith made to the following publishers for their kind permission to quote from titles published by them: to D. Appleton-Century Co., Inc., publishers of Ian Ferguson's *Philosophy of Witchcraft*; to CIBA Pharmaceutical Products, Inc., Summit, N. J., publishers of William J. Wilson's 'The Greek Alchemical Papyri', which appeared in *CIBA Symposia*, vol. 3, No. 5 (1941); to the Columbia University Press, publishers of A. V. William Jackson's *Zoroastrian Studies*; to the Dial Press, publishers of C. L'Estrange Ewen's *Witch Hunting and Witch Trials*; to Houghton Mifflin Co., publishers of *The Making of the Modern Mind*, by John H. Randall, Jr; to the Macmillan Co., for material from *Folklore in the Old Testament* and *The Golden Bough*, both by James G. Frazer; to Charles Scribner's Sons, publishers of James H. Breasted's *A History of Egypt*.

The quotations from Philostratus are reprinted by permission of the publishers from the Loeb Classical Library edition of *The Life of Apollonius of Tyana*, vol. I, translated by F. C. Conybeare, Cambridge, Mass., Harvard University Press, 1917; for which kindness grateful acknowledgement is herewith made.

Thanks are also due to the British Museum, the Metropolitan Museum of Art, New York, the University Museum, Philadelphia, and the Mansell Collection, London, for their courtesy in allowing the reproduction of some of their pictorial material.

Introductory Note

The aim of this book is to present to the general reader a condensed account of the magical ideas and operations in the civilized Western world. Because of the character of the book a vast material had to be sifted and reduced to what I considered most typical. Such a condensation, however, may convey more to the lay reader than a lengthy dissertation on an inexhaustible theme.

Magic has been treated mainly in two different ways. The specialized works of scholars are confined to specific types, aspects and eras; generally, they are written for the scientific reader. On the other hand, there are innumerable publications of questionable value expounding ideas rarely based on fact, but twisting the truth into a narrow system of a special brand: that of the sectarian of the occult. Only a few authors on magic have written for the general reader, a fact which will perhaps justify this publication.

I make no great claim to original scholarship; my investigation has been guided by such scholarly works as those of J. G. Frazer, A. von Harnack, G. L. Kittredge, Fr J. Boll, L. Thorndike and others. In addition, my personal library of old books on magic and witchcraft facilitated the investigation and permitted me to select a wealth of illustrations which the reader will no doubt welcome. As an artist, I was concerned with the aesthetic value of magic and its influence upon man's creative imagination. The relics of ancient peoples indicate that religio-magical beliefs have given a great impulse to artistic activities, a stimulus which outlasted paganism and produced belated flowers in the era of Christianity.

I wish to express my gratitude to the following persons who have helped me in assembling and coordinating material for this book: Miss Henrietta Weigel, Ralph Hyams, Martin James, Miss Edith Porada, Marc Pagano

THE HISTORY OF

Magic
AND THE
OCCULT

MESOPOTAMIA

The Forgetful Gods

From time immemorial, man has felt himself to be confronted with evil supernatural beings, and his weapon against them has been the use of magical rites. Spirits lurked everywhere. Larvae and lemures lived beneath the earth; vampires escaped from the dead to attack the living; Namtar (pestilence) and Idpa (fever) plagued the cities. Night was ruled by the demons of evil, of the desert, of the abyss, of the sea, of the mountains, of the swamp, of the south wind. There were the succubi and the incubi, carriers of obscene nightmares; the snare-setting Maskim; the evil Utuq, dweller of the desert; the bull demon Telal; and Alal the destroyer. People's minds were dominated by malign demons who demanded sacrifices and prayers. But the sages of ancient civilizations knew also that good spirits existed, ever ready to come to the rescue of the afflicted. In the higher magical religions, the priests conceived a supreme deity, a wise controller of the world's harmony.

Amid such fears and wonders lived the river peoples of the Tigris and Euphrates: the legendary Sumerians who had settled in the lower Euphrates valley five thousand years before Christ; the dark-skinned Akkadians who had established themselves in the region of Babylon three thousand years before our era; the Elamites, ancestors of the Persians whom we can trace back to the fourth millennium; the star-wise Babylonians, founders of a world empire; the Assyrians, first vassals of Babylon, subsequently conquerors of western Asia and Egypt; and again the Medes, whose glory had seemed everlasting until the Persians achieved hegemony over all Asiatic lands.

In the broad plains, on terraces of temples and towers, the priests scanned the night sky, pondering over the riddle of the universe – the cause of all being, of life and death. They offered their prayers to the spirit of Hea, the earth, and to the spirit of Ana, the sky. By conjuration, by the burning of incense, by shouts and by whispers, by gesture and by song, the priests sought to attract the attention of the fickle gods who had forever to be reminded of the misfortunes of mortals. 'Remember,' the incantations were always reiterating: 'Remember him who makes sacrifices – may forgiveness and peace flow for him like molten brass: may this man's days be vivified by the sun! – Spirit of the Earth, remember! Spirit of the Sky, remember!'*[1]

Not only were the demons to be feared; but also within man

* References are listed on p. 323.

himself lived dangerous powers. If magic was a protector, it was likewise a destroyer, a formidable weapon in the hands of criminals who used it to attain evil ends. The sorcerer believed himself to be beyond laws and religious commandments, casting spells and reciting incantations to kill at random:

> The imprecation acts upon man like an evil demon. The screaming voice is upon him. The maleficent voice is upon him. The malicious imprecation is the cause of his disease. The maleficent imprecation strangles this man as if he were a lamb. The god in his body made the wound, the goddess gives him anxiety. The screaming voice, like that of the hyena, has overcome him and masters him.[2]

Some sorcerers were believed to possess the evil eye, which enabled them to kill by merely glancing at their victims: of others it was said that they created images of their enemies which they burned or punctured with pins, depending upon the amount of harm they desired to inflict.

> He who forges the image, he who enchants –
> The spiteful face, the evil eye,
> The mischievous mouth, the mischievous tongue,
> The mischievous lips, the mischievous words,
> Spirit of the Sky, remember!
> Spirit of the Earth, remember![3]

There were incantations against the innumerable operations of black magic, against the ever-present demons which pass like snakes furtively into the house, preventing women from conceiving, stealing children, sometimes descending upon the land like pillaging Asiatic warriors.

> They fall on one land after the other,
> They raise the slave above his rank,
> They cast the freewoman out of the house where she gave birth,
> They cast the young birds out of their nests into emptiness,
> They drive the oxen before them, they drive away the lamb,
> The evil, the cunning demons.[4]

But voices of peace are also heard amid the fear and the tumult, and hymns of worship alternate with conjurations. A broken tablet still reads in cuneiform characters: 'The garlands . . . exalted shepherd . . . on the thrones and altars . . . the marble sceptre . . . exalted shepherd, King, shepherd of the peoples. . . .' These peaceful songs cease when Namtar, the pernicious demon, unfolds his black wings. Then the afflicted are reminded of Mulge, lord of the abyss, and the planets, his kin. In deadly terror they call upon the gods and the spirits whom they had forgotten in their prosperity, for men are forgetful just as the gods whom they shaped in their image.

> Spirit of Mulge, Lord of the countries, remember.
> Spirit of Nin-gelal, Lady of the countries, remember.
> Spirit of Nindar, mighty warrior of Mulge, remember.
> Spirit of Paku, sublime intelligence of Mulge, remember.
> Spirit of En-Zuna, son of Mulge, remember.
> Spirit of Tishku, Lady of the hosts, remember.
> Spirit of Udu, King of Justice, remember. . . .*[5]

* Mulge is the master of hell; Nin-gelal is the earth; Nindar is Saturn; Paku is Mercury; En-Zuna is the moon; Tishku is Venus; Udu is the sun.

Such is the nature of the cuneiform inscriptions that have come to us from the royal library at Nineveh, which, in the seventh century B.C., King Ashurbanipal had compiled from the ancient Akkadian texts. These had long since become unintelligible, but precisely for this reason even greater powers were ascribed to them. It was taken for granted that, since these mysterious formulas had been recited for ages, they were still efficacious. Similar beliefs that the magic word must not be altered existed among other nations of antiquity, beliefs which, indeed, with slight modifications, survive in our day. Veneration for the original word of the Scriptures is stressed in our time by Catholics and Jews who recite their prayers in Latin or Hebrew, in spite of the fact that these languages are dead, just as Akkadian was during the reign of Ashurbanipal.

The ancient Akkadian texts clearly show these people's conception of the supernatural. For them, good and evil are caused by good or evil spirits sent forth by good and evil gods. Their world is dualistic, the stage of undecided combat between the forces of light and dark. No moral distinction is made in this perennial struggle, in the belief that it is only through fatality that these forces are either good or bad. Good may well engender evil, as illustrated by Mulge, who, although not belonging essentially to the evil principle, yet begot Namtar, the most cruel of all demons. Good and evil are not even necessarily encamped in separate abodes: beneficent powers dwell in the dark abyss of Mulge, and spiteful forces live side by side with charitable ones. In these beliefs, man would have been the prey of chaos had he not employed magical arts to protect himself against evil influences.

Through magic, he established his society; it coordinated his daily life. The arts flourished, merchants attended to their business, troops manoeuvred in the plain, from the temples rose the smoke of sacrifices, hunters roamed the northern mountains, and in the king's palace the wise assembled to discuss affairs of state. These nations have left behind vestiges of their high culture; a refined taste, a sharp sense of beauty were predominant. Artisans made marvellous things from metal, stone, wood, shells and other materials; their works harmoniously united elegance with simplicity, ostentation with intimacy, humour with cruelty.

The ancient Elamites had created their gods in animal forms. But among the Sumero-Akkadians, human gods emerge from the beast. The animal is subdued and is made to conform to human ways. On the harp of the king of Ur is engraved the mythical hero Gilgamesh, embracing two rampant man-headed bulls. Lion and dog are depicted on their way to the sacrifice; a bear is holding a harp 'that fills with joy the temple courts', while a donkey is playing upon it, a jest that was also dear to the Middle Ages. On the bear's paw, a fox makes himself at home, drumming on a board and shaking his rattle under the muzzle of the carved bull's head which adorns the sounding box. A creature – half man, half scorpion – is about to dance. Standing on his hind-legs, a chamois shakes the rattles. These scenes represent the wild spirit of the dance.

1. Shell plaques from Ur

Joyous feasts alternate with solemn sacrifices, and everything is accomplished by magical operations that free the soul from fear and stimulate man's imagination. It was for magical purposes that images were carved, poems written, music played and public monuments erected.

Divinatory Arts

Demons were powerful, capable of killing man and beast, but they could not altogether destroy life, nor could they permanently disrupt the order of nature. An eclipse of the sun might cause panic; but ultimately the sun emerged victorious from this struggle against evil, for did it not rise and set day after day, with the seasons following one another, bringing sowing and harvesting? Man stimulated the rhythm of nature by incantation, dance and gesture; and the stars moved in accordance with immutable laws as if to bear witness to the harmony of the world.

With the progress of civilization, the early dualism was modified. In Chaldea, wise men discovered a higher order and a better law. By contemplation of the night sky, the Chaldean priests conceived a supreme god from whom sprang the other deities. This god was a creative power chained to the eternal law which he embodied, and submitting to his own decrees. A purer religion, based upon a philosophical system, was born from Akkad's demoniacal world.

About two thousand years before our era, a reform took place: a caste of priests was founded in whom all occult knowledge was concentrated. They were masters in the arts of prescience, predicting the future from the livers and intestines of slaughtered animals, from fire and smoke, and from the brilliancy of precious stones; they foretold events from the murmuring of springs and from the shape of plants. Trees spoke to them, as did serpents, 'wisest of all animals'. Monstrous births of animals and of men were believed to be portents, and dreams found skilful interpreters.

Atmospheric signs, rain, clouds, wind and lightning, were interpreted as forebodings; the cracking of furniture and wooden panels foretold future events. Such cracking was called Assaput, the prophetic voice; it did not always bode ill, sometimes presaging the 'rejoicing of the heart'. Flies and other insects, as well as dogs, were the carriers of occult messages.

If a red dog enters the temple, the gods will desert it.
If a dog is found lying upon the king's throne, the palace will be burned down.
If a white dog enters the temple, it will stand for a long time.
If a grey dog enters the temple, it will be deprived of its possessions.
If a yellow dog enters the king's palace, the palace will be destroyed.[6]

The Chaldeans sought also to prognosticate the future through arrow divination. In the writings of Ezekiel we read: 'The king of Babylon stands at the parting of the ways, at the fork of the two roads, practising divination; he shakes the arrows. . . .'

According to St Jerome, the king used the arrows for a strategic purpose. In order to know which city he should attack first, he marked his arrows with the names of his enemies. He put them into the quiver and, after shaking them, took out one of the arrows; the name it bore directed the army to its first attack.

The practices of divination may seem puerile or at least so primitive in character as to appear irreconcilable with the elaborate Chaldean cosmogony. However, such reasoning does not take into account the world concept of the Chaldeans, which was essentially magical, akin to that of the Egyptians, the Greeks and the Romans. We find similar 'superstitions' among all these peoples, where divination is the logical application of their theory of magic. To the magus, there exists no accidental happening; everything obeys the one law, which is not resented as a coercion but rather welcomed as a liberation from the tyranny of chance. The world and its gods submit to this law, which binds together all things and all events. *Certa stant omnia lege*: everything is established solidly by that law which the wise man discerns in happenings that appear accidental to the profane. The curve observed in the flight of birds, the barking of a dog, the shape of a cloud, are occult manifestations of that omnipotent coordinator, the source of unity and harmony.

The Mystery of Stars and Numbers

In the search for a supreme standard, a prototype of order and harmony, the priests looked to the heavens where, inaccessible, the stars move along. A minute and continuous observation of the heavenly bodies led them to that wisdom which we call astrology. In their everlasting round, the planet-gods were performing a pantomime, expressive of the law which ruled the universe. The stargazers understood the meaning of this harmonious play. They could foretell the configurations of the grandiose rondo and they knew also in what way the heavenly movement would affect happenings on earth. In the world hierarchy, the superior rules over the inferior, and the star-gods were the heavenly rulers of all that lay below.

Among them, the seven planets were the most powerful, 'the interpreter gods'. Jupiter-Marduk was the creator, the awakener of the dead, the victor over chaos. His bright star was a torch, 'a ruler of the sky'. When appearing in the moon aura, he bestowed male offspring. His influence was always favourable. The forebodings of the moon, Sin, were ambiguous because of its irregular phases. Growth was hindered by its contraction, stimulated by its expansion. The sun, Samas, carrier of life and light, was likewise ambiguous, bringing sometimes scorching and drought. Uncertain was Mercury, Nebo, the scribe and god of wisdom, who wrote down the deeds of men: knowledge can bring forth good and evil. Saturn, Adar, the god of hunting, was propitious to public affairs as well as to family life. But he too seems generally to exert evil influence; they called him the great misfortune.

Evil was Mars, Nergal, the god of the dead and of pestilence, causing war, and foretelling death to the king. He destroyed the wheat and the date harvest; he stunted the growth of cattle and fish roe. He was called the fiend, the Persian, the Fox, etc. Venus, Ishtar, the goddess of motherhood and love, was beneficent. From her emanated great healing power, by her vegetation is brought forth; however, she was dangerous to widows and to sucklings.

Besides the planets, the signs of the zodiac also are offsprings of Chaldean astrology, and six of its original figures still exist to this day. They are the Bull, the Twins, the Lion, the Balance, the Scorpion and the Fishes. Although little is known of their symbolism, it may be surmised that these figures originally were closely connected with earthly affairs. Thus the price of wheat was fixed according to the position of the heavenly Balance, rather than according to the quantity produced by the harvest. When the sign of the Fishes shone weakly, it meant that fish roe was affected adversely; when Nergal, the evil planet, approached the sign of the Scorpion, it meant that the king was about to die from a scorpion's sting.

In the astrologer's language, symbols and allegories were adopted which were enigmas to the profane. The sun sheds tears; Jupiter is surrounded by courtiers; the moon travels in a carriage and accepts various crowns from the stars she approaches, crowns of the evil wind, of anger, of happiness, of iron, of bronze, of copper and of gold. Venus seizes foreign goods and wears crowns of different colours according to her conjunction with Mars, Saturn, Mercury or Jupiter.[7]

These enigmatic images were expressed in the old tongue of Akkad or Sumer, the 'language of the gods', in which only the initiate conversed. The cosmic secrets were hidden from the people, because of the fear that knowledge of the future might either discourage them or cause them to abandon their daily work from joy. Those who had knowledge of the stars were more influential than king's ministers, and foreign rulers consulted them frequently. Diodorus of Sicily (first century of the Christian era) gives witness of their prestige: 'Having observed the stars during an enormous number of years,' he says, 'they know more precisely than anyone else the movements and the influence of the stars, and they predict with accuracy many things to come.'

From ancient times, the known world had been divided according to the four quarters of the sky. The south was Akkad (Babylonia); the north, Saburtu (Assyria); the east, Elam (Persia); the west, Syria and Palestine. The movements of the stars and other events in the sky were interpreted according to this astrological geography. Thus it was considered a natural thing when thunder resounded in the south, Akkad, whereas thunder from other directions was considered as an omen. On the twenty-ninth of the month, the moon was favourable to Akkad, but unfavourable to Amurru, etc. Of still greater intricacy was the Chaldean concept of star substitution. Its meaning has been a mystery until a recent discovery cast light upon it. In certain cases of star interpretation, a planet or a fixed star might be replaced by a constellation or zodiacal figure. Thus Saturn might be replaced by the Balance, by Cassiopeia, by Orion or by the Raven. This enigmatic relationship was based upon similarities of colour and strength of light among the stars. Heavenly bodies of the same luminosity and colour were believed to be related to one another, a theory which permitted many variations and subtleties in star interpretation.[8]

As far back as memory reached, metals were related to the underworld. They lay hidden in the hollow of the earth and no heavenly stars shone upon them; yet, in the wish to relate all earthly things to heaven, the astrologer saw an affinity between metals and planets, an idea which still haunted the medieval alchemists. To the Chaldeans gold was the metal of the sun, silver that of the moon, lead that of Saturn. Tin had its correspondence in Jupiter, iron in Mars and copper in Venus.

Like a mysterious incised seal representing the pre-established mathematical harmony of the universe, certain sacred numbers are to be found in the skies, numbers which seem to confirm the basic idea of astrology. They appear to assist each other and lend themselves to many speculations. Thus the number seven occurs in the main stars of the Great Bear and in the Lesser Bear, in the Pleiades and in Orion. Seven are the days of the moon quarters, seven are the planets of antiquity. Twelve and thirty seem to be mystically connected. Twelve are the zodiacal signs, thirty is the number of a moon period, and thirty are the years of Saturn's circuit. The product of twelve and thirty is the approximate number of the days of the year. Many such relations can be found. They offer to the indefatigable astrologer a wide field for his inquiries and quests. Together with astrology, the concept of mystic numbers came into being and, like astrology, numerology has survived through the ages with astounding vitality.[9]

Since the Chaldeans were such keen observers, it is difficult to believe that all their wisdom was of an arbitrary nature. No doubt many features of their knowledge were based on a true notion of meteorology, physics, chemistry and medicine. Let us not forget, however, that astrology, which has been the stimulus to many scientific discoveries, was also theology. In its vast domain there is nourishment for both spirit and soul, and there can be no doubt that astrology owes its longevity to its psychic rather than to its intellectual value. Yet it is good to remember also that the great astronomer Kepler made his discovery at the end of his vain search for that law which unifies the universe. His desire for unification was similar to that which had animated the Chaldean astrologers, whose early wisdom still exerted a powerful influence at the dawn of modern science. Astrology and numerology are such great discoveries that no epoch has escaped their influence. At the end of the eighteenth century the romanticist Novalis still believed in the mystical essence of numbers. 'It is very likely,' he says, 'that in nature a marvellous mysticity of numbers is at work, and in history also. Is not everything of significance, symmetry and strange connection? Can God not reveal Himself as well in mathematics as in other sciences?'[10]

The Tower of Babel

In relating the things of the earth to the celestial, and those of heaven to the inferior, the Chaldeans have shown in the mutual affections between these parts of the universe (which are separated in space but not in essence) the harmony that unites them in a sort of musical accord.

Philo Judaeus

In the search for a plastic expression of their cosmogony, the Chaldean rulers devised the temple tower, the ziggurat. Built in steps, it expressed the degrees of hierarchy on which heaven and earth were established. The ziggurat was actually a miniature world; its structure represented the 'mountain of earth'. In Babylon they erected the El-Temen-An-Ki, the house of the foundation stone of heaven and earth. This magical monument, known in the Bible as the Tower of Babel, had seven stages, each one dedicated to a planet. Its angles symbolized the four corners of the world, pointing to Akkad, Saburtu, Elam, and the western lands. Four, according to old Sumerian traditions, was the number of the heavens, and the square or rectangle was accepted by Babylon as the basis of their system. The seven steps of the tower were painted in different colours which corresponded to the planets. The 'great misfortune', Saturn, was black. Saturn, the 'nightly sun', was at the base, opposed to the highest degree, the gilded top of the tower where the sun resided. The second storey up was white, the colour of shining Jupiter; the third, brick-red, the colour of Mercury. Then followed blue for Venus, yellow for Mars, grey or silver for the moon. These colours boded good or evil, like their planets. This explains why a yellow dog entering the palace foretells destruction, for yellow was the colour of Mars-Nergal, the war god. In the same way a white dog brings luck, because he is the colour of the beneficent planet, Marduk-Jupiter.

The height of El-Temen-An-Ki corresponded to its length. The square, though divided into seven, was again respected, and the old tradition of a fourfold world was reconciled with the seven heavens of later times. For the first time in history numbers expressed the world order. Such calculations became frequent among later philosophers. A legend depicts Pythagoras travelling to Babylon, where he is taught the mystery of numbers, their magical significance and power. The seven steps often appear in magical philosophy. At the beginning of the seventeenth century Heinrich Khunrath, in his *Amphitheatre of Eternal Wisdom,* depicts wise men ascending the seven steps before they reach the hidden lights of wisdom. As the Chaldean priests may have warned the impious against entering the temple tower, Khunrath had these words engraved over the entrance of his marvellous cave: 'Stay away, keep out from here, ye profane.' An earlier woodcut shows a learned man wrapped in a doctor's mantle, setting his foot on the first of the seven steps. Through ascending these he will attain the knowledge of God, whose name is at the eighth degree, the threshold of God's heavenly

2. The gateway to eternal wisdom

dwelling. According to this image, which illustrates Lully's book *On the Ascent*, the seven steps are stones, fire, plants, animals, man, the starry heavens and the angels. Starting with the humble study of stones, the man of wisdom will attain higher and higher degrees of knowledge, until he will be able to apprehend the sublime and the eternal.

The Babylonian commonwealth was administered according to the law which the priests had discovered in the universe. Nothing could disturb the world order but the impiety of man. Once angered, the gods would leave the temples and choose a dwelling in a foreign country. Then chaos would reign, and Chaldea would become a prey to evil. The temple towers are the symbols, the very embodiment of ancient wisdom. In the conviction that their knowledge was valid for all time, the kings had the towers constructed so that they might be invulnerable to decay. Thus the ziggurat were never built higher than three hundred feet. The royal seal was imprinted on each brick and the kings compared the raising of these structures to the superhuman, boasting that they were 'like heaven'. This may be the reason for the erroneous belief that the Tower of Babel was of an enormous height.

Among the temple towers restored by Nabopalassar, who reigned 625–604 B.C., was that of Babylon. An inscription recording this pious deed reads as follows:

3. The steps leading to the celestial city

As for the temple tower of Babylon, El-Temen-An-Ki, which before my time had become weakened and had fallen in, Marduk the lord commanded me to lay its foundation in the heart of the earth and to raise its turrets to heaven. I caused numerous workmen to be assembled in my land to carry them. I set to work, I made bricks, I manufactured burnt bricks. Like the downpour of heaven which cannot be measured, like the massive flood, I caused the Arabtu to carry bitumen and pitch. With the help of Hea, with the insight of Marduk, with the wisdom of Nebo and Nisaba . . . I came to a decision. By means of exorcism, in the wisdom of Hea and Marduk, I cleared away the place and on the original site I laid its platform foundation.[11]

The image of the king is then placed in the foundation together with silver, gold, jewels, 'goodly oil' and herbs. The royal family carries precious tools and baskets in a solemn procession. In this inaugural ceremony, mortar is mixed with wine; and the king continues:

I built the temple in front of Esharra with rejoicing, and like a mountain I raised its tower aloft; to Marduk my lord, as in days of old, I dedicated it for a sight to be gazed at. O Marduk, my lord, look with favour upon my goodly deeds. At thy exalted command, which cannot be altered, let the performance of my hands endure forever. Like the bricks of El-Temen-An-Ki, which are to remain firm forever, do thou establish the foundation of my throne for all time. O

El-Temen-An-Ki grant blessing to the king who has restored thee. When Marduk with joy takes up his abode in thee, O temple, recall to Marduk, my lord, my gracious deeds.[12]

The tower, however, decayed rapidly. King Nebuchadnezzar, Nabopalassar's son and successor (ruled 605–562 B.C.), refers to its restoration in this inscription: 'The temples of Babylon I have restored. As for El-Temen-An-Ki, with burned bricks and bright ugnu-stone I raised on high its turrets.'

However, bricks, bitumen and magical incantation could not prevent its ultimate decay. The famous tower perished together with the splendour of Babylon. Its sand-covered ruins seem to confirm the legend of Genesis which tells of the confusion of languages, brought about by Elohim in order to stop this 'sinful' construction. In the symbolic language of the Orient, its builders say: 'Come, let us build ourselves a city with a tower, whose top shall reach to the heavens, so that we may not be scattered over all the earth.'

Was it not indeed to conquer the heavens and their secrets that the ziggurat was erected? These magical attempts were destined to fail because the workmen were scattered and disunited, says the book of Genesis, contrary to the true aim of magic, which is to achieve unity.

PERSIA

Zoroaster

In the primitive dualistic world the powers of light and darkness
are worshipped alike. The equal strength of both good and evil
may have arisen in the mind of man when he observed nature
and meditated upon his own life. Man is inhabited by contradictory forces; in his thought and action, good and evil are so
intimately mingled that he cannot always distinguish between
them. Moreover, good intentions sometimes generate evil, or
criminal desires become the servant of the good. Both principles
seem to be everlasting, and in nature nothing carries out the
idea that light should overcome darkness. In the east, good rain
falls, fertilizing the land, while in the west evil rain falls, causing
destructive inundation. The south wind carries pestilence and
fever whereas the north wind cleanses the air and chases away
disease. No wonder that primitive man discovers good and evil
spirits everywhere. He calls upon them, flatters them, lies to
them, and uses every means which he deems fit to bring about
good influences and to avert the evil ones. Out of fear he pays
more respect to evil spirits. When the hunter's arrow fails his
prey, such failure is rarely attributed to lack of skill but rather to
a nefarious intervention of evil. Little power is given to man in
such a primitive world.

With growing civilization, man became increasingly aware of
his capacities and his responsibility. The Chaldean star religion
taught that luck and disaster are no haphazard events depending
on the caprices of spirits; rather they derive from the heavenly
bodies which send good and bad according to mathematical
laws. Man, it seemed, was incapable of fighting the will of the
planet divinities. Yet the more this system evolved, the more did
the wise men read ethical values into man's fate; the will of the
stars was not completely independent from man's demeanour.
His deeds were mysteriously linked with the happenings above,
and they were of importance in the interplay between heaven
and earth. In the seventh century B.C. the king of Assyria, Ashurbanipal, sent his prayer to the star Sirius:

> Speak, and the gods may assist thee,
> Judge, give thine oracle,
> Accept the raising of my hand, harken to my imprecation.
> Take away the enchantment, blot out my sin.[1]

A spell had been cast upon the ruler, who asked himself whether
he deserved this misfortune because he had committed a sin.
The favour of the star is invoked to remove not only the spell, but
its cause as well, the evil deed. And Sirius is addressed as the

messenger of higher gods who assist him in his beneficent course, and whose will he announces.

It was probably in Ashurbanipal's time that Zoroaster the Median prophet preached the doctrine that evil, though powerful and ever present, can be avoided and lastly defeated. Zoroaster purified the ancient belief in the hosts of good and evil spirits, rulers of a split universe. He traced these legions back to their principles: Ormazd (Ahura Mazda), king of light; Ahriman (Ahura Mainyu), prince of darkness. The good demons of older traditions were dethroned by Zoroaster; however, since they could not be eradicated from popular beliefs, they were granted a place in the hierarchy of evil spirits. Led by Ahriman, these spirits no longer oppose good in unruly swarms. The kingdom of evil has become organized like that of good. The two armies are marshalled in warlike array. As in the game of chess, whose white and black figures oppose each other in equal strength, the armies of light and of darkness face one another. Victory, however, is not followed by peace, because the struggle continues to the end of time. In heaven as on earth resounds the battle cry: Here Ormazd – There Ahriman!

Six archdemons are Ahriman's principal underlings, corresponding to the six archangels surrounding the king of light. These archangels are divine wisdom, righteousness, dominion, devotion, totality and salvation. The archdemons are the spirits of anarchy, apostasy, presumption, destruction, decay and fury. The last-mentioned archdemon's name is Aeshma Daeva, known to the Hebrews as Ashmadai and to Christian demonologists as Asmodeus. The riddle of why this demon has attracted more interest in the Occident than other Zoroastrian devils is still unsolved. According to Pierre de Lancre (died 1630) Asmodeus is the 'chief of the fourth hierarchy of evil demons', who are called 'the avengers of wickedness, crimes and misdeeds'. The learned Brabantian doctor John Wier (1515–88) gives in his *Pseudo-Monarchy of Demons* a curious description of Asmodeus. 'He is

4. Asmodeus

a great and powerful king. He appears with three heads, a bull's head, a human head and a ram's head. He has goose feet and a snake's tail. He exhales fire and rides upon a dragon of hell. He carries a spear and a banner.' Truly the goose-footed fiend will give goose flesh to whoever calls upon him. Asmodeus is, however, not to be feared. Say to him: 'In truth thou art Asmodeus,' and he will give you a marvellous ring; he will teach you geometry, arithmetic, astronomy and mechanics. When questioned, he will answer truthfully. He can render man invisible and reveal hidden treasures. Many other demons in the Zoroastrian religion, daevas of lower rank, tempt one away from the true worship of Mazda: Paromaiti, arrogance; Mitox, the falsely spoken word; Zaurvan, decrepitude; Akatasa, meddlesomeness; Vereno, lust.[2] Still lower in this fiendish hierarchy rank the Drujs, the Yatus, the Nasus, enchantresses, malevolent beings, deceivers and monsters. Just as great is the circle of heavenly legions, the good Yazatas.

So far it is only by its detailed organization that Zoroaster's dogma is distinguishable from that of primitive dualism. But the reformer's originality resides in something beyond his elaborate angelology and demonology. He conceived periods of time in which the fate of the material world and of the good and bad principle would be decided. The outcome was to be good; defeat awaited Ahriman. Zoroaster distinguishes between two types of time: boundless time or eternity, and sovereign time, a long period which Ormazd 'carved out' from the immeasurable bulk of eternity. Sovereign time will last twelve thousand years; it is divided into four cycles of three thousand. Each millennium is presided over by a sign of the zodiac, an indication that sovereign time is thought to be an enormous celestial year whose smallest fraction is the circle of twelve daily and nightly hours. Three, four and twelve are the mystical numbers of this cycle. They are the base upon which evolves the number seven, the six archdemons together with Ahriman their ruler, and the six archangels and Ormazd. The first three thousand years are those of spiritual creation, during which all creatures remain in their transcendental form. The second triad is that of material creation, of celestial beings, of spirits, sky, water, earth, plants, animals and mankind. The third period is that of the irruption of the evil one, that dominated man's history before the coming of revelation. The last period, that which started with the advent of Zoroaster, will end with the day of judgement.

Dualistic Zoroastrianism tended towards monotheism. Evil was originally thought to have sprung from a doubting thought of the good god. In later versions of the sacred scriptures, those accepted by the Zarvanite sect, there exists a single power, whence sprang Ormazd and Ahriman, the ill-matched brothers. This single power is Zrvan Akaran, boundless time, which rests in its glory, so incomprehensible to man that we can but honour it in awed silence.

In this manner creation began: Akaran produced light by emanation; from light sprang Ormazd, the first-born, who created the pure world. Then he ordered the hierarchy of angels and the

myriad concepts of things he intended to bring into being.
Another emanation of boundless time was Ahriman, second-
born of the eternal, who was jealous and hungry for power. He
envied Ormazd and was banished to the realm of darkness, where
he is to reign in night while the struggle between good and evil is
being fought. The war began thus. After a thousand years,
Ormazd created light, patterned after the supermundane, the
celestial light. He fashioned the source of life, a power he called
bull, and Ahriman destroyed the bull-being. From its scattered
seed, Ormazd then fashioned the first man and the first woman.
With milk and fruit Ahriman seduced the woman, and man fell
into sin. And as evil counterparts of the 'good animals', Ahriman
created harmful beasts, reptiles and snakes, the Khraftstras. And
the war goes on; the strength of evil grows overwhelming. Yet,
at the moment when Ahriman seems to triumph, redemption is at
hand.

Redemption awaits the day of judgement, the advent of the
saviour, when a flood of molten metal shall sear the wicked, while
the righteous shall pass unharmed. As good and evil are parted
finally from one another, Ormazd will establish his good kingdom. The dead shall rise, and hell shall be purified and claimed
for the enlargement of a regenerated world, deathless and everlasting.

Zoroastrian thought has exerted a greater influence upon the
Western world than many wish to believe. Though this religion
is nearly extinct today, many of its ideas continue to live in
Christian doctrine. A. V. William Jackson says that 'anyone
who has even a superficial knowledge of the Iranian religion
cannot but be struck by the parallel that may be drawn between
it on the one hand and Judaism and Christianity on the other'.
He points out how intimately related in both types of religion are
the doctrines of angels and demons, how the manifestations of the
doctrine of a new kingdom, the coming of a saviour, the belief in
resurrection, a general judgement and a future life, are almost
identical in both dogmas, the Zoroastrian and the Christian. The
question of who was the originator of these ideas has not yet
been satisfactorily answered. We are inclined to believe, however, that most of these ideas germinated in an older tradition
and were shaped by Zoroaster, whose teachings began to spread
shortly before the Hebrews returned from their Babylonian
exile.

It must have been in Babylon that the Hebrew sages became
acquainted with Zoroastrianism and incorporated some of its
features into the older creed. There is also no doubt that the
Gnostics accepted many Zoroastrian ideas, especially Hellenistic
Gnosticism, which attempted to reconcile Greek thought with
that of the Orient. Infinite light, by which deity is expressed, the
doctrine of the all-powerful and eternal word by which Ormazd
created the world, the emanation of divine light bringing forth the
good, and numerous other features of Zoroastrianism lived on in
more or less altered form among Gnostics and Neo-Platonists –
Mithraicism and Manicheism were offspring of Zoroastrian
religion. Even the Mohammedans, whose persecution caused the

decay of the Zoroastrian creed, accepted some of its features. Today, about two hundred thousand Parsees in India and Persia still perform the magical rites prescribed in the holy books attributed to the Iranian prophet.

Though practically extinct, the old doctrine sprang up anew in the Middle Ages. Towards the end of the twelfth century, the dualistic creed of the Albigenses spread in France like wildfire. Though suppressed in a pitiless crusade, it lived on surreptitiously. Today the people in Carcassonne and Albi sometimes tell you in dark words of the struggle still being waged between good and evil. Again and again, the dualism of old brought forth the fruit of a vanished civilization, comparable to the ancient grain found in the tombs of the pharaohs: planted in the earth they arise from the sleep of ages, and yield their long-delayed harvest.

Magic about Hair and Nails

... not to pare our nails, whilst we are present at the festival of the gods.

Hesiod

Not all the sacred books of Zoroastrianism have been preserved, and only a small part of the surviving sections can be ascribed to the Magus himself, namely the seventeen psalms or *Gathas*. The laws of worship and sacrifice are of early date. Other books of the Magian cult are the hymns, the daily prayers and the liturgies. The books called *Vendidad*, compilations of anti-demoniac lore, were written after the middle of the fifth century B.C. They contain rituals which are of a more purely magical type than some others, and which therefore attract our special attention. The dogmatic theology of Zoroastrianism is essentially religious, but the ritual of dealing with demons is magical. Two instances will illustrate the magical aspect of cleansing rites, the ritual applying to hair and nails, described in this section, and that applying to the fly demon, treated in the next.

In the seventeenth chapter of the *Vendidad* there is a prescription devoted to parings of nails and clippings of hair, which as soon as they are separated from the body belong to the evil one as abodes of uncleanliness. Hair and nails taken from the dead are mentioned in the fable of how Zoroaster converted the royal family to the new doctrine, and how he escaped a plot against his life. According to the story, courtiers hid bones in his room, together with hair and nails robbed from the dead. Zoroaster, accused of wizardry, was condemned to be hung. At this moment the king's horse fell sick; its legs had entered its body. 'Free me,' said the prophet, 'and I will restore one leg.' Freedom was granted, and the leg came forth. 'Lord,' said Zoroaster, 'if thou wilt embrace my creed, I will restore the second leg.' After the king's conversion, the two remaining legs were also restored, but only after the rest of the royal family and the court had become Zoroastrians.

Hair and nails, which were used by wizards for conjuring up the deceased, live 'a life apart' from that of the body. They lack sensibility and are seemingly dead. Yet they grow, and grow much more rapidly than the rest of the body. This individual tempo of growth together with a complete lack of sensibility may have led them to be regarded as individuals, growing upon people like parasitic plants. In such a belief their independence would be sufficient cause for disquiet.

1. Zarathustra [Zoroaster] asked Ahura Mazda [Ormazd]: O Ahura Mazda, most beneficent spirit, maker of the material world, thou holy one. Which is the most deadly deed whereby a man increases the most baleful strength of the daevas, as he would do by offering them sacrifice?

2. Ahura Mazda answered: It is when a man here below, combing his hair or shaving it off or paring his nails, drops them into a hole or into a crack.

3. Then for want of the lawful rites being observed, daevas are produced on the earth which we call lice, and which eat up the corn in the cornfield and the clothes in the wardrobe.

4. Therefore, O Zarathustra, whenever here below thou shalt comb thy hair or shave it off, or pare thy nails, thou shalt take them away ten paces from the faithful, twenty paces from the fire, thirty paces from the water, fifty paces from the consecrated bundles of baresma [holy twigs].

5. Then thou shalt dig a hole, ten fingers deep if the earth is hard, twelve fingers deep if it is soft; thou shalt take thy hair down there and thou shalt say aloud these fiend-smiting words: Out of his pity Mazda made plants grow.

6. Thereupon thou shalt draw three furrows with a knife of metal around the hole, or six, or nine, and thou shalt chant the Ahuna Vairya three times, or six, or nine.

7. For the nails, thou shalt dig a hole, out of the house, as deep as the top joint of the little finger; thou shalt take the nails down there and thou shalt say aloud these fiend-smiting words: The words are heard from the pious in holiness and good thought.[3]

Zoroaster's concern with hair and nails has given full scope to the ironical humour of many who regard this as superstition unworthy of the wise. It is true that similar rites exist among primitive tribes whose level of civilization is far below that of the ancient Iranians. Cut hair and nails are hidden away by many primitive people, or deposited in sacred places and burned, to prevent their falling into the hands of sorcerers who would use them for evil spells against their former owners. According to Frazer, the belief is widespread among these tribes that men may be bewitched through the clippings of their hair and the parings of their nails. Among primitives, the custom existed and still exists of releasing war prisoners after their hair is shorn. The hair is kept as 'hostage', a warrant for the future behaviour of the defeated. Thus they can be punished easily from any distance. Whatever punishment the victors inflict upon the hair, its owners too will suffer.

Our scepticism about Zoroastrian superstitions may subside when we learn how many similar beliefs still exist in Europe and America. Chilean gauchos stuff their hair into walls, as do the Turks. Armenians hide it in churches, hollow trees and columns. French peasants of the Vosges Mountains bury their hair secretly, together with extracted teeth, and mark the spot so that they may find them on the day of resurrection. In the village of Drumconrath, in Ireland, some trustworthy people, having learned from Scripture that their hairs were all numbered by the Almighty, expect to have to account for them on the day of judgement. The good people of Liège in Belgium remove their hair carefully from their combs, lest it should come into the possession of some witch.[4]

Zoroaster's belief that hair and nails produce insects or other animals did not spring from his own imagination. The belief was older than Iran, and it was still alive in the sixteenth century of the Christian era. Women's hair buried in dung was thought to produce snakes. In his book on witchcraft, published in 1603, the famous French judge, Henri Boguet, recalls St Thomas's opinion that rotten sticks can turn into snakes. Though Paracelsus had declared; '*Nihil est sine spermate*' (nothing exists without semen), the old belief lived on into the epoch of Leibniz and Newton. Today, spontaneous generation of insects is held possible by people in Brittany. Hair carried away by wind, they think, will produce flies.

Snakes, bugs, frogs, lice, flies, etc., were considered imperfect animals which are reproduced by corruption and not by semen. This implies that these animals were in relation with the infernal powers. According to Zoroaster, they were created by Ahriman, since nothing imperfect could derive from Ormazd. Imperfection was, in Christianity, ascribed to the devil. Popular tradition warns that he can never appear in perfect human form: either he limps or has a horse's hoof, betraying his true nature. Satan was, like Ahriman, the master of imperfect animals. Did he not give a silver louse to his devotees as a token of his friendship? Great mystery surrounds the belief that hair and nails are specially susceptible to corruption, for in fact the contrary is true: in the grave they continue to 'live' for some time independently of the decaying corpse.

Christianity, like Zoroastrianism, correlated hair and hell. Pious Jews think similarly about nails, a belief which causes them to pare them as short as possible. They profess that nails are abodes of evil, and that they are the only part of the body incapable of serving God. Analogous beliefs do exist in Madagascar, where natives think that the devil dwells under unpared fingernails. 'Witches,' says Paracelsus, 'give their hair to Satan as a deposit on the contract they make with him. But the evil one does not waste this hair, for he cuts it up small and mixes it with the exhalation from which he forms hail; thus it has come to pass that we ordinarily find little hairs in hail.' The conviction that hair is a refuge *par excellence* for devilish spells was shared by the persecutors of witches. Before going to the torture chamber, suspected witches had all their hair shorn, a practice which made many a witch confess before the torture was applied. The French legal authority Jean Bodin (1530–96) records such an instance. In 1485 forty witches in northern Italy simultaneously confessed their crimes, after having undergone this procedure. In defence of the custom, he reminds us that Apollonius of

Tyana was treated in the same way when the Emperor Domitian had him arrested for wizardry.

The shocking happenings in liberated France, where women who had dealings with the Germans saw their locks fall under the scissors of patriots, may likewise be traced to primitive magic. It is a cleansing rite performed upon a taboo person. Their hair was infected with the virus of the taboo which France had placed upon the invader.

Casting out the Fly Demon

'The Lord of rats and eke of mice Of flies and bed bugs, frogs and lice. . . .'

Goethe, *Faust*

Flies, we know now, are imperfect animals, generated from corruption, which they spread everywhere, carrying disease and contaminating foods. Anyone who has travelled in the East knows to what degree they constitute a true calamity. Zoroastrian demonology has made of the fly a female demon, the Nasu, embodying impurity, putrefaction and decay, feeding in preference upon the dead. The Nasu may be smitten 'by corpse-eating dogs and birds' – beneficent creatures of Ormazd, whose glance can cast out demons. Expelled by their gaze, the demon, disguised in the shape of an abominable fly, leaves the corpse. This forms the basis of the Sag-did ceremony, which must be performed before anyone may touch the dead. An infringement of the taboo makes necessary a complicated cleansing rite, called the Barashnum, which the polluted must perform during nine days. 'The worshipper of Mazda shall dig three holes in the ground and he shall thereupon wash his body with gomez [ox urine], not with water. They shall then lift and bring my dog; they shall bring him in front of the man.' This is done three times, and the third time the defiled one is to be washed not with gomez, but with water. 'He shall first wash his hands. If his hands be not washed, he makes his whole body unclean. When he has washed his hands three times, thou shalt sprinkle with water the forepart of his skull.'

This cleansing water will cause the Nasu to jump from one part of the head to another and chase her from the head to the chest. One after another, each part of the body is to be sprinkled with holy water in an oft-repeated and elaborate ceremony which ultimately drives the demon to the earth: from the right shoulder to the left shoulder, from the right armpit to the left, upon the chest, upon the back and so on until she is driven into the sole of the foot, 'where what is seen of her is like the wing of a fly'. From the sole, Druj-Nasu is finally driven to her last stronghold, the toe.

He shall press his heels upon the ground and shall raise his right toe; thou shalt sprinkle his right toe with water; then the Druj-Nasu rushes upon the left toe. Thou shalt sprinkle the left toe with water; then the Druj-Nasu flies away to the region of the north, in the shape of a raging fly, with knees and tail sticking out, all stained and like the foulest Khraftstras [devilish beasts].

And thou shalt say aloud these fiend-smiting and most healing words: The will of the Lord is the law of holiness. . . . Whom hast thou placed to protect me, O Mazda . . . while the hate of the fiend is grasping me . . . Who is he who will smite the fiend in order to maintain thy ordinances? . . . Perish, O fiendish Druj! Perish, O brood of the fiend! . . . Perish away, O Druj! Perish away to the regions of the north, never more to give unto death the living world of the holy spirit![5]

The resemblance of this Zoroastrian cleansing rite to the Catholic rite of exorcism upon individuals possessed by demons is striking. In A.D. 1582 Jerome Mengo published his *Whip for the Demons*, which deals with this difficult matter. This curious work was tardily (1709) placed upon the papal index. Up to that date, the priest-exorcist may have used rites such as are recommended in Mengo's treatise, which includes advice about washing the possessed frequently with holy water, not unlike the ritual Zoroaster prescribes. As in the Barashnum, the demon is driven away systematically from every part of the body. As anatomy was better known in Mengo's time than during that of the Iranian prophet, the enumeration of anatomical parts is far more complete, which adds to the intricacy of the ceremony. At the end of the exorcism, the patient is bathed in a mixture of holy water and other liquids so 'as to cleanse him of some malignancy against which no remedy has been foreseen, some spell which may lie hidden in the hair of the enchanted'.

Other peoples of the East also resorted to supernatural powers for protection against the fly plague. The Canaanites worshipped Beelzebub, whose temple was never polluted by these unclean insects. Beelzebub signifies 'lord of flies'. The Hebrews called him prince of demons (Matthew 12:24; Luke 11:15), and the Pharisees accused Jesus of driving out other fiends with his help. Beelzebub was well known to the theologians and demonologists of the West. Pierre le Loyer (1550–1634), first councillor to the king of France and an expert in such matters, tells us of a possessed woman in the city of Laon. Beelzebub, having been duly exorcised, escaped from her mouth in the form of a fly.

5. *Beelzebub*

'This is well testified to,' he says, 'by notaries and many goodly
people, so that no one can doubt this happening.'

In Christianity, Beelzebub is considered by many the sovereign of the empire of darkness. His prestige brought forth other fly demons, imps that were suckled by English witches, and the big fly that stung Cunibert, king of Lombardy. This incident occurred while the king was discussing with his favourite how best to rid the court of two noblemen who had defied him. The royal court gave chase, but succeeded only in cutting off the fly's legs. Meanwhile, the two noblemen were approached by an exhausted, one-legged man who warned them of the king's wrath; and they were able to escape.

THE HEBREWS

Jehovah's Warriors

In the fertile Tigris and Euphrates valleys, ruled by Babylonian and Assyrian masters, lived a people who disdained the hordes of good and evil demons. They opposed the ostentatious, vain and terror-inspiring idols, worshipping instead a single deity, a spiritual godhead that did not reside in images but was at once both invisible and omnipotent, reigning above the material world. In the eighth century before Christ, the most prominent Jews were deported to Assyria, and the Assyrians forced strange gods upon Jerusalem. In 605 B.C. Babylon rose again to establish a new Chaldean world empire, and King Nebuchadnezzar banished more Jews to the Euphrates valley. Then as the people in Palestine continued to rebel, still more Jews were deported to Chaldea. After the murder of a Babylonian governor in Jerusalem, the remaining Hebrews escaped the king's wrath by fleeing to Egypt. These kings of Mesopotamia thought perhaps that the vanquished would merge with the populations of their own kingdoms. But this stubborn minority, preserving its individuality, held its own against foreign ways.

Perhaps a feeling of guilt among the captives caused a temporary tightening of morals. For they thought that surely this banishment to a heathen land was sent by Jehovah to punish His people for their uncleanness in the past. The greatest uncleanness of all consisted in the cult of idols and the practice of magic. Had not the Hebrew prophets repeatedly warned their people that the Holy Land would no longer suffer these abominations, that it would spew forth its sacrilegious inhabitants? The false gods proved powerless before fate; none had prevented the devastation of Palestine. The dispersed Jews could now reflect with shame and disgust upon these faithless gods.

They had learned from the Egyptians to worship Beelsephon. A mare or dog, tradition says, was in his likeness set up according to the rules of astrology. Impure, Ammonitic Beelphegor dwelt in pits and rocky clefts, and at the time of the Exodus the Jews, seduced by the women of Sittim, were dissolutely sacrificing to Beelphegor's idols. Moral purity was not his strong point, and Hosea thus protests against his disruptive influence:

> Therefore your daughters play the harlot
> And your sons' wives commit adultery.
> I will not punish your daughters when they play the harlot
> Nor your sons' wives when they commit adultery,
> For they themselves go with harlots
> And sacrifice with temple prostitutes
> And people without insight must go to ruin . . .

The Jews had also worshipped Dagon, the fish woman, goddess of the Philistines.[1] Her gigantic bronze image was in the
form of a beautiful woman, whose body, like the Syrian goddess
Derceto and Dirce of Ascalon, ended in a huge fish tail. Then
there was the Babylonian goddess, Succoth Benoth. She was
represented, the legend says, as a hen with her chicks. Asima,
god of the Emathites, had the figure of a he-goat; Anamelech,
that of a horse; and the Samaritan Nergal, that of a cock. In
Accaron Beelzebub's image was that of a fly, and the Israelite
King Achaz sent for him in vain, to cure his sickness.

6. *Dagon*

The most gruesome deity was the Ammonitic Moloch,
gobbler of children. He alone of all the idols had no temple in
Jerusalem. Even during the time of greatest decadence, he did
not venture into the holy city. The near-by valley of the sons of
Hinnom sheltered his iron image; leading his followers astray
in wantonness, he rejoiced at their doom. Moloch is identical
with the Hebraic '*melech*' (king). The purpose of his cult was
originally to gain health and long life for the king, who was
expected to use his magic powers for the benefit of the people, in
particular to obtain good harvests.[2] But Moloch's price was too
high, and the people had to burn their own children to please
him. Gorged with the lives of his victims, Moloch dominated
over Hinnom. Cymbals, trumpets and drums filled the air with
barbaric din, drowning out the shrieks of his victims.

In spite of all these waverings and regressions to the old idol
worship, the Jews were an exception among the nations of antiquity. Ever and again, enlightened prophets arose to remind them

Vallis

Gehinnom

7. *Moloch*

of their ancient compact with the Eternal. And during times of misfortune and persecution, the Jewish people remembered the one Lord, recognizing in their misery the stern and righteous hand of the 'jealous God'. In this conception of misfortune the Jews differed from their neighbours, who believed that ill fortune stemmed from evil powers with whom they must compromise when all their counter-magic had failed.

Today we know that Israel had no monopoly of the idea of one God; nor can the chosen people claim to have been the first to conceive monotheism, which, we know also, became the Egyptian state religion under the young monarch Amenhotep IV. He declared the old deities deposed (1375 B.C.), and over priestly opposition, enforced the religion of the one god, Aton, a name which may have lived on in the Hebrew '*adonai*' (lord). Aton would suffer no images, and the disc of the sun was his only symbol. Amenhotep, who with the new cult changed his name to Ikhnaton, also abolished the cult of the dead with all its magical rites. Yet Aton's cult was short-lived. The kingly reformer died in 1358 B.C., and soon afterwards Aton was overthrown, having never gained popularity among a people so fond of the sculptured image.

Neighbouring peoples, whether friends or enemies, learn from one another and an exchange of ideas takes place between them, so that for good or for evil they are linked. In spite of their stubborn resistance, the exiled Jews were not able to withstand foreign influences. If the apocryphal book of Tobit can be relied on, the Jews at Nineveh were not confined to separate communities. Many attained dignity and wealth. Tobit was buyer for King Shalmaneser V (ruled 727–722 B.C.), journeying to Media on official business, and apparently to other lands of western Asia. Under the succeeding king, Essarhaddon, the conqueror of Egypt, Tobit's nephew became secretary of the treasury, in charge of all the accounts of the kingdom. Many forgot their homeland, only a few, perhaps, remaining steadfast in their faith. Thus Tobit could complain: 'All my brothers and relatives ate the food of the heathen, but I kept myself from eating it, because I remembered God with all my heart.'

Even those who had remained in Palestine were hardly better able to withstand Assyro-Babylonian influences. From the incensed writings of Ezekiel (sixth century B.C.) we learn of Israel's countless relapses into the various beliefs of its conquerors. With few exceptions, the people were fascinated by foreign religions and magic practices, which were carried into the very temple at Jerusalem. 'Lo, there were all sorts of loathsome forms of reptiles and beasts, together with all the idols of Israel.' And at the north gate of the temple, 'lo, there sat women weeping for Tammuz'. Still greater sacrilege was to be seen. 'Between the vestibule and the altar about twenty-five men, with their backs to the tabernacle of the Lord and their faces to the east, were worshipping the sun of the East.'

The abhorred gods of the Mesopotamians, the cult of the Persians, had invaded the Holy of Holies, and at its gates the shrill pipe and plaintive flute were being played in honour of the ancient god Tammuz, whom the Sumerians had worshipped in the past as Dumu-Zi, the true son. They gave Tammuz to the Hebrews. Tammuz was the youthful lover of Ishtar, the great mother goddess, the embodiment of productive power, the female principle. Like Astarte, Cybele, Aphrodite and Isis, she was the receptacle of life and growth. As Tammuz, the man-god, dies and descends into the underworld, he is bewailed by all that is female. Ishtar follows her dead lover and wrests him from the infernal powers. Tammuz comes back to life for the sake of all life, and when the couple return to the light of day, nature rejoices, and vegetative activity, which had stopped during Ishtar's hell-journey, starts anew.

From time immemorial Ishtar had been honoured by the women and maidens of western Asia. A magical custom which aimed at stimulating the goddess's productive power accompanied the ancient cult in the form of prostitution. The usage probably dated back to the time when marriage was unknown or forbidden as an infringement upon old communal rights.[3] And the goddess Ishtar was thought to be unchaste and unwed, an abomination to the true believer in Israel.

The Jewish people passed through many crises and many relapses into various old and abolished cults, such as that of Tammuz; and they borrowed new elements which attached themselves to the monotheistic religion. The notions of Daniel and of Ezekiel have quite a Persian character, and there is a thoroughly Persian flavour[4] to Tobit's story of his daughter-in-law Sarah, a Median Jewess. She was possessed by the evil demon Ashmadai, who had killed seven of Sarah's betrothed. Ashmadai must be cast out. To this end, incense was mixed with the heart and liver of fish and put on a burner. 'And when the demon smelled the smoke, he fled to the farthest part of upper Egypt, and the Angel Raphael bound him there.'

After the rise of Zoroastrian Magianism, Israel witnessed the collapse of her oppressors, when during the mid-sixth century Mesopotamian might was shattered and the Persians rode into Babylon. Forty thousand Jews returned to the now deserted and gutted Jerusalem. Through their political defeat, the Jews had lost faith in the stability of earthly things. God's kingdom was not on earth. Palestine, they recognized, was the crossroads through which marched the armies of powerful empires; and only the coming of the Messiah could free them from their political misery. Like the Zoroastrians, they were preoccupied with the life to come after death, unknown to the old religion of Moses. They longed for the establishment of the heavenly kingdom which would mark the end of their hopeless struggle.

Magic in Holy Writ

The Scriptures speak of magic as something whose existence no one doubts. Here, magic is a reality. The widespread condemnation of the occult does not arise from the suspicion that its magical operations are exploited for deception, but because magic is morally and socially harmful, indulging in what is forbidden and doing violence to divine teaching. Holy Writ recognizes God as a governor having jurisdiction over mankind. Piety and good deeds, it is true, influence Him favourably, but men's destinies are ultimately in his hands, and when He strikes the good man, it is not from injustice, for His ways are inscrutable, beyond mortal comprehension. The Mosaic religion, like the Christian, opposed magic as an illicit tampering with God's power. But being itself an outgrowth of magic, its ritual contains many elements whose magical origin can hardly be denied. The Biblical miracle is not entirely unlike the magical prodigies recorded in Holy Writ, the distinction being that the one is performed by the will and with the help of Jehovah, whereas the other is brought forth with the assistance of the evil one.

Jannes and Mambres, conjurors of the pharaonic court, are wizards capable of imitating many of Moses's miracles, changing staffs into serpents and conjuring up swarms of frogs. The devil, who is the 'ape of God', taught them to counterfeit the divine miracles of the prophet. The devil's power, however, is limited: the conjurors were able to bring forth frogs, but it lay beyond their wisdom to make them disappear again. In this way, the Bible distinguishes between the miracle and the prodigy of black magic. The onlooker in pharaoh's court must have regarded Moses simply as the more able magician.

An unmistakably magical operation is performed by the

patriarch Jacob. When they divided the herds, Jacob and his father-in-law Laban agreed that Laban was to have the unspotted animals, while all spotted goats should be Jacob's. 'Then Jacob procured some fresh boughs of poplar, almond and plane and peeled these rods in alternate stripes of white and dark, and he put them in the gutters in the watering troughs when the flocks came to drink.' The animals copulated duly and 'the flocks conceived before the rods and brought forth cattle ring-streaked, speckled and spotted'. Jacob was using his striped sticks according to the magical principle that like produces like: striped boughs produce stripes upon the animals' hides. He did not gain his wealth through divine intervention; it was not a miracle which produced the spots upon the patriarch's cattle, but rather Jacob's knowledge of magic.

We learn from the Biblical narrative that Joseph practised divination by hydromancy, that is, he wanted to discover hidden things by gazing into water. When his brothers were leaving the land of Egypt with their sacks of grain, Joseph caused a silver goblet to be hidden in Benjamin's sack. This vessel was not for drinking purposes only. 'In fact,' the Bible says, 'he used it for divination.' The practice of hydromancy must have been general in Joseph's time. He speaks about it as of something well known, not only to the Egyptians but also to the Hebrews. 'Did you not know that a man like me would be sure to use divination?'

Moses, seeking to free his people from the plague of serpents, set up the bronze image of a snake in the wilderness. This statue had the character of a talisman; such images were used at all times as a protection against various evils. According to conceptions of magic, like not only produces like, but also propitiates it. Gregory of Tours (A.D. 538–94) tells how the Parisians, excavating for a bridge, found strange medals whose significance was unknown to them. One of these magical coins depicted a rat, another a snake and a third a flame. These talismans, Gregory says, were lost or destroyed, and since that time Paris has known rats, snakes and conflagrations, three plagues which formerly had spared the city. The magus Jacques Gaffarel (1601–81), the learned librarian of Richelieu, reports that during the capture of Constantinople by Mohammed II, the jaw of a bronze snake chanced to be broken. This image had a talismanic virtue, and from that time on the city's snakes began to multiply in an uncanny way. Gaffarel also mentions the snake of Moses, but pronounces it not to have been a magical image since it was made of copper, the sight of which, according to him, aggravates snake bites. He argues that Moses must have fashioned the statue in this metal to convince his people that it was no talisman but that its effects were divinely rather than magically wrought. This argument seems somewhat weak.

In the book of Numbers we find a custom which must be classified as magical since it does not merely *pray* for a divine verdict, but *insists* on obtaining one. The jealous husband suspecting his wife of unfaithfulness brings her before the priest. After performing some ceremonies, the priest summoning the woman bids her to 'take her stand before the Lord, loosening the hair of her head'. Then the priest pours the consecrated water into an earthenware jug, and after further ceremonies orders her to drink thereof. 'When he has made her drink the water, if she has defiled herself and has been unfaithful to her husband, then the water that brings the curse upon entering her shall cause her pain, her womb shall become easily fertile but she shall have miscarriages, so that the woman shall become an execration among her people. But if the woman is not defiled, she shall be immune and shall bear children.'

Another custom of the Jews, one prescribed by their cult, arose from the belief that evil could be discharged into an animal. In the New Testament Jesus cures a demoniac 'night and day shrieking among the tombs and cutting himself with stones'. The Messiah casts out these sons of darkness who thereupon rush into a herd of swine. A very old ceremony was connected with this belief. Before the Hebrews could give themselves over to the Feast of the Tabernacles and its joys, a purification rite had to be performed on the preceding Day of Atonement. The high priest cast lots over two he-goats, one falling to Yaweh, the other to Azazel. They offered up the Lord's goat in the usual manner, but the scape-goat, that was Azazel's, they sent into the wilderness with the sins of Israel. The suffix '*el*' (lord) suggests that in an earlier age Azazel had been a deity, perhaps a local god of primitive Semitic tribes. On being discarded as a god, Azazel was banished to the wilderness as an unclean being, an object of scorn, upon which the people might purge their misdeeds.

Of all magic usages, divination of future and hidden things gained the strongest foothold in Israel. We learn from the Scriptures that the Syrian Laban, Rachel's father, possessed the Teraphim, the household gods. He thought their oracle to be of unfailing truth. When Rachel eloped from her father's house with Jacob, she took with her the idols whose reliability she had learned to trust when still a child. In her simple belief, she feared the Teraphim would tell Laban the direction of their flight. And

8. Azazel

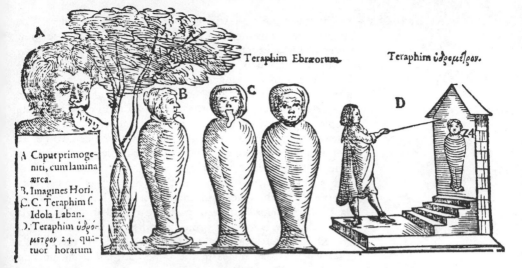

Teraphim Ebræorum.   Teraphim ὑδροεμέλρον.

A Caput primoge-
niti, cum lamina
ærea.
B. Imagines Hori.
C.C. Teraphim ſ.
Idola Laban.
D. Teraphim ὑδρό-
μετρον 24. qua-
tuor horarum

9. *Teraphim*

when Laban, unaided by the oracles, overtook the pair, Rachel resolved to keep the Teraphim, concealing them beneath her skirts. The idols were the only things of her home that Rachel would not forego in the outside world. This survival of the pastoral faith passed into the popular magic of Israel. We do not know how one questioned the Teraphim nor how they answered, but like the Lares in Rome the Teraphim were to be found in many houses of Israel. In vain the prophet Zechariah argued that 'the Teraphim have given vain answers'.

The interrogation of God was a good and legal thing when it took place in the temple. Prior to a weighty transaction of state, His will had to be discovered through the Ephod oracle. The high priest wore shoulder pieces set with onyx stones, and a woven sash embroidered with gold. Over this outer garment called the Ephod he donned the square breastplate with the Urim and Thummin, twelve jewels through which Jehovah spoke, giving strategic counsel in time of war, pointing out transgressors and predicting things to come. But often God would withhold His advice; when angered, He not infrequently denied help to His blaspheming people. Then the kings in despair might turn to soothsayers, who deserved the death penalty, according to the law: 'A man or woman in whom there is a pythonic or divining spirit, dying let them die.'

King Saul turned to necromancy when the Ephod remained mute. He was seeking foreknowledge of the battle in which he was to be fatally wounded. With a few trusted men, he stole out by night to visit the witch of Endor. 'Divine now for me by the familiar spirit,' he said, 'and bring up for me whom I shall indicate to you. . . .' 'Whom shall I bring up for you?' said the woman. 'Bring Samuel up for me,' said he. Then the spirit of Samuel rose from the ground . . . 'an old man, wrapped in a mantle'. He confronted the terrified king with his approaching death. Was this the real Samuel, sent by God to frighten the anxious king, or was it a phantom from hell? This much-debated question is left unanswered in the Scriptures.

Saul had always fought sorcery and witchcraft in his kingdom.

Yet he was more superstitious than other Hebrew rulers. Too often he had consulted the Ephod oracle, and the Lord grew weary of his questioning. Neither could his virtuous successor David rid himself of these magical beliefs. Once when there was a blight in the kingdom, David interrogated the Ephod, which placed the blame on Saul. Saul, having been gathered to his fathers, lay beyond the reach of the hungry and irate people, but many of his sons were still alive. David ordered seven of them to be sought out. 'And they were hanged before the Lord', at the beginning of the barley harvest in the spring. When the autumn rains came at last, falling upon their dead bodies and upon the scorched earth, their bones were gathered and buried with honour in their ancestors' sepulchre. King Saul's descendents had been used as a rain charm. The magic power that dwelt in their princely bodies, in their bones, had proved efficacious, as David had anticipated. In the Middle Ages witches used bones to the same end, conjuring up rain and storms. They perpetuated the old belief that the bones of the dead, when handled properly, induce rain.[5]

We are told that Manasse, thirteenth king of Judah, encouraged the most sacrilegious kind of divination. 'Manasse shed much innocent blood till he filled Jerusalem up to the mouth.' This king of the chosen people saw prophecies of good or evil in the quivering entrails of the slaughtered. Even the great and legendary Solomon did not always behave according to the Lord's behest. In his old age he turned away from the God of his fathers and worshipped the wanton Elilim. He had peopled his harem with foreign women who worshipped their native gods, and in the holy city he had built temples for every creed. His theological and demonological wisdom has become legendary; his magic lamp and celebrated seal enabled him to command the spirits of hell. A thousand legends concerning Solomon (Suleiman) are scattered through the East. His throne was of ivory, flanked by two sculptured lions overtopped by eagles; when he approached, the lions would roar and the eagles would spread their wings above his venerable head. However, this and other marvellous accounts cannot conceal the fact that after Solomon's reign Jerusalem fell into a magico-religious chaos. The Scriptures, so eloquent concerning Solomon's wealth and magnificence, his wisdom, his horses and chariots, leave unanswered the question as to whether Solomon ever returned to the faith of the one Jehovah.

The Sphinx

The Sphinx: 'I am the child of yesterday; the Twin Lion Gods have made me come into being.'

Book of the Dead

In the undulating desert near Giseh rise three mighty pyramids, the tombs of three kings – Khufu, Khafre and Menkure. At the foot of the pyramids crouches the Sphinx, with talons outstretched over the city of the dead, guarding the magical secrets gathered therein. 'In front of the pyramids,' says Pliny, 'is the Sphinx, a still more wondrous object of art, but upon which rests a spell of silence, as it is looked upon as a deity.' The Sphinx imposes silence. The thirteenth-century Arab writer, Abd-al-Latif, tells us that 'the true reason why all mention of this monument had been avoided was the terror it inspired'. During that epoch, its face and figure were still beautiful, and its mouth, Abd-al-Latif relates, bore 'the imprint of grace and beauty, as if it were smiling'. The huge head refulgent with red varnish was still untarnished at that time. The Arabs named it Abu'l-hawl, father of terror. Fourteen centuries before Christ, so we read on the flat stone leaning against its breast, this giant already lay buried in the shifting sand. By that time the Sphinx was already ageless, its origin blurred in legend.

Fourteen hundred years before our era, a prince, later Thutmose IV, took his siesta in the shadow of the half-submerged Sphinx. He had been throwing spears and hunting in the neighbourhood, when the hour came in which he granted rest to his followers. Alone in the noontime solitude, he offered flower seeds to Horus, 'for a great enchantment rests upon this place from the beginning of time'. Whereupon the Sun-god (whose image the Sphinx was then believed to be) appeared in a dream to the prince and spoke to him as a father to a son; after promising that he would succeed to the throne and enjoy a long and happy reign, the god urged the prince to have the Sphinx cleared of sand: 'Promise me that thou wilt do what I wish with all my heart; then I shall know whether thou art my son and my helper.' When later, contrary to his expectations, the prince was raised to kingship, he remembered his dream and obeying the god's will, ordered the Sphinx to be dug out of the sands.[1] However, the sands of the desert continued their ceaseless labour, and a few hundred years later the monster was again buried beneath the dunes, as man and desert fought to possess the hewn rock.

In his book *Isis and Osiris* Plutarch (A.D. 45–126) says that the Sphinx symbolizes the secret of occult wisdom. Elsewhere he describes it as a magnificent creature having wings of ever-changing hue. When turned towards the sun, they glitter like gold; when towards the clouds, they shine with the reflection of rainbow colours. But even Plutarch, that assiduous investigator, failed to penetrate the mystery. For countless ages, the Sphinx remained the guardian of Egyptian magic. Plutarch assures us that, in their desire to converse with its priests, many Greek thinkers – Solon, Thales, Pythagoras, Eudoxus, even Lycurgus himself – undertook the arduous journey to Egypt.

The Egyptians believed that each priestly word, each priestly gesture, had a marvellous effect. Mysterious magical power resided in certain persons, and the greater the Mana or magic tension, the more astounding the marvels they could induce. The pharaoh was so charged with this power that by merely raising his hand he could make the earth tremble. For this reason perhaps, the king, when not depicted in the midst of a well-defined action, was usually portrayed in a pose of immobility so that no danger might result from an involuntary movement of his. For the Mana resided not only in the person but in the image too.

In the Nile lands, images had from ancient times been treated as living, active beings. Since the beginning Egypt had been the home of magical statues whose occult powers could affect the physical world. Thus the awesome figures of the guardian Sphinxes before the temples did more than frighten away the profane. They could reward and punish, as could the king himself whose image they originally represented. The Sphinxes opened their stone mouths and revealed the will of the gods. The fathers of the Christian church distinctly vouch for the phenomenon that statues could speak. The king and the assembled people were often present at this oracle, and scribes wrote down the words on their papyri. In the Siwa oasis stood the image of Ammon, to which Alexander the Great once made a pilgrimage. Ammon promised something dazzling to the Macedonian: mastery over the earth. Images accomplished still greater wonders. Often they would descend from their pedestals to walk among men. Thus during the reign of Queen Hatshepsut the god Ammon strode through the temple halls at Karnak, stopping before a youth, later to be Thutmose III (ruled 1501–1477 B.C.). The young man knelt before the god, but Ammon raised him up and bade him take the place that was the king's. Through this divine coup d'état Thutmose became sovereign. Human reason is silenced when Ammon intervenes in a dynastic matter.

Whenever the sculptor's chisel moulds the amorphous mass into an image, whenever he portrays an organism, magical power flows into the statue – a power which may be imprisoned within it by incantation and magical gesture, and which gives life to the image so long as it remains whole. When it is broken its soul escapes. Demons hostile to men are for this reason cut through on the hieroglyphic reliefs, so that the sign may have no evil influence.

But what power can disturb the magic virtue of the Sphinx or drive away the spirit that inhabits it? Thousands of chisels carved the rock. When nature failed, masonry was introduced

This colossus, half hewn, half sculpted, has defied millennia.
Never in the history of mankind has a statue so lastingly caught
the imagination of peoples. The thoughts of countless generations dwell in it: numberless conjurations and rites have built
up in it a mighty protective spirit, a soul that still inhabits this
time-scarred giant.

Mortuary Magic

As Osiris died and rose again from the
dead, so all men hoped to arise like
him, from death to the life eternal.

J. G. Frazer, *The Golden Bough*

When Ikhnaton overthrew the Egyptian gods and demons,
making the cult of the one god Aton a state religion, he also
suppressed mortuary magic. The reformer king did not believe
in a life beyond the grave. Yet it was upon the afterlife that
Egyptian magic centred. In the course of the ages, this magic had
become an elaborate science whose aim was to win for the dead a
pleasant life in the hereafter. The massive pyramids and tombs
built for the deceased pharaohs and their ministers, for priests
and other dignitaries, suggest the power that the dead wielded
over all minds. Looking at these monuments, we can sense the
impossible task that Ikhnaton faced when he sought to banish
mortuary magic from the Egyptian religion.

In the west, the Egyptians believed, lies the world of the dead,
where the sun-god disappears every evening; they spoke of the
departed as 'westerners'. The belief in a world of the dead often
mingled with the notion of an underworld. It is through this
subterranean world that the ship of the sun sails during the
night: the dead await it impatiently and rejoice when its divine
radiance appears. Then the dead souls, filled with delight, seize
a rope from the ship and tow it through the depths. It was also
believed that the dead, disguised as birds, soar into the sky
where in his heavenly barge Ra, the sun-god, awaits them and
transforms them into stars to travel with him through the vault
of the heavens. Or again, a lentil field lies high in the northeast,
where the grain grows taller than it does on the banks of the
Nile, and where the dead live on in peace and abundance. However, this blessed land is water-locked, and none but the just
and righteous may persuade the obdurate ferryman to row them
across.[2]

The cult of the dead reached a peak when it incorporated the
Osiris myth. Osiris, divine brother and husband of Isis, was
born to save mankind. At his nativity, a voice was heard proclaiming that the Lord had come into the world. But the diabolical, vengeful Seth shut him up in a chest which he conveyed
to the sea by the Tanaïtic mouth of the Nile. Isis wandered in
search of the body, and at last, near the city of Byblos in Syria,
she found the coffin in a tamarisk tree which had grown up
around it. She carried it back to Egypt, but now Seth dis-
membered the body and scattered its parts far and wide. A
second time the grieving Isis set out upon her arduous search

for her husband's scattered limbs. She interred the fragments wherever she found them or, as others believed, buried an image in all these spots, pretending that it was his body, to the end that Osiris might be honoured in many places. According to this version, she fastened the limbs together with the help of the gods Nephtis, Thot and Horus, her son. She fanned the body with her wings, and through her magic art Osiris rose again to reign henceforth as king over the dead.

There he was assisted by the forty-two helpers, hideous representatives of the sins, with Osiris exercising power over the souls of the departed. Before this tribunal, in the 'hall of both truths', appear the dead, to have their hearts weighed in the scales of righteousness. According to the verdict, they receive everlasting life or are punished for their sins. Those whom Osiris brings to reckoning are condemned to hunger and thirst, to lie in the dark and solitary grave from which they may never return to sunlight; or they are tossed to abominable executioners in the shape of crocodiles and hippopotami eager to tear them asunder. The good and the righteous, however, now receive their reward. In the course of ages, these diverse traditions concerning the blessed and their afterlife have tended to mingle. According to belief, the dead will live on in the fields of Yaru or soar to Ra the sun-god; or they will descend to Osiris in the underworld, or again to Abydos, city of the dead, whose sovereigns were once the living rulers of Egypt.

Whereas the soul known as Ba passes into the afterlife, the Ka remains with the mummy. The Ka is a mysterious life force, a tenuous counterpart of the soul, which continues to live a magical reflection of life in the grave, among the tomb possessions of the deceased or among the pictures of such objects. Images, statuettes, imitation utensils, miniature houses take the place of real things. Magical operations give them their efficacy, and the small-scale replicas of reality attract the Ka, since the Ka is unable to detect the difference between them and reality. Or rather, through the magical operations of mortuary priests, the replicas become reality. The priest could thus assure the Ka of

10. *The Ka and the mummy*

the deceased a serene life in the silent depths of the grave, from which it might at times emerge to be gladdened by the sun. But what advantage did these promises gain if the Osiris tribunal condemned the Ba soul?[3]

Here too priestly magic offered a solution. The Egyptian gods could be deceived, menaced and forced into obedience. So implicitly did the Egyptians trust the power of magic, the virtue of the spoken word, the irresistibility of magic gestures and other rituals, that they hoped to bend even the good gods to their will. The priests would bring dreadful retribution to the deities who failed to deal leniently with the dead. They threatened to shoot lightning into the arm of Shu, god of the air, who would then no longer be able to support the sky-goddess, and her star-sown body would collapse, disrupting the order of all things.

The priests filled papyrus scrolls with magical formulas enabling the deceased to withstand his judges in the world beyond. The *Book of the Dead* told precisely what the soul would encounter during its journey into the shadowy kingdom, and how the deceased might plead his cause. This scroll revealed the secret names of the demons and inquisitor-gods; knowledge of the spirit's true name gave to the deceased power over that spirit. The answers to the examiners' questions were transcribed word for word, and knowing them was sufficient to obtain a favourable verdict: 'I have always shunned evil; I have given bread to the hungry, water to the thirsty, clothes to the naked, a ship to the stranded; to the orphan I was a father, to the widow a husband, to the roofless I gave a home.' These answers, uttered with the correct intonation and in the prescribed phraseology, would pass for truth. But what if the deceased should find himself unable to pronounce the words? What if the spirits of the air robbed him of breath, or other evil spirits stole his mouth, his head, his heart, or even his name, without which he lost all identity? For this emergency, too, the *Book of the Dead* contains formulas and incantations. A guidebook placed in the sarcophagus or inscribed on it conducts the wayfarer into the next life.

Despite these arts, one fear remained. In the tribunal hall, before the terrifying judges, might not the conscience of the traveller rebel within him and cause his heart to rise against the deceitful words issuing from his mouth? Here too priestly magic provided assistance. On the mummy's breast a sacred beetle, a scarab, was fastened, with a charm to pacify the restive heart. 'O my heart, rise not as a witness against me.'[4]

Journey to the Underworld

The mouth of the dead had to be 'opened' before he could journey to Osiris, so that he might plead and answer in accordance with the priests' instructions. The 'opening of the mouth' was of the greatest importance: it was performed upon the statue that had been made of the deceased and set in the tomb. The statue was placed on a mound, symbolizing the funeral mountain.

There, leaning against the arch beyond which the mummy lay, it received the fluid, the Ka of the deceased, that entered the image through the nape, causing the statue to come to life. Its mouth was opened by the priests according to a ceremony described in the *Book of the Dead*.

A vignette in one of the papyri which have come to us shows a man seated upon a pedestal which has the shape of the emblem of right and truth, the Maat. The dead man, we learn from the scroll, is a scribe named Ani, now called Ani-Osiris, for like all the blessed deceased he was supposed to have become one with the great Osiris. This fusion with the godhead was in Ani's time considered the reward of those who had escaped punishment. Standing before the statue of Ani-Osiris, a priest clad in a panther skin holds in his right hand a wand with which he is about to touch the statue's lips. Below the image is this text:

Osiris, the scribe Ani, triumphant, sayeth: May the god Ptah open my mouth, and may the god of my city loosen the swathings, even the swathings which are over my mouth. Moreover, may Thoth, being filled and furnished with charms, come and loosen the bandages, even the bandages of Seth which fetter my mouth: and may the god Tem hurl them at those who would fetter me with them and drive them back. May my mouth be opened, may my mouth be unclosed by Shu with his iron knife wherewith he opened the mouths of the gods. I am the goddess Sekhet and I sit upon my place in the great wind of heaven. I am the great goddess Sah who dwelleth among the souls of Heliopolis. Now as concerning every charm and all the words which may be spoken against me, may the gods resist them, and may each and every one of the company of the gods withstand them . . .[5]

11. Magical operation of the priest on the effigy of the deceased

Ptah, the patron-god of artists and artisans, and Thoth, whose magical words became flesh when they brought the world into being, are invoked as the protectors of statues and incantations. They will put to flight Seth the destroyer, the enemy of Osiris. Shu, the god of the air, is called upon, since he is the breath necessary for speaking. He stands erect, supporting the heavenly vault, whose curve is like the hollow of the mouth. In early time the gods too had their mouths opened, and Shu performed this magical act. Ani identifies himself with several deities, for instance with Sekhet and Sah. This stratagem endows him with supernatural power, as we shall discover.

Once having had his mouth opened, Ani will begin his perilous journey. He will meet evil spirits, but powerful words will drive them away. In his guidebook, the *Book of the Dead*, Ani will find the answers to all the questions with which the underworld will burden him. When he reaches the river where the old ferryman is waiting, Ani will speak thus to him:

'O thou guardian of the mysterious boat, I hasten, I hasten, I hasten. I come to see my father Osiris.'

Then speaks the boat's hull: 'Tell me my name.'

'Darkness is thy name.'

Then the voice of the mast commands: 'Tell me my name.'

'He who leadeth the great goddess on her way is thy name.'

The sail says: 'Tell me my name.'

'Nuit, goddess of heaven, is thy name,' replies Ani, and his answers, if uttered in the right tone, are accepted. The boat seems to stand for the universe. Its hull is Keb, the god of the dark earth, in which are the caves of the underworld. The mast is Shu, the air-god, who stands upright, holding in his outstretched arms, as if they were the sail's yard, the arched body of Nuit, goddess of heaven, symbolizing the sail.

After having left the boat, the scribe is called upon again: 'Who then art thou?' Several voices ask: 'What is thy name?'

'I am he who lives under the flowers; the dweller in his olive tree, is my name.'

'Pass thou,' the gods say, and Ani reaches the city 'to the north of the olive tree'.

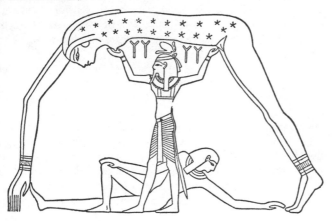

12. The Egyptian gods of the earth, the air, and the heavenly vault

New questions assail him which, like the answers, are clad in the code of occult wisdom, whose beholder alone will pass freely the twenty-one pylons, the fifteen doors, and the seven halls that lead to the judgement chamber.

'What, then, didst thou see there?' meaning in the city through which Ani has passed.

'The leg and the thigh,' is the enigmatic answer.

'What didst thou pay to them?'

'Let me see rejoicings in those lands of the Fenkhu.'

'And what did they give unto thee?'

'A flame of fire and a tablet of crystal.'

'What then didst thou do therewith?'

'I buried them by the furrow of Manaat, as gifts for the night.'

'What then didst thou find by the furrow of Manaat?'

'A sceptre of flint, the name of which is giver of words.'

'What then didst thou do to the flame and the tablet of crystal after thou hadst buried them?'

'I uttered words over them in the furrow, I extinguished the fire, I broke the tablet, and I made a pool of water.'

'Come then,' they say, 'and enter through the door of the hall of double Maati [the judgement hall], for thou knowest us.'

But the wanderer is not yet free, since the bolts of the door, the lintels, the threshold, and the sockets ask to be told their names. Ani, however, has learned the answer from the *Book of the Dead*, and thus at last the door opens to allow him entrance to the judgement hall, where Osiris will try him.

The Word

Whatever a man calls his own is magically a part of him. His cut hair and nail parings remain bound up with his being; objects with which he has shared contact are imbued with his personality; and his name is just as much a part of him as a limb is of his body. Objects with which he has had no contact may likewise carry influence; likeness has the most powerful ties with the man it represents. An individual's magic tension flows into his portrait or image. The reluctance of primitive people to be photographed is well known; they are afraid to leave fragments of themselves in strangers' hands.

J. G. Frazer analyses the principles of thought upon which these magical beliefs are based. They are of two kinds: 'First, that like produces like, or that an effect resembles its cause; and second, that things which have once been in contact with each other continue to act on each other at a distance after physical contact has been severed.' Using the first of these principles, called by Frazer the law of similarity, the magician seeks to produce the desired effect by imitating this effect. Using the second, the law of contagion, the magician does to a thing which has belonged to a person whatever he wishes to do to the person himself.

By mistreating a portrait, the magus will cause its subject, no matter how far away, to suffer. If the magician adds a lock of the victim's hair or his walking stick to the image, he will be combining the two principles, similarity and contagion, thus building up greater magical power. Calling the enchanted one by his name strengthens further the effect of the operation. The name is the only part of a person with which the magician can work when his victim is remote and no other belongings of his are available. This is why a name is a precarious possession, to be guarded jealously. Innumerable people have believed and still believe in the magical power of a name. This belief was especially powerful among the Egyptians: at birth everyone was given two names, the true name and the good name, or the greater and the lesser. Only the lesser name was made public; the greater belonged to the Ka, and embodied all the individual's magical power. The evil spirits and the gods would vent their anger upon the lesser name, leaving the man himself unharmed.

In the light of this belief, the priests of Egypt sought to discover the names of the gods, and thereby the ability to wield a supernatural power. At the sound of the true name, the powers of the god stood ready to perform the invoker's bidding. 'This name being uttered on a river bank, the stream will dry up. And if pronounced in the fields, sparks will spring forth. If the magician who knows the secret name of a god is attacked by a crocodile, the virtue of this name will cause the earth to fall into the water; south will become north, and the earth will be overturned.'

In the magic incantations of the Egyptians, not only the name but every spoken word had its supernatural effect. Nothing could come into being before its name had been uttered. Not before the mind had projected its idea upon the outside world could a thing have true existence. 'The word,' the hieroglyphics tell us, 'creates all things: everything that we love and hate, the totality of being. Nothing *is* before it has been uttered in a clear voice.' To accomplish its full effect, the word must be spoken correctly. Magic conjuration prescribed the intonation, the secret rhythm which Thoth, god of magic and inventor of language, had taught to the wise men. Success depended on the exact delivery of the formula. Rhythms and melodies were studied in the Egyptian college of magic or 'house of life', where the various other arts of magical conjuration also had their home. For in time primitive beliefs become framed in an elaborate technique. More and more knowledge was needed for an effective conjuration.

Thoroughgoing preparations had to be made before one was ready to begin. For nine days, the magician had to undergo cleansing rites; then he anointed his body and washed his mouth with natron. Fresh clothing was obligatory, new and white. All the garments were thoroughly fumigated before the magician donned them. On his tongue, in green ink, the magician drew a feather, the sign of truth. And finally, in the colour appropriate to the god of the hour, he traced a circle on the earth. Only then could he proceed with his incantation.

To make an enemy harmless, the magician would smear his own feet with clay, placing between them the severed head of an ass and rubbing his mouth and hand with its blood. He turned to the sun, and having put one arm forward, the other back, he addressed Seth-Typhon, the evil one, in magical rhythmic speech: 'Thou terrible, invisible, all-powerful one, god of gods, assailer and destroyer. . . .' In many ceremonies, the magus would utter strange, incomprehensible sounds, words foreign to the Egyptian tongue. With these names, either of Semitic origin or fancifully compounded, the gods were summoned. Since the word was charged with magical power, it had to remain unaltered. The words of the magical language were handed down through centuries, although there were few who still knew to what gods the bizarre expressions referred. An incantation from the time of Ramses II (1292–1225 B.C.) contains the following jumble of ancient verbage:

> O Ualpaga. O Kemmara. O Kamolo. O Karkhenmu.
> O Asmagaaa, The Uana. The Uthun [enemies] of the sun.
> This is to order those who are in your midst, the enemies.
>
> He died by violence who murdered his brother.
> To the crocodile he has vowed his soul.
> No man laments him.
> But he brings his soul before the tribunal of double justice
> Before Mamuremukahabu [Osiris]
> And those absolute rulers who are with him,
> Who thus answers his enemy:
>
> O lion, black face, bloody eyes [venom],
> Into his mouth who destroyed his own name . . .
> His Father's. These have not yet lost their power to bite.[6]

This is doubtless addressed to the formidable judges of the underworld, lest they be deceived by the magical formulas offered by the murderer. It is a powerful counter-magic, designed to fathom the wiles of the criminal's soul in order to make certain that he receives his punishment: to the crocodile he has vowed his soul! Only one thing could resist the virtue of a word: still more powerful words, more powerful magic.

Often the evil spirits would appear unbidden. Particularly fearful were the dead condemned to wander until their souls were annihilated. They were recognizable by their mummy noses, flattened by the swathings. Eluding watchful mothers, they would steal up to the cradles of sleeping children. One had to be wary when undressing: at night, the ghosts spied upon the living, waiting for the unguarded moment when a careless one might be dragged away. Against this danger was used the formula: 'The beauties of N. [speaker of the formula] are the beauties of Osiris. His upper lip is that of Isis. His under lip is that of Nepthis. His teeth are little swords. His arms are those of the gods. His fingers are like divine serpents. His back is like that of Keb. . . .'[7]

Despite the elaborate ritual for the passage of the dead to the afterlife, it was ever to be feared that the departed would return to the home they had left. Complicated formulas had to be recited:

> O ewe, ewe's son, lamb, ewe's son who suckest milk of the mother ewe, do not let the deceased be bitten by any serpent male or female, nor by any scorpion, nor by any reptile. Do not let the venom become master of his limbs, nor let any of the dead, whether male or female, enter into it. May it not be haunted by the shade of any spirit. May the mouth of the serpent Em-kkahu-ef have no power over him. He is the ewe.
> You who enter, do not enter into any of the deceased limbs. O you

who hear him, do not hear him with you. O you coilers around, do not coil yourselves around him. . . .

I have uttered these words over the sacred herbs placed in all the corners of the house, whereafter I sprinkled the whole house with the sacred water at evening and at sunrise. He who hears this [the deceased] will remain stretched out in his place.[8]

All-powerful words also helped to resist earthly perils. On the edge of the pale desert one awaited nightfall uneasily. True, one's house was well guarded by dogs to ward off any nocturnal visitor, but it was more certain if, before turning them loose, one strengthened them with the magical words:

Up, savage dog. I shall prescribe to thee what thou art to do this day. Thou wert tied up. Art thou not set loose? By Horus thou art commanded to do this: let thy face be as the open sky. Let thy jaws be merciless. May thy strength immolate like that of the god Har-shefi. Kill like the goddess Anata. Let thy mane rise in iron rods. For this, be Horus and be Seth. . . . I invest thee with the power of fascination; take away hearing. For thou art the courageous, threatening watcher.

In many conjurations, the magician identifies himself with a god or with several gods. A man attacked by crocodiles cries out: 'Be not against me. I am Ammon. I am Amhur, the guardian. I am the great lord of the blade. I am Seth', etc. The potentates of the land believed themselves to be close relatives, sons of the gods. In battle, the pharaohs would turn to Ammon-Ra, the sun-god, to remind him of this bond. The king did not pray for victory, but demanded it as something that was his right. And the 'father of battles' might respond: '. . . Ramses-Meriamun, I am with you! It is I, thy father! . . . My hand is with thee and I am better for thee than hundreds of thousands.'[9] The highest powers of all, the supernatural rulers of the world, are obedient to mortal words. The world order is perpetually in danger. A foolhardy priest might overturn the earth and the sky to satisfy his own or his client's wishes. 'How is it possible,' we must exclaim with Porphyry the Neo-Platonist, 'that the gods should be subject to extortion, like men?'

Quite different was the magic of the Mesopotamians. True the Chaldeans were aware of the existence of the name of the highest god. Although it remained unknown to them and therefore unutterable, it was invoked by them in times of great peril. This name was a distinct person, a divine hypostasis endowed with a personal existence, and hence having a power of its own over the other gods, over nature and over the spirits. Not even the priests could learn it through initiation. No constraint could be exercised over it.

As children recognize their parents to be their masters yet seek to obtain from them the gratification of their innumerable wishes, so did the Egyptians behave towards their gods. The world revolved around their own problems and wishes, and the gods, like parents, had to succumb to their pressure. Like children, the Egyptians lied to their god-elders without the feeling of remorse or without diminished confidence in the omnipotence of these supernal beings. And they knew that the gods could withhold neither their favour nor attention.

Isis

One element of the old cosmogony was destined to outlive
Egyptian magic: the cult of Isis. The great goddess evokes gentle-
ness, maternal constancy, devotion to husband, and the fertility
and grace of woman. She fosters everything born, everything that
grows. Her tears swell the waters of the Nile which, overflowing,
fertilize the earth. Her soul dwells in the star Sirius. And for
thousands of years the appearance of Sirius in the dawning sky
during the summer solstice was a signal to the Egyptians for the
return of the Nile flood. Restored by the grieving Isis, Osiris,
the husband, rose again. The ever-recurrent procreative act took
place: Osiris, the sacred Nile, fertilized the green-growing land
of Egypt.

Isis had many names, and she united the qualities of many
local divinities. The faithful sought her protection, and the alien
recognized in her the traits of the mother goddesses of his homeland: Minerva, Aphrodite, Ceres, Hecate. . . . Isis towered above
them all. Her motherliness contrasted with the wanton, cruel
behaviour of Astarte, Anaïtis, Cybele, the formidable goddesses
of the Orient, and the holocaust of maidens and mutilated youths
whom they subjected. These goddesses loved human sacrifice,
war, barrenness; but it was *life* that Isis loved and protected.

Her cult spread throughout Europe and western Asia, and
traces of it merged finally with nascent Christianity. Many
attributes of the Holy Virgin were borrowed from Isis; 'the
immaculate': '*mater domina*', an appellation that survives in
the form 'Madonna'. 'Indeed,' says J. G. Frazer in describing the
cult of Isis, 'her stately ritual, with its shaven and tonsured
priests, its matins and its vespers, its tinkling music, its baptism
and aspersions of holy water, its solemn processions, the jewelled
images of the mother of god, presented many points of similarity
to the pomp and ceremony of catholicism.'

There was significance in everything pertaining to the goddess's
figure and dress. On the base of her statue in the city of Saïs
these enigmatic words were carved: 'I am everything that was,
that is, that shall be. . . . Nor has any mortal ever been able to
discover what lies under my veil.' Apuleius (second century of
the Christian era) vividly portrays the goddess, and from his
description the Jesuit Athanasius Kircher (1601–80) had a woodcut made, in which Isis is crowned with a coil of hair, symbol of
the moon's influence upon herbs and grasses. Wheat adorns her
head, as a reminder that she was the discoverer of grain and
taught us how to cultivate it. Her hair is drawn through a sphere
which represents the world. This sphere rests on a garland of
flowers, denoting her rule over the plant world. The rich head-
dress is completed by two snakes, signifying doubly the moon's
generative power and its sinuous path. Isis's flowing hair means
that she is the nurturer of the whole world. In her left hand, she
holds the pail, symbol of the Nile flood; in her right, the
sistrum, a jingling instrument sacred to her. This, according

ISIDIS
Magnæ Deorum Matris
APVLEIANA DESCRIPTIO.

Nomina varia Isidis.

Isis
Minerua
Venus
Iuno
Proserpina
Ceres
Diana
Rhea seu Tellus
Pessinuncia
Rhraminusia
Bellona
Hecate
Luna
Polymorphus dæmon.

Ἴσις παυδεχὴς πο-
λύμορφ⊙. δαί-
μων.
Μυσ'ήριμ⊙. φύσις,
ὕλη.

Explicationes symbolorum Isidis.

A Diuinitatem, mundum, orbes cœlestes
BB Iter Lunæ flexuosum, & vim fœcundatiuam notat.
CC Tutulus, vim Lunæ in herbas, & plantas.
D Cereris symbolum, Isis enim spicas inuenit.
E Byssina vestis multicolor, multiformem Lunæ faciem.
F Innentio frumenti.
G Dominium in omnia vegetabilia.
H Radios lunares.
I Genius Nili malorum auerruncus.
K Incrementa & decrementa Lunæ.
L Humectat. vis Lunæ.
M Lunæ vis victrix, & vis diuinandi.
N Dominium in humores & mare.
O Terræ symbolū, & Medicinæ inuentrix,
P Fœcunditas, quæ sequitur terram irrigatam.
Q Astrorum Domina.
R Omnium nutrix.
S ⎫ Terræ marisque
M ⎭ Domina.

Ἀπερὶ Θιῶν Μῆτηρ ταύτη πολύτιμ⊙. ΙΣΙΣ.

13. Isis

Kircher, reveals her as the genius of the Nile and guardian against evil. Her robe glows with all the colours of the moon, and being the queen of the firmament, she wears a star-sown mantle, the hem of which is decorated with flowers, symbolic of the soil and recalling that Isis is the discoverer of healing herbal juices. On her womb she wears a half-moon, whose magic rays fertilize the earth. Her right foot is on land, her left in the water: she presides over both elements. She is the *stella maris*, star of the sea, guardian of all that journey upon the ocean. And the ship, a feminine symbol, is consecrated to Isis.

All these attributes the believer regarded with curiosity; they excited his imagination. The figure of Isis preoccupied both the simple-minded and the philosophic. He who sought higher

14. *The soul of the world*

philosophers: it meant little to him that the myth symbolized
the overflowing Nile, an eclipse of the moon or other astronomical events. From the world of matter, he withdrew to the sphere
of ideas, seeking a transcendent key to the legend of the world
mother.

Plutarch, whose ideology is deeply tinged with Platonic and
Oriental esoterism, speaks in mysterious terms of the holy trinity
of Osiris, Isis and the son Horus. They corporealize, he says,
intelligence, matter and cosmos, and they are called the most
perfect triangle. The proportions of this triangle express a divine
secret: the base, equal to four, is Isis, the female conceiving element: the vertical, equal to three, is Osiris, the male creative
principle; the hypotenuse, five, is Horus the offspring.

Any triangle traced in these proportions is a sacred diagram
endowed with magic power; and similarly are the three numbers,
carrying supernatural forces. The Egyptians and the philosophers of the Pythagorean school were devoted to the wisdom of
numbers, as we shall see in the following chapter. Wherever in
later times numbers and geometrical figures appear in magic
circles and on talismans, we may trace them back to ancient
numerology. 'Numbers,' Plutarch says, 'allude to something
which the founder of this sect had observed in the Egyptian
temples; they refer to some ceremonies performed in them, or
to some symbols exhibited there.' The secret, however, Plutarch
cannot or does not want to reveal, though he affirms repeatedly
that all this has a profound meaning. Everything in the Egyptian
religion, he says, is to be understood allegorically.

Isis lived on in the Christian West, not only in the cult of the
Madonna but also in the occult doctrine of the magicians. Following Plutarch's ideas, they discovered in the god-mother of
antiquity an occult allegory, that of the world soul, which nur-
tures the entire creation at God's behest. Cast out of the Christian
heaven, she continues in the world of the stars and upon earth to
sow the essence of life. 'She is the feminine part of nature, or that
property which renders her a suitable subject for the production
of all other beings.' A seventeenth-century engraving shows the
world soul still with some of the symbols of the ancient Isis:
flowing hair, the half-moon on her womb, one foot in the water,
the other on land. She is chained to God, according to Plutarch's
saying: 'Isis always partakes of the supreme.' And man (the ape
of God!) is chained to her, as he owes his very life to the seed
that flows from her breast.

Centuries passed and still her image persisted. At the end of the
eighteenth century, she was remembered by men who seemed
closed to every magical sentiment, the leaders of the French
revolution. At the solemn ceremony performed in honour of the
supreme being, Robespierre, in a vague remembrance of the
mysterious inscription of Saïs, put the torch to a veil that covered
the gigantic statue of a woman, Isis, whose generative power was
interpreted now as reason, the nurturer of progress.

GREECE

Magic in Philosophical Garb

... let us not boast, lest some evil eye should put to flight the word which I am going to speak.

Plato, *Phaedo*

More than other nations of antiquity, the Greeks relied on inductive reasoning which framed poetically the sombre images of mythology and pervaded their philosophy. Natural phenomena were approached from the higher realms of the mind, which was thought to partake of the divine. This explains why the Greeks were poor experimenters; despite their masterly logic, they evolved only vague and unscientific explanations for happenings in nature. Mind subjugated matter. This negligence and even abhorrence of experimentation resulted from indulgence in what was 'superior', the unreserved acceptance of the authority of reason which could exist without material proof. The West inherited this unscientific procedure from Hellenic philosophy. Throughout the Middle Ages, during the Renaissance, and even in more recent times, the natural sciences were hampered by this tradition.

Plato says that there are four species of beings – those of the air, the birds; those of water, the fishes; those of earth, the pedestrians; and those of the heavens, the stars, whose element is fire. During the Renaissance Agrippa von Nettesheim, reluctant to accept the idea that the stars were related to the earthly fauna, modified Plato's statement. Agrippa, basing his opinion on Aristotle, Dioscorides and Pliny the Elder, said that fire shelters salamanders and crickets. A simple experiment would have proven that salamanders and crickets die in fire, like any other animal, but Agrippa shared with the past an aversion to experimentation. From Pliny we learn that similar beliefs concerning the marvellous virtues of salamanders existed in Egypt and Babylon. Without doubt Aristotle had gathered his wisdom from Oriental neighbours, and did not find it necessary to submit the salamander to a scientific test. Thus did a superstitious belief perpetuate itself for about two thousand years. That the fiery nature of the salamander was accepted generally in Agrippa's time is illustrated by the fact that his contemporary, Francis I of France, adopted as his royal emblem the batrachian surrounded by flames.

The reasoning of the philosophers produced the most startling, and poetic, absurdities. Plato says that the head, the abode of ideas, is spherical in the image of the stars. Unlike the rest of the body, the head is linked to heaven. A small isthmus, the neck, between the intelligible and the corporeal, was made in order to separate neatly these two things. Plato's world is a magical one:

for it is unified and all things are interrelated. The universe is an animal endowed with soul and mind. It has no eyes, as nothing is to be seen beyond it; it has no ears, for there is no place outside of it in which anything could be heard. It has no breath as the atmosphere is within it. Hands are useless to the world animal, as it has no enemy against whom it would use them. It has no feet, for they are not necessary to revolving movement, etc. Thus the world animal is shaped in the most perfect form: the sphere.

The soul is older than the body and therefore superior to it, says Plato. It is composed of three elements: the indivisible, which partakes of the divine, and the divisible, which partakes of the earthly. Both are related through a third element partaking of each and placed between the two. The three were made one by compression! The compound was cut into strips which were crossed or interwoven, and bent into a spherical shape. Such was the world soul in which God has placed the corporeal universe. The human soul is made of the same elements as the world soul. The star-gods are the children of the creator; they form man who will return after death to his star. The world soul pervades everything; in man, it circulates in a proper motion, which can be perfected by him who observes the motion of the heavenly gods, the planets.

Plato believed in the influence of the stars. He is cited frequently by the astrologers of the sixteenth and seventeenth centuries. Moreover, he gave an impetus to alchemy when placing the world soul in all bodies. The alchemists were striving to extract the soul of substances: using this essence, they wanted to produce marvellous effects with minerals. Just as the Persian Zoroaster believed that the good god Ormazd shaped the world with ideas, similarly Plato attributed a divine character to ideas. Since they dominate the body, the magicians of the West concluded that they could induce marvels in the corporeal world through the omnipotence of sovereign ideas.

Since in Plato's world heaven and earth, the elements, the soul and the spirit, the divine and the terrestrial are interrelated and partake of one another, it is no wonder that magicians wanted to make use of such mysterious consanguinity. Similarly, they used Pythagorean numbers in their magic circles, as numbers were also, according to Pythagoras, older than bodies and hence more powerful. The world is formed according to a mathematical scheme, and is harmonized according to proportion. Beauty and order were to these philosophers impossible to achieve without numbers. In the size, weight and intervals of the stars lurk mystic numbers; and around these, the creator built the cosmos.

The Pythagoreans called arithmetic the study of numbers and their relation to natural phenomena, so that scientific study was fused with philosophic speculations and fantasy. When the Pythagoreans became inebriated with their own imagination, arithmetic was lost in the marvellous, and numbers became living beings, divine hypostases in their own right. At times the number four answered to Hermes and Dionysus; seven, one of the oldest number divinities, was Pallas Athene; ten represented Atlas who upholds the vault of the sky. According to the poet

Hesiod (eighth century B.C.), chaos or the primeval mass whence all things were formed found its embodiment in the monad, the number one. Five was the number of justice, uniting the 'feminine' number two with the 'masculine' three. Six was Aphrodite, goddess of love, as this number was composed of two times three, the multiplied first numbers of each sex. Plutarch, as we have noted, has a different interpretation for the numbers three, four and five, and we may suppose that more than once in the course of time the meaning of numbers has changed. The Pythagoreans were not only theorists of magic but they practised it publicly. Empedocles (fifth century B.C.) performed wonders among the people. He believed firmly that he could resuscitate the dead, induce rain and drought, etc.

The magical beliefs of old which had enriched peoples' lives were clothed by the philosophers in the beautiful garments of reason. Most philosophers, however, like the members of all classes, indulged also in popular magic or superstitions. Thales (640–548 B.C.) believed in demoniacal apparitions, and Plato in ghosts – deceased people who were compelled to return to the living because they were unable to disassociate themselves from their bodily passions. Democritus (fifth century B.C.), who could laugh so heartily at human folly, recommended that a man stung by a scorpion should sit upon an ass and whisper in the animal's ear: 'A scorpion has stung me.' He thought that the pain would thus be transferred to the ass.

All the philosophers of old believed in the reality of magic. Heraclitus, Thales, Pindar, Xenophon, Socrates were unable to elude the enchanted circle. The later Greek philosophers, like Porphyry (A.D. 233–303), were entirely devoted to magical practices. They have bequeathed their elaborate demonology to the early Christians, whom they had fought so bitterly. For Porphyry there existed innumerable beastly demons who haunted men and houses in their hankering after blood and filth. At meal times the demons swarm around us like flies, and only a complicated ritual can keep them away. These ceremonies were initiated not to please the gods but solely to repel devils.

Greek magic has been influenced from time immemorial by Oriental beliefs. No nation welcomed foreign ideologies more warmly than the Hellenes. Priests, philosophers and historians roamed foreign lands. The quest for knowledge led the wonder-worker Apollonius of Tyana to the shores of India. Plato tells of cultural ties with Egypt and Crete. Greeks accompanied the Persians Darius and Xerxes on their expeditions. They admired the wisdom of the Persians. In the *Alcibiades* Plato causes Socrates to say that their educators are superior to those in Athens, and he speaks admiringly of the brilliant tutelage given to the young Persian princes and of the virtues of their teachers, the wisest of whom is a Magian, a disciple of Zoroaster. Mythical figures and gods of the Orient have been hellenized. The Delphic cult originated in Crete; Adonis sprang from the Hebrew Adonai; Aphrodite is the embellished and pacified Astarte; Isis became Athene; and Dionysus hardly veils his alien origin.

Like the wise men of the Orient, the Hellenic philosophers

were believed by the people to be magicians. It was commonly accepted that Socrates possessed a familiar spirit that kept him informed of the future. According to Socrates's friend Xenophon (*ca.* 427–355 B.C.), many of the philosopher's confidants would consult the spirit about their own problems. Plutarch says that the familiar replied with sneezes directed either to the right or left, according to whether the answers were affirmative or negative. Apuleius says that Socrates's demon was visible to all, an opinion which Maximus of Tyre disputed vigorously. The latter asserted that it merely symbolized Socrates's psychic power. This controversy as to the appearance and character of his demon continued to the eighteenth century. In *An Essay on the Demon or Divination of Socrates* (London, 1782) the author, Nares, arrives at the disappointing conclusion that Socrates employed the word 'demon' merely to describe his divinatory gift. Nares decides reasonably that despite their wisdom the Greek philosophers were after all only children of their time, and like lesser men subject to the beliefs and prejudices of their fathers.

Dreams, Ghosts and Heroes

In the Greek mind, side by side with the Apollonian dwelt the Dionysiac; along with the harmonious, rational world of plastic form and intellectual clarity there dwelt among the Greek people the dark, the eerie and the undisciplined. The Dionysiac conjured up the dead and induced a belief in witches, ghosts and other apparitions.

The nightmares of the Greeks shared the repulsive qualities that later characterized medieval ghosts and devils, not unlike those which exist in our own time, bringing to our dreams hybrids, witches and grotesque animals. Apuleius (second century of the Christian era) describes a harrowing nightmare in his *Metamorphoses*. After a hearty dinner, Aristomenes and his friend retired to a shabby hostel in Thessalonia. Sleep had scarcely come to Aristomenes when the door opened and two witches entered the room. Aristomenes's bed collapsed, pinning him beneath it. From this uncomfortable position, he saw the two hags stab his friend and afterwards neatly pour his blood into a leather flask. One of them plunged her arm into the wound and drew out the victim's heart, after which she closed the orifice with a sponge, while murmuring these magic words: 'Beware O sea-born sponge, how thou dost pass through a river. . . .' Whereupon the two creatures turned their attentions to the fearful Aristomenes and defiled him. Then they vanished. On the following morning, however, the dream proved to have been real, for when the friend stooped to drink at the river, the wound opened, the magic sponge fell into the water, and with it the corpse of the bewitched traveller. Just as this dream became reality, so among the imaginative Greeks the real merged with the illusory. In their dreams they saw the mythical monsters whose images they had observed during the day, and afterwards they believed that the visit of the magic creature was no hallucination but had actually happened.

But even when the dream was recognized as one, it still furnished enough substance for conjecture. In their dreams, they saw the forerunners of the future, experienced divine revelations, and had premonitions of impending danger. Most of these nightly visitors filled them with terror. Pan the goat-footed, the goat-horned, son of the nymph Dryope, was the reputed sender of nightmares.[1] To the early Christians, the devil appeared as a Panic figure and inherited the attributes of the Grecian shepherd-god.

Seafarers, before sailing, would sleep in the temple of Poseidon, praying to the sea-god for a prophetic dream wherein they might glimpse the outcome of their voyage. The temples of Asklepios too were famous, where the god of healing would reveal remedies to his believers during sleep. God-sent dreams were not only for the individual; magistrates and generals were often sent to the temples to dream of official business and to learn the will of the gods. When Alexander the Great lay mortally stricken, several of his generals visited the temples of Asklepios to ask whether the king should be left in his palace or be carried to the sanctuary.[2] Asklepios replied that it was best to leave the dying hero where he was.

A remarkable feature of this Asklepian dreaming is that it formed the basis for medical science among the Greeks. After each successful cure, the case history together with the god's prescription was recorded in writing or carved upon the temple walls. As the centuries passed, a reliable archive was created of significant therapeutic dreams. The great physician Hippocrates is said to have been indebted for his knowledge largely to the temple records of Cos, his native city.[3] We are reminded at this point of a dream which saved the city of Athens from a plague: the nightly apparition which came to a dreaming woman in the form of a deceased Scythian, who counselled that wine be poured into the streets and alleys of the stricken town. Following the Scythian's advice, the foul air was 'cleansed' by wine, and the pestilence disappeared.[4]

The importance of dreams is reflected in the stress placed upon their correct interpretation. Considerable rewards awaited whoever possessed that gift. A work that soon became famous is the dream book of Artemidorus Daldianus, Apuleius's contemporary. Many dreams, says Artemidorus, represent a simple and direct image of the event which they foretell. Others show symbols whose meaning must be ascertained. The interpreter should know every detail of the dream which he wishes to explore; if the beginning is confused, he should start his interpretation at the end and reascend to the source. Moreover, he should know the dreamer's state of mind, his social standing and his state of health. It is important to know whether the dreamer is a master or a slave, a rich man or a pauper, an old man or a youth. They may have similar dreams which should, however, be interpreted in various ways.

If an old man dreams about being wounded in the chest he

must expect bad news. If a young girl has a similar dream, she may expect a devoted lover. If a poor man dreams that he is changed into a woman this is a good sign, for someone will take care of his needs; yet to the rich this same dream announces the end of his authority: he will retire from public life into a petty domestic existence. A slave will be pleased to dream of being assisted and comforted, whereas the master's similar dream announces misery and insult. A sick person will die when a dream shows him an innkeeper, for the latter, like death, receives whomsoever; but to the healthy, the innkeeper means travels into many countries. Certain dreams, says Artemidorus, are a good omen to people specialized in a craft or profession. The nightly vision of ants invading one's ears is favourable to educators and professors who will be listened to by the public, symbolized by ants. For other people this same dream signifies death: like ants they will dwell in the earth.

He who eats books in a dream will die soon. To lawyers, teachers and statesmen, however, eating books allegorizes the increase of knowledge. To have donkey ears is a good dream only for philosophers who will interpret it in this flattering fashion · they will be indifferent to gossip and vain rumours, 'because the donkey seldom moves its ears'. To other people the donkey dream announces servitude; they will have to toil like domestic animals. To be dressed up ridiculously is a disagreeable presage for everyone who dislikes to be ridiculed; for comedians and dancers, such a dream predicts great success on the stage.

Dreams of horror, which Artemidorus enumerates carefully, may well signify good luck. To hold one's head in one's hand is only favourable for him who has neither wife nor children. However, to be burned at the stake is a good omen for all; the sick, when dreaming of such execution, will readily recover, and young people will know the passions of love. Whipping is also a good omen. To be fustigated by a wealthy and capable person predicts favourable and profitable things. Similarly favourable is the dream of crucifixion. Whoever sees himself crucified will enjoy a fairly serene married life. To seafarers it indicates a good voyage, 'because the cross, like the ship, is made of wood and nails, and because the misery of the crucified is not unlike seasickness'. To a politician, crucifixion announces an office: he will be 'raised' at the very place where the cross was elevated in the dream. For slaves, the same dream signifies that they will soon be free men.

The cult of the dead among the Greeks at this time was also widespread. Often the deceased would return from their graves, having neglected to complete some act during their lifetime, or because an important part of the mortuary rites had been omitted. Usually they spread terror throughout the house, and we rarely find in these apparitions the tenderness and poetry of that which came to Eukrates's dwelling: Eukrates had lost his beloved wife, and together with the body, her dress and ornaments had been burned on the pyre. On the seventh day, as the widower was reading Plato's *Phaedo* to escape his grief for a while, she entered and sat by him, complaining that one of her golden sandals had not been burned. It had, in fact, fallen behind the chest and escaped the flames. As she spoke, the Melitian dog barked, and she vanished. The sandal, being found later, was burned, and the dead woman never returned again.[5]

Graveyards always aroused in the Greeks an uncanny feeling. Some remnant of life might still inhabit the body: thus who could be sure that the deceased might not leave the grave, or at least send forth a spectre. In the funereal avenues and the necropoleis, there also appeared superhuman phantoms of the night, such as the infernal Hecate, whose repulsive figure was accompanied by souls and howling dogs swarming over the graves.[6]

A similar spectre showed itself to Dion, a pupil of Plato and ruler of Syracuse (409–354 B.C.). Having finally rid himself of the villainous Herakleides, Dion was resting in the vestibule of his house and absorbed in his thoughts, when something stirred behind him. He turned and beheld a powerful woman whose face and black garments recalled a goddess of vengeance. She was sweeping the hall with a besom. As he cried out for help, the apparition faded. A few days later, Dion's son committed suicide, and the ruler himself was assassinated shortly afterwards.

On his journey to India, Apollonius of Tyana had crossed the snowcapped Caucasus and wandered now by moonlight with his companion Damis through the plain. They reached the Indus river, where they met Empusa, a hobgoblin that was continually changing form, and sometimes vanishing into limbo. 'And Apollonius, realizing what it was, abused the hobgoblin and instructed the members of his party to do the same, explaining that this was the remedy for such a visitation. The phantasm fled, shrieking even as ghosts do.'[7]

Later, after his return from India, Apollonius journeyed through Greece, stopping at Athens, Ephesus and Corinth. According to Apollonius's biographer Philostratus, the philosopher, while in Corinth, met a lamia, a vampire. One of Apollonius's followers was Menippus, a poor young student whose sole possession was the philosopher's cloak. Apollonius had been attracted by the youth's beauty and good judgement. It was rumoured by his friends that Menippus was loved by a foreign lady, a Phoenician, who was beautiful and extremely rich. She wanted to marry Menippus despite their contrasting social rank; Menippus was happy to make her his wife, for he loved her devotedly. He invited Apollonius to be the guest of honour at the wedding breakfast and the master, sensing danger for his disciple, declared that for the special occasion he would break his habit of abstaining from rich meals and wine. When he arrived at the lady's house, he asked to be introduced to the bride. He looked at her searchingly and, turning to Menippus, he asked to whom the silver and gold vessels and decorations of the banqueting hall belonged. 'To the lady,' replied the youth, 'for this is all I possess,' and he touched the mantle that he wore. 'All this adornment,' Apollonius said, 'is not reality but semblance, and thy fine and dainty bride is not a mortal but a vampire, a lamia. These beings are devoted to the delights of Aphrodite, but still more to devouring human flesh.'

The lady pretended to be disgusted with such nonsense. Obviously amused, she said that philosophers were always spoiling the pleasures of honest people, frightening them with evil omens; and she commanded her unwelcome guest to leave. But Apollonius took one of the silver goblets from the table and weighed it in his hand: it was light as a feather, and soon it vanished. In a similar way the other plate disappeared; the cooks and servants fell to dust when Apollonius uttered a magical imprecation; the house tumbled into ruins. The lady, imploring the philosopher to torment her no longer, was forced to confess that she had intended to fatten Menippus before devouring him, 'for it was her habit to feed upon young and beautiful bodies, because their blood is pure and strong'.

The fear of spectres and other apparitions did not prevent the conjuring up of the dead at special places that were chosen for these rites, such as Manteia, Psychomanteia and Psychopompeia. The conjurors of the deceased were called psychagogues. Little is known of their ritual, but we may take it for granted that they demanded fasting and concentration. Blood and burned offerings were surely necessary for the ceremonies in the silence of night. The psychagogues must have had considerable influence. Among them there was one who did not fear to announce the bad tidings to the tyrant Periander (625–585 B.C.), when his wife spoke from the underworld. She was cold and naked, for at her funeral her clothes had been interred with her and not burned according to custom. Whereupon the wise Periander ordered a public feast for all Corinthian women. Arrayed in their best garments they gathered in a public square, expecting a brilliant show or some other treat. However, they were ordered to undress, and their fine raiments were gathered and burned in a pit for the benefit of the deceased. Periander's wife announced through the mouth of the psychagogue that she was warm now and comfortable in the kingdom of Hades.

Although some of the philosophers, notably Plato, protested vigorously against necromancy, its practice remained an integral part of the Hellenic religion.

Together with the cult of the dead and the conjuring up of the deceased, magical rites were used to propitiate dead heroes. These demigods were feared, yet they were considered benevolent patrons during danger. The heroes were as a rule connected with a city or a district; in earlier times they may have been the family ancestors or the house-god, worshipped with the fire of the hearth. Their tombs were small buildings surrounded by colonnades, venerable trees and orderly gardens. Others were invisible, hidden beneath some public building, and the location of their shrines was kept secret because it was feared that the heroes' bones might be stolen. Like the relics of Christian saints, these bones were endowed with beneficent power that brought luck to the city or to the province where they were buried. This belief may be illustrated by the weird myth of Oedipus, the murderer of his father and spouse of his mother who, in expiation for his monstrous deeds, wanders distractedly through Hellenic lands. Though abhorred by all, and despite his atrocious crime, the hero is offered an asylum by rival cities, because it is generally known that wherever Oedipus is buried, he will bring luck to that land and its inhabitants.

Hero magic was accomplished at night, and solemnity accompanied it. Its ritual was different from that used for the worship of the gods. A groove was opened at the west side of the tomb, and magical formulas were recited. The sacrificial offering consisted of wine, milk and pomades; blood was poured into a crack of the tomb, as it was believed to revive the dead. An active force emanated from the shrine, guiding the destinies of the living, influencing the welfare of the city, and exerting its mysterious power within the landmarks of the country. In Aeschylus's *Choephores*, the entombed Agamemnon, though never visible, is a co-active power, and without him the play could not be concluded. In the *Persians* the hero-king Darius rises from his tomb and takes part in the action. In this play, Aeschylus creates the imposing image of the magical rites, the evocation of the dead.[8]

It is but a short step from the sublime to the ridiculous. The Greeks created heroes from bizarre, allegorical beings, who became the clowns of the cult. In Munychia they offered these honours to the mythical Akratopotes, who drank undiluted wine. No doubt he was a drunkard, for the Greeks used to add water to their wine. Keraon and Matton, the wine mixer and the baker, were Spartan heroes, and in Boeotia, bread and cake were worshipped as heroes. This self-irony is typically Greek. In the Near East the cults were clad in pathos. We search the Old Testament in vain for a conscious humorous note. The rites of the Phrygians, the Babylonians and the Assyrians are awesome; those practised by the Persians and the Hebrews are severe and sober.[9]

Omens, Oracles and Astrology

The Christian church condemned magical operations even when they aimed at good. A magician who by magic words healed a neighbour's cow might suffer a fate similar to that of a witch who had placed the curse of sickness. The Greek religion was less rigid; no ecclesiastical authority ruled. While having strong links to the old usage, it welcomed fresh revelation. All that mattered was that the magic should have a beneficent purpose, and serve the commonweal. This applied both to practitioners of magic who were members of the priesthood and to freelance magicians.

Plato, in his *Laws*, ordains: 'He who seems to be such a man who injures others by magic knots or enchantments, be he a prophet or a diviner, let him die.' But in the *Timaeus* he declares divination from the liver of slaughtered animals to be a good and legitimate deed, a remedy 'which god combined with the liver and placed in the house of lower nature [the body] . . . in order that [in the liver] the power of thought, which proceeds from the mind, might be reflected as in a mirror which received the like ness of objects and gives back images of them'. Death punished similar acts when practised criminally; Apollonius of Tyana was brought to trial in Rome when 'it was declared that he had sacrificed a boy to divine the secrets of futurity which are to be learned from youthful entrails'. This could hardly have been an exceptional practice, for a law provided specifically against it.

Spontaneous prophecy was interpreted as a divine gift bestowed upon the worthy. Plato, in his *Apology*, causes Socrates, under sentence of death, to say: 'And now, O men who have condemned me, I would fain prophesy to you; for I am about to die, and in the hour of death men are gifted with prophetic power.'

And in the *Symposium*, Plato terms the divinatory arts, as a whole, 'communion between gods and men'.

Mythical Orpheus was thought to have fathered all prophecy and founded all initiations and mysteries. 'His melodies brought back the dead.' The Orphic religion was already flourishing in Greece six hundred years before Christ. Orpheus's head was preserved in the isle of Lesbos, with its magical power still alive; it foretold the future. Melampus understood the language of birds that the snakes had taught him. Epimenides lived three hundred years, and had slept thirty of them. Melisangus, the divine soothsayer, practised his art in Athens. Bakis was possessed by nymphs, and the daughters of springs and sources spoke through his lips. Last of this elect company was Apollonius of Tyana, who lived in the first century of the Christian era. His power was hailed as that of a god, and many communities in Asia Minor raised temples and shrines to this rival of Jesus the Nazarene.[10]

Clairvoyance was most intimately bound up with daily religion. The oracles were consulted as to the future, and old seers witnessed sacrifices and other religious ceremonies. From the intestines of the animal, from the way its entrails burned, from the sacrificial flame, one sought first to know whether the sacrifice was acceptable and pleased the gods; then, avid for more knowledge, one searched these phenomena to find the wisdom of the immortals.

The word oracle means 'answer'. Priests might speak with the god through the Pythia, a female medium. Narcotic smoke or natural fumes rising from the earth brought the medium into a state of trance. In Argos, to achieve the same end, the Pythia drank the blood of lambs. Once the godly spirit had entered the body of the Pythia, the priest posed his questions, receiving the replies of the Olympians through her mouth. Most of these answers, produced in a strangely altered intonation, were ambiguous. Lucian (second century of the Christian era) scoffed at the ambiguity: 'Only a second Apollo could have elucidated the statements of the first.' Thus the Pythia is said to have warned Nero, 'Beware of the sixty-third year.' Nero interpreted the caution as applying to his own age. But it referred to the sixty-third year of Galba, who overthrew him.

The most celebrated oracle was at Delphi, on a slope of Mount Parnassus. Surrounding boulders gave back a wondrous echo;

vapours emanated from a natural grotto, and in a crypt stood the image of Apollo, framed by laurel. When the oracle was to be rendered, the Pythia, sitting on a golden tripod, moved closer to the steaming crevasse. Soon she was overcome by a divine delirium – her neck swelled, her body writhed in convulsions, her head jerked violently. The crisis was shocking enough to fill all who beheld her with religious awe.

These mantic phenomena are seen in their full importance when we recall that any religious ecstasy was believed to be divinely inspired. People among the crowd at the Orphic and Dionysiac festivals would, in a state of hysteria, utter prophetic words; in daily life, the flight of birds, the whispering of the trees, the sneeze of a neighbour were premonitions sent by the gods. Centuries of anticipating such portents must have sharpened the senses of the Greeks. Constant alertness added not only to their occult knowledge, but also to their powers of observation in the broadest sense.

Oracles and omens played an influential role in political life. No war was declared before consulting the gods. And more than once the oracle, which also confided strategic advice, started a war. One might say that at times the soothsaying Pythia of Delphi served as Greek minister of war and foreign affairs.

Generals were ever anxious lest an evil omen should bring panic to their armies. In the fourth century B.C. when Timotheus was about to sail with the entire Attic fleet, the sneeze of a soldier caused a standstill. The army hesitated to board ship until Timotheus – laughing, though scarcely in a jovial mood – asked: 'What kind of omen is this, if it caused only one man to sneeze?' Whereupon the warriors laughed too, and the embarkation proceeded.[11] Agathocles (361–289 B.C.) carried with him 'lucky owls', birds sacred to Pallas Athene, on a foolhardy expedition to Libya. And as his army somewhat dejectedly took up its position for battle, he released the birds. The owls perched on the shields and helmets of the soldiers, restoring courage to them.[12] Doves are set free to this day during the religious processions in southern Italy. This custom stems directly from the bird omens of antiquity.

Unusual occurrences in the temples were also interpreted as portents. The disappearance of sacred weapons, sweating images, the opening of the temple doors, etc., boded ill. Perhaps the priests, wishing to guide public opinion, may have contrived these miracles. A singular book ascribed to Hero of Alexandria (second century of the Christian era) explains how such 'wonders' could be brought about by mechanical means. Incense, driven by the pressure of warm air, fell from the hands of bronze statues and burned upon the altar. A water syphon might produce mysterious trumpet tones as the temple shutters opened. When the fire was lit before the sanctuary door, heat accumulated in the hollow altar, and the expanding air caused water to flow into a bucket. This made the bucket descend, and its motion acted upon the pivots, opening the door. This mechanical device was of course invisible to the spectators.

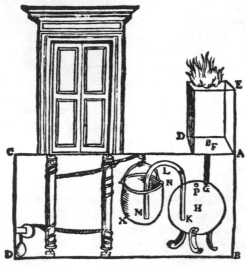

15. A fire automaton

It would, however, be a mistake to believe that all magical operations of the ancients were calculated to deceive. Not even the most ardent champions of the new Christian religion doubted the supernatural powers of the Hellenistic gods or demons, although they condemned them as work of the devil. Among the Greeks, as with all peoples, religion merged with magic. Observing these practices, we must first ask ourselves what were the ethical implications in each case; and where the outcome was not evil, or could in some way be defended, one may justify them. Doubtless the magicians and priests were, as a whole, earnest men, believers in what they professed. Many, rendering oracles, may have acted by suggestion upon the medium, Pythia. However, they might have done this unintentionally, as modern students of occult phenomena have shown. Today, even the sceptical do not doubt the reality of premonition or clairvoyance. During an era when large numbers of people concentrated their thoughts upon such phenomena, they must have taken place more readily than today. The Greeks, certain that these powers existed, wished to avail themselves of them. Yet it was difficult to know what benefit there might be in making use of this power, since the Greeks thought that fate could not be avoided. Some of them may have later arrived at the opinion expressed by Iamblichus, the Greco-Syrian: 'Better not to know the future and to await with patience the calamities of fate.' Still, much interrogation of the future continued into Christian times. Iamblichus, despite his belief, was credited with the invention of alectryomancy – divining by means of a fowl. After certain magical rites, one traced the letters of the alphabet on the sand, sprinkling a handful of wheat or barley across the characters. One listed the signs in the order made by the bird's picking, and then sought hidden meanings in the words thus produced.

Ptolemy, the great astronomer and interpreter of the stars, a contemporary of Iamblichus, vigorously defended the use of foreknowledge. A thoughtful chapter in one of his four books,

On the Influence of the Stars, is devoted to this. In general, he says, it is good to know both the human and the divine, and to rejoice. Prescience, it is true, will bring neither fame nor riches; yet the art of prognostication shares these traits with all other arts. When something unforeseen occurs, we are either overwhelmed by terror or our composure is destroyed by the sudden knowledge; but forewarned, we may await the future with dignity.

Not all events of human life are caused divinely nor are they all inevitable; neither do they all stem from a single relentless fate, as there are also natural events. Man is subject not only to disasters inherent in his own personality, but also to those born of general causes – plagues, floods and fires, which destroy multitudes. Such occurrences must be explained by the absence of any opposing heavenly influence which might prevent them. Whoever exercises prognostication must take care to foretell only those events belonging within the realm of natural causes. These subtleties of Ptolemy are a late product of Greek thought. Originally, the Greeks may well have thought otherwise about astrology, for the course of the stars suggested rather the mathematical precision and relentlessness of fate.

Although astrology was no creation of the Greeks, not having been introduced to them until late by Alexander who had brought it from Babylon and Egypt, it soon gained tremendous popularity. Not only was the hour of birth considered important because of its astrological influence, but horoscopes also were made the bases for all important decisions. Chaldean astrologers settled in Athens and won wealth and favour. Berosus, a Babylonian, founded a college for astrology on the isle of Cos; so great was his success that in their gymnasium the Athenians erected his statue, holding a golden lyre, the symbol of divine prophecy.

The Mysteries of Eleusis

Demeter the Earth-goddess journeyed through all lands in search of her daughter Kore, and found her in the city of Eleusis at the end of her long quest. There Demeter founded a secret worship, teaching her mysteries to the city elders. The initiates were to be both good citizens and wise men. So runs the story as to the origins and purpose of the cult. These rites contained a hidden meaning guarded from the masses, a deep secret of magical nature. Similar secret institutions existed in other Greek cities, but Eleusis was the most famed and the most venerated, even down to the first centuries of the Christian era. For ages the arcane Eleusinian temple lived through the changing fortunes of the Greek people, and cruel wars had left it unprofaned. The imparting of the secret was at the same time a promise. What this privilege was appears in the Homeric hymn to Demeter: 'Happy he of the mortals who has seen this; in the dark kingdom of shadows, the fate of the initiate and of the uninitiate is not the same.' Such was its great pledge: an afterlife happier than for other men.

It is not astonishing then that eventually so many people wished to receive this initiation that a special building had to be erected, since the temple could no longer house all the candidates. A rite which promises privileges in the afterlife is a magical one. Similar promises were made by the priests of Egypt. The Egyptians sought mainly to cover up man's bad actions by secret formulas, conjurations and talismans so as to deceive the gods and bias their judgement. But in the Greek mind a light was kindled: true good deeds rather than counterfeit ones were the best guarantee for a happier hereafter.

The sacred rites began with a cleansing, a lustration, in the sea nearby. 'To the sea, ye mystics!' cried the leader of the festivities, and the hopeful group plunged into the water. How the rite itself proceeded remains unknown to us. Even those converts to Christianity who had formerly received the Eleusinian rites kept the pledge of secrecy. But various allusions suggest that a sacrament was administered. A potion was drunk, symbolic objects being taken from a basket and set in a chest. The novice's lips were 'locked' with a golden key, and the experience began. What Aristotle said of mysteries in general must hold true for those of Eleusis: 'The initiates had not to learn, but to experience.' A sacred pantomime would seem to have acted out the history of the gods: the rape of Kore, the wanderings of Demeter, the marriage of Pluto and Kore, Demeter's return to Olympus. In this silent drama each gesture was a revelation. The enactment of age-old traditions in the flesh, this was certainly no ordinary performance. The showing of sacred objects should be understood in like manner.

Then followed the initiation itself, of which Plutarch gives a veiled account. Modern occultists who have read between Plutarch's lines give us colourful descriptions, interesting to be sure, but on the fanciful side. The little that we may take for granted is that the candidates were made to roam through winding subterranean passages. It was a peregrination through the dark, a journey to an invisible end, which put to the test all one's presence of mind. And then, at the moment of decision, the initiates were subjected to terrors. They experienced shudders and trembling, they sweated with fear and were paralysed with terror, until light was gradually admitted, and the day restored. With sacred chants and dancing choruses a magnificent place was opened before them. There noble things were seen and heard. The initiated was crowned with garlands, and by the side of pure and holy men he enjoyed the festival of rebirth. Regenerated and freed, he could now leave the temple; and certain it is that pensive natures would carry away from Eleusis a new, a consoling faith.

Many students of the occult have stated that the Eleusinian rite contained the one great magic secret, the kernel of all wisdom; yet the democratic nature of the gathering, the presence of large numbers, rules out the possibility of any doctrine calling for great intelligence and philosophical skill. The mystery must have been a matter of faith rather than of knowledge.

GNOSTICISM

The Way to Blessedness

The unity of religion and that of political authority are two correlative ideas.

Louis Menard

Expansion into world empires, the conquests of Asiatic and Egyptian rulers, brought nations into ever closer contact. An understanding of the foreigner's mind became an important factor in the administration of conquered territory, for wherever possible victorious kings preferred to govern by peaceful means. This toleration of the ways of subject peoples was however opposed by another interest: that of fusing all the provinces into a unit over which the monarch would reign as an inviolable, divinely ordained ruler. Such a king, who would ascribe his power to the will of the gods, had first to elicit unchallenged respect for these gods, and his subjects would have to recognize them as the highest divinities.

The policy of ancient kings seems to have been torn between these two aims. Government would swing from one extreme to another: violence and persecution would alternate with kindness and tolerance. Both had the same goal: supremacy of the state religion. One would try to persuade the subjects that their faith was hardly different from the king's religion, that their gods were actually identical though worshipped under other names. Thus, for political reasons, the wise men of the court learned about the ways of foreign peoples. The knowledge thus gained was superficial, gathered from the needs of the moment and not from a deeper quest.

Wisdom and philosophy travelled along strategic and commercial routes. Alexander's conquests had opened Asia to an astonished West. When finally Rome mastered the subtle art of governing, the intercourse of the nations reached its peak. Universal religious toleration was Rome's traditional policy. The doctrine of Buddha spread to the Mediterranean and exerted its influence, since Buddhistic teaching had been sanctioned by treaties under the Seleucidan and Ptolemaic rulers. Buddhism revealed to the West that the acquisition of wealth was not necessarily a blessing, that salvation could also be gained in absolute chastity and poverty. The highest morality of the monks of India rested no longer in the strength to maintain oneself in the struggle for existence, but in the surrender of all strife and the renunciation of self.

Judaism also exerted a strong influence upon many provinces of the Roman empire, and the Roman emperors lost no time in gaining a new patron, Jehovah, by instituting daily sacrifices to him at their own cost. Augustus highly commended his grandson's conduct, when during his stay in Palestine he had visited the temple of Jerusalem. Jewish influence in Rome continued even after the fall of Jerusalem and, in fact, grew stronger. In Alexandria, the Jews were for some time leaders in science and philosophy. Their ideas mingled with those of the Greeks. The Hellenizing Rabbi Aristobulos saw a connection between Greek philosophy and Jewish theology. Alexandria became the most prolific intellectual centre, where East and West joined hands. Here the great spiritual currents met and merged. Babylonian astrology, Zoroastrian Magism, Egyptian secret knowledge, Hellenic philosophy, Judaism and Christianity produced a movement unique in the history of mankind: the syncretism of many doctrines and religions. Gnosticism arose from the widely held belief that revelation and wisdom of the divine were not the prerogatives of one particular nation, but were to be found among all civilized nations, and that every faith contained a germ of the great truth which culminated in Christ.

The Greeks were well prepared for the acceptance of religious internationalism. The ideas of evil, sin, hell, salvation and immortal life had been familiar to them before Plato. The philosophers opposed the primitive polytheism of their nation. Through the legends of Hercules, Bellerophon and Prometheus, they had become familiar with the idea of salvation. They understood that Hercules performed his heroic deeds not for his own sake, but for that of mankind. And Prometheus suffers for humanity; his myth resembles – not accidentally – the history of Golgotha. The Greek mind conceived the idea that the redeemer of mankind was to suffer martyrdom. Did not Plato say that the perfect one, the righteous, shall be tortured and whipped? 'They will blind him, and when he has suffered the most excruciating torments they will hang him on a stake.'

Many Babylonian ideas had long since influenced the West, particularly their astrology. It became known also that the priests of Babylon knew the 'one god', Ilu, primary and unique, from whom spring all the other gods. Ilu formed the holy trinity: Anu, the time-god, Nuah, intelligence, and Bel, the coordinator. This first triad represents the genesis of the material world which emanated from the divine being. To each of these gods corresponds a feminine divinity: Nana, Belit and Davkina. They are the passive forms of the triad. Their significance is not quite clear. Belit, however, is distinguishable as the female principle of nature, the womb which generates gods and men. The godly emanation continued and formed a second triad, the most magnificent external manifestation of god. They are Sin, the moon, son of Bel; Samas, the sun, son of Nuah; and Bin, the god of the atmosphere, wind, rain and thunder. Bin was Anu's son. As the Chaldeans never accepted a god without dividing him into the male and female principle, the gods of the second triad are accompanied by their spouses. In the descending scale follow the gods of the five planets: Adar, Saturn; Marduk, Jupiter; Nergal, Mars; Ishtar, Venus; and Nebo, Mercury. The planets, like the higher gods, have their spouses. The complicated hierarchy of powers or gods, culminating in the one god, attracted deep interest among the syncretists. They too conceived a single deity enthroned above a still more intricate hierarchy of heavenly cycles, the aeons.

As Gnosticism originated on Egyptian soil, we may be sure that many elements of the antique Egyptian magic were adopted by the founders of the new doctrine. Magical incantations, powerful words, had opened in times of old the underworld: formulas had driven away evil powers which threatened the deceased on his journey to Osiris. Similar words, letters and phrases were now pronounced by the Gnostic on his ascent to Paradise. For the attainment of eternal life, this word-magic was indispensable to him. He believed that after his death he was to ascend to heaven through the aeons and this ascent, he thought, was as difficult and dangerous as was the descent of the ancient Egyptians into the world beneath. Without knowing the magical words, the righteous could not hope to find their way to paradise. So important was this knowledge that Christ returned to earth after his crucifixion and dwelt there many years, teaching men the mysterious path to heaven.

Two outstanding features of the Gnostic world image are borrowed from Zoroastrianism or from its offspring, namely dualism and the doctrine of emanation. Like Ahura Mazda, the Persian god of the good, so did the highest Gnostic god manifest himself through a mystical light that penetrated the aeons of the invisible world and was mingled, though imperceptibly, with the corrupt matter of the visible world. The idea of perennial strife between the good and the evil principles is inherent in all Gnostic sects. Towards the end of the third century, waning Gnosticism was succeeded by Manicheism, which attempted to reconcile the religion of Zoroaster with that of Christ. Adopting many Gnostic features, Manicheism stressed again the irreconcilability of good and evil: 'Before heaven and earth existed, and all that is in them, there existed two principles, one was the good and the other the bad.'

Of the alleged teachings of Christ, collected in innumerable books by the leaders of Gnosticism, only one, discovered in a Coptic manuscript towards the middle of the last century, entitled *Pistis Sophia* (Faith-Wisdom), has come down to us. The author claims to be Philip the Apostle, writing at the Saviour's behest.[1] The soul, this book says, must traverse aeons, circles of celestial powers and virtues. When Christ ascended to heaven again, he found at the thirteenth aeon the forlorn and weeping Pistis Sophia who, having glimpsed the highest light, had an irresistible desire to reach it and flew to its source. Adamas, ruler of her circle, punished her for this rebellion by making a false light shine upon the waters, so that Pistis Sophia was led astray by it and plunged into the abyss. By the Saviour's intervention she was rescued and together with Christ she ascended the aeons, singing a confession at each step. After the reinstatement of Pistis Sophia, the book turns to a precise interpretation of doctrine. Mary Magdalene, the chief speaker, questions the ultimate cause of sin, to which Jesus replies with a dissertation on man's soul. This is followed by an estimate of the powers ruling the place of torment, which is also known as the dragon of 'outward darkness'.

The book speaks in veiled terms of twenty-four mysteries contained in twenty-four aeons.[2] There are also five marks, seven vowels, five trees and seven amens, which the voyager to paradise must know. Scattered through the *Pistis Sophia* are allusions to seals, numbers and other symbols borrowed partly from the faith of the Hebrews and partly from Egyptian worship. Repeating themselves in mysterious sequence, they are impenetrable.

Finally, the *Pistis Sophia* contains a long portion of the prayers of Jesus. Now on a mountain, now at sea, now in mid-air, the Saviour, attended by his disciples, makes invocations to the Father. These invocations are preceded by magical formulas; Jesus also celebrates a communion of wine and water. He then explains the influence of the zodiac upon man's soul, as well as the good and evil influences of the planets, the names of which are borrowed seemingly from the Magian religion of Zoroaster. Some Egyptian deities are among those mentioned: Bubastes and Typhon-Seth, and the Syrian goddess Barbelo, who is the heavenly mother of the Saviour.

The following is from the last part of the *Pistis Sophia*, written independently of the others. The words put into Jesus's mouth are pure magical incantation, not a fantasy as might at first sight appear, but a jumble of Hebrew, Egyptian and Persian, copied and recopied until it became incomprehensible. The masses uttered these words without knowing their origin. In this they followed the ancient rule of not altering foreign and obscure texts, for fear of destroying their magical power. This trust in the efficacy of the word is paralleled by a belief in the mystical power of numbers, of the 'true names', and in other elements of the Egyptian or Babylonian magical apparatus:[3]

Then Jesus stood up with his disciples at the water of the ocean and He invoked it with this prayer, saying: 'Hear me my Father, the Father of every Fatherhood, the boundless light:

aeeiouo-iao-aoioia
psinother-therinops-nopsither-zagoure-
pagouri-nethmomaoth-nepsiomaoth-markhkhhatha-
thobarran-tharnakhakhan-zoroko-thora-jeou-sabaoth.'

But Jesus thus saying them, Thomas with Andreas with Jakobos with Simon the Kananite were being west, their faces being turned to the east. . .

But Philippos with Bartholomaios, were being on the south, being turned onto the north. But the remainder of the disciples, with the women disciples, they were standing behind Jesus. But Jesus was standing at the altar and cried out, 'Jesus, Jesus'; turned himself about it unto the four corners of the world with his disciples, all being wrapped in linen garments, saying: 'iao, iao.' This is its interpretation: Iota – the universe came out of Alpha; they will turn them. O – will become the completion of all completions. But these he having said them, Jesus said:

'Japhta raphta mounaer, mounaer, ermanouer, ermanouer', which is this: 'O Father of every Fatherhood whom I brought into thy presence, because they shall believe every word of thy truths.'

It would abuse the patience of the reader to describe the intricate heavenly organization of the Gnostic doctrines. The Gnostics, no doubt, wished by plunging into the meander of a most complicated system to reach the divine light. Blessedness, they believed, could not be attained without strenuous effort. The Jews had wandered thirty years through the desert before they reached the promised land, and it was the will of their God which had caused this long journey of purification; how much more difficult must be the journey to heaven.

This heaven was the domain of numerous deities taken from many religions of that day. Three hundred and sixty higher rulers depended on five great rulers: Kronos, Ares, Hermes, Aphrodite and Zeus. Among all these celestial powers the Greek gods occupied the highest rank. Their clear Hellenic names mingle with barbarian Oriental ones. The Hebrew Jehovah and the Greek Zeus had their assigned rank. To Ares, the god of war, was bound a power called Jpsantakhounkhainkhoukheoc. Hermes, the mediator-god, is endowed apparently with a power of lesser importance. Its name is only of two syllables: Khainkhookh. Still, Khainkhookh is among the three triple-powered gods who still are mighty enough. Sophia, the daughter of Barbelos, is bound to Aphrodite, the most amiable of these forced alliances. And Kronos is bound to a power without a name, a virtue drawn from the 'great invisible'.

The wide diffusion of Gnosticism shows clearly how much it appealed to the masses. It is also true that the intelligentsia of the time had been attracted by the new faith, which strove towards the reconciliation of the ancient world with nascent Christianity. St Paul (died A.D. 67), fully aware of the dangerous spread of Gnosticism, warns the church of Ephesus against being seduced by 'these vain discourses and newly coined apellations'. Other men of the church were less cautious, as for example Synesius (370–413), who was chosen bishop of Ptolemaïs in North Africa. His commentary on the alchemical book ascribed to Democritus was dedicated to the high priest of Serapis in Alexandria. His alchemical writings and his Gnostic hymns were certainly not orthodox.

The Gnostic Sects

According to Valentinus, the most prominent of the Gnostic leaders (died A.D. 161), matter is not separated originally and irretrievably from the spiritual, celestial world. Thus Pistis Sophia's temporary fall from grace is accomplished within the world of heaven. Two highest aeons exist, that of the father and that of the primal man who, according to the myth, sank into matter and raised himself again to heaven. This fallen aeon begot a soul, Christos, who is not the Christ. Redemption came through Horos, the limiter, whose name is derived from the Egyptian Horus, the son of Isis.

The chief sacrament of the Valentinians was that of the bridal chamber, where the pious were to witness the celestial marriage of Sophia and the redeemer, and the faithful to experience mystical union with his angel. A formula was used at this sacrament:

I will confer my favour upon thee, for the father of all sees thine angel even before his face . . . we must now become as one; receive now this grace from me and through me; deck thyself as a bride who awaits her bridegroom, that thou mayest become as I am, and as thou art; let the seed of light descend into thy bridal chamber, receive the bridegroom and give place to him, and open thine arms to embrace him. Behold, grace has descended upon thee.

Mystical eroticism is also manifest in the doctrine of Simon Magus, the most ancient of the Gnostics. His numerous followers thought that the supreme god, the father and most exalted power, had produced by emanation a female, generative principle. She in her turn gave birth to the angels who then fashioned the visible world. These inferior beings were jealous of their mother, and they drew her down to earth and forced her to endure degrading incarnations. She had been Helen of Troy and lived in Simon's time in Tyre as a prostitute. Simon married her for the salvation of mankind; salvation comes not through good works but through the grace of Simon and hope in Helen.

Simon has become in the West the prototype of the evil wizard. According to Acts 8:9–24, he was converted to Christianity by Philip, whose wonders and preaching had deeply impressed the magician. The magic of Philip appeared to him more powerful than his own. When he saw Peter and John baptizing people by laying their hands upon them, Simon asked that he be taught this rite so that he too might dispense the Holy Spirit. And he offered them money for their instructions. Humbly he accepted Peter's rebuke and begged him to pray for his forgiveness. Simon's name has been branded, and 'simony' has since this episode been the word to describe the acquisition of ecclesiastic charges. According to the legend, Simon wanted to demonstrate that he, like Christ, could ascend to heaven. He flew into the blue sky of Rome. Many people were seduced by this prodigy, and Peter feared that his flock might be attracted to this false prophet. He prayed to God, imploring Him to end this scandal. Driven away by Peter's prayers, the demons supporting Simon abandoned him and the magus fell to the earth and broke his legs.

The most celebrated Gnostic was Basilides who flourished *ca.* A.D. 125. Early Catholics have written much about him. Hippolytus in his account of the Basilidian faith describes the 'father' as the supreme being – his essence is beyond words, and nothing can be predicated about him. He created the seed which contains the germs of all things, and wherein were also embedded three degrees of divine sonship, consubstantial with the father. The first sonship ascended to the supreme; the second, being less, made only half this ascent; the third sonship was immersed in matter and became the spiritual heritage of the chosen. From the world seed, the great ruler, the higher Archon, was generated, who believed he was the highest being. His son, however, wiser and better than himself, laid the foundation of the universe. He and his father ruled the upper firmament to the moon area. The sublunary world was ruled by the god of the Hebrews, who also had a son. The higher Archon's son became the Christ.

Among the innumerable and widespread Gnostic sects – far too many to be mentioned here – some beliefs were held in common. They all agreed that creation was not the work of the highest god but that of the demiourgos. He was below the highest god, the 'unknown father' or 'boundless power', as Simon called him. The demiourgos was also called Iadalbaoth. Since he had created the visible world from matter, it was imperfect in its very nature. According to the sympathy or antipathy for the Hebrew faith, the various sects assigned to Iadalbaoth a higher or lower rank, but never considered him as the highest divinity who had created the spiritual world, heaven and the angels. The large sect of the Ophites took a decided stand against the Hebrew god. Their dogma ascribed to Iadalbaoth traits unworthy of a divine being. He was proud, ignorant and vengeful. Dissatisfied with his creation, he wanted to destroy his work through a woman, Eve. But Sophia sent the serpent that enticed man to eat the fruit of the tree of knowledge, upon which Iadalbaoth had placed a taboo, hoping thus to keep man in a state of ignorance. Wisdom enabled man to wage war against Iadalbaoth; the inner meaning of the Old Testament lies in this ruthless struggle. When the father sends Christ to save mankind, Iadalbaoth instigates the Jews to kill Christ; but only Jesus, the human form of the redeemer, died and not Christ, who is divine and cannot die.

The serpent, Ouroboros, was worshipped by several sects of the Ophites. The coiled dragon-like creature biting its own tail forms a circle, the symbol of the endless cycle of metamorphoses. Good and bad is united within the Ouroboros.

16. Gnostic gem:
Abraxas

THE ROMAN EMPIRE

Magic Under the Roman Emperors

The Jew can send you any dream you choose.

In A.D. 77 Pliny the Elder dedicated his books on natural history to the Emperor Titus. Though recognizing the powerful influence of magic upon many nations in the past and present, Pliny declares that magicians are either tricksters or fools whose doctrines are born from the contempt they have for mankind. Magic is vanity and nonsense; humanity is indebted to the Roman government for abolishing that monstrous magical rite, the human sacrifice. Pliny asserts that the founder of magic was a Persian, Zoroaster, but by ignoring the fact that the Zoroastrians abhorred human sacrifices, he defeats one of his stronger arguments. In general, his discussion of the whole matter reveals confusion and uncertainty. Despite his scorn for that 'invalid and empty' wisdom, his own book is full of magical elements and follows the tradition of praising the virtues of herbs, stones, animals, amulets, etc.

In rallying arguments against magic, Pliny cites the Emperor Nero, who had performed many occult experiments, but never successfully. Furthermore, he notes with satisfaction that the Emperor Tiberius suppressed magicians in Gaul. Most of the Roman emperors, it is true, were openly opposed to magic, and Pliny, an admiral of the Roman fleet, may have found it politic to agree with the *status quo*. His salvo on magic seems to lack objectivity, as do his repeated attacks on Greek philosophers, whom he accuses of vanity, credulity and falsehood.

Nero, whom Pliny presents as a sceptic, was certainly hostile to magic as well as philosophy, whose study he forbade, saying it was frivolous and served as a pretext for those who wished to know the future. He believed that magic was dangerous to the government, and it would indeed have been so, had citizens been allowed to read in the stars the destiny which awaited their rulers. The stars might predict conspiracies. Nero's wife, Poppaea, had a diviner attached to her household, and astrologers cluttered her private chambers. Nero, despite his official stand, consulted magicians in political matters. The astrologer Babilus read from the sky the names of Nero's enemies, who thereupon were annihilated by the emperor.

Tiberius, whom Pliny credits with the abolition of magic in Gaul, consulted the star-wise Thrasyllus. This astrologer predicted not only the impending elevation of Tiberius to the throne but his own imminent danger as well. Tiberius, in order to test Thrasyllus's veracity, had decided to kill the astrologer if he failed. Therefore, when he asked Thrasyllus to prophesy his own destiny, the astrologer, growing pale, declared himself to be in impending danger. 'That is true,' replied Tiberius, 'and the exactness of the prophecy guarantees the one concerning my person.' He reassured the trembling prophet and embraced him.

Quod licet Jovi, non licet bovi – what is suitable to Jove, is not permissible for the oxen: Caesar may consult the soothsayers, but the people should abstain from doing so. Tiberius prohibited public and secret divination from the entrails of slaughtered animals, and during his reign magicians and astrologers were banished from Italy. Four thousand Romans were exiled to Sardinia for having practised magical arts, and others were condemned to death on the charge that they had made horoscopes that would foretell the honours they would attain. But privately the emperor resorted to this same method when he wanted to know his rivals' plans. And so did Titus, Domitian and Otho, to whom Ptolemy had predicted the imperial crown. Vespasian reinforced the law of banishment, but he exempted his own astrologer from it. His predecessor Vitellius had ordered all magicians to be gone from Italy by a set date. The answer of the astrologers was a poster announcing that the emperor would leave the earth before their departure from Italy – and the prediction proved to be true.

As a rule, famous astrologers were well received at court. So long as their oracles were agreeable to the emperor, they were honoured. Among them, however, were many bad courtiers whose predictions were contrary to the ruler's projects. Their originality rarely found favour. Accused of being responsible for the adverse stars, they faced exile, gaol or execution. Those who had miraculously escaped death were certain to gain wealth. 'So long as an astrologer,' says Juvenal, 'has not endured chains and dungeons, he has no credit, and is an ordinary man. But when he has escaped death, everyone wants his advice.'

Aristocrats, like the emperor, had their household prophets. When Livia was bearing Tiberius, she consulted her astrologer, who foretold the unborn infant's brilliant future. A similar prophecy was made about the suckling Octavian, Livia's future husband. Octavian, better known as the Emperor Augustus, was the first in the lineage of Caesars. His reign established the most brilliant epoch of Roman history. Originally a sceptic, he was converted to astrology when Theogenes, almost against the future Caesar's will, set up his horoscope. Theogenes had barely examined it when he knelt worshipfully before the future master of the empire. Augustus later ordered the coining of medals representing the lucky stars under which he was born.

If such an enlightened man indulged in magic arts, we can understand how it happened that the philosopher-emperor Marcus Aurelius, the most virtuous of all Roman rulers, sought help from a Chaldean magus. His wife Faustina had fallen in love with a gladiator. After having fought her infatuation in vain, she revealed her misery to Marcus Aurelius and the couple decided to have a philtre concocted that would free her untimely

passion. The remedy prescribed by the magician was simple;
the gladiator should be killed and Faustina was to rub her body
with his warm blood. After having accomplished this loathsome
rite, the empress could not but think with horror of her past
love.

The fearless soldier and friend of the muses, Septimius
Severus, was ruthlessly ambitious. Having lost his wife, he
wanted to marry a woman who would help his ascent to the
throne. From Chaldean astrologers he knew that in Syria lived
a maiden to whom the stars had promised a royal spouse.
Accordingly Septimius married her. In his impatience, he found
that his political advancement was proceeding too slowly, and in
him arose the fear that he had wed wrongly because of astrological miscalculation. In order to secure advice on this affair, he
went to Sicily to consult a famous stargazer. When the Emperor
Commodus, son of Marcus Aurelius, heard of this scandal, he
was enraged. Septimius narrowly escaped death, but he ascended
to the throne after Commodus's assassination and ruled for many
years. It must be added that his own horoscope had not been
interpreted correctly, as none of the astrologers had told him that
he would die by strangulation.

The rulers of the empire suspected all magicians, foreign as
well as native. Soothsayers and philtre-brewing wizards might
uncover dangerous secrets. Jewish magi sold dreams in the
streets of the capital; at night, the people fulfilled the illegal and
criminal desires repressed by day in fear of the Caesar. The clan
of philosophers discussed 'the eternal', 'the everlasting', and
found unworthy of words the ephemeral splendour of the emperor. A few among them dared to criticize the government and
offered their unsolicited advice upon political matters. Before
long, foreign gods with newly coincd names were to be worshipped in ceremonies of which the sacred books do not speak.
Had not Maecenas given this golden advice to Augustus:
'Chastise the authors of foreign religions, not only from respect
to the gods, but because, by introducing foreign divinities, they
instigate many to follow foreign laws. From them are born conspiracies and secret societies, dangerous to the reign of a sole ruler.
Tolerate no person who despises the gods, anyone who devotes
himself to the arts of magic.' As early as 139 B.C. the Chaldean
magi had been banished from Rome, but they always managed to
return. Augustus followed Maecenas's admonition, but punishment was lenient: only two thousand Chaldean books were
burned.

Pliny looked upon magic as a parasite that had fattened itself
upon science; the historian Tacitus defended it, saying that the
charlatans who practised magic ought not to serve as proof
against true magic; Seneca, though uncertain, believed at any
rate in astrology and divination; the satirist Juvenal ridicules the
Chaldeans and the Roman ladies who believe in such nonsense.
Only a short time before, Maecenas had called magic an instigator to revolt. These conflicting opinions, uttered in the first
century of the Christian era, bear witness to the fact that magic
was then still exerting a strong influence upon every mind: it

caused laughter and fear, scorn and admiration. Everybody was concerned with *private* magic; no one found it timely to criticize the *official* cult, in spite of the fact that the codified religion of the state was nothing more than legalized magic. Did it really matter whether the priest or the magician interpreted omens? Before Tiberius abolished the law, no state action could be decided upon without interrogation of the entrails, the haruspicy. Of a similar magical character were the other divinatory arts, taught in the priest-controlled schools – prediction of the future through interpretation of the flight or the cries of birds, of the lightning, of the trees. There was little in Roman religion which could not already be found among the earlier Etruscans and the Greeks. It was an antiquated religion of nature, full of the relics of 'savagery'. In defending it the Caesars pursued only one aim, the consolidation of their authority.

The early Christian emperors began their persecutions where the pagans had ended theirs. Under Constantius people who adhered to the old cult (which had now become illegal) were declared to be magicians and made to suffer martyrdom for their beliefs. In the east Roman empire, under Valens, the terrorized citizens burned their books, fearing they might be indicted for witchcraft. Valens's investigators resorted to a method which was then not new and which has since that time too been employed. In the houses of suspects, they 'discovered' magical writings which they themselves had placed there – an easy way of ridding the emperor of annoying subjects and of filling the treasury with the gold of the executed.

Neo-Platonism

In Rome private magic had become a trade; in exchange for money, the Chaldeans meted out good and evil. Their knowledge was degenerating steadily. But magic still exerted a powerful influence, and Gnostics and Neo-Platonists who accepted magical ideas and ceremonies gathered believers everywhere. The latter, alarmed by expanding Christianity, appointed themselves the new champions of pagan magic. An integral part of their cult was *theurgy*, the calling down of good demons.

Originally, demons had been mortals of extraordinary merit whom the gods claimed after death. Under the influence of Greek philosophers, especially of Pythagoras and Plato, this concept changed, and now the demons were thought to be divinities. The gods and heroes of ancient polytheism became the servants of the one god, who was infinite and universal, incomprehensible to man. Thus a compromise was reached between primitive polytheism and the monotheism of the philosophers. The demons, though partaking of the divine, appeared in human form. They protected man against evil influences and carried his prayers to the highest heavens. Neo-Platonism also recognized evil demons, fond of bloodshed and strife. Their evocation was considered a crime.

An important feature of Neo-Platonic ethics was the belief that god had manifested himself not only to one, but to many nations. 'His spirit had breathed wherever one discovers traces of divine revelation.' Specially venerable at that time were older religions, as being the receptacles of god's earliest manifestations to mankind. Neo-Platonic syncretism, however, differed from that of most of the Gnostics in that Christianity was not accepted. Hellenic philosophy was to be saved by grafting upon it religious beliefs and other wisdom of the Orient.

In Alexandria, which had become the laboratory of the expanding communication between East and West, a Jewish philosopher, Philo (born 20 B.C.), had translated the Old Testament into Greek, attempting to show a relationship between the old Jewish creed and Greek philosophy. Philo had declared that Greek philosophy was superior to the Jewish religion; but he asserted that most of the great ideas in philosophy had originated among the Hebrews and had been borrowed from them by the Occident. Philo's philosophy culminated in the belief that true wisdom and morality are superior to intellectual apprehension, and that knowledge alone does not confer blessedness.

Together with Philo, early Christians like Athenagoras and Justin paved the way for Neo-Platonism. In their ambition to exhibit Christianity as hyper-Platonic, they strove to connect the new faith with Platonism and Stoicism. They referred to philosophy in order to prove that the Christian revelation was true. The mysticism of Plotinus contains less magical and religious elements than that of later Neo-Platonists. He and his disciples still exhibit confidence in the presuppositions of philosophy. Their successors, however, did not share this view; and to the achievements of the human intellect they opposed the higher wisdom of divine revelation.

The soul, partaking of the divine, strives to return to its source, god, from whom has emanated nous, who is at once created in his image and the archetype of all existing things. This return, however, according to Plotinus, cannot be hastened by magical rites, but only by the practice of virtue, ascetic observance, chastity and by the contemplation of god. From Porphyry, Plotinus's disciple, we know that the master attained this ecstatic union with god four times. Porphyry popularized his master's teachings, placing the emphasis on religio-magical rites, thus accelerating the transition of Neo-Platonism from mystical philosophy to religious practice. In the hands of Iamblichus, Porphyry's pupil, this process was completed: philosophical theory was transmuted into a theological doctrine.

Plotinus, who lived from about A.D. 204 to 262, was opposed to magic. He charges the Gnostics with believing that the spoken word can influence the higher and incorporeal powers. He also attacks their conviction that diseases are demons who can be banished by exorcism. Although Plotinus recognizes the efficacy of incantations and talismans, he calls them the works of magicians and sorcerers and in his *Aeneid* (IV, 4, 44), he concludes that the life of reason is free from magic.[1] He concedes an occult meaning to the stars and to their motion, which though 'not causing everything, signify the future concerning each'. Like Plato, he considered the stars as divine and eternal animals endowed with souls and with an intelligence superior to that of man. They dwell closer to the world soul, and therefore their nature is beyond that of earthly beings; but by no means do they shift from good to evil upon entering the different signs of the zodiac.

Thus he denies emphatically the Chaldean star wisdom. His world image, however, is essentially a magical one. For him, harmony and sympathy draw together all the existing parts of the universe. Between beings having no apparent relationship there exist secret sympathies, a concept which the later Neo-Platonists were to make use of in producing marvels. Plotinus's conception of astrology was the same as that of many Christian scholars of the Middle Ages: the stars exert their influence, which, however, the human will – being free – can overcome. His followers saw a connection between demons and magic; they drew a distinction between theurgical arts and the evil practice of sorcery on the one hand and science on the other. Theurgy uses 'arcane signatures' and 'the power of inexplicable symbols, consecrated from eternity'. These are more sublime than reason, and their origin is known only to the god whom they invoke. In other words, the old belief in seals and strange words is upheld once more and, though they are transformed to suit the needs of a changing world, they are truly the implements of magic.

In the book *Of the Mysteries of the Egyptians*, ascribed alternately to Iamblichus or to Porphyry, we read that natural objects are related to demons ethereally, aerially or aquatically. This leaves a wide field open to magical operations, covering objects already familiar to us for such purposes. Stones, herbs, aromatics and animals are used to attract spiritual powers, while the efficacy of prayer rests in its power to purify the conjurer of passion and profanity. It is little wonder then that the Neo-Platonic magicians of the Renaissance operate similarly, preparing themselves with devout prayers and Christian symbols prior to conjuring up the demon who shall reveal hidden treasures to them. A sixteenth-century magician recommends that these operations be suspended until the half-moon rises in the sky; that the conjurer observe chastity for nine days; that he attend to his confession and communion, and so forth.

The Neo-Platonists, fearing injury from evil, used counter-charms, employing tactics which might thwart the demons. Porphyry (A.D. 232–304) reports on an imperfect conjuration conducted by his master, Plotinus, in the temple of Isis in Rome. The sober views that Plotinus held about magic did not prevent him, in this case at any rate, from indulging in theurgy. The god who appeared in this instance vanished soon because a friend of Plotinus, who had held two birds as counter-charms, strangled them when the apparition became visible. The god, shocked by this action, remained mute and disappeared quickly.[2]

The influence which theurgy exerted upon the Occident was powerful, and stronger still was the imprint which Neo-Platonism left upon Church dogma. However, it is not within the scope of this book to describe its evolution in the Christian Church. It may suffice to remember that St Augustine and Plotinus, both being products of the same philosophic tradition, had arrived independently at similar conclusions. The dogmas were formulated through philosophic methods; the theologians and the Neo-Platonists at times drew so closely together that they appear completely in accord.

During Plato's time, any magic that served the commonwealth could be fused with religion. Under the Roman emperors of pagan times, the official cult was legalized magic; private practices were feared because they escaped government control. Neo-Platonism had introduced rites hitherto unknown to Rome, which could be considered in the nature of reforms as well as taken for some new, forbidden magic. When Apuleius was accused of witchcraft, he declared that his operations were nothing more than those sanctioned by state religion. And not long afterwards, Neo-Platonism became factually identified with the theology of paganism. No one could be certain whom the Christian emperors might condemn through their laws against magic; this ambiguity proved practical for the rulers. Apparently, they revived the ancient decrees which Rome had formulated against wizardry. Their belated application, however, in a profoundly changed society, produced other results: those same laws which had originally been created to protect the state religion now caused its destruction.

In Rome, when the persecution of Christians was at its height, Tertullian (*ca.* A.D. 160–240) exclaimed: 'All those of ours who fell into your hands you have destroyed, and still more perish daily through your abominable tortures. Should we call for revenge, what a war of reprisal we could wage against you, we who have not been weakened by debauchery and the enslavement of the mind.'[3] The reprisal was then not far away, and the old Roman laws were to constitute its most powerful weapon. The ancient Twelve Tables, the oldest Roman legislation, had never lost their validity. They ordered death for the crime of witchcraft. The Cornelian Law confirmed the sentence: 'Soothsayers, enchanters, and those who make use of sorcery for evil purposes; those who conjure up demons, who disrupt the elements, who employ waxen images destructively, shall be punished by death.'

When they found it expedient, Christian emperors now stigmatized as soothsayers the prophetesses of the sacred temples; as conjurers of coiled demons the philosophers who conversed with the intermediary gods. This double-edged sword of justice was not always of equal sharpness on both sides. The emperors either enforced or disregarded these laws, according to circumstances. Constantius, son of Constantine the Great, upheld tolerance in Italy and in Africa, whereas in Asia Minor he persecuted the heathens under various pretexts. In 357 he forbade absolutely every kind of divination: 'There shall be no more divination, nor curious inquiry, for evermore. Whosoever dares disobey shall lose his head by the avenging sword of the executioner. He who refuses to comply with this decree shall be smitten.' People who had practised the old religion were now accused of attempting to take the emperor's life by evil spells.

Julian the Apostate

From such procedures we may gather that the early Christian emperors considered themselves, before all, the rulers of the empire, the foundations of which they consolidated by every political means that suited their purpose. On the other hand, the Church, to whom the majority of the lower classes now flocked, saw itself compelled to compromise with popular superstitions. Many of the spiritual leaders indulged in these superstitions, and numerous clerics exhibited a corruption which contrasted strangely with the virtue of the last pagan philosophers. No longer burdened with the problem of how to attract the masses, the latter retired into the highest realms of philosophy.

It is necessary to bear these facts in mind in order to understand the popularity which the Emperor Julian enjoyed when he abandoned the Christian faith and reinstalled pagan worship. Julian was the only survivor of his family, which had been massacred by his cousins, the sons of Constantine. He had been spared, probably because of his apparent inoffensiveness. He had known a joyless youth on the eastern border of the empire. No princely education was given him, and the bishop of Nicomedia was ordered by Constantius to direct Julian's inclinations towards the clerical profession.

Julian must have concealed his resentment skilfully, as Constantius had no suspicion that he might become dangerous. According to the legend, Julian secretly instructed himself in Neo-Platonism. Eusebius the philosopher had instilled in him reliance on reason, 'since nothing is closer to error than the beliefs of a feeble mind'. Chrysantius, on the contrary, was loud in the praise of theurgy and spurred his pupil's interest in supernatural manifestations. The venerable Maximus finally initiated the future emperor in the philosophy of Neo-Platonism, and as supreme proof of his wisdom he evoked a few beneficent demons. The initiation, which took place in an abandoned temple near Ephesus, was the beginning of Julian's career. It was as incredible to him as it was to many others that his cousin Constantius called upon him. Still more marvellous was his nomination as Caesar, that is, commander-in-chief of the armies in Gaul. When he entered the first Gallic village, arrayed gaily by the friendly inhabitants, a laurel wreath accidentally fell upon his head. When riding through Vienne, an old woman blocked his way to greet him as the emperor and the favourite of the gods. These were good omens, which became confirmed when Julian fought victoriously against the invading Germans.

The events of Julian's life are well-known: his victory over the German tribes, his *coup d'état* in Paris, which made him Roman

emperor, his startling career as ruler of the empires of East and
West, his recantation of the Christian faith. In Eleusis, he descended into a pit, where ox blood was poured on him in accordance with the rites of the Mithraic religion. Then he offered a
sacrifice in the temple of Fortune, and was present at the
haruspicy, the inspection of entrails for knowledge of the future.
As Pontifex Maximus he decreed that the temples be reopened, and
sacrifices and divination were declared to be an integral part of
the state religion.

In 362 he travelled to Persia, the only country which for
centuries had resisted Rome. He reached Antioch by the end of
July, at the time of the festival of the mourning for Adonais. This
coincidence was considered an evil omen. In Mesopotamia he
worshipped the goddess of the moon and, after mysterious nocturnal ceremonies, he ordered her temple doors to be walled
up 'until his return'. The Persian war was an unlucky undertaking. Fatally wounded, Julian addressed his confidants, affirming
he knew that the soul was above the body. Fearing that his
waning spirit might make a mistake fatal to the empire he did
not designate his successor. 'Why,' he said, expiring, 'bewail a
soul ready to join the genii of the stars?'

In his writings, Julian reveals himself to be a true Neo-
Platonist and an admirer of Iamblichus, whom he praises in his
Hymn to the Sovereign Sun. This work contains many astrological ideas. The planets are the visible gods; and the sun, the
highest among them, is the link between the visible and the intelligible world. Behind its shining disc is the great invisible. He is
the first cause, the supreme principle, acting upon the world by
means of emanation, whose highest embodiment is the sun.[4]
'The doctrines of Aristotle,' Julian says, 'are incomplete until
they become harmonized with those of Plato, and even that is
not enough; they must agree with the revelations granted by the
gods.' He wanted to use Neo-Platonism for the revival of Greek
philosophy. As an advocate of this school, he considered man's
soul to be imprisoned in the body for the expiation of sin.
Matter is evil, and one ought to flee from it. One should blush to
possess a body whose grossness is offensive to man's soul.
Knowledge of God is attained through ecstasy, a Bacchic frenzy
which the initiated alone may witness. The world is a trinity,
composed of matter, of the planets which are not marred by imperfection, and of the supreme good that evades the grasp of the
intelligence.

Julian's main interest was the glorification of his favourite
deity, the sun. His worship of the radiant provider of all life we
can trace to Eastern sources that sprang from Zoroastrianism,
the religion of light. Julian worshipped the sun-god under the
name of Mithra, the mediator, as King Helios, the king of all
things, who 'fills the heavens with as many gods as are comprehended by his intelligence'.[5] All the gods of the other religions
shall play their parts on the intelligible scene, as manifestations
of the power and the beneficence of Helios. He ends his discourse on King Sun with these exalted words:

May the gods grant me the privilege of celebrating many times the sacred feast, and may the sun-god, king of the universe – he who proceeds through all eternity from the generative substance of the good, who in the midst of the intellectual gods fills them with infinite harmony and beauty, with fruitful substance, perfect intelligence, and continually and without end with every good – bless me. I beseech thee, sun, king of all things, because of my devotion, to be benevolent to me, and give me a happy life, a steady mind, a divine intelligence – and, finally, at the desired moment, a most tranquil liberation from life, and allow me to ascend and remain near him, possibly through eternity and, if this be beyond my merit, at least for many harmonious years.[6]

Julian was not the only promoter of sun worship. Such beliefs must have been popular in Rome and caused perhaps the spreading of the Mithraic cult in Europe. Sun worship was connected with the faith of Mithras. A relationship of Mithraicism with Christianity was also alleged by the priests of the Oriental creed. A witness to this is St Augustine: 'I remember,' he says, 'that the priests of the fellow in the cap [that is, Mithra, who wore a Phrygian bonnet] used to say at one-time, "Our capped one is himself a Christian." '[7] The first Christian emperor, Constantine the Great, adopted for the most common type of coinage the figure of the sun with the legend, 'To the invincible sun, my guardian,'[8] retaining it long after his conversion.

Julian's religion rested upon the ancient beliefs of the Orient and recalls the earliest monotheistic religion, that of Ikhnaton who had arrived, thirteen hundred years before Christ, at similar conclusions, praying to a supreme deity whose emblem was the disc of the sun.

The Ruin of Pagan Magic

. . . announce that the great Pan is dead.

Attributed to Plutarch

It was during the fourth century that Christianity overcame the pagan cult and its magical rites. Julian died in 363 and his successor Jovian in 364, the year in which the brothers Valens and Valentinian ascended to the thrones of East and West Rome. Under Valens, pagan resistance was still powerful, centring upon the old Iamblichus whose sobriety was combined strangely with enthusiasm and the love of the marvellous. His doctrine and that of Plotinus were the pillars supporting the pagan sanctuary. Paganism was smouldering beneath the ashes of burned temples, sacred trees and images. In the cities, many found it wise to accept under pressure the religion of Christ. But these converts, though adding to the number of Christians, were dangerous, as is demonstrated by Libanius, the Greek rhetorician (314–91). He says:

If they tell you that there are many newly converted, be sure that their sudden conversion is only simulation. They remain what they were. They show, when in the company of true Christians, their new religious feelings. They seem to swell the number of worshippers of Christ with whom they pray. . . . No doubt they do pray – with words tyrant in the tragedy: being no tyrants at all yet wearing his mask.

In the country such a mask was not always necessary since there official vigilance was relaxed. Pagan signifies villager (Latin '*pagus*', village); and in Valentinian's laws the old creed is called *religio paganorum*, the religion of the country people. It was in the country that the philosophers met secretly to deliberate on how to face the oppression. One of these meetings, under the guidance of Iamblichus, has often been described. Twenty-four philosophers met in an abandoned mansion to exert their divinatory arts. By alectryomancy, divination by a fowl, they wanted to explore the future, anxious to know whether Valens was to be succeeded by a more worthy monarch. They scattered grain on their alphabetical circle and the cock picked from the Greek letters, in the sequence ΘΕΟΔ, Theod. . . . The philosophers concluded that Theodorus, an official of high rank at court, was to be chosen emperor.

When Valens had been informed of this meeting, he reinforced the persecution of all philosophers, seers and magicians. Not only were philosophers sentenced to death but also others whose mantles were fringed in the style of the philosophers' garments. This persecution was not considered unusual in these barbaric times. However, the remainder of the story as it has been reported can only find its prototype in the realms of legend: Valens commanded the death of all people whose names began with Theod, the Theodores, Theodules, Theodotes, Theodosites, Theodorites, etc. The slaughter was initiated by the execution of the courtier, Theodorus. By the hysterical way in which the emperor sought to eradicate superstitious beliefs, he exposed his own subservience to superstition.

The venerable Iamblichus, it is said, poisoned himself in order to escape an ignominious death. Secret police roamed the countryside searching for victims. At court Heliodorus, an astrologer, gave Valens lessons in eloquence, in this way disguising his true function, which was to cast horoscopes, to predict the future from the stars. But he did not reveal that Iamblichus's ill-starred alectryomantic oracle was to come true. Valens, fighting the Goths at Adrianople, was killed (378), and Theodosius (346–95), called the Great, ascended to the throne. It was Theodosius who dealt the death blow to paganism, for his Draconian decrees prohibited the most inoffensive old customs: the burning of incense and the lighting of a fire at home in honour of the house-god, the pouring of wine with a similar intention, and the adorning of trees. Many of these rites were hardly connected with the pagan cult. There was, for instance, the sacrifice called the '*propter viam*' (because of departure). It consisted in the burning of remainders of food. This 'sacrifice', or rather hygienic measure, was dictated more by the necessity of getting rid of waste than by piety. Such rites, or rather traditions, were punished by confiscation of the house and prosecution for high treason. The new laws were reinforced sternly by magistrates and judges. The third of a field in which a pagan fire had been kindled was confiscated, even though its owner had not participated in the rite. 'Prejudice disguised itself in religious fervour, and many accused their neighbours of paganism in order to despoil them.'

Festus, former governor of Syria and proconsul of Asia, who had always been an enemy of paganism, was so horrified by these abuses that in his old age he embraced the religion of the persecuted. In vain did Libanius exhort the emperor to be tolerant. In his *Speech in Defence of the Temples* Libanius, who had been councillor under Julian, exposes with humanity misdeeds committed through fanaticism. It was useless, however, for the fate of paganism was already decided. Under Theodosius II it struggled feebly for existence and lingered on into the fifth and sixth centuries. The demons of Neo-Platonism grew ever less powerful. A single word, 'Christ', could drive them now into the abyss. With prayers and holy water the air which they had polluted was purified. They seemed to be driven away forever, yet they were to avenge the persecution of their worshippers. As devils, they reappeared in the Occidental world, where they dwelled in the imagination both of the learned and of the simple. The persecutions of which they were the cause rank among the major misfortunes that have visited the West.

ALCHEMY

Origins of Alchemy

There is evidence that the art which was later called alchemy came to the West at the beginning of the second century of the Christian era. The most important testimony substantiating this is that of Pliny the Elder (A.D. 23–79), who writes extensively on metallurgy but does not mention ideas which could be included among those related to alchemy. The various beliefs concerning metals and their treatment mentioned by Pliny do however indicate a climate of thought favourable to the emergence of the art.[1] Despite the alchemists' claim concerning the age of their art, it is in point of fact the youngest magical wisdom. The notion that it flourished during the time of the pharaohs has been abandoned, along with the etymology '*chem*' or '*qem*' (black), an Egyptian word employed occasionally to describe Egypt, whose black soil contrasted so sharply with the red earth of the desert.[2] It was in the fourth century, amidst the merciless fight which Christianity was waging against paganism, that alchemy flowered. Zosimus of Panopolis, a writer of that epoch, appointed himself the apologist of the alchemical art. His allegories and comments are cited by medieval experts as the most profound and venerable documents of the arcana. Zosimus declared that the knowledge of metals, precious stones and scents dated back to the epoch mentioned furtively in the Genesis: 'The sons of God saw the daughters of men, that they were fair.' The mysterious sons of God were believed to be fallen angels who had mated with the women of antediluvian times. In gratitude, the angels taught these women various arts, obviously with the intention that their companions make jewels, colourful garments and perfumes with which to adorn their beauty. Thus the wise men of ancient times decided that the fallen angels must have been evil, perverters of morals and manners. Tertullian confirms these early beliefs, saying that the sons of God bequeathed their wisdom to the mortals with the evil intention of seducing them to 'mundane pleasures'.

According to Zosimus, these happenings marked the beginning of alchemy. He was repeating what late Jewish and early Christian writers had already declared. Zosimus elaborates upon the subject and gives also the name of a very early master of the alchemical art, the mysterious Chemes, though this legendary ancestor of the gold-makers has left no evidence that he ever existed. However, it was accepted that Chemes had written a book which he called *Chema*, and that the fallen angels had given lessons to the daughters of men with the aid of this book. From Chemes and *Chema* was derived Chemia, a name which was given consequently to the art itself. This accounts for the legend thus far. The Greek word '*chemia*' was the designation for alchemy until the Arabs added to it the article '*al*' of their native tongue.

In an early alchemical manuscript a priestess who calls herself Isis and who addresses her writings to her son Horus declares that she owed her knowledge to the first of the angels and prophets, Amnael. Isis does not hesitate to tell us that she acquired her wisdom as a reward for intercourse with Amnael. Her book is of great interest to the student of alchemical tradition, and still more revealing are the writings of a woman known by the pseudonym of Mary the Jewess. Mary, a Greek, is apparently the earliest alchemist of the West. None of her writings have survived in complete form, but she is cited by her colleagues, like Zosimus, as if she might be identified with Moses's sister Miriam. The alchemist Olympiodorus (fourth century of the Christian era) quotes the famous passage on the strength of which she has always been called a Jewess. Speaking of the 'holiness' of her book, she says:

'Do not touch it (if you are not of the Abrahamitic race), unless indeed you are of our race.'[3]

The passage is confused, as the sentence in parentheses seems to be a gloss that had worked itself into the text. The question of Mary's faith is of minor importance. She is a most capable chemist, and the invention of a series of new technical devices is ascribed to her: the vessel enclosed in a box of hot ashes, producing a low and steady heat; the dung bed which retains its warmth for an indefinite time; the double boiler, still called in French '*bain-marie*'.[4] Speaking of women alchemists, we must not forget the early scholar who called herself Cleopatra; and Theosebia, Zosimus's sister. There will be further discussion in following chapters of Cleopatra's book, *Chrysopeia* (*Gold-Making*). The participation by so many women in the study of the newly invented art is like a confirmation of the fable that wills the fair sex to be connected with the origins of alchemy.

Most of the alchemical manuscripts which were written in the third and fourth centuries of the Christian era have come to us in copies of later dates. Cleopatra's *Gold-Making*, for instance, is preserved in a manuscript of the tenth or eleventh century. But there are also early Greco-Egyptian texts, like the famous Leyden and Stockholm Papyri. They date back to about A.D. 300. Most, if not all, of them were found in a tomb at Thebes in Egypt, but the name of the alchemical master who wanted his library to be buried with him is unknown. To this early literature must be added the theoretical and apologetic writings of Zosimus, Stephanus, Olympiodorus, Synesius and others, whose authenticity cannot be questioned. Zosimus and Olympiodorus wrote in the fourth century, Synesius in the fifth, and Stephanus continued the lineage in the seventh century. This literature provides a clear picture of the early alchemical art. By these authentic writings it is possible to unwind the silky

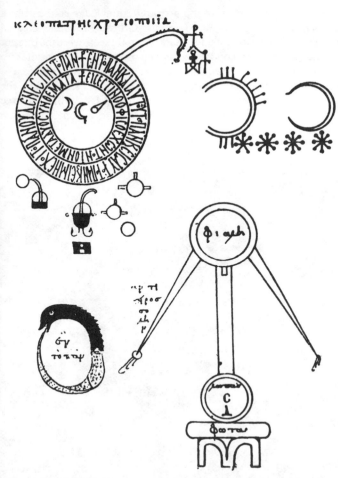

17. The Chrysopeia of Cleopatra

thread which fable has spun into a marvellous cocoon, and to unravel its mystery.

Together with magic and other illicit arts, alchemy was revealed to mankind by the cursed angels, betrayers of God's secrets. They had been punished for this indiscretion; a curse lay upon the forbidden knowledge which enabled man to rival his creator. Investigation of the hidden works of nature was sacrilegious. St Augustine shares this conception when he censures 'the vain and curious desire of investigation, known as knowledge and science'. The rivalry between knowledge and faith had likewise been perceived by Roman writers. In his book *On the Nature of Things* Lucretius (*ca.* 98–53 B.C.) exclaims triumphantly: 'Thus is religion trod down, by a just reverse; victory makes us akin to the gods.' And he adds, hypocritically: 'Do not think that I wish to teach you the principles of impiety, or to lead you to the path of crime.'[5]

Throughout the first centuries of our era, the tree of knowledge of the Genesis remained the symbol of such sinful investigation. With the eating of the forbidden fruit, man had become like God, knowing good and evil. No doubt the alchemists accepted such views, yet they proceeded with their investigations just the same. Isis's boast of how she acquired knowledge sounds like a challenge to the passage of Genesis. Gnostic teachings created this entirely new attitude, for many Gnostic sects were indifferent to the problem of good and evil upon earth. The Ophites in like manner worshipped the serpent of the Bible as a beneficent being, since it had rightly directed man to knowledge, the weapon used by him against his creator Iadalbaoth. The tree of knowledge and the serpent were thus to become the most cherished emblems of alchemy.

18. Alchemical tree

It is not surprising that the first alchemists were treated as badly as the heathen. Their persecution was initiated when the art was still centred in Alexandria. The study of medicine and alchemy was carried on in buildings adjacent to the Serapeum, the temple of Serapis. When Theophilus, archbishop of Alexandria, ordered the destruction of this temple, he met with resistance; but a direct command by Emperor Theodosius forced the scholars to retreat. Together with the other temples of the empire, the Serapeum perished in flames. The library, once already destroyed under Caesar, was saved and the studies continued in the museum, until the woman-philosopher, Hypatia, was murdered (415).

Her death marked the end of pagan learning in Egypt. The persecuted philosophers sought refuge in Athens, where Proclus, the Neo-Platonist, was then teaching. With them, alchemy travelled to Greece. In 529 Justinian ordered the official suppression of ancient learning, science and philosophy. Pagan culture disappeared, but alchemy survived, though the Theodosian law had ordered that alchemical books be burned publicly, in the presence of a bishop.

New writers continued the filiation of the cursed. Fusing some orthodox elements into their doctrine, they made it acceptable to the emperors. Stephanus of Alexandria dedicated his *Nine Lessons in Chemia* to Heraclius, emperor of the East (575–641). Well versed in the philosophy of Pythagoras and Plato, yet a Christian mystic, Stephanus marks the transition between ancient alchemy and that of a new Europe. Not far away were the times when Byzantine monks would set to work copying such old writings as might fall into their hands. Among these assiduous compilers who worked for several centuries at the reconstitution of the wisdom fanaticism had destroyed, Nicephorus (758–829) was concerned mainly with Greek authors. In the eleventh century Psellus restored Platonic philosophy. Together with the reappearance of this early literature, the number of alchemical commentators increased, including the 'Christian Philosopher', pseudonym of a highly trained monk who in his work fused Christian culture with pagan studies, alchemy with theology.

Inspired by Stephanus's writings, alchemical poets appear upon the literary stage, praising in exalted verse the marvels revealed by the Hermetic art. Zosimus and Olympiodorus are cited again, together with Synesius, the ingenious and wise bishop of Ptolemaïs. Mythical alchemists like Trismegistus, Petesis and Agathodaemon reappear in the texts, also pseudo-Hermetics such as Zoroaster and Democritus. Those who in fear of persecution had hidden behind pseudonyms – Cleopatra, Mary and Isis – are now the objects of veneration. Iamblichus, the unfortunate champion of Neo-Platonism, was credited with two alchemical treatises. These Byzantine manuscripts of Hermetic texts made their way to Italy; some were ultimately acquired by Francis I and brought to France.

However, this trickle of old wisdom would not have saved Europe from falling into the depths of ignorance, had not the conquering Arabs introduced to Spain the learning of antiquity.

Hermes Trismegistus

As early as 2900 B.C. the Egyptians had mined gold, *nub*, in Nubia. The precious metal, obtained from quartz, was ground by handmills, and as technical skills progressed, gold was refined and standardized. The refining process had been discovered after laborious research, and its secret was closely guarded by the priests.[6] They reserved it for the inheritor of the throne or for those of the highest virtue and wisdom. Zosimus says: 'The good of the whole kingdom is upheld by these arts of exploiting metals and sand, but no one but the priests may exercise power over them.' In Egypt chemical operations were accompanied, as everything important was, by magical incantations. If we combine the three facts, namely, that the Egyptians worked with gold ore and other metals, that they kept these operations secret, and that their chemistry was endowed with magic, we draw close to alchemy.

Were the Egyptians adept at the arcane art itself? There is no evidence nor any likelihood that they were. Everything relating to alchemy, however, leads us back constantly to Egypt. Zosimus dedicated his book on alchemy to Imhotep, the wise poet and councillor, who lived not much later than 3000 B.C. In Imhotep's beautiful verses we recognize that at an early date the Egyptians already knew the mundane pleasures which the sons of god had taught to the daughters of men:

> Follow thy desire while thou livest,
> Lay myrrh upon thy head,
> Clothe thee in fine linen
> Imbued with luxurious perfumes,
> The genuine things of the gods. . . .[7]

Stephanus, who wrote in the seventh century of our era, says that sulphur and lead are synonymous with Osiris. This god, Isis, and the evil Typhon are mentioned often in alchemical writings, and most of them name Hermes Trismegistus as the master of alchemical philosophy. Hermes is the Greek god who conducts the souls to the dark kingdom of Hades, the underworld. 'He opens the doors of birth and of death.' He controls exchange, commerce and learning: he is the gods' messenger, the mediator, the reconciler.

'Trismegistus' means 'three times the greatest', an epithet that reveals in what high esteem he was held. He is not a Greek god but a divinity of the Greek colonists in Egypt. These Greco-Egyptians admired the ancient religious doctrines of the Nile land, which did not appear to have changed since the remote times of the pharaohs, but which in reality had decayed, so that when the Greeks began to study them, not even their symbols were understood by the Egyptian priests.

The Hellenic settlers did not make up the largest portion of the population in Alexandria, but they were certainly the most intelligent. In the amalgamation of Egyptian religion and Greek philosophy, resulting in constant exchange between these two peoples, Hellenic ideas were predominant, so that we can rightly speak of an Hellenized Egypt. The Greeks accepted readily whatever they could understand among the remnants of the old Egyptian religion, and the result of this process was an Egyptian philosophy in which were mingled both elements, together with religious fragments of the Jews and the other peoples of the East.[8] The Greeks recognized in the Egyptian gods their own deities; thus they identified their Hermes with Thoth, the divine inventor of magic, of writing and of the spoken word.

Thoth is the scribe in the judgement hall of the underworld, writing down Osiris's verdict which is pronounced after the deeds of the deceased have been weighed. Thoth-Hermes became humanized, developing into a mythical king who had reigned for 3,226 years and who had written 36,525 books on the principles of nature. Iamblichus brought this fantastic number down to 20,000, and Clement of Alexandria (fl. A.D. 200) reduced it to a sober forty-two, which he had seen carried in a solemn procession. These books were nothing else but the anonymous writings on Egyptian philosophy, the offspring of Greco-Egyptian intercourse. According to Iamblichus, the authors of such works signed them with the name Thoth, probably to give them the venerability of age. Thoth-Hermes, assumed to have been their author, was credited with founding the doctrine which consequently was called Hermetic. No one doubted the authenticity of the mythical adept, whose existence had been confirmed by Plato, by Diodorus of Sicily, by Tertullian, Galen, Iamblichus and many others.

From the colossal amount of writing ascribed to Hermes Trismegistus not very much has survived, beyond fourteen short texts written in Greek and a series of fragments preserved by Christian authors. These express mystical and philosophical ideas inherent in this early epoch which, viewed as a whole, recall Gnosticism. The best known among them is called *Poimandres, the Good Shepherd*, some passages of which bear a striking resemblance to the Gospel of St John, while others are reminiscent of Plato's *Timaeus*. Jewish thought, such as is expressed by Philo, can also be discerned in them. In addition to these writings, a few magical treatises are ascribed to Trismegistus. Their main theme is astrology; alchemy is treated somewhat vaguely.

The Hermetic books were considered by the alchemists as Hermes's bequest to them of the secrets which were veiled in allegories to prevent the precious wisdom from falling into the hands of the profane. Only the wise were able to find their way in this mystical labyrinth. The passage of Hermes most frequently cited, the credo of the adepts, was the inscription found on an emerald tablet 'in the hands of Hermes's mummy, in an obscure pit, where his interred body lay', situated, according to tradition, in the great pyramid of Gizeh. The document is called the *Emerald Tablet* and is too intimately connected with alchemy not to be reproduced in its entirety.

'Tis true, without falsehood, and most real: that which is above is like that which is below, to perpetrate the miracles of one thing. And as all things have been derived from one, by the thought of one, so all things are born from this thing, by adoption. The sun is its father, the moon is its mother. Wind has carried it in its belly, the earth is its nurse. Here is the father of every perfection in the world. His strength and power are absolute when changed into earth; thou wilt separate the earth from fire, the subtle from the gross, gently and with care. It ascends from earth to heaven, and descends again to earth to receive the power of the superior and the inferior things. By this means, thou wilt have the glory of the world. And because of this, all obscurity will flee from thee. Within this is the power, most powerful of all powers. For it will overcome all subtle things, and penetrate every solid thing. Thus the world was created. From this will be, and will emerge, admirable adaptations of which the means are here. And for this reason, I am called Hermes Trismegistus, having the three parts of the philosophy of the world. What I have said of the sun's operations is accomplished.

19. *Alchemical allegory:* *'The wind hath carried it in his belly.'*

In these allegories, the alchemists recognized the various stages in the process of gold-making, and the ambiguity of the sentences lent itself to infinite interpretations. We know that there was no Hermes Trismegistus; no emerald slab was found in the master's tomb. It is an interesting coincidence, however, that the old fable met the truth halfway, for the earliest recorded copy of the *Emerald Tablet* can be found in the Leyden Papyrus, mentioned already, which was discovered in the tomb of an anonymous magician in Egyptian Thebes in 1828.

In the *Emerald Tablet* one sentence emerges as a possible clue to many alchemical theories: 'Because of this, all obscurity will flee from thee.' The alchemists knew that gold appearing in their retorts would radiate a beautiful light. The heavy, congealed material was to become animated. It would not be ordinary but living gold that would grow as 'gold grows in the earth'. The goldsmith's metal, they thought, was dead, like the limbs severed from a tree, and with a tree they compared the subterranean ramifications of the ore. Living gold 'engenders gold, as corn engenders corn'. Once the Hermetics had grasped the truth, they radiated like living gold and 'obscurity flew from them'. Thus the transmutation of base metals into gold was accompanied by another transmutation, that of man, and the seven steps, or path to blessedness.

In this struggle, the alchemist sought a union of soul and mind with the divine. Scientific achievement was without value when not accompanied by an ennoblement of the soul. And the mastery was the proof that the adept was now among the chosen. The symbol of this final stage was the figure of Christ, appearing within the retort. The alchemists thought that in this world the most perfect substance was imperishable gold. Nature, which always tends towards perfection, wants only to produce gold. Lead, copper, iron and other metals are miscarriages of nature. God has imbued man's soul with a longing for perfection. Like nature, man should strive for the divine within him. The best that existed below, the adept believed, could only be linked to what was lowest above. The most perfect thing on earth was gold; and above, the only body whose rays reached into the heaven of the angels was the sun. Among the divine things, the sun was the lowest. Thus gold was linked with the sun, which is halfway between the supreme and the earth, the mediator between man and God.

Hermetica

One loses science when losing the purity of the heart.

Nicholas Valois

True alchemy was infinitely superior to a craft or a science, for transmutation could not be produced by ability alone; neither was knowledge by itself adequate to attain mastery. Moral virtues were required, and only when he had attained the sublime state of perfection could man utilize the wonders of nature. St John was thought to have been an alchemist, for according to the Byzantine legend he had transformed the pebbles at the seashore into gold and precious stones. Medieval and Renaissance alchemists did not stress the scientific part of their wisdom; as they turned away from magic more and more, the inquiring spirit of their ancestors released its hold upon them. Many declared that the contemplation of nature was far more important than the study of learned books. They recommended that one recapture the simplicity of heart, affirming that a child could make gold, and that the primary ingredient for alchemical work – the *prima materia* – could be found everywhere. But the ignorant trod upon it daily, and the cornerstone of alchemy is rejected by the unworthy. 'It is manifest to all men,' says Paracelsus concerning *prima materia*, 'the poor have more of it than the rich. The good part of it people discard, and the bad part they retain. It is visible and invisible, children play with it in the lane. . . .'

Such images are borrowed from the Gospel, and even the apparent nonsense of the *materia* being at once both visible and invisible can be shaped to accord with passages of the Evangelist: 'And they had closed their eyes so as never to see . . . for blessed are their eyes, for they do see. . . .' (Matt. 13:11–15.) The Gospel and the writings of Hermes are akin to each other.

Both were written in the second century, and independent of each other, their authors have discovered similar ideas and modes of expression. This resemblance impressed the early leaders of the Church. Together with the Sibyls – who also are apocryphal – they invoked Hermes Trismegistus as a witness of the truth. In the third century, Lactantius exclaimed: 'Hermes has found, I do not know how, almost the whole verity.'

The medieval and Renaissance Hermetics stressed still more this parentage. Apparently pious Christians, their books exalt the Almighty, 'who still creates wonders in our days'. Verses in the Gospel are quoted so frequently that one begins to suspect that Writ is nothing more than an alchemical book. Even the obscure imagery of the seven stages of gold-making could be justified by Matthew's text: 'I will open my mouth in figures. I will utter things that have been concealed since creation.' (13:35.)

But this figurative speaking of the Hermetic lacks the vigour of Biblical images. The writer's imagination was hampered by established symbols, allegories and metaphors which were not to be altered, for everything had been articulated and accomplished from the beginning. New discoveries were not to be made; the perfect art could not be perfected. However, it was different with alchemical graphics, as we shall see in the following pages.

In all the ramifications of society, alchemy had taken root, yet it did not participate in its life. The alchemists lived in seclusion, as if protesting tacitly against their environment. The soul of the alchemist could find no peace in the teachings of the established dogma. For the truly pious, *faith* was blessedness; but the alchemist wanted to *understand* God through knowing the marvellous force that God had given to matter. With his intellect he wished to grasp the supreme, and through study and contemplation to ascend gradually to the divine light. Wisdom builds its own house, they used to say, and such a proud device contrasts oddly with the simplicity of the heart which they desired to achieve. Yet both things have been professed by the adepts. Their way to blessedness was a sinuous one, and their ideas an alloy of contradictions.

An engraving in Khunrath's *Amphitheatre of Eternal Wisdom* (1609) illustrates this fusion of ideas. Khunrath, the alchemist and Rosicrucian, is kneeling before a tabernacle, reminiscent of the tent of the Hebrews in the desert. In it, an inscription says: 'Do not speak of God without enlightenment.' Upon the table are two open books, the Bible opened at the psalm: 'Then they were in great terror; for God was with the righteous generation.' 'Generation' alludes probably to the production of the philosopher's stone. The other book contains Hermetic formulas. Smoke escaping from an incense burner nearby is inscribed: 'The prayer may rise like smoke, a sacrifice agreeable to God.' At the right, in a sumptuous hall, a huge fireplace contains the laboratory. The mantelpiece is sustained by two columns: experience and reason. And above, on one of the heavy beams which support the wooden ceiling, we read: 'Nobody is great without divine inspiration.'

Prayer and work are confined to opposite walls, for the

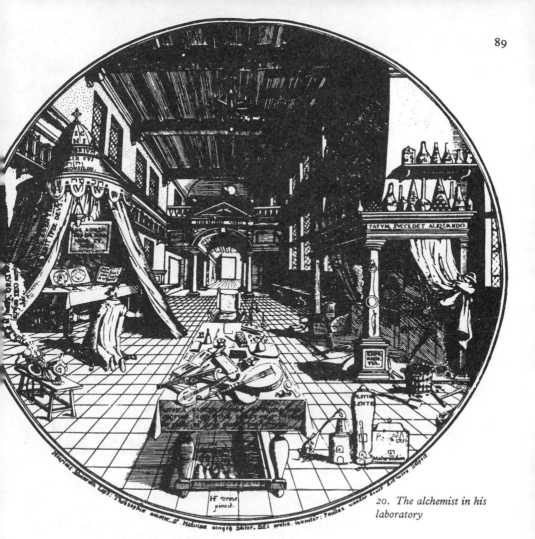

20. *The alchemist in his laboratory*

alchemist's laboratory, the *laboratorium*, is consecrated to both – the word composed of '*labor*' and '*oratorium*', meaning both 'labour' and 'a place devoted to prayer'. Between these activities are those of relaxation – musical instruments are piled upon the centre table, inkwell, pen and paper inviting one to indulge in leisurely writing. In order that music should not lead to pleasures too worldly, on the tablecloth is inscribed: 'Sacred music causes flight to sadness and to the evil spirits because the spirit of Jehovah sings happily in a heart filled with holy joy.' Amidst these manifold activities the secluded Khunrath could not have known boredom. He had stored his princely dwelling generously with provisions that fed his mind and his soul. Alertness must have been one of his outstanding characteristics, for over the portal of the hall he had written: 'Be vigilant even when asleep.'

The division in the Hermetic's activities is similarly made clear by an etching of the *Musaeum Hermeticum*, a compilation of alchemical treatises, published in 1625. In a library an abbot, a monk and a philosopher are discussing Hermetic problems.

Their garments and expressions reveal that they do not intend to do any alchemical work; it is obvious that they are merely theorizing. The adjoining laboratory is filled with alchemical apparatus. This room shows no sign of scientific conjecture or mystical speculation, but is apparently the place for experimentation, and the vigorous old man – a new Vulcan – his heavy hammer swung over his shoulder, is concerned solely with the air pipes he has driven into the flame. The alchemist's oven in the centre is the link between work and study, practice and theory. Absorbed in thought, the three philosophizing adepts are unaware of what is happening in the retort on the oven. One of them points to the glass bowl in which a snake has appeared.

21. Hermetic philosophers and a practising alchemist

This miniature reptile, which in 1625 still haunted the alchemist's retort, can trace its ancestry back to the earliest times of our era, when Paul was warning his Corinthian flock of the dangerous Gnostic teachings, of 'scurrilous talk, secret practices and sham apostles'. Some sects of Gnosticism, it may be recalled, worshipped the serpent of paradise who had planted in man's heart the yearning for knowledge. This snake, the Ouroboros, became an alchemical emblem. It is found in Cleopatra's book on gold-making, the *Chrysopeia*. The serpent's body, divided between light and dark, signified to the adept that in the material world good and bad, perfection and imperfection, are bound together in matter. For matter is One, or as the alchemists used to say: 'One is All.' In Cleopatra's book, this axiom is encircled by the Ouroboros. In the three concentric circles in the upper left, a mysterious text elaborates this idea: 'One is All, by him is all, and for him is all, and in him is all. The Serpent is one; he has the two symbols (good and bad). . . .'

The evil serpent of paradise was transformed by the Gnostics into the beneficent Ouroboros. The Ouroboros was changed into the alchemist's dragon, and its body being light and dark found a chemical interpretation. A beautiful etching in Lambsprinck's book on the *Philosophical Stone* shows such a dragon, that 'lives in the forest'.

Most venomous is he, yet lacking nothing,
When he sees the rays of the sun and its bright fire,
He scatters abroad his poison,
And flies upward so fiercely
That no living creature can stand before him. . . .

His venom becomes the great medicine.
He quickly consumes his venom,
For he devours his poisonous tail.
And this is performed on his own body,
From which flows forth glorious balm,
With all its miraculous virtues.
Here do all the sages rejoice loudly.[9]

For him who has not yet grasped the meaning of this imagery, Lambsprinck has added a short and prosaic explanation: 'The mercury is precipitated, dissolved in its own water, and then once more coagulated.' But before the miracle can be performed with this marvellous metal, containing its own 'medicine', the dragon must be killed.

22. The Hermetic dragon
23. Alchemical allegory:
The killing of the dragon

> The sages say
> That a wild beast is in the forest,
> Whose skin is of blackest dye.
> If any man cut off his head,
> His *blackness* will disappear
> And give place to a *snowy* white. . . .[10]

This allegory alluding to the change of colour of the chemically treated mercury is explained by Lambsprinck with one word: putrefaction. In the alchemist's work the first stage is decay. The dragon, mercury, must be killed. 'Sacrifice him,' it is written in a manuscript of the tenth century, 'peel off his skin, separate the flesh from the bone, and thou wilt find that which thou seekest.' The perfect philosopher's gold cannot be produced without preceding decay.

And this was not only valid for transmuting matter, since the alchemical mystic thought, as we have already seen, that man had to endure the same ordeal. He cannot attain the state of blessedness without first destroying his bodily passions. When he has vanquished the black Hydra in his heart, then he will be cleansed, and the blackness will turn white:

> When the beast's black hue has vanished in a black smoke,
> The sages rejoice. . . .[11]

Such speculations carry us into Catholic mysticism. Man's body is impure; Adam's flesh is putrefied. But the Saviour's flesh is hidden in every man. From the putrefied flesh of Adam, a seed blossoms into eternal life. Without sin there is no salvation; without death there is no resurrection. Man has to descend to the darkness of the grave before rising to eternal clarity. Or, as we read in Paul (I Cor. 15:36): 'That which thou sowest is not quickened, except it die.'

Basil Valentine, the pious monk of the fifteenth century, interprets as follows the first stage in the alchemical process. In his book *Azoth* a woodcut shows a decayed cadaver lying in the alchemist's globe. Below, cold and warm perform their task, 'gently with great care'. Above are the sun, the moon, and the planets with their signs. Among them is black Saturn, under whose auspices the first step towards gold is made. Hopeful, the corpse raises his head to heaven; Black Raven 'separates the flesh from the bones', while soul and mind, small white bird-monsters, have left the body together with the last breath.

24. *Alchemical allegory of putrefaction*
25. Ex libris *of E. A. Hitchcock*

Eugenius Philalethes, a Hermetic writer of the seventeenth century, describes his search of the marvellous treasure hidden in the decaying dragon. 'This treasure is real,' he says, 'but by the magical art of God it is enchanted.' Thus Philalethes restores the magical power to God, from whom the fallen angels had wrested it to please the daughters of men. The circuit of alchemy is moving to its close. In his book *Light of All Lights* Philalethes describes his subterranean wandering in search of the philosopher's stone. Guided by a woman, the alchemists' muse, or nature, he reaches a hall where below the altar is the green dragon, the mercury of the magi, encircling with his coils a treasure of gold and pearls. 'This is no dream or fantasy, but truth. . . . Above the treasure was a child, and the device, *Nil nisi parvulis* (only for the humble ones).' Philalethes's comments on the image echo earlier teachings: the adept must be free from falsehood, and his heart like that of a child.

The device *Nil nisi parvulis*, together with Philalethes's allegory, was to serve as the bookplate of a retired American army officer E. A. Hitchcock. In 1865 he published his *Remarks on Alchemy and the Alchemists*, which attracted considerable attention. Hitchcock, marshalling an impressive series of quotations from old alchemical books, undertakes to demonstrate that the only object of alchemy was man himself. 'The genuine alchemists,' he says,

were not in pursuit of worldly wealth and honours. Their real object was the perfection or at least the improvement of man. According to this theory, such perfection lies in a certain unity, a living sense of the unity of the human with the divine nature, the attainment of which I can compare to nothing so well as to the experience known in religion as the new birth. The desired perfection or unity is a state of the soul, a condition of being, and not merely a condition of knowing.

It is unnecessary to point out the importance of Hitchcock's discovery. He denies the likelihood that any real chemical operations were performed by the adepts and affirms that all chemical processes were symbols for the ennoblement not of the metals but of man himself.

While we do not share such ideas, believing that both mystical contemplation and alchemical operations can coexist, yet the impulse which Hitchcock gave to psychological and psychoanalytical inquiry into Hermetic art produced a rich harvest. We may even call the lonely Vermont Hermetic a forerunner of modern psychology. Silberer, in his *Problems of Mysticism* (Vienna, 1914), refers frequently to him. Hitchcock's early suggestions of the psychic values of alchemy have been justified and elaborated in several psychoanalytical essays, of which the most voluminous work is C. G. Jung's *Psychology and Alchemy*, published in 1944.

The Principles of Alchemy and the Philosophers' Stone

What was the fundamental theory upon which the adepts based their practice? They have claimed that two principles – the theory of the composition of metals, and that of their generation – have served as the basis for their system. To them, metals were composed of diverse substances, and all of them contained sulphur and mercury: varying proportions produced gold, silver, copper, etc. Gold was supposed to be composed of a large proportion of mercury and little sulphur; in copper, both ingredients existed approximately in equal quantities. Tin was an imperfect mixture of a small quantity of impure mercury and a large proportion of sulphur, and so forth.

The Arab, Geber, had professed this in the eighth century, and affirmed that according to the ancients one could by efficacious operations vary the contents of metals and transmute one into another. The theory of generation is formulated quite clearly in the medieval alchemical treatises. The theorists compared the process that was taking place in their vessels to the generation of animals and vegetables. Thus, for the producing of metals, it was necessary to discover their seed.

For the adept there existed no such phenomenon as an inorganic substance; every substance was endowed with life. Life was influenced secretly by the stars, silent artisans working towards the perfection of metals. At first imperfect, they changed gradually into perfect substances, and the process ended when they were ultimately transformed into gold. A few Hermetics who had comprehended the meaning of the serpent biting its tail supposed that there could be no cessation in nature's work and that the perfect metals were to undergo new transformations only to return again to base metals. Thus they were to perpetuate the circuit of molecular change.

However, these were only theories, and transmutation had to be accomplished in order to prove them. From the twelfth century on, the alchemists declared that for their transmutations an agent was necessary. This agent they called by many names – the philosophers' stone, the philosophic powder, the great elixir, the quintessence, etc. When touching the liquid metals, the philosophers' stone was thought to change them into gold. The descriptions of this marvellous substance vary among different writers. Paracelsus calls it solid and dark red; Berigard of Pisa says it is the colour of poppies; Raymond Lully observed its colour to be like that of carbuncles; Helvetius had held it in his hands, and claimed it was bright yellow. These contradictions are reconciled by the Arab Khalid, or rather by the author who wrote under that name: 'This stone unites within itself all the colours. It is white, red, yellow, sky-blue and green.' Thus all the philosophers were brought into accord.[12]

Besides its power to transmute metals, the philosophers' stone had other marvellous virtues: it could cure all diseases and prolong life beyond its natural limits. These virtues of the philosophers' stone have their counterpart in the Far East. China also had its adepts, indeed before alchemy was known to the West. Although it is not planned to include in this book the complex problems of magic in India and in the Far East, Chinese alchemy is mentioned here because it possibly promoted Occidental alchemy.

The Chinese, believing that gold was immortal, thought that when it was absorbed by the human body it could render man immortal. The problem was to discover the 'wonder preparation of medicine', for gold powder could not be digested. They wanted to find means other than that of breaking the metal up into small particles. It was to be dissolved into a marvellous powder, a gold dust which 'spread mistily like wind driven by rain' through the five organs. Such a powder could be obtained only through an alchemical operation. The universal medicine, 'huantan', freed its owner from all worldly miseries. New teeth would grow, dark hair would cover the old man's baldness, and his sick wife would regain her girlhood.

'Like produces like' is the old axiom of sympathetic magic: the most perfect and imperishable metal will produce immortality and perfection. The Chinese alchemist used magical formulas in his work, and he trusted in the beneficent influence of the stars on his various and laborious procedures.

Contrary to Western beliefs, the Chinese supposed that artificial gold, not true gold, was endowed with great magical power. From cinnabar, a mercury ore, and other metals, the masters of the East strove to develop alloys which *resembled* gold. It was sufficient to eat regularly from vessels made of such alloys to have immortality granted. But the great Wei Po-Yang (*ca.* A.D. 100–150) did not have recourse to such artificiality. He succeeded in manufacturing the true gold medicine, and he and his pupil Yu became immortal, together with the wise man's dog which had eaten the scraps left on the plate. The Chinese aimed 'only' at rejuvenation and eternal life, and the philosophers' gold was unknown to them. Their art can be traced back to about 100 or 150 B.C., an epoch when alchemy was unknown to the West.

Here transmutation was the main topic, and the problem of how much gold the transformed metal would yield. Johann Kunkel (1630–1703), an adept when alchemy was declining, and more chemist than alchemist, is modest in his evaluation. He thinks that the base metal when tinged with the stone would yield twice as much gold. The Englishman, Germspreiser, believes that lead will change so as to yield fifty times more gold. Roger Bacon says a hundred thousand times more, and Isaac, the Dutchman, a million times more. Lully calculates an astronomical amount of multiplied gold, and he exclaims: 'I could transmute the seas, were there enough mercury.'

Wonderful creative powers such as these resided in the philosophers' stone, but what was its essence? Could it be a composition akin to the sacred stones which the Egyptians manufactured in antiquity? It is unlikely. The Egyptians used to fashion magical stones which were objects of worship. They were endowed with supernatural power, like the Kaaba of the Mohammedans. Plutarch reports that Kyphi, the sacred stone of the Egyptians, was made of many substances, of gold, of silver, of *chesteb* and of *mafek* (blue and green stone). Other writers name the various minerals that were fused to produce the substance sacred in the city of Edfu: they are gold, silver, *chesteb, chenem, mafek, hertes* and *nesenem*. What all these minerals were it is difficult to know, and the meaning of such alloys is still more mysterious. The Kyphi was sacred, therefore magical.

The philosophers' stone contained marvellous virtues which may be called magical. This is what the learned Agrippa has to say about it:

An operation cannot proceed from a mere body. All famous Poets and Philosophers affirm therefore that the world and all celestial bodies must have a soul, and also intelligence; hence, Marcus Manilius, in his *Astronomy to Augustus*, sings of:

> 'The great corporeal world, which doth appear
> In divers forms, of air, earth, sea and fire,
> A divine soul doth rule, a deity
> Doth govern wisely. . . .'

. . . And Virgil, richest in philosophy, sings thus:

> 'And first the heaven, earth, and liquid plain,
> The moon's bright globe and stars titanian
> A spirit fed within, spread through the whole
> And with the huge heap mix'd infused a soul;
> Hence man and beasts and birds derive their strain
> And monsters floating in the marbled main;
> These seeds have fiery vigour, and a birth
> Of heavenly race, but clogg'd with heavy earth.'

What do these verses seem to mean other than that the world should have not only a spirit-soul but also should partake of the divine mind; and that the original virtue, vigour of all inferior things, depend upon the soul of the world? All Platonists, Pythagoreans, Orpheus, Trismegistus, Aristotle, Theophrastus, Avicenna, Algazel, and all Peripatetics confess and confirm this. . . .

There are four essences in the universe upon which not only Agrippa but all the learned through the centuries have agreed. These are fire, water, earth and air. However, there is a fifth essence, or quintessence, which permeates everything above in the stars and below upon earth. It is the world soul-spirit which animates all bodies. It is 'clogg'd with heavy earth', and never free or visible. Yet it is omnipresent, and he who can free this fifth element from the matter that it inhabits shall hold in his hand the creative power with which God has endowed the world of matter. The ancient goddesses of growth and vegetation, like Isis, were nothing more to the alchemist than the emblems of the quintessence, the generative power that resides in the philosophers' stone.

'Vas Insigne Electionis' . . . Rejoicing not in the many but in the probity of the few. . . .

William of Conches

According to Hitchcock, the seven stages of the alchemical process have been described by the adepts with, at least, comparative simplicity. There is, however, one exception: complete secrecy is maintained concerning the *vessel* in which the process must take place. Hitchcock conjectures, as we have learned, that this vessel was the key to the hidden treasure, that it was nothing more than the alchemist himself. An adept of the sixteenth century, Denis Zachaire, describes in his *Memoirs* the vain search of the Parisian alchemists for the true recipient: 'The one worked with glass retorts, the other with earthenware vessels, another with bronze vases or pots, cans, jars, jugs of copper, lead, silver, or gold.' None of them succeeded.

Hitchcock's idea of a process of purification which leads to a mystical union with the divine seems to recall the Gnostic sacrament of the bridal chamber, the supreme spiritual achievement as professed by the Valentinians: the pious will witness the divine marriage of Sophia with Soter, the redeemer, and he will experience, in the image of the heavenly marriage, the union with his angel. The generative, active male element and the vegetative, passive female element must be united in order to become the perfect unity. We have said that the sun was considered by the adept to be male, its warm radiance was active, and heat and dryness were thought to be male attributes. On the other hand, the moon was female as it does not send forth rays other than those it has received from the sun. The moon is the receptacle, and its expansion was pregnancy.

Often the alchemists represented in their allegories the union of sun and moon, prototypes of both sexes. In Michael Majer's *Chemical Secrets of Nature* (1687) a curious etching shows sun and moon embracing in front of a cave which symbolizes the hollow of the retort. The etching is explained thus: 'He is conceived in water and born in air; when he has become red in colour, he walks over the water.' The offspring of the sun and the moon is the philosophers' red stone, floating upon the liquid in the crucible. Another emblem of the philosophers' stone is that of the androgyne, a being half male, half female, half sun, half moon, holding in its hands the philosophic egg, which symbolizes, like the serpent, the universe.

The alchemical furnace expresses similarly this union. It was not without reason that this apparatus was called the cosmic oven. Did it not perform that generative process which the adept

26. *The Hermetic androgyne*

had observed in the cosmos? In Cleopatra's drawing, the oldest of its kind, the separation of the two elements is already obvious. Below, the furnace, the producer of heat, symbolizes the male, the upper retort the female part. From the bowl, resting upon the fire, the seed is projected into the upper recipient. There it is cooled off, condensed and liquefied. The 'nuptial diagram' is still more distinct in later graphics, where the oven and the convex vessels are depicted as a couple. Three miniature retorts, the offsprings, are suckling their 'mother'.

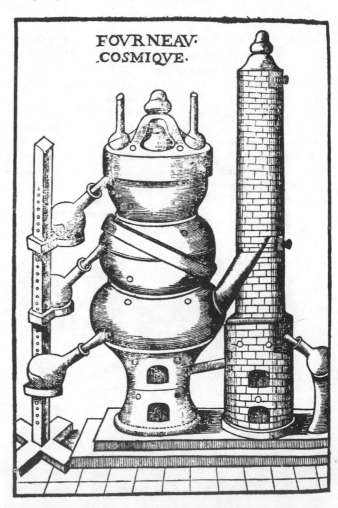

27. *The cosmic oven*

Hermetic Enigmas

> They were pleased to speak by figures, types and analogies, that they might not be understood but by the discreet, religious and enlightened.
>
> Synesius

Some alchemists accused themselves of having been too explicit in their writings, of revealing more than was permissible, thus profaning their sacred art. The indiscreet might be expelled from the circle of the chosen and condemned to eternal misery.

But in reading these books, such indiscretions are in no way apparent. When the assiduous reader has grasped a meaning, he will search immediately for a still deeper one which he suspects is hidden in the newly discovered truth. He can thus devote a lifetime to these mysteries without ever reaching the bottom of the enchanted well. With his imagination constantly directed towards the marvellous, the Hermetic philosopher was undoubtedly pleased with his studies. It is not difficult to understand why alchemy is called an art – it relied upon imagination as well as upon manual dexterity. To produce the philosophers' gold was the goal. Only a few succeeded, but those who failed did not consider their efforts futile. From daily meditation and experimentation was born a silent bliss. There was pleasure in handling various substances and tools, in the feeding and surveying of the oven, as well as in learned discussions with neighbourly colleagues who followed all this activity. More than one adept may have preferred the passage leading towards perfection to its actual attainment.

When gold appeared in the alchemist's crucible, his quietude must have been disturbed. Fearing the indiscretion of others, his joy over achieving the ultimate was mingled with anguish. Kings were ever eager to know of these prodigies, which could miraculously refill their empty treasuries, finance their wars and otherwise assist them in shady activities. Such princely plans, however, horrified the chosen. The masters of the art were courted by monarchs until they declared that their wisdom could not be revealed; then they were imprisoned, tortured and executed. They endured pain and death, but they remained undefeated. Incurable egocentrics, they preferred martyrdom to admitting that their studies had been futile and their gold an illusion.

These threats to their lives and the danger of profanation justified their enigmatic style, which is illustrated by a few examples. In Abraham Lambsprinck's book *On the Philosophers' Stone*, there is an etching of two fishes, 'without flesh and bone, swimming in our sea'. Lambsprinck recommends that these fishes be cooked in their own water; then they will become transformed into a sea, 'the vastness of which no man can describe'. The fishes, says Lambsprinck, are the soul and the spirit; the sea is the body. When cooked, i.e., purified, they will attain an indescribable state of felicity. Lambsprinck adds that the fishes are not two but one. The meaning of this may readily be explained.

The following figure in Lambsprinck's book shows a unicorn and a deer hidden in the forest. The unicorn is the spirit, the deer the soul, and the forest the body.

> The sages say truly
> That two animals are in this forest;
> One glorious, beautiful, and swift,
> A great and strong deer;
> The other a unicorn.
> They are concealed in the forest,
> But happy will be the man
> Who shall capture them.[13]

*28. Alchemical allegory:
Soul and spirit in the
body*

*29. Alchemical allegory:
Body, soul and spirit*

Lambsprinck's next figure and text reveal what must be done when the two, soul and spirit, are caught.

> The sages faithfully teach us
> That two strong lions, to wit, male and female,
> Lurk in a dark and rugged valley.
> These the master must catch,
> Though they are swift and fierce,
> And of terrible and savage aspect.
> He who, by wisdom and cunning,
> Can snare and bind them
> And lead them into the same forest,
> Of him it may be said with justice and truth
> That he has merited the need and praise before all others,
> And that his wisdom transcends that of the worldly wise.[14]

The two lions are again symbols of the soul and the spirit. When they are caught, says Lambsprinck, 'they must be united in their body'. In the state of man's perfection, his soul and spirit must become one.

> A nest is found in the forest
> In which Hermes has his brood;
> One fledgling always strives to fly upward,
> The other rejoices to sit quietly in the nest;
> Yet neither can get away from the nest,
> As a husband in a house with his wife,
> Bound together in closest bonds of wedlock.
> So we rejoice at all times also,
> That we hold the female eagle fast in this way,
> And we render thanks to God the Father.[15]

The spirit strives towards God, but it is held down by the body. In the same way, mercury must be sublimated repeatedly, fly up, and 'return to the nest', until at length fixation is attained. The alchemist, like the snail, proceeds slowly on his journey. Spirit and body will become one in the nest, i.e., the heart. 'From a rhetor [man] has become a consul.'

> Yet I was of ignoble birth,
> Till I was set in a high place.
> To reach the lofty summit
> Was given me by God and nature.[16]

The master has been able to separate soul and spirit from the body, with which they had been mingled imperceptibly. He knows himself! Soul and spirit, the young king and a winged old man, have climbed the mountain; the body. But the conflict between father and son is not at its end: the son is longing for the father, who cannot live alone. A new union must take place. The spirit will unite them and dwell with them constantly. 'When the son enters his father's palace, the latter is overcome with joy.' Now the mysterious unification takes place.

*30. Alchemical allegory:
Body, soul and spirit
31. Alchemical allegory:
The soul rising towards
God*

> 'My son, I was dead without thee,
> And lived in great danger of my life.
> I revive at thy return,
> And it fills my breast with joy.'
> But when the son entered the father's house,
> The father took him to his heart,
> And swallowed him out of excessive joy. . . .[17]

The son has risen to heaven, as Hermes Trismegistus has expressed it, and descended again to earth, after having received the power of the superior. Lambsprinck's last figure shows the father and the son united through the spirit, 'to remain so forever'.

The Biblical happenings of the advent and the ascension of Christ have happened here in reverse; the son has returned to earth, to dwell upon it eternally. Hermes Trismegistus says that the below is like the above. But this was to be interpreted not as an earthly replica independent of heavenly things but as a reflection. As in a mirror, everything is seen in reverse. The sage and the scholar are having a discussion under the tree of knowledge, whose branches are the sun, the moon and the planets. The triangle above is the soul, the spirit and the body of the universe. The triangle below is reversed. Its three minerals are identified with man's threefold essence. Valentine depicts the planet Mercury as the top of the tree and unlike the other planets, Mercury has eight branches. Already in Cleopatra's book we find the emblem of the eight-branch star. Eight recalls the Gnostic Ogdoas, a group of the highest celestial powers, peculiar to the systems of Basilides and Valentinus. According to Plutarch, the

32. *Alchemical allegory:*
The achievement of the
work
33. *Alchemical allegory:*
Soul and spirit separated
from the body

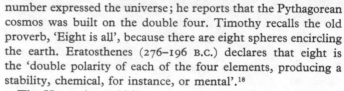

34. *Hermetic conversation*

number expressed the universe; he reports that the Pythagorean cosmos was built on the double four. Timothy recalls the old proverb, 'Eight is all', because there are eight spheres encircling the earth. Eratosthenes (276–196 B.C.) declares that eight is the 'double polarity of each of the four elements, producing a stability, chemical, for instance, or mental'.[18]

The Hermetic world image may be exemplified by a scheme invented by Thomas Norton (died A.D. 1477), which is suspected of being not only a plan of the universe but also that of the perfect alchemical oven. Its hearth is Satan, the lower rectangle chaos, the abyss, darkness, etc., i.e., the uncreated world, according to the Bible. The hearth is the residence of fire. The kingdom of Satan is surmounted by a triangle representing the created world, which is divided into four smaller triangles: earth, water, air and heaven. In the centre is man, halfway in heaven since his soul and spirit partake of the divine. The apex of the triangle reaches into God's heaven, called the world's archetype. Its centre is God, the infinite good. The finite good is the lower threefold heaven, angelic, elementary and ethereal, which encircles the fourfold triangle. The latter's angles are sulphur, salt and mercury: soul, body and mind. Thus was the world created. Its hierarchic construction is comparable to the world architecture of the ancients, the Egyptians, Persians and Babylonians.

Norton's treatise begins thus:

A most wonderful magistery and archemagistery is the tincture [the stone] of sacred alchemy, the marvellous science of the secret philosophy, the singular gift bestowed upon men through the grace of the Almighty, which men have never discovered by the labour of their hands but only through revelation – and the teachings of others. It was never bought nor sold but has always been granted through the grace of God alone to worthy men, and perfected by long labour and the passing of time.

Neither drawing nor text reveals anything beyond generalities. No suggestion is given on how to proceed in the making of the philosophers' stone, and allegories take the place of weights, lapses of time, temperatures and similar technical data. Such minor items the adept had to discover alone. If he was not

35. *Alchemical allegory:*
The father (body)
devouring the son (spirit)
36. *Alchemical allegory:*
Body and soul reunited
by the spirit

MVNDVS ARCHETYPVS
DEVS
IEHOVA
Bonum
Infinitum

II. ANGELIC? III ETHE RE? IIII ELEMENTARIS.

Bonum

COELVM

Finitum

Mercurg

Angeli
Stellæ

HOMO

Meteor
Aues

Bestiæ
Pisces

AER

TERRA
AQVA

Sulphur
Lapides
Plantæ
Metalla
Sol

3
Ignis:
5
Procellæ
Z

Inane: Tenebræ: Abyjs

CHA
O
S

LIS
VN
FER
VIN

Malum
SATAN

37. *Hermetic scheme*
of the universe

successful, he could always bestow upon his son the little he had uncovered; and so it happened frequently that the results of alchemical efforts were transmitted through several generations.

When the alchemists' treatises are more explicit than usual, they justifiably arouse suspicion. In Cremer's *Testament*, a short treatise of the fourteenth century, a series of very strange procedures are explained: 'Take the water of an unpolluted youth, after his first sleep for three or four nights, until you have three pints. . . . Add two glasses of very strong vinegar, two ounces of quicklime, half an ounce of living water, of which the preparation has been described. Put the mixture into an earthen pot, and place over it an alembic, or distilling vessel, etc.' A very simple drawing illustrates the process. Is this the great secret, that one should evaporate the prepared sulphur and mercury in the vessel's womb and allow the steam to escape through a chimney? There is doubt about what has to be done with this evaporated mixture, as the little alchemist on the hilltop is operating in a mysterious manner. Cremer, the abbot of Westminster, stands nearby. With his wide cloak, he resembles the alchemical hill, and, self-assured, he points at his invention. Did he know the secret? He could not have, because there has never been an Abbot Cremer at Westminster, and the Benedictine is wholly invented by an anonymous adept.[19]

38. Allegory of the Great Arcanum

Basil Valentine, prior of St Peter's in Erfurt, is credited with several alchemical treatises on the philosophers' stone. The subtitle of his book *Azoth* is certainly not lacking in clarity: '*The means by which the hidden philosophers' stone can be made.*' But the contents are disappointing to him who expects technical information. Valentine writes in alchemical metaphors. The Hermetic dragon speaks in the usual manner: 'I am old, sick and weak. My pseudonym is the dragon. Therefore I am imprisoned in the pit in order to be rewarded with the royal crown, and to make my family rich; being the fugacious servant yet able to accomplish

such things; we will possess the treasures of the kingdom. . . .'
A woodcut accompanies this enigmatic text. The centre of the
alchemical disc is man – his face is compressed within a triangle
representing sulphur, mercury and salt. Salt is the base of the
process: it is identified with heavy Saturn whose black ray points
at the cube, symbol of the body. Body may also mean the philosophers' stone. As in Babylonian colour magic, the yellowness of
sulphur is identified with Mars, whose sign is pointing at a hand
holding a candle or torch: the soul. Mercury is connected with
another hand, holding a bag or matrix: the spirit. Thus, body,
soul and spirit are the angles of the big triangle, the universe.
The triangle framing man's face is a microcosm, shaped in the
world's image. Soul is male, active, fiery, and is usually identified
with the sun. Spirit, the female principle, is the moon. Again,
the male fiery essence is symbolized by the salamander, 'which
lives in fire'; and the female fugitiveness by an eagle. To the
left, seated upon the earth, is the ambivalent figure of King
Sun and Jupiter; to the right, a goddess rides a dolphin; she
embodies both Venus and Diana, travelling across the water.

The mystical meaning of the large triangle is that the sun is
the father, and the moon the mother – the male and the female
principles. In nature, they are always separated. Through the
alchemical art, the two principles should be united, and from

39. Hermetic circle

this marriage will be born the philosophers' stone, female and
male simultaneously, a hermaphrodite. The emblem of man's perfection is also the hermaphrodite, since soul and spirit, as we
have learned already, must be merged into one. Below, in Valentine's image, two feet are shown, one in the water, the other on

land, participating in the male and female elements: the process
is to be applied to man, whose ultimate perfection is perhaps
identified with the hermaphroditic philosophers' stone.

Upon the disc, between the planets' rays, are the seven allegories of the process, starting from the left below with putrefaction, and ending at the lower right with resurrection. Seven
words suggest how the work must be done, each word being
related to one stage of the procedure: '*Visita interiora terrae rec-
tificando invenies occultum lapidem*' (Investigate the interior of the
earth. Rectifying, thou wilt find the hidden stone).

How can such perfection be attained? To this, the adept
answered paradoxically: 'Make the fixed volatile – unite the
fugitive female with the fixed male.' The answer is but another
riddle. The emblem of the fixed volatile is at the top centre of
Valentine's figure: two wings tied together. The volatile is the

*40. Alchemical allegory :
The fixed volatile*

evaporating mercury. The fixed is the mercury remaining at the
bottom of the vessel. When condensed on the vessel's vault, the
volatile will drip and whenever 'the water comes back, it brings
a blessing with it'. This rising and sinking of the volatile, Valentine compares with ebb and flow. The process, sublimation, aims
at separating the male and female elements contained in mercury,
the fixed and the volatile. They must be joined in marriage,
but first they have to cleanse themselves, as do the bride and
the bridegroom before they enter the nuptial chamber. In Valentine's engraving, the dual essence of mercury, speaking in
alchemical terms, is represented as the crowned genius holding
in each hand a caduceus. The opposing male and female are
depicted allegorically as two fencers – upon the sword of one
rests a young eagle, symbol of the volatile; on the other's sword
perches a crowned snake, the fixed mercury. The combative
parties are characterized by sun and moon. The alchemist must
end this merciless struggle of kin – the adversity residing in one
and the same metal was symbolized by the swan which, according
to Aristotle, fights its own kind. The reconciliation of the
irreconcilable is the fixed volatile whose emblem, the joined wings,
is set in the foreground. The allegory is interpreted without

difficulty; but the chemical recipe it supposedly personifies is
illegible.

Neither will Nazari's alchemical dragon utter comprehensible
words. Gifted with a human head, he should be able to speak the
language of man, but all that this does is merely complicate further
the riddle of Hermetic philosophy. We can hardly recognize in
this monster the descendant of the old Gnostic Ouroboros.
Though the art was immutable and the symbols were retained
through centuries, many curlicues embellished or disfigured their
established forms. How modest Cleopatra's serpent is in comparison with Nazari's baroque creature. Fantasy, with which the
Italians seem more gifted than other people, has produced an
alchemical emblem which is fluidly and fastidiously drawn.
Mercury's winged sandals remind us that the monster symbolizes
the corresponding metal. Additional tails and signs attempt to
create a new alchemical synthesis. The tails are strangely knotted
and knotty is the problem of how to unravel the dragon's obtuse
speech:

> Raising myself from death, I kill death – which kills me. I raise up
> again the bodies that I have created. Living in death, I destroy myself –
> whereof you rejoice. You cannot rejoice without me and my life.
> If I carry the poison in my head, in my tail which I bite with rage
> lies the remedy. Whoever thinks to amuse himself at my expense, I
> shall kill with my gimlet eye.
> Whoever bites me must bite himself first; otherwise, if I bite him,
> death shall bite him first, in the head; for first he must bite me –
> biting being the medicine of biting.

One would have to be a new Alexander to cut this Gordian
knot with the sword – and such bold means have been recommended by Michael Majer (1568–1622). 'Learn about the egg and
cut it with a flaming sword. In our world, there is a bird more

*41. The Mercury of the
philosophers*

*42. Alchemical allegory:
The philosopher's egg*

43. *Alchemical allegory:*
    Ablactatio

sublime than all others. To search for his egg be thy only concern. Vile albumin surrounds its soft yolk; heat the egg according to custom, then with thy sword search for it cautiously; after
Vulcan, Mars will accelerate the work; and when thenceforth
has come the chick, it will overcome fire and sword.' Fire and
ore – Vulcan and Mars – are needed for the transmutation. Majer's
recommendation seems so far quite clear, but what he counsels
next is truly astounding. In order to make perfect the 'noble
medicine' a woman must be suckled by a toad. 'Apply a toad to
the woman's breast, that it may take milk from her; and the
woman will die, when the toad is full of milk.' This is certainly
an odd chemical formula, compared with the sober signs and
numbers of modern chemistry!

44. *Alchemical allegory:*
    The golden rain

But Majer's imagination has not yet reached its fullness. His twenty-third emblem depicts in breathless simultaneity several events of mythology associated with the alchemist's work. The adept (or is it the god Vulcan?) splits sleeping Jupiter's head. In his right hand, the maltreated god holds the sign of his power: the flame of lightning. He is leaning against his bird, the eagle. From the wounded head arises naked Pallas Athene. A shower of gold falls upon her. Like the sun, the head of Apollo's statue in the background rises above the horizon. The god Apollo himself embraces Venus in an improvised tent. They are observed by Eros. The explanation of the representation is given as follows: 'It rained gold when Pallas was born in Rhodes, and the sun mated with Venus. This is a marvel, and its truthfulness is affirmed by Greece. The happening was celebrated in Rhodes where they say that the clouds yielded a golden rain. And the sun was joined to Cypria, the goddess of love. At the time when Pallas emerged from Jupiter's brain, from the vessel fell gold as if it were rain-water.'

The myths of Greece and the legends of the Bible are melted together in the alchemist's retorts. Jason, who took the golden fleece from the venomous dragon, was an alchemist, and Bezalel, the Hebrew artisan whom Moses had blessed, was also a gold-maker; Job must have known the great arcanum, as his wealth increased in such an astonishing way after God blessed him. Alexander and Solomon possessed the philosophers' stone, as did likewise Pythagoras, Democritus and Galen. Wherever the word gold occurred in accounts of history, the alchemists were on the lookout for marvellous interpretations. Wherever they recognized the report as mythology, it was interpreted as an Hermetic allegory. As in the age of Gnosticism and Neo-Platonism, fable and philosophy of East and West were syncretized into an astounding world image. The heaven of theology and that of Greek philosophy, the monsters of the Orient and the mythical figures of Hellas, were joined under the sign of Hermes.

Mylius's Hermetic world plan depicts such a syncretism. Above is the Heavenly Trinity, the lamb, the dove and the Hebrew Jehovah. Surrounded by angels, they send forth rays of divine light. Below is the world of matter. The starry heaven encircles the Hermetic work, which is 'half above and half below'. Its centre is the philosophic stone, a triangle inscribed by the double sign of mercury and gold. The symbol is flanked by the three signs of the alchemistic procedure: a triangle, air, signifying the volatile mercury; a reversed triangle, water, i.e., the fixed mercury. In the third sign, the two qualities of mercury are superimposed, forming a six-branched star which symbolizes the 'fixed volatile'. Seven concentric circles surround the signs. The innermost contains the recommendation to use four degrees of fire for the work. Then follow the trinities of mercury, sulphur and salt. Mylius is discerning about the philosophers' mercury, which is not corporeal, but spiritual. One circle signifies time, which Mylius divides into the solar year, the year of the stars, and that of the winds. They refer to the influences of sun,

45. Hermetic cosmos

stars and atmosphere upon the Hermetic work. The outermost circle, finally, shows that these influences must be directed. Favourable constellations have to be awaited: here are the twelve signs of the zodiac, and the five signs of the planets (sun and moon having special places). The sphere of the fixed stars encircles five Hermetic emblems: the raven, the swan, the Hermetic dragon, the pelican which feeds its children with its own blood and the phoenix which resuscitates in the flames.

The world below is dualistic, divided into light and darkness, day and night. Man and woman are chained to the world above. They are the two principles of procreation, with which God has endowed the world of matter. Here below everything is divided into two, male and female; in God alone both principles are united, as he is the cause of everything. Various meanings are superimposed on these two figures: the male is the sun, gold, the fiery dry essence; he is the soul, the generative principle. With him is the lion of the zodiac, presiding over the month when the heat is strongest; he is Jupiter and Apollo, and fire and air are his elements, because they are dry and warm. The fiery phoenix is his emblem, and the lion is the symbol of gold. Lion and man hold the sun, which is the philosophers' gold as well as the heavenly star, and the emblem of generation.

Woman is the moon, silver, the moist and cool essence; she is the spirit, bearing fruit, conceiving, giving birth and nourishing. In her hand she holds the grape whose many fruits are her true symbol. She is connected with evaporation, rain, and earthly moist exhalation, for her elements are earth and water. From her

breast flows the Milky Way, the seed which penetrates everything in this world of bodies, and which the wise men also called
the world spirit or world soul. In her left hand she holds
the moon in its two extreme phases. Her fugitiveness is symbolized by the eagle. The silvery moon she shares with the Hellenic
Actaeon of the myth. He had surprised Diana when she was
bathing, and was changed by the goddess into a deer. But Diana
being cleansed was a symbol of alchemical volatization, the sixth
degree of the process which is marked by the appearance of
silver in the alchemist's retort. Actaeon's horns are both six-
branched, and his metamorphosis into a deer is but an allegory
of the transformation occurring in the vessel. Silver, moon,
Diana and night are connected ideas. Other alchemical allegories
of the sixth stage represent the Holy Virgin, immaculate like
Diana, standing upon the half-moon.

Mylius's cosmic symbols stress the twofold quality of the
material world. In the centre of his plan, however, he shows the
mystical union of the two essences. Lambsprinck's lions are
united here: they have two bodies, but only one head. This head
sputters the water of life. The sage is standing upon the lions'
bodies, resting upon both male and female, soul and spirit. He is
clad in dark and light, day and night, man and woman. He is
like God. The Hermetic's eyes are opened now, he knows good
and evil. From the tree of knowledge he has taken the fruit; and
the tree of paradise has multiplied and produced the orchard
which covers the Hermetic hill. Bathed in the light of the sun and
the moon, receiving as well the divine light, this hill is a suitable
dwelling for the Hermetic master. Fire and water emerge from
its sacred soil, whose trees reach to the heavenly vault. Mylius's
stunning image is accompanied by this text: 'What heaven shows,
is found on earth. Fire and flowing water are contrary to each
other. Happy thou, if thou canst unite them. Let it suffice thee
to know this.'[20]

46. *The alchemist at work*

The Alkahest

The *prima materia*, the alchemists declared, can be found everywhere. It was considered the essence of all substances, 'the
underlying something that always remains identical and one'.[21]
It was the world soul, the world spirit, the quintessence from
which had sprung the elements.

The alchemists wanted to capture this ever-present and yet
unseizable power and to confine it in the philosophers' stone.
They dissolved various substances in order to seize the *prima
materia*, which was not only fugacious but also very fragile.
Greatest care was necessary for this operation, a care which the
simple chemists disregarded when they dissolved bodies with
acids. 'The chemists destroy,' said the Hermetics, 'but we build
up; they kill, and we resurrect; they burn with fire, and we burn
with water.'

This burning water was an all-dissolvent liquid, the alkahest, mentioned for the first time by Paracelsus. In his book on the *Members of Man* he says: 'There is also the spirit alkahest, which acts very efficiently upon the liver: it sustains, fortifies and preserves from the diseases within its reach. . . . Those who want to use such medicine must know how the alkahest is prepared.' And in his book *On the Nature of Things* Paracelsus speaks of an elixir which matures metals and makes them perfect. However, whether this elixir is the alkahest, he does not say.

These casual references would not have been sufficient for bringing fame to the alkahest, had not the famous Belgian doctor, Jean Baptiste van Helmont (1577–1644), enriched the subject with new marvels. It is he who proclaimed the dissolving characteristic of the alkahest, which he calls a new wonder medicine, fire water, hell water. He says: 'It is a salt, most blessed and most perfect of all salts; the secret of its preparation is beyond human comprehension and God alone can reveal it to the chosen.' Van Helmont was one of the chosen, for he affirms by oath that he possessed the alkahest. 'As warm water dissolves ice', it dissolved all bodies.

During the seventeenth century and the first half of the eighteenth many adepts searched for the alkahest, and one could fill a library with the writings concerning the universal dissolvent. The alchemist Glauber, who discovered sodium sulphate, still known as Glauber salts, believed that his discovery was this wonder elixir. The adepts generally imagined that the word alkahest was an anagram veiling the secret, and for this reason Glauber used alkali; he alkalized nitre.

The research continued without abatement until the middle of the eighteenth century, when the alchemist Kunkel declared: 'If the alkahest dissolves all bodies, it will dissolve the vessel which contains it; if it dissolves flint, it will render liquid the glass retort, for glass is made with flint. The great dissolvent of nature has been discussed often. Some say its name means *alkali est*, "it is alkali"; others say it is derived from the German *All-Geist*, "universal spirit", or from *all ist*, "it is all". But I believe that such a dissolvent does not exist, and I call it by its true name, *Alles Lügen ist*, "all that is a lie".' Kunkel gave the death blow to the alkahest, for after his declaration the dissolvent is no longer mentioned in alchemical writings. Adepts who still wanted to lay their hands on the *prima materia* had to resort to other means.

Early Attacks on Alchemy

An art which good men hate and most men blame.

Agrippa

In the second part of the *Roman de la Rose* Jean de Meung (*ca.* 1240–1305) shows Lady Nature complaining about the foolishness and the sophistication of those alchemists who make use only of mechanical practices in their operations. He is fully convinced that gold can be produced, but he reprimands the adepts for their negligence in spiritual matters. Science without

morality for him was lacking in wisdom, and nature too is
ashamed of this:

> I am suffering great grief
> For the stench of thy sulphur.
> With hot fire that burns man
> Thou wilt fix the quicksilver....
>
> Poor man, thou deceivest thyself!
> For by these means thou wilt do nothing.
>
> And the artist is ashamed and affectionate;
> Kneeling before Lady Nature
> He begs humbly for forgiveness
> And gives her thanks.

He had been misled by 'oblique words and parabolic sentences'
instead of following nature.

Geoffrey Chaucer (1340?–1400), who translated the *Roman de la
Rose* into English, is more sceptical. In the Canon's Yeoman's
Prologue we read:

> They take upon them to turne upside downe
> All the earth betwixt Southwarke and Canturburie towne,
> And to pave it all of silver and gold ...
>
> But ever they lacke of their conclusion,
> And to much folke they doo illusion,
> For their stuff slides awaie so fast,
> That it makes them beggars at the last
> And by this craft they never doo win,
> But make their pursse emptie, and their wits thin.[22]

During the Renaissance a few writers protested against
alchemy, declaring that the great art was a chimera. The most
violent attacks came from the Protestant north. Here the power of
the orthodox Church had been secularized, its wealth confiscated
and monasteries and nunneries closed. This was a difficult
period for individuals who wanted to live in loneliness and
meditation. The rising bourgeoisie stressed the virtue of common sense. What the Church had censured formerly as sin, the
bourgeois now called folly. Catholic and Protestant citizens
appointed themselves as the inquisitors of human folly, and they
discovered it everywhere. Satirical writers rampaged through
human activities, and neither the magicians nor, more especially,
the alchemists escaped their invective. Through the invention of
printing, a wider circulation of alchemical writings was possible; and many who had blindly admired the Hermetic art discovered now, when able to read the masters' works, that they
were foolish and pretentious.

Erasmus of Rotterdam (1467–1536), whose witty and cultivated pen excelled that of his contemporaries, describes in a
dialogue between two priests, John and Balbine, to what extent
'fair words make fools and how large offers blind the wise'.
John, the alchemist, succeeds in having his experiments financed
by Balbine, a wise man who speaks little. John finds numerous
ways of extorting money from his silent friend, and the more
Balbine invests in this adventurous enterprise, the more he is

bound to John, to whom he clings like the gambler does to his dice. After the modest and reasonable demands for retorts, coals and tools, John asks for larger amounts. His experiment being unsuccessful, he advises his pious friend that a prayer to the Virgin would hasten the work, that those matters would proceed much better if he sent Our Lady a few French crowns in reward: for the art being holy, the matter cannot proceed prosperously without the favour of the saints. On his short voyage John dissipates every penny among bawds and knaves. After his return he prepares another swindle. Lamenting his misfortune, he tells Balbine that it has become known at court that they are making alchemical experiments without having a licence. They will be cast into a dungeon, condemned to fabricate gold for their sovereign. The learned Balbine prepares his defence, beating his brains in devising how the accusation might be answered and the danger averted.

John proposes that the courtiers be silenced with bribes, for they are greedy for money. In this way Balbine loses thirty ducats more. Finally, his alchemical friend is involved in an ugly scandal; he has been found with a neighbour's wife. This affair offers many opportunities for tapping Balbine's purse. And he who would rather have lost thirty-two teeth than one ducat is now compelled to spend half of his wealth sending the alchemist abroad secretly, and bribing him not to gossip about their unsuccessful partnership. Erasmus's description of the wise fool, the easy prey of every cheat, is a happy stroke. Balbine, who speaks little and thinks much, incorporates a type of folly which escaped the observation of the satirist's less subtle contemporaries. Indeed, learnedness and discretion do not exclude vice and folly.

Sebastian Brant (1457–1521) dedicates in his *Ship of Fools* a few malicious verses to the alchemical imposters whose most common trick was to hide gold in the stick with which they stirred the molten metal; little wonder, then, that the amazed witness was able to find gold in the cauldron!

> And so as here not to forget
> The ugly lie of alchemy,
> Which conjures up silver and gold
> First hidden in the stirring stick;
> It's only trick and jugglery.
> They show a lump to you as proof,
> And soon, behold, out comes a toad!
> This blindness drives him from his home,
> Him who was sitting soft and warm;
> He stuffed his wealth in the retort
> Till it is ashes all and dust—
> And at the end his mind was lost.
> Many a man has perished thus,
> And hardly one acquired wealth.
> For Aristoteles declares:
> 'The form of things will never change.'

Brant refers to Aristotle's declaration in his *Meteorology* that artificers cannot alter species, but can only make other metals seem like silver or gold. His mention of Aristotle is significant,

for medieval scholasticism (which had been supplanted in
Brant's time by Platonism) was based upon Aristotelian theories.
Most arguments against alchemy revealed the dryness of a
scholasticism which had outlived its usefulness and, especially
in its ultimate form, lent itself to senseless speculations and syllogisms based on false premises.

At the end of the seventeeth century these syllogisms were
still cultivated. 'If alchemy,' declares a superfine scholar, 'were a
reality, King Solomon would have known of it. For does not
Writ affirm that in him was united all wisdom of heaven and
earth? But Solomon sent his ships to Ophir, in search of gold.
And he also made his subjects pay their taxes. Had Solomon
known the philosophers' stone, he would have acted differently.
Thus – there is no alchemy!'[23] To this an apologist of alchemy,
John Becher, replied with arguments likewise born from idle
fancy:

It is true, Solomon possessed every wisdom. But did he know plainly
every detail of human activity? Was he a specialist in all arts and crafts?
Did he paint, carve, make shoes, weave rugs? It is certain also that he
ignored many things to come, for instance the printing press and gunpowder. Solomon may well have possessed the philosophers' stone.
It is not known for what reasons he sent away his ships. And uncertain
also is whether this legendary expedition ever happened in an epoch
when the mariner's needle had not yet been invented. The German
Emperor Leopold I is known to have made gold. Did he on that
account recall all his ships and reduce his subjects' taxes?[24]

Becher's book was published in 1664. Earlier, in 1572, a
scholar from Heidelberg, Thomas Erastus, published his
Explanations. They were directed mainly against Paracelsus.
Thomas Erastus is the prototype of learned sterility and quarrel-
someness. He makes a considerable effort to disprove the
reality of transmutations, with the use of the same futile syllogisms. Incredulous in alchemical matters, Erastus defended belief
in witchcraft. In his *Dialogues* he venomously attacked the doctor, John Wier, who had dared to write that witches were, in
the main, mentally disturbed women.

Pierre le Loyer, the learned magistrate of Angers, refused to
believe in transmutation. In 1605 he wrote: 'As to transmutation,
I wonder how it can be reasonably defended. Metals can be
adulterated, but not changed. . . . Blowing [the bellows], they
exhaust their purses, they multiply all into nothing. Yes, I do
not believe, and may the philosophers excuse me if they wish,
that the alchemists can change any metal into gold.' This testimony of a sceptic le Loyer published in his heavy quarto, *Discourse and Histories about Spectres, Visions and Apparitions of
Spirits, Angels, Demons and Souls that appeared visibly to Men*.
The resounding title makes clear that le Loyer was not equally
sceptical in other matters.

Similarly, many scholars who believed firmly in witchcraft
denounced the vanity of alchemy. They were convinced that the
devil could appear in the form of a goat, that witches could
transform themselves into cats, wolves, snails, etc. Proclaiming
that the metamorphoses of spirits and humans were a matter of

DEBENT IGNARI RES FERRE ET POST OPERARI QUATUOR INSERTA NATURIS IN NUBE REFERTA
IVI LAPIDIS CARI VILIS SED DENIQ RARI NULLA MINERALIS RES EST UBI PRINCIPALIS
UNICA RES CERTA VILIS SED UBIQS REFERTA SED TALIS QUALIS REPERITUA UBIQS LOCALIS

47. *The laboratory of the alchemist*

fact, they railed against the credulous who accepted the possibility of metals being transmuted from one into another. In such a way, Pierre de Lancre, the famous witch-burner, ridiculed those who believe in transmutation: 'Considering the multitude of Hermetic ideas,' he says, 'there would not be a sick man in the whole kingdom, nor a poor, nor an ignorant one. The adepts were more fortunate when *ideas* were able to cause transformation.'

Agrippa, the magus and Neo-Platonist (1486–1534), author of *Three Books on Occult Philosophy*, surprised the learned of his time when he published a work on the *Vanity of Sciences and Art*. Having believed in all marvels, he found himself lost now in confusion, and reached the radical decision that all human enterprise was folly. He who had been alchemy's champion now proclaimed its madness, exposing the tragicomic character of the adepts. His prejudice blinded him, and he failed to see that these men who had devoted themselves so ardently to the quest of the unknown might deserve interest and compassion rather than ridicule. 'There is no greater madness,' says Agrippa,

'than to believe in the fixed volatile or that the fixed volatile can be made – so that the smells of coal, sulphur, dung, poison and piss are to them a greater pleasure than the taste of honey – till their farms, goods and patrimonies are wasted, and converted into ashes and smoke; when they expect the rewards of their labours, births of gold, youth and immortality, after all their time and expenses; at length old, ragged, famished, and with the use of quicksilver, paralytic; only rich in misery, and so miserable that they will sell their souls for three farthings; so that the metamorphosis which they could have produced in the metals, they cause to happen in themselves – for instead of being alchemists, they are *cacochymists*; instead of being doctors, beggars; instead of unguentaries, victuallers; a laughing stock to the people; and they who in their youth hated to live meanly, at length grown old in chemical impostures, are compelled to live in the lowest degree of poverty, and in such calamity that they receive nothing but contempt and laughter, instead of commendation and pity; at length compelled thereto by penury, they fall to ill courses, as counterfeiting of money.

'And therefore this art was not only expelled from the Roman Commonwealth, but also prohibited by the decrees of the sacred canons of the Church.'

Agrippa's sarcasms are less pleasing than Pieter Brueghel's drawing, engraved so masterfully by Hieronymus Cock of Antwerp. Brueghel the Elder (1525–69), the painter of human folly, found the alchemist a suitable model for his cherished theme. The drawing depicts the appalling disorder of the adept's house, which reflects the state of the alchemist's mind. His wife with her empty purse is the image of mute despair; two assistants perform their operations according to the master's directions; one wears a fool's cap that suits his moron's face; the other, emaciated and ragged, works with apparent displeasure and distrust. In search of food, the children climb into the cupboard, but all they find is an empty cauldron. Through a wide opening in the wall we look into a square, where in front of a poorhouse a nun greets some famished newcomers. They are the members of the unfortunate adept's family: after an ultimate attempt – and failure – he has disappeared, and one of the helpers has brought his wife and children to this public shelter. This happens immediately after the scene in the foreground, as one of the children is still capped with the cauldron he had found in the larder. Brueghel's figures seem to represent allegories of sterile learning, folly and misery. They contrast strikingly with the proud Hermetic allegories.

The caricature of Dr Rauchmantel ('smoke-mantle'), engraved by Wilhelm Koning and published in 1716, depicts the alchemist in similar style. The small amount of liquid which he has been able to distil is not very promising, and his plump hands seem hardly suited to such subtle operations. Rauchmantel's attitude reveals painful effort, which manages to squeeze out two drops, the symbol of the alchemist's sterility. It is difficult to recognize in this short-legged and unintelligent gold-cook a descendant of Roger Bacon and Albertus Magnus. When Rauchmantel's image was engraved, the heroic times of alchemy were past and the art was the object of raillery and witticism. We shall see in another chapter whether the epoch of reason that was to follow in the eighteenth century was really as reasonable as many have judged it to be.

Famous Transmutations

He produces an inexhaustible treasure
Who from rods made gold,
And from stones made gems.

Hymn to St John the Baptist

Louis Figuier, an authority on medieval alchemy, wrote in 1856: 'The present stage of chemistry does not allow us to

48. Pamphlet against the alchemists

consider impossible the transmutation of metals; from notions
recently acquired and from the current character of chemistry,
we may assume that the transformation of one metal into another
could be attained.' He adds, however, that this has not yet been
achieved. Similar views are expressed by M. Berthelot in 1884.
In his work, *The Origins of Alchemy*, he devotes a chapter to the
comparison of old alchemical and modern theories, and he
concludes that both, though unlike, are not completely alien to
one another. 'Alchemy,' he says, 'was a philosophy explaining
rationally the metamorphosis of matter.' Berthelot mentions also
the atomic conceptions of those 'who consider so-called simple
bodies as being formed by association of a certain number of
analogous elements, and the efforts to reduce all equivalents of
simple bodies to a series of numerical values'. He mentions his
colleagues – Chancourtois, Mendeleef, Newlands and Meyer –
who tried to group together all numbers that express the atomic
weight of elements, and he refers to the problems in arithmetic
resulting from such attempts.

Transmutation, which Berthelot and Figuier believed possible,
was proven a reality by Mme. Curie, whose work was published
at the end of the nineteenth century. Today, we know that not
only can we transmute one substance into another, changing
mercury into gold, for instance, but that through chemical operations we are able to produce new metals. The seventeen-hun-
dred-year-old dream of the adepts has thus become true, and

we can only wish that the men who know the secret may possess that 'purity of heart' without which, according to the alchemists, there can be no science.

Did the alchemist have valid scientific knowledge about transmutation? That is difficult to believe, for alchemy's principles were not scientific. Hermetics had to be eradicated before the tree of chemistry could be planted. Unlike other ancient knowledge – for instance surgery, which was gradually perfected as its errors were eliminated – it had to be discarded altogether. The principles of surgery were correct scientifically; those of alchemy did not belong to science but to a philosophic wisdom which directed it from its inception towards mysticism. Alchemy's chief values were of a psychic nature; the Hermetic was the brother of the mystic.

It is curious to remember, however, that the experiments of the adepts resulted in an impressive series of chemical discoveries, whereas under the unsterilized scalpel of medieval surgeons most of their patients died. If alchemy failed to discover what it had been seeking, it certainly stumbled upon things it had not anticipated finding. It may be worthwhile to mention some of these discoveries.

Albertus Magnus (1193–1280) is credited with the preparation of caustic potash. He was the first to describe the chemical composition of cinnabar, ceruse and minium. Raymond Lully (1235–1315) prepared bicarbonate of potassium. Basil Valentine (fifteenth century) discovered sulphuric ether and hydrochloric acid. Theophrastus Paracelsus (1493–1541) was the first to describe zinc, till then unknown. He also introduced to medicine the use of chemical compounds. Jean Baptiste van Helmont (1577–1644) recognized the existence of gas. Johann Rudolf Glauber (1604–68) discovered sodium sulphate, i.e., Glauber salts, which he believed to be the philosophers' stone. Brandt (died 1692), a burgher of Hamburg, is said to have discovered phosphorus. Giambattista della Porta (1541–1615) prepared tin oxide. Johann Friedrich Boetticher (1682–1719) was the first European who made porcelain. Blaise Vigenère (1523–96) discovered benzoic acid. These few examples suffice to illustrate that the alchemists' researches, though lacking scientific direction, produced a benefit to humanity at large, not merely for the chosen.

Some reports on transmutations will now be considered, selected from amongst many of those recorded by serious contemporaneous scientists whose honesty cannot be doubted, and by rulers who could not easily be deceived. These reports are truly astounding, since they apparently preclude every possibility of deception.

John Frederick Schweitzer, called Helvetius, one of the most violent adversaries of alchemy, reports that in the forenoon of 27 December 1666 a stranger came to his house, a man of honest, grave countenance and authoritative mien, clothed in simple garb, like that of a Mennonite. Having asked Helvetius whether he believed in the philosophers' stone (to which the famous doctor answered negatively), the stranger opened a little ivory box, 'in which there were three pieces of a substance resembling glass or pale sulphur'. Its owner declared this was the stone, and that with such a small quantity he was able to produce twenty tons of gold. Helvetius held a piece in his hand and, having thanked the visitor for his kindness, begged the alchemist to give him a small amount of it. He refused brusquely, adding in a milder tone that he could not part with any of it for all the wealth Helvetius possessed, 'for a reason which was not lawful for him to divulge'.

Asked to give proof of his assertion by performing a transmutation, the stranger replied that he would return in three weeks and show Helvetius something that would amaze him. He arrived punctually on the promised day, but refused to operate, saying that he was not permitted to reveal the secret. He condescended, however, to give Helvetius a small piece of the stone, 'no larger than a grain of rapeseed'. And as the doctor showed doubt as to whether such an infinitesimal quantity could produce any effect, the alchemist broke the grain in half, threw away half and returned the other, said: 'Even now it is sufficient for you.' The honest scholar admitted now that at the stranger's first visit, he had managed to extract a few particles from the stone, but that they had changed the lead not into gold but into glass. 'You should have protected your spoil with yellow wax,' the amused alchemist answered, 'then it would have been able to penetrate the lead and to transmute it into gold.' He promised to return again the next morning at nine o'clock and to perform the miracle – but he did not come that day nor the following day. Thereupon Helvetius's wife persuaded him to attempt the transmutation himself.

Helvetius proceeded according to the stranger's directions. He melted three drachmas of lead, enveloped the stone in wax and dropped it into the liquefied metal. It turned into gold! 'We immediately brought it to the goldsmith, who declared at once that it was the finest gold he had ever seen, and offered to pay fifty florins an ounce for it.' Helvetius, in concluding his report, tells us that the gold was still in his possession as proof of the veracity of transmutation. 'May the holy angels of God watch over him [the anonymous alchemist] as a source of blessing to Christendom! This is an earnest prayer on his behalf and ours.'

The news spread like wildfire. Spinoza, whom we cannot include among the credulous, wanted to inquire into the matter. He visited the goldsmith who had tested the gold. The report was more than favourable: during the fusion, the silver which was added was also transmuted into gold. Brechtel, the goldsmith, was the Duke of Orange's minter. He surely knew his craft. It is hardly credible that he could be the victim of a subterfuge or that he wanted to deceive Spinoza. Many trustworthy people were present when Brechtel made the assay. Spinoza then visited Helvetius, who showed him the gold and the crucible which had served for the operation. Some gold still clung to the inside of the crucible; and like the others, Spinoza was convinced of the reality of this famous transmutation.

In 1621 Professor Martini, lecturing at the University of

Helmstedt in Germany, explained to his students why transmutation was impossible. One of the students replied to the incensed scholar with subtle arguments, and the verbal duel continued for some time. Finally the student demanded a crucible, a stove and lead and, forthwith, under the scrutiny of Martini and the students, he performed the transmutation: the lead turned into gold! He handed the vessel to the astonished professor, saying: '*Domine, solve mi hunc syllogismum*' (Sir, confound *this* syllogism). But Martini had nothing to say. In his *Treatise on Logic* published after this event, he expresses his complete credulity in alchemical matters.

In 1648 an adept, Labujardière, felt that he was going to die. He wrote to his friend Richthausen in Vienna to come and get the philosophers' stone which he kept in a special casket. Richthausen hastened to Prague; he arrived too late, but the casket was found. Count Schlick, a nobleman of Bohemia, in whose service Labujardière had been, demanded that the famous box be given to him. Richthausen, however, returned a replica of the box, and brought the original to the emperor's court. Ferdinand III, himself an alchemist, knowing well the adepts' subterfuges, employed all precautions against deception. Count Rutz, director of mines, was present at the experiment, which the emperor conducted in person. Richthausen was not permitted to assist at the operation. With one grain of Labujardière's powder, Ferdinand transmuted two and a half pounds of mercury into pure gold. A medal was coined to commemorate the transmutation; it represented Apollo, the sun-god, holding Mercury's caduceus. The coin bore this inscription: *Divine Metamorphosis Caused in Prague, 15 January 1648, Witnessed by His Holy Imperial Majesty Ferdinand III*. Still doubtful, the emperor made a second transmutation, and again it was successful. Richthausen was ennobled with the title of Baron of Chaos; he travelled through Germany, performing transmutations here and there until his wonder powder was exhausted.

49. *Medal commemorating a transmutation at Prague in 1648*

Wolfgang Dienheim, professor at Freiburg University, a great sceptic in alchemical matters, was forced by evidence to admit the possibility of transmutation. The alchemist who succeeded in changing his mind was the famous Scotsman, Alexander Sethon. Sethon had learned the secret from a ship-wrecked Dutchman, James Haussen, whom he had sheltered. In 1602 Sethon started his ill-starred journey through Europe. After having furnished ample proof of his capacities in transmutation, he was imprisoned by Christian II, Elector of Saxony. The unfortunate adept was pierced with pointed irons, scorched with molten lead, burned by fire; but he exhausted his torturers and did not reveal his secret. He finally escaped with the aid of Sendivogius, a Polish nobleman who was also an adept. Sethon died soon after his liberation.

During his journey through Switzerland Sethon had met Wolfgang Dienheim. They travelled together by boat from Zurich to Basel. 'You have attacked the alchemical art constantly during our trip,' Sethon said when they reached Basel. 'I have promised you an answer; it will be a demonstration. I expect somebody else whom I wish to convince too.' He was referring to Zwinger, professor of medicine at the University of Basel, author of a *History of German Medicine*. The three went to a mineworker, the two professors carrying some lead plates which Zwinger had brought with him; a crucible was borrowed from a goldsmith, and ordinary sulphur was purchased on the way. Sethon had not chosen the goldsmith or the apothecary, nor did he touch anything. In the goldminer's house, the hearth was lit and the lead and the sulphur heated in the crucible. After a quarter of an hour had passed, Sethon said: 'Drop this little paper into the molten lead, but well in the middle as nothing should fall into the fire.' This was done. The paper, according to Dienheim, contained a yellow powder, but so little that he could scarcely see it. For another fifteen minutes, the mass was stirred with iron sticks. Then the fire was extinguished, and the lead had changed into pure gold. 'Now,' Sethon said to the two overwhelmed scholars, 'where are your pedantries? Do you see the verity of the fact and this truth, which is stronger than your sophisms?' The gold was cut. Zwinger received a piece as a souvenir which was retained by his family through several generations until an alchemist, unable to perform the transmutation, sold it in order to pay his debts. Dienheim adds in his report: 'You disbelievers will probably laugh at this true story. But I am alive and ever ready to testify to what I have seen. And Zwinger is also alive. He will not remain mute, but be a witness to what I affirm.'

When Alexander Sethon died from the injuries inflicted upon him by his torturers, he bequeathed the remainder of his philosophers' stone to his liberator, Sendivogius. By accomplishing numerous transmutations, Sendivogius soon became as famous as his deceased master. Emperor Rudolf II sent for him, and in Prague Sendivogius was received graciously and highly honoured. Courtesy demanded that the adept acknowledge this recognition; he deemed it best to present some philosophers' stone to the emperor. With a small amount of the yellow powder, Rudolf accomplished a successful transmutation. A marble plate was affixed to a wall in the chamber where it had taken place. The plate read: 'May others accomplish what the Pole Sendivogius has done.' The court's alchemical poet, Mordecai of Delle, praised the event in bombastic verses, and Sendivogius received the title of Councillor of His Majesty, together with a medal bearing the emperor's effigy. He left Prague and, after a series of unfortunate adventures, reached Poland. In 1604 Frederick, Duke of Wurttemberg, sent for him. In Frederick's castle at Stuttgart the Polish adept performed several astonishing transmutations, which greatly disturbed the court's alchemist, the Count of Mullenfels.

To rid himself of such a formidable competitor, Mullenfels persuaded Sendivogius that the duke was planning his imprisonment; Sendivogius, recalling his master's fate, was convinced without too much difficulty. He escaped at night – and Mullenfels's horsemen captured him. They robbed him of his valuables, not forgetting the philosophers' stone. Sendivogius's wife complained at court; the emperor sent a dispatch to Stuttgart,

Mullenfels be hung. Mullenfels was executed in a garment
covered with gold spangles, and the gibbet was gilded. The
philosophers' stone could not be found, however, and Sendivogius, unable to replace his loss, ended in misery.

A famous transmutation, though not confirmed by witnesses,
will be related here for two reasons: the report of its author seems
to bear the stamp of truth, and the reality of the transmutation
appears plausible since the adept's wealth increased suddenly.
The hero of this story is the famous Nicolas Flamel (1330–1418)
whose name has long been venerated by Hermetics and by the
French people. In many ways, Flamel is an exception among the
adepts:

> Whilst in all ages and nations, the majority of the alchemists have
> derived little beyond deception, ruination and despair from their
> devotion to alchemy, Nicholas Flamel enjoyed permanent good for-
> tune and serenity. Far from expending his resources in the practice
> of the *magnum opus*, his moderate fortune swelled to a vast treasure
> within an amazingly brief period. He used his wealth to endow
> charitable and pious foundations that survived him and sanctified his
> memory.[25]

Flamel was a scribe. Among the books he copied there were, no
doubt, many alchemical treatises, but none of them attracted his
interest so much as the one he acquired for two florins and 'which
was gilded, very old, and large. It was not made of paper or
parchment, like other books, but of admirable rinds of young
trees.' With the aid of this book and the advice of a Jewish doctor
whom he had met during a pilgrimage to Spain, Flamel discovered, as he says, the secret of transmutation. His wife assisted
him in his experiment, and was present when gold appeared in
the vessel. Flamel describes the memorable event as follows:

> This was upon a Monday, the 17th of January, about noon, in my
> house, with Perenella [his wife] present only, in the year of the restora-
> tion of mankind, 1382.
> Afterwards, following always word for word in my book, I projected
> the red stone upon a similar quantity of mercury in the presence, like-
> wise, of only Perenella, in the same house about five o'clock in the
> evening – which I transmuted truly into almost as much pure gold,
> better assuredly than common gold, being more pliable.
> I may speak with truth: I have made it three times with the help of
> Perenella, who understood it as well as I, because she assisted me in
> my operations, and without doubt if she would have attempted it
> alone, she too would have attained at the end perfection thereof.
> I had indeed accomplished enough when I succeeded once, but I
> found great pleasure in seeing and contemplating the admirable works
> of nature within the vessels. . . .
> I was afraid for a long time that Perenella could not hide her exces-
> sive joy, which I measured by my own, and feared lest she should let
> some word escape amongst her kindred of the great treasures which we
> possessed:
> For excessive joy robs one of understanding as well as of great
> heaviness; but the goodness of the most great God had not only filled
> me with this blessing: he gave me a wife chaste and sage – for she was

moreover capable not only of reason but also of doing all that was reasonable, and was more discreet than women usually are:

Above all, she was exceedingly devout and, therefore, being without hope of bearing children and now well-advanced in years, she began, as I had, to think about God and to give herself to the works of mercy.[26]

Nicolas and Perenella founded and endowed with revenues fourteen hospitals, three chapels and seven churches in Paris. 'We have also accomplished in Boulogne about as much as we have in Paris, not to speak of the charitable acts which we both performed, specially with regard to widows and orphans. If I were to divulge their names under the guise of charity, my reward would be only in this world and it would not be pleasing to the persons involved.' Flamel's words have a convincing tone of being forthright and humble, and it is difficult to regard them as the testimony of an imposter. In an archway which he had built in the Cemetery of the Holy Innocents, a mural symbolizes the great secret. The painting was an object of pilgrimage for the Hermetists of the seventeenth and eighteenth centuries. Flamel's alleged success gave a decisive impetus to alchemy and added to the popularity of the art.

One is inclined to believe in the reality of transmutation when reading these reports. What can be said against them? It is possible, though unlikely, that the rulers honoured the adepts' talent of deception and not their true ability for transmutation. Were not many magicians in later times rewarded royally at court for their art of legerdemain? The custom still existed at the beginning of this century. The question is whether Ferdinand, Rudolf, Frederick and other royal alchemists believed in the art. In that case, it seems unlikely that they honoured those who wanted to deceive them. What interest could they have had in championing alchemy? To make other European potentates believe that they were rich enough to wage war for an unlimited time?

And what about the sober statements of scholars, like Martini, Zwinger, Dienheim, Helvetius, and others? Could they be as easily deceived, even when they themselves were operating? As a solution to the riddle, it has been proposed that by some subterfuge contrived by a crony, an auriferous substance had been introduced into the crucible. Such an argument drives the devil out with Beelzebub. Who would believe that these scholars were the victims of such grossness!

Furthermore, one would like to know what was the proposed auriferous substance which made possible changing large quantities of base metal into gold. Where did the base metal go? Such a powder would be as marvellous as the stone itself. Did all these seemingly honest scientists wish to deceive their friends; and if not, why would they interpolate their scientific tracts with practical jokes? Perhaps they had other reasons for promoting the belief in alchemy, which formerly they had fought so violently. Their motives would surely have been weighty, as none of these grave men would have risked compromising their honest careers for a bagatelle. In whatever way we approach the problem, it

Les Figures du   Juif Abraham

NICOLAS FLAMEL ET PERRENELLE SA FEMME
Figures de

COMMENT LES INOCENS FVRENT OCCIS PAR LE COMMANDEMENT LV ROY HERODES
Nicolas Flamel.

remains a mystery, and no reasoning has yet robbed these happenings of their marvellous aura.

50. The frescoes of Nicolas Flamel in the charnel-house of the Innocents

The Inheritance of the Accursed

With all thy likeness to God, thou'lt yet be a sorry example!

Goethe, *Faust*

Many scholars of the past have studied alchemy together with other sciences: geometry, mathematics, etc. But there were also adepts whose sole preoccupation was the philosophers' stone. Was it necessary to probe other fields of learning when from the stone all moral and intellectual qualities emanated? They did not study Hermetics as a part of knowledge; for them, this art embraced all things, including the guidance of the soul and the nourishment of the mind. These 'specialists' were mystics without being orthodox Catholics, scientists without following the learning of their time, artisans unable to teach others what they knew. They were sectarians, problem-children of society.

Psychoanalysts have pointed out the neurotic character of alchemical allegories and practices: the fondness of the adepts for putrefaction, their experimentations with offensive substances, their peeping-tom curiosity in erotic matters, their glorification of the hermaphrodite, and so forth. If this is true, the alchemist could be compared to the artist, according to Freud's analysis of the latter. In both cases the abnormal produces what is valuable, the good. Speaking in alchemical terms, we could say that putrefaction was followed immediately by sublimation.

The moral and intellectual postulates of the doctrine were not merely theoretical to the adept. He wanted to live purely, to be charitable and pious, for the stone, he knew, was revealed only to the *worthy*. But the alchemist's conception of the good was not identical with that of the society in which he lived. The spiritual and secular rulers were always hesitant about deciding whether to welcome the Hermetic as a pure sage or to destroy him for being a sacrilegious impostor. The question as to whether gold could be made was considered a minor one. From the middle of the fourteenth to the sixteenth centuries, the reality of the art was accepted generally; the incontestable fact of transmutation is often mentioned in laws. As late as 1668 the Chancellory of Breslau rewarded the alchemist Kirchof with a diploma authorizing his practice of alchemy.[27]

Most of the medieval popes were not concerned openly with alchemy, and few shared the remarkable scepticism of John XXII whose edict against the art (1317) begins like this: 'The unfortunate alchemists promise what they have not. Though they call themselves sages, they stumble into the pitfalls which they have dug for others. Ludicrously, they pretend that they are masters of alchemy. And they offer proof of their ignorance when citing older authors; though they have not discovered what those were unable to find, they still believe that it is possible to discover it in the future.'[28] Only a few years before this edict, Arnold Villanova had accomplished two successful transmutations at the Holy See. The witty reply which Pope Leo X is supposed to have given to the alchemist Aurelius Augurelli when the latter dedicated a poem on alchemy to him is well known. Augurelli had expected a princely reward in return, but Leo, who had never been fond of gold, gave him a most beautiful – but empty – purse: he who can make gold needs only a receptacle for storing it!

The medieval kings had been less indifferent to the matter. In 1380, Charles V of France proscribed all alchemical research. An unfortunate adept who disregarded this law was arrested, and had a narrow escape from the gibbet. After the king's death, the law became obsolete. Henry IV of England made the following decree in 1404: 'From now on, nobody shall, under penalty of felony, multiply gold and silver, or make use of fraud in order to succeed in his designs.' Although this law makes a distinction between true and fraudulent transmutation, neither jugglers nor Hermetics paid much attention to it. In 1418 the Venetian Republic prohibited the practice of alchemy, but the law had no more effect than that of the English king. With the rise of capitalism, the attitude of monarchs towards alchemy changed. Wherever they scented gold, i.e., power, the kings and princes became very gracious. Disappointed, they resorted to penalties whose cruelty far exceeded the severity of the medieval

laws against Hermetism. The desire for gold and scientific
interest caused a few potentates themselves to study the
problem of transmutation. Among them, Rudolf II (1552–
1612) and Ferdinand III (1608–57) protected and financed the
alchemists.

Many theologians felt that Hermetic philosophy did not conform to the Church's dogma, though they rarely objected to
alchemical practice itself. They were not deceived by the
alchemists' frequent citations of Bible verses. The apparent
modesty of the Hermetics veiled an offensive pride. Their teachings pointed out a path to felicity unlike the one recommended
by the Church.

In a former chapter, it has been shown that the art, like all
inquiry into natural phenomena, had been considered a vain
and cursed knowledge. It was connected with two great crimes:
the intercourse of women with fallen angels, and Adam eating
the forbidden fruit, i.e., original sin. Furthermore, we have seen
that Hermetism was related closely to Gnosticism: the serpent
is a symbol borrowed from the Gnostics.

The fundamental difference between Gnosticism and Catholicism is their opposing concept of *guilt*. Humbly, the orthodox
Church accepted original sin and professed that the only possible
salvation lay in conciliating the offended Father. This had taken
place when the Son offered himself as a voluntary sacrifice: His
blood had washed away Adam's sin. But there were others, in
fact many Gnostic sects, who did not admit their own culpability,
justifying Adam's deed as being caused by God's injustice. As
previously pointed out, they declared that the creator of the
material world was but the imperfect maker of an imperfect
universe. He was the God of the Old Testament, the jealous one
who had incensed the Jewish people to destroy Christ. Through
the father's intrigue, the son was killed. Thus the Gnostics
reversed the accusation and projected their feeling of guilt
upon the accuser: the offended father.

The early alchemists must have shared these conceptions, and
their emblems – the tree and the serpent – may have also symbolized to them the happenings in the garden of Eden. Whether
the later adepts were aware of this significance and whether they
knew the true origin of their doctrine is not clear. At any rate,
alchemy had retained this heretic notion, that the achievement of
the supreme is attained through knowledge (*sophia*); soul and
spirit must become one, i.e., faith and science are to be identical.
For the adept, intellect, like the soul, is of the divine; and often
the Hermetics do not distinguish between them.

In the alchemists' rich imagery, the crucified Saviour does not
appear, though the flowing blood is the symbol of the fourth
stage of the transmuting process. Instead of Christ, the alchemists
depict the killing of the holy innocents by King Herod, the
iniquitous *father* of the people. Flamel represents the sixth stage
of the process by a crucified serpent, as if to allude to Gnostic
salvation, which is achieved through wisdom. In Lambsprinck's
Hermetic figures, father and son are shown in open conflict, and
their reconciliation is caused both by the spirit and by the

51. *Hermetic allegory:*
Nature teaches nature

intellect. But before the two can be reconciled, they have to be separated. The spirit says:

Come hither, I will conduct thee everywhere,
To the summit of the loftiest mountain,
That thou mayest behold the greatness of the earth and of the sea,
And thence derive true pleasure.[29]

The Gnostic trinity, father, mother and son, appears in Cleopatra's early design. The mystical circles in the upper left are inscribed with the old signs of gold, silver, quicksilver, which are to be identified with the heavenly family. Hermes Trismegistus alludes similarly to the female element in the trinity when he says, 'The sun is his father, the moon is his mother.' The alchemists have always maintained this trinity in the macrocosmic triangle whose angles are the sun, the moon and the stone.

Noticeable also is the importance given to women by the Hermetic. In Majer's etching the virgin is, like her ancestor Eve, the instigator. And a woman is the alchemist's symbol of nature. He follows her tracks, which lead to perfection. It may be recalled that Magdalene and Sophia are the most important and active figures in the *Pistis Sophia*, and that the earthly incarnation of the heavenly mother is a main feature in the dogma of Simon Magus. Flamel's transmutation took place when his wife was present; and in the *Liber Mutus*, an alchemical tract, it is

recommended that before starting the operation the alchemist
and his wife should kneel and pray before the oven. The union
of soul and spirit, of the male and female essence, has its counterpart in heaven: the sun is the father and the moon, the mother.
Sophia is wed to her divine lover.

The importance that is given to women is connected with the
Ophites' gratitude to Sophia, who had pointed out the way to
knowledge. The leaders of the orthodox Church fought from the
very beginning of Christianity against such glorification of
women. In his first letter to the Corinthians, Paul says bluntly:
'Women are to keep quiet in church, for they are not allowed to
speak. They must accept a subordinate place, just as the Law
says. If they want to find out anything, they should ask their
husbands at home, for it is disgraceful for a woman to speak in
church.' (14:34, 35.) Moreover, Paul affirms that man 'is the
image of God and reflects His glory; while woman is the reflection of man's glory'. (I Cor. 11:7.)

THE MIDDLE AGES

Magical Miscellany in Pre-Arabic Times

Leaving the art of Hermes and its remarkable adepts, we shall return to the early Middle Ages. For about seven hundred years, magic seems to have been repressed and even annihilated. The Church is built upon solid rock; its representatives know that nothing can endanger it. From this feeling of safety is born a relative tolerance, replacing the cruelty of old, a fact which is demonstrated by the dealings of the authorities with the popular superstitions and customs of the past. Among the early laws against magic, a few are amazingly lenient. That of the Salic Franks, the *Lex Salica*, stipulates that 'a witch, having eaten human flesh and being convicted of this crime, shall pay eight thousand denarii, i.e., two hundred gold pennies.'[1] The amount is high, but the crime is horrible in an epoch when necrophagous habits in a man could not be explained as a psychic disorder but only as a most dreadful and punishable perversion.

This Salic law was sanctioned by Clovis I (466–511). It inflicts a fine of seventy-two pennies and half a gold coin for enchantment by magic knots. Strangely enough, most of the fines for evil operations of magic are lower than those specified for defamation, the unjust accusation that a person is a witch. The Ripuarian law ordained that any wrong inflicted by a sorcerer – harming limb or property – must be compensated by money. In doubtful cases, the accused might clear himself by oath. The code of Charlemagne provided imprisonment for enchanters and wizards and a season to be devoted to repentance. The law of Withraed, king of Kent (in 690), ordains: 'If a theow make an offering to devils, iet him make a bot of six shillings, or his hide!'[2]

It is remarkable that the punishment meted out to the higher classes was more severe than that to the lower classes. The earliest collection of ecclesiastical disciplinary measures, the *Liber Poenitentialis* of St Leonard (seventh century), provides imprisonment for what the Church must have judged to be a dreadful crime – the sacrifice to demons: 'One year of penance, if he is a clown of low estate; if he be of a higher degree, ten years.'[3] When the life of the king was at stake, or that of any member of the royal family, things were different. A magical attempt to kill the ruler was punished cruelly. Sometimes witchcraft was the pretext used for ridding the court of some displeasing figure. The rigour displayed during such trials, however, cannot be interpreted as a measure provided for by established jurisdiction.

The formulation of a law implies the existence of a crime. That the annihilation of magic was not complete has already been surmised above with respect to alchemy. Hermeticism was cultivated mainly in the East, and early scholars in France, Spain and England hardly mention it. But from the writings of the West, we learn that many pagan customs survived among the lower classes: enchantment, magical knots, the use of disguise as mythical animals, nightly assemblies of sorcerers, the use of talismans, herbs, stones and poisons, incantations, spells, demon-worship, and many other practices of witchcraft which were common in these seemingly pacific centuries. Everybody believed in the power of magic, the scholars as well as the worldly rulers and the clergy.

The writers do not define clearly the difference between magic and witchcraft. Most of them censure such operations and only a few find them worthy of investigation. In astrological matters, however, they were less certain. Acting on their knowledge of philosophy, they assigned a higher rank to the stargazers and mathematicians than to the common sorcerers. Thus Boethius (480?–524), the famous author of the *Consolation of Philosophy*, believed that the stars were superior, influencing men and things upon earth.

Less versed in philosophy and more concerned with witch-craft pure and simple was Isidor of Seville (*ca.* 560–636), who believed that there are signs of things to come, prodigies and monstrous births. In his historical survey he calls Zoroaster and Democritus the inventors of magic. Magic is identical with witchcraft, arts which cause disturbances in the air, incantations that cause death. The future may be known through divinatory arts, etc. In his censure of magic, he derives his arguments from the Church fathers.

The English historian and monk, Bede (675–735), also believed in prodigies and divination. Gregory the Great, pope from 590 to 604, dwells mainly upon ecclesiastical matters. His preferred theme is the possession of man by devils. He reveals an amazing credulity for superstitious tales and dwells also upon the miracles performed by the saints. In addition to such writings, there existed also some confused compilations of classical fragments. These books were ascribed incorrectly to various famous authors of antiquity, crumbs of ancient wisdom which had become the nourishment for those arid times.[4]

The Arabs

European learning changed utterly when the Arabs entered Spain. Endowed with an insatiable curiosity concerning foreign learning, guided by a truly Oriental imagination, and filled with the energy of a people who had extended their boundaries from the Indus to the Pyrenees, the Arabs in their writings show a dynamism which contrasts sharply with the passive wisdom of the West. In the seventh century Mohammed carried his message

into the Arabic world. Before his coming the Arabs had lived
and died with magic – they spoke to the good genii, the Djinns,
they used charms, wax figures and incantations. Talismans were
to them powerful protectors, and the wise men foretold the
future in their sacred songs. After Mohammed had established
the new faith, they continued all their magical practices, adding
to their incantations some verses of the Koran, employing thus
the power of religion together with that of traditional magic.

Mohammed himself had frequent dealings with demons. He
was the victim of a powerful magic spell, the enchantment by
knots, an operation of witchcraft already censured by Plato.
Lucaides, a Jew, had knotted a cord, uttering mysterious words
while doing so. By these means he hoped to rob Mohammed of
his virility. Then he stuck needles into a wax figure that represented the prophet. Fortunately, Allah appeared to Mohammed
in a dream and revealed the cause of his ailments. The wax
figure and the cord were found in a sacred well, and when the
prophet recited some verses from the Koran the punctures in the
wax disappeared, and the knots became untied.

*53. Arabic talisman with
inscriptions such as 'Allah
is with us, the almighty,
by this magic sign, in the
name of Allah, you, the
believers of Islam, shall
not be harmed by magic.'*

Mohammed composed the Koran in verse, the rhythmic prose
called *sadj*. This he had done for a weighty reason, for the Arabic
seers had always offered their oracles in the *sadj*, and the people
would not have accepted Mohammed's laws had they not been
written in the language of the gods. Like all great men, Mohammed had moments of doubt. Did he truly fulfil a divine mission
or had he been seduced by an evil spirit? One night he heard
a voice which commanded: 'Announce!' Its owner claimed to be
the angel Gabriel. Utterly disturbed, the champion of Islam
confided this to his wife. She found a way by which he could
ascertain the truth. Undressing, she told him to do likewise. The
angel disappeared modestly, proving that he belonged to the
good spirits.[5]

In the centuries which followed the establishment of Islam its
leaders, the sultans, exhibited great interest in the knowledge of
the conquered nations, and many foreign books were translated
into the Arabic. Alkindi (died 850 or 873) translated Aristotle.
He wrote on philosophy, politics, mathematics, medicine, music,
astronomy and astrology. Albumasar (died 886) treated various
problems, and his occult writings strongly influenced the later
medieval magi. Costa ben Luca (ninth century) translated Hero
of Alexandria's book *Mechanics*. He wrote also on physical ligatures, i.e., talismans and enchantments. His quotations from
Greek and Roman writers reveal that he was well versed in
classical literature. His book *The Difference of Soul and Spirit*
was translated into Latin by John of Spain (twelfth century).
Medieval scholars, Arnold of Villanova for instance, were indebted to him.

The encyclopedist, philosopher and astronomer, Thebit ben
Corat, exerted a still greater influence. He is frequently quoted
by celebrities of the thirteenth century – Albertus Magnus,
Roger Bacon, Cecco d'Ascoli, Peter of Abano – and we are
indebted to him for a treatise on images. Thebit was one of the
most prolific translators: by him the writings of Archimedes,

54. *Arabian astrologers*

Apollonius, Aristotle, Euclid, Hippocrates and Galen were made available in the Arabic tongue. Rasis (died 924) is credited with having contributed a fabulous number of works, two hundred and thirty-two! He wrote on medicine, physiognomy, drugs, cosmetics, hygiene, surgery, diseases and so forth. Among numerous others may be mentioned also Khalid ibn Jazid (635–704), Geber (ninth century) and the legendary Morienus who wrote treatises upon the Hermetic art. Thus it was through Arabic writings that alchemy was introduced to Western Europe.

Avicenna (980–1037), 'prince of the physicians', explored matter and soul with the intent to prove that there are no miracles, but that all happenings derive from natural causes. He wrote on the wonderful virtues of nature, on diseases, poisons, the influence of the mind upon the body, on the power of the stars and talismans. The Arabic encyclopedia *Kitab-Fihrist* (988), devotes several pages to the enumeration of Hermetics, mentioning among others the Egyptian Chemes, the Median Osthanes – presumably the teacher of Democritus – Hermes Trismegistus, Mary the Jewess, Cleopatra and Stephanus of Alexandria.[6]

Vanquished in France in 732, the Arabs retreated to Spain and settled there until the fifteenth century. Through them Spain became the European centre of learning. Under Alfonso the Sage, in the thirteenth century, foreign learning attained so high a level that it could be compared with that of the Renaissance.

Dante saw Albertus Magnus in Paradise:

> He who at my right is closest to me:
> My brother and master, Albert of Cologne. . . .

But in his verses Dante imprisoned other contemporaries in hell – Michael Scot (*ca.* 1170–1232) and Guido Bonatti (died about 1300). Scot expiates his crimes of magic, a magic doubly criminal since according to Dante it was a fraud. Little is known of the Scotsman's life. He died early in the thirteenth century, and now he wanders in the eighth circle of the Inferno, looking back over his shoulder, because here those who attempted to predict the future are not allowed to look forward.

According to his own statement, Scot was astrologer to Emperor Frederick II, the extraordinary ruler who invited to his court seers and magi of the East and of the West. At Frederick's request, Scot wrote his extensive works dealing with the occult – the books *Introductions*, *Particularis*, and also one on physiognomy, the study of man's face, where the planets have marked the events of each individual's life. Scot also translated Avicenna. Among his contemporaries, Scot was considered a great scholar. Bacon believed – erroneously – that Scot had introduced Aristotle to the West. Leonardo da Pisa dedicated his book on numbers to him. Thomas of Cantimpré, Bartholomew of England and Vincent of Beauvais called him an authority, but Albertus, the saintly man, was more cautious, for he censured his writings severely, saying that Scot had failed to understand Aristotle.[7] Yet Albertus used Scot's translation of Aristotle's *History of Animals*.

What crimes did Scot commit that caused his eternal banishment to hell? Although he disguised many magical operations as experiments and condemned magic and especially necromancy, the conjuring up of the dead, he spoke too much and in too detailed a way of all these evil practices. The full description and publication of forbidden arts had been condemned throughout the centuries in the fear that people might become inspired by them. Whatever magic arts existed in his time were described by Scot. Conjurors mix blood with their ritual water, because demons are attracted by blood. They sacrifice human flesh and bite off their own flesh or that of corpses. They cut off doves' heads, and seek their bleeding hearts with which to draw magic circles; they make use of Biblical verses in their diabolical incantations.[8]

In his book on astronomy Scot speaks of spirits of the air and of the planets, of images, prayers and conjurations for each hour of the day and night, things which we will encounter frequently in the black books of the Renaissance and of more recent times. His treatise on physiognomy contains the traditional elements of the subjects: the stars influence the generation of man and imprint their seals upon the face of man. Therefore we can read in man's features what the heavenly bodies have decided concerning him. Scot interprets dreams and believes like everyone in his time that stones, herbs, etc., are endowed with marvellous virtues. He accepts alchemy and divination. In short, he is a great expert of magic, concerned solely, apart from his medical practice, with the occult arts. No theological treatise counterbalances this prodigious amount of suspect learning.

Guido Bonatti, a citizen of Forlì, whom Dante also consigned to hell, was a promoter of astrology, of the talismanic arts, and of all wisdom that derives from the stars. A violent and self-assured man, whose magic power fascinated his fellow citizens, Bonatti worked zealously – and magically – for the welfare of his town. He derives his learning from the Arabs mainly, from the Greek astronomer Ptolemy and from Hermes Trismegistus. His publications enjoyed great popularity. He recommended his book on astrology to the spiritual and secular leaders of the states, but not all of his ecclesiastical readers can have been pleased by his assertions: for instance that the foundation of churches should be laid at the propitious hour, calculated by a capable astrologer; to him who does not believe in astrology, God must undoubtedly appear unjust, but the pious astrologers recognized that they are not afflicted by Him, since misfortune comes from the stars; Christ was an astrologer; when his disciples dissuaded Him from returning to Judea, He answered: 'Are there not twelve hours in the day', alluding to the fact that He would not be molested, having chosen the right hour.

Bonatti tampered dangerously with theological problems. The miracle of St Francis's divine love he declared to be caused by a favourable conjunction of the planets. Similar assertions proved unlucky for the astrologer Cecco d'Ascoli, who died at the stake in Florence, because he had deduced from Christ's horoscope that He was predestined to die at a given time upon the cross. But Forlì and Bologna were not Florence, and Bonatti felt sufficiently secure there in railing at the ignorance and the 'idiocy' of the Franciscans. 'Fortune rules everything,' he said, 'although some fools in tunics [the friars] may say the contrary.' John of Vicenza, of the Order of the Preaching Friars, he called a silly fool and a hypocrite – and what is worse, Bonatti defended his town against the Pope's armies.

Forlì had been girdled with new walls. The event was celebrated by both the Ghibellines and the Guelfs, who embraced each other and forgot their old feud. Bonatti, however, did not trust this bond, and in order to protect the city from any evil that might result from human inconstancy, he fabricated a brass horseman according to the rules of astrology. Before the construction of the new walls was begun, Bonatti had convinced the inhabitants of Forlì that the right hour for this enterprise should be awaited. The fortunate constellation, he said, should be used simultaneously for an eternal reconciliation of Ghibellines and Guelfs. One member of each party was elected for the ceremony: both held a foundation stone in their hands while the masons stood by with mortar. When the decisive moment had arrived, Bonatti gave the signal and the Ghibelline did as he had been told. But the Guelf, fearing that he was being tricked

into some operation contrary to the interests of his party, with-
held his stone. Now the angered Bonatti cursed him together
with all the Guelfs, saying that this sign would not appear again
in the sky for five hundred years. The chronicler adds with
satisfaction that God had afterwards destroyed the Guelfs of
Forli, just as Guido had predicted.[9]

At times the astrologer was also inclined to help an individual,
like the apothecary with whom he used to play chess, and who
had lost his wealth. Guido made a wax image for his friend, a
ship endowed with astro-magic power. 'Store it away,' he said,
'and do not speak to anyone about it.' The apothecary regained
his wealth but was troubled by the thought that his lucky ship
might be the evil work of magic. He confessed the story and the
priest told him to destroy this product of superstition. He did so
– and, as Bonatti had warned him, the apothecary once more lost
his possessions. This time when he asked Bonatti to make him
another ship, he was called a fool. The propitious hour, the
astrologer said, would not return for fifty years.[10] It is quite
astonishing how this headstrong magician managed to escape the
vengeful arm of the Inquisition. He was killed by bandits, as he
was returning from Paris to Bologna.

A man who could not avoid open conflict with the ecclesiastical
authorities was Peter of Abano, famous translator of Abraham
Aben Ezra's book *Nativities*. Peter was the author of a work on
physiognomy, on geomancy, on prophecy and on the elements of
magic. He lived from 1250 to 1318. This peaceful and most
learned scholar travelled widely. From Padua, where he was
lecturing, he went to Paris; from there to Sardinia, thence to
Constantinople where he discovered a volume of the *Problems*
of Aristotle, which he translated for the first time into Latin. In
Paris, where he spent several years at the university, he wrote his
book on physiognomy. He was acquainted with Marco Polo,
from whom he obtained information on Asia. He also carried on
a lucrative medical practice.

Such wisdom and wealth soon brought him into trouble. He
became the victim of a colleague's envy. A medical doctor
denounced him to the inquisitors of Padua. His books were
burned, and he barely escaped the stake. After his death his
corpse was burned upon the pyre. The public, however, did not
share the inquisitors' views. Frederick, Duke of Urbino, had his
statue erected at the portal of the palace; Trithemius and Agrippa,
in the sixteenth century, published Abano's treatises together
with their own works. A hundred years later Gabriel Naudé,
referred to previously as the defender of Zoroaster, attempted to
clear the name of the unfortunate scholar of the stain of heresy.

Peter believed in geomancy, the divinatory art that uncovers
the future through the design formed by earth tossed hap-
hazardly upon a table. Geomancy can also be manipulated by a
simpler method, i.e., marking, at random, a paper with four rows
of dots. By cancelling two of them simultaneously, the remaining
dots will be two or one. From the four lines will result four of the
following figures: 2222, 2221, 2211, etc.; sixteen variations are
possible, eight of them being favourable omens, eight unfavour-

able. These numbers are connected with the planets, the signs of the zodiac, etc. They predict the future. The process proposed by Abano is still used today. Like many divinatory operations, it has degenerated into a game, and who would believe that such a harmless operation could have endangered the life of its promoter in early days!

From the innumerable books ascribed to Raymond Lully, only a few can be identified as the writing of the Catalan martyr. His chief work, the *Universal Art*, contains magic merely as an incidental. It is a treatise on a perfected scholastic method of argumentation supposed to serve as a tool for the conversion of the Mohammedans. The Doctor Illuminatus, as he was called, believed like all his learned colleagues in the power of the stars, which he sought to employ for medical treatment. He also held numbers in high esteem, believing like the Pythagoreans that they were endowed with marvellous virtues.

His life story is that of a fervent Christian whose temperament forbade him to live peacefully within the walls of a monastery. A forerunner of the Jesuit missionaries, he wished to travel to the heathens, to learn their customs and wisdom, which he hoped to make use of in propaganda for their conversion. All this does not seem typical of a magician. His most ardent desire was to die like a martyr. He was stoned at Tunis by a mob of angry Arabs whom he had tried to convert. A few Christian merchants carried the badly wounded Lully to their ship and set sail for Majorca, the martyr's homeland. Just as the island was sighted, he died, on 29 June 1315.

Oddly enough, Lully, well-versed in the art of arguing in abstractions, soon won reputation as an experimenter. Just as later the archway in Paris dedicated to Nicolas Flamel was the object of alchemists' pilgrimages, so now Lully's tomb became an object of worship. Later alchemists were wont to count the columns of the tomb and to examine its sculpture, hoping to find a key through which they could attain the famous perfection. Many wrote treatises on the philosophers' stone, signing their work with Lully's name. They bequeathed to their master more than he had given them, for in the few authentic writings available Lully seems to be rather opposed to alchemy. He had, however, attained perfection, if not in the crucible, at any rate in his person, as he changed from a frivolous and vain courtier to a learned and active defender of his convictions.

Starting as a country practitioner and lacking literary culture, Arnold of Villanova achieved astounding fame. Two kings and three popes were his patients, admirers and defenders. Arnold was indeed in need of protection from the clerical judges, who though ready to accept his medical innovations did not appreciate his originality concerning matters of faith. It is not clear why he wanted at any cost to be more than a great scholar, why he insisted on being also a counsellor in spiritual matters. His preaching impressed James II of Portugal and Frederick II, James's brother, King of Sicily. Even the popes were forced to listen to his sermons if they wanted to be treated by Arnold. Arnold of Villanova had the great ambition to cure not only individuals, but even states and the Church itself. He criticized severely the condition of the clergy, and predicted the advent of the antichrist and a precipitous end for this corrupt world, for he had read in the stars that a catastrophe would occur in the middle of the fourteenth century.

Arnold was also a great traveller. We find him in Montpellier, Valencia, Barcelona, Naples, in Gascony, in Piedmont, at Bologna, Rome, and even on the African continent. He was often called abroad on official business, carrying messages for kings and popes. He interpreted dreams for James and Frederick, impressing them both with his weird predictions. James had been disturbed by a nightly apparition of his deceased mother. He wrote about it to Frederick, who advised his brother to read Villanova's books. The magus exhorted the king to reform his country's administration. He advised that he endow hospitals and give alms to the poor, that he should proscribe the divinatory arts and witchcraft; justice should be exercised equally to both the rich and the poor; taxes were to be diminished. He summed up his arguments by pointing out that the king in order to preserve his interests had to yield to the will of the people.

In his works, Arnold emphasizes the reality of alchemy. He performed a successful transmutation at the Holy See, in the presence of Pope Boniface VIII. John André, a witness, reports: 'In our days, we had at the See master Arnold of Villanova, an authority in theological and medical matters. He is a great alchemist, and he submitted the gold sticks he produced to everyone for examination.' Villanova spoke Greek, Latin and Arabic, and was well-versed in mathematics, philosophy and medicine. He translated Costa ben Luca's treatise upon physical ligatures, a compendium of talismans, charms, herbs and stones. In his *Disapprobation of Sorcerers* he enumerates the remedies of counter magic. They are none other than those used by wizards and at times reveal Gnostic influences:

Take the purest gold and melt it as the sun enters Aries. Later, form a round seal from it and say while so doing: 'Arise Jesus, light of the world, thou art in truth the lamb that takes away the sins of the world.' . . . Then repeat the psalm, *'Domine dominus noster'*. Put the seal away, and when the moon is in Cancer or Leo, and the sun in Aries, engrave on one side the figure of a ram, and on the circumference, *'arahel juda v et vii'*, and elsewhere on the circumference engrave the sacred words, 'The Word was made flesh' . . . and in the centre, 'Alpha and Omega and St Peter'

We will meet similar prescriptions in later black books of magic. Their mingling of magic and religious elements had a soothing effect upon those who feared heavenly punishment for their unorthodox operations. Such counter-magical ceremonies and prescriptions were shocking to the authorities, though Arnold accompanies all this with passionate arguments against witchcraft. Magic must be excluded from medicine, he says; enchanters, conjurors, invokers of spirits and diviners, should be rejected as being ignominious, producing marvels of a character unlike those of natural science.

However, even during his lifetime – in 1305 – the inquisitors forbade the reading of his books. And his conflict with the Catalan Dominicans was not his only one with the authorities. James sent him as an ambassador to Philip the Fair of France. When Arnold arrived in Paris he was arrested. An influential friend bailed him out the following day. During the trial before the Parisian theological faculty and the bishop he learned about the grudge the theologians bore against him because of his prophecies concerning the world's end and also for his treatise upon the Holy Name, in which he seems to revive the old word-magic of Gnosticism. The verdict was that his books should be burned publicly. Arnold protested to Philip and Boniface; and in 1301 he was allowed to leave France. Shrewdly he tried to enlist the pope in his behalf by submitting to him a modified copy of his work. But the Parisians had anticipated such a move and sent to His Holiness the original version which they had condemned.

Arnold was imprisoned by the pope; and after a while, he had to abjure his errors before a secret consistory. The pope gave him this friendly advice: 'Occupy thyself with medicine, leave theology alone, and we will honour thee.'[11] Boniface needed him as a doctor and, perhaps for this reason, showed an extraordinary leniency towards Arnold, who had declared that he received his ideas for reforming the Church from Christ. Such communication with the divine, without the mediation of the Church, would have been sufficient to bring the illuminated culprit to the stake. He might have ended tragically had the pope not at that moment become ill. Arnold treated him successfully, was rewarded with the castle of Anagni, and his next book was well received.

Clement V was favourably disposed towards Arnold. In Avignon the seer was permitted to expound his theories before a 'sacred college'. His uncompromising ideas eventually brought about his estrangement from James II of Portugal, whom he had cured in 1303. In his arguments the reformer probably denounced temporal governments, in order not to antagonize the sacred college. He returned to Frederick, and in 1310 he died en route to Clement, to whom he was carrying a message from Frederick.

Such was the life of this extraordinary man, who is rightly ranked with magicians, for he operated magically, as is confirmed by his own writings: 'The human operator can accomplish great things by availing himself of the stars' influence.' Like the ancient Egyptians, he chose the hours for gathering healing plants. He used cabalistic signs and every kind of talisman in treating his patients. He did not reject ceremonial magic, including conjurations and unorthodox prayers. Following the Greek Galen (A.D. 131–210), he brewed unsavoury concoctions for his patients. His treatment of kidney stones is most dreadful, and Pope Boniface's trust in him must have been great to accept it.

In one important point, however, Arnold was unlike his scholastic colleagues: despite his criticism of popular remedies, he admitted that many of them were effective. Unlike Bacon and Albertus, he defended popular experiments, and to some extent his tolerance can be compared to that of Paracelsus (1493–

1541) who learned from barbers, surgeons, witches and vaga-
bonds whom he met during his wanderings through Europe.

Papal pressure increased with the spreading of heretical beliefs
which the Church was unable to eradicate. From the East the
dualistic heresy, possibly imported by the Crusaders, filtered
in for many years, and from the eleventh century on, sectarians
paraded their theories openly in Italy, especially in Lombardy,
where two movements met: on the one hand that which had originated in the sea ports of southern France, on the other that
from the east reaching the valley of the Po. In 1080 Pope
Gregory VII still recommends moderation to worldly leaders in
prosecuting heretics and witches. But numerous sects grew up
with a disquieting speed: the Paulicians, Bogomiles, Kathari,
Paterini, Vaudois, Albigenses, Tartarins, Beghards, the Pauvres
of Lyons.

In 1209 Pope Innocent III ordered a crusade against the
Albigenses and the Kathari. Crusaders ransacked Béziers and
Carcassonne, and the Albigenses, though protected by the Count
of Toulouse, were defeated at Muret and at Toulouse. This
terrible war, in which the king of France participated, came to an
end in 1229. The Albigenses suffered a military defeat which
was accompanied by cruel persecutions, but the faith continued
to exist, and only a few years after the peace treaty a papal bull
refers to the Luciferians, who worship the principle of evil.
The struggle between the orthodox Church and the dualists
continued throughout the thirteenth century. In 1233 Gregory
IX established the Inquisition, a special tribunal of Dominicans
who were to combat all heresies. The Inquisition condemned
culprits to the stake on grounds of heresy. However, the dualists
were not mere heretics but actually members of a faith independent of Christianity. In 1274 the earliest 'example' of an inquisitorial condemnation of a witch occurred. She was burned in
Toulouse, the centre of the Katharan movement.

Then, in the years 1318, 1320, 1331 and 1337, additional papal
edicts against witchcraft and heresy were published.[12] The
example set by the Church was later followed by the secular
authorities, but mass persecution was most drastic during the
sixteenth and seventeenth centuries, when the burning of witches
became an economic factor.

Albertus Magnus (1193–1280)

The thirteenth century was far from being a dark epoch in the
Middle Ages. Christendom was united, and under the Church,
European civilization constituted a homogeneous society with
common institutions and aspirations. 'The supreme Pontiff,'
Dante says, 'shall lead the human race to life eternal by means of
revelation, and the emperor guide it to temporal felicity by
means of philosophical instruction.'[13] Philosophy, though controlled by the dogma of the Church, flourished again. The early
days, when philosophers were persecuted as magicians, were for-

gotten, and now their venerable images were carved on the portals of cathedrals. The century was enlightened by scholars of a truly universal wisdom, men such as William of Auvergne, Vincent of Beauvais, Thomas of Cantimpré, Bartholomew of England, Robert Grosseteste, Roger Bacon, Lully, Aquinas, and the great Albertus (to mention only a few of the outstanding scholars). Their treatises differ from those of the past because of their greater thoroughness and the larger number of subjects treated.

These men were not magicians, in the true sense of the word, but they showed an interest in magic; they found it worthy of investigation, and a few among them made magical experiments. The sacred fear of the occult arts, which had previously been considered the works of the devil – the shrewd one who is ever ready to set his traps for the learned as well as for others – existed no longer. The cunning of the devil could be defeated by wise or holy men, his power exploited for the good of mankind. Here he was called upon to build a castle, there, a bridge; and the chroniclers rejoice when telling how his services were finally ill rewarded and how mortals escaped his voracious fangs by some humorous trickery.

The epoch was, however, profoundly religious. All the above-mentioned scholars were members of the clergy. William was Bishop of Paris, Thomas lecturer of the Dominicans who played an important role in this renaissance of wisdom. Bartholomew lectured for the Franciscans; Grosseteste was Bishop of Lincoln; the Dominican Vincent of Beauvais was chaplain to Louis IX; St Thomas Aquinas, the great teacher and author of *Summa Theologica*, became a Dominican when he was sixteen years old. Bacon joined the Franciscan order; Albertus, who was canonized in 1932, was Bishop of Ratisbon, and Raymond Lully died as a martyr for his faith.

These men were the faithful servants of the Church, under whose mantle the wisdom of the past and the present met. How wide this mantle was, we can judge from the painting by Andrea da Firenze (fourteenth century) representing St Thomas Aquinas enthroned in glory, holding upon his knees the open Bible. At his side are the champions of the faith: Job, David, St Paul, the four Evangelists, Moses, Isaiah and King Solomon. Below, fourteen female figures seated in choir stalls personify the theological sciences and the liberal arts. At their feet sit celebrated students of art and science: Emperor Justinian, Pope Clement IV, Peter Lombard, Dionysius the Areopagite, Boethius, John the Damascene and St Augustine representing the theological branches of wisdom. Then follow Pythagoras, Euclid and Zoroaster (astronomy), the Biblical Tubal Cain (music), Aristotle, Cicero, and the Latin grammarian Priscianus. The men of the faith dwell peaceably together with the wise men of antiquity, admitting even the presumed inventor of magic, Zoroaster. A more profound understanding of the past, a wider conception of wisdom, produced this world, which although not as universal as that of the early syncretistic religions, is well ordered, with all its elements fully understood.

55. Philosophical allegory of the Catholic religion

In Albertus's writings we often read such phrases as 'I have tested this', or 'I have not experienced this', or 'I have proved that this is not true'. Such an attitude is new; it shows that the authorities of the past were not accepted blindly. Albertus's relative objectivity is seen when he criticizes his beloved Aristotle, the pillar of scholasticism. Often he enumerates facts, adding that they have not been proved adequately by certain experience, 'though found in the writings of the ancients'. These ancients were philosophers, and the goal of philosophy is to attain truth by observation and reason, and not by experimentation.[14]

Although Albertus recommends the making of conjectures and their testing, he is still a man of philosophy. His reasoning is good but his experiments are superficial and his conclusions often wrong. Albertus's importance in scientific matters lies more in his attitude than in his achievements. His description of the marvellous virtues that dwell in crystals may serve as an example. If you hold a crystal towards the sun, you can light a fire. This is true, but Albertus forgets to tell us the most important thing, that the crystal must be of a convex shape. He seems to believe that it is the crystalline substance that produces the marvel, not the refraction of light. But at times, he plucks the right fruit from the tree of knowledge. 'The ostrich eats and digests iron,' the ancients say, to which Albertus answers that it eats stones but not iron, for he himself has observed the fact. Such apparently humble observation is more important than one might think. Despite Albertus's thoughtful remark, the ostrich three hundred years after his time was still depicted with a horseshoe in its beak. Albertus united within himself a curiosity which was laudable, together with the disciplined methods of a scholar. These methods, as we have said, test particular statements by the general law concerning living beings, as they are established by Aristotle.

A work published in honour of Albertus's canonization does not mention the master's views on magic. Some writers have contested that he even manifested interest in alchemy and astrology. But in Albertus's treatises are found many allusions to the magical arts. An early scholar, the Abbot Trithemius (1462–1516), says that this 'most saintly of saints' was not ignorant of natural magic, holding that this is not evil: 'For not the knowledge but the practice of what is bad is evil.' The question arises how can one master an art without practising it? Trithemius's sentence seems to be the key to an understanding of the medieval scholars' interest in magic: they wanted to study the evil in order to be able to recognize and to judge it. But so strong a curiosity indicates also that the forbidden wisdom attracted them powerfully. Whether Albertus's magical experiments were good or evil depended upon his intention, and we may take it for granted that his operations were motivated by only one purpose: knowledge.

He never doubts that magical wonders can be effected. True, there exists for him jugglery and illusion: people believe they are seeing things which do not exist. True, also, that evil demons lead man astray with magic, which is considerably worse than the deception of the eyes. Yet there also exists in Albertus's opinion natural magic, which is of the good, and a great deal of this good can be found in the writings of the Arabs as well as in Hermetic literature. Furthermore, there are wonderful virtues in herbs and stones of which the patristic writings do not speak. Betony confers the power of divination; verbena can be used as a love charm; the herb meropis opens the seas; and many other marvels can be induced with plants, as is written in Costa ben Luca and Hermes. There are also magical stones which cure diseases. In his work on minerals – according to the edition of 1518 – Albertus speaks extensively of the hidden virtues of stones. Some of the marvels he has experienced himself. '*Lapides preciosi praeter aliis habent mirabiles virtutes*' (precious stones have more miraculous virtues than others). He enumerates carefully these marvels.

The amethyst is found in India; it acts against inebriation, as Aaron says; it creates alertness and appeases quarrels. It fosters the acquisition of knowledge and produces intelligence. The beryl helps to overcome laziness. It soothes the pain in the liver and stops hiccoughs and belching, and is also good for watery eyes. When a rounded beryl is exposed to the sun, it will kindle a fire. It is said also to preserve peace at home. The emerald is of a chaste nature. In order to ascertain whether a girl is chaste, a mixture which contains emerald fragments is prescribed as a potion; if she is chaste, she will retain the potion, if not, she will vomit. It is also said that the emerald increases its owner's wealth and that, in court, it encourages persuasive words. When worn in a necklace, it cures epilepsy. The agate is found in Libya and in Britain. It strengthens the teeth, drives away phantoms and melancholy and is good for stomach-aches. Snakes flee from it. The magi make much use of the stone *diacodos*, which is said to excite phantasms but loses its virtues when brought into contact with a corpse. In the works of such magi as Hermes, Ptolemy and Thebit ben Corat there is more information about this stone.

All this Albertus professes with assurance, apparently unaware that it is pure magic, not unlike that used by Chaldeans, Egyptians and Persians. In the same treatise he asserts also that engraved gems are endowed with mysterious powers, especially those which nature has formed without man's aid. Such ideas lead to the making of talismans, magical images, medals and signs which protect their owners.

The existence of all these marvellous virtues is derived from the stars, for, according to Aristotle, the heavenly bodies govern things upon earth. Believing this, Albertus has already betrayed himself as an astrologer. Repeatedly he asserts that the stars influence objects and men, recognizing their power over the earth, which is manifested by the marvels he likes to enumerate. There is still more to be said about their influence: they are the base of all the divinatory arts, for he who can read the stars' imprints upon bodies will be able to calculate his fate. Whether it is the grooves in man's hand or forehead, whether the veins of a leaf, the form of stag-horns, the shape of a stone, they are 'physiognomies' moulded by the planets.

The question as to whether Albertus was an alchemist must likewise be answered affirmatively. Like his pupil St Thomas Aquinas, he believed that alchemy was a difficult but true art. In his chemical experiments he is less hampered by philosophy, perhaps because the early Greeks were not acquainted with alchemy. He describes his operations with accuracy and expresses original ideas. Among the numerous volumes he bequeathed to posterity, his alchemical treatise is perhaps the best. In the book on minerals he finds much to criticize in alchemical theories, and sometimes he seems opposed to the art of Hermes; but in his treatise *On Alchemy*, which probably is authentic, he champions alchemical operations and the idea that gold can be produced artificially. This is what he recommends in his book to his fellow-alchemists:

The alchemist must be silent and discreet. To no one should he reveal the results of his operations.

He shall live in loneliness, remote from men. His house should have two or three rooms consecrated entirely to the work.

He shall choose the right hour for his operations [meaning that the favourable heavenly constellations should be awaited].

He must be patient and possess perseverance.

He will operate according to the rules: the trituration, the sublimation, the fixation, the calcination, the solution, the distillation and the coagulation.

He will use only glass vessels or glazed pottery.

He must be rich enough to afford the expense which such works demand.

And finally, he will avoid all contact with princes and rulers.[15]

Albertus knew that the Hermetic wisdom was a source of constant danger to the alchemist: neighbours might report a successful operation to the prince, and once the latter knew about the philosopher's gold, the worker of such miracles was doomed, as were Alexander Sethon and others. The alchemist must be rich enough to support his work during his lifetime, for there was no certainty that he might ever succeed, and poverty might then compel him to abandon his studies or resort to deceit and falsification.

Albertus does not tell us whether he made gold or not. According to popular traditions, he had owned the famous stone and could accomplish other marvels which the people readily called magical. When William II, Count of Holland, dined with him in Cologne, Albertus had the table set in the garden of the convent in spite of the fact that it was mid-winter. When the guests arrived they found a snow-decked table. But as soon as they sat down, the snow disappeared and the garden was filled with fragrant flowers. Birds flew about as if it were summer, and the trees were in bloom. The legend has credited a less saintly man of later times with similar magic, Dr Faustus, but the latter produced his winter flowers not with natural magic, as Albertus did, but with black magic and with the help of the devil.

Contemporaries of Albertus affirm also that he built an automaton, the android. Shaped like a man, with each part of its body welded under the influence of a particular star, the android was Albertus's servant. He was endowed with the gift of speech, so much so that his gibberish disturbed the studious Aquinas, who destroyed the machine. Did such an automaton really exist, and if so what was its nature? Eliphas Lévi, the nineteenth-century occultist, has remarked subtly that it was only a symbol of Albertus's scholasticism: human in form, but an artificial being controlled by a mechanism and not by life.

Roger Bacon (1214–94)

Without experience, nothing can be sufficiently known.

Roger Bacon

Like Albertus and other contemporaries Roger Bacon, the Franciscan friar, based his knowledge upon Aristotelian philosophy. Not only did he gather wisdom by philosophical methods, i.e., through observation and reasoning, but also, like Albertus, he emphasized the importance of experimentation. It must be borne in mind, however, that what we call experience today has little relation to that of the Middle Ages. Bacon says, for instance: 'We have established by experience that the stars cause generation and decay upon earth, as anyone can see.' This is not so evident to us, and we may also ask ourselves in what way Bacon could experience the mysterious forces of the planets which influence, supposedly, man's life and death. The friar concludes impetuously: 'Having established by experience what philosophers have made evident before, it follows immediately that all knowledge here below depends on the power of mathematics.'

Another instance of Bacon's scientific attitude is his hazel experiment. In his work on *Experimental Science* he recommends that a sapling of one year's growth should be severed from the root of a hazel tree. It should be slit longitudinally and the divided parts, separated by the space of a palm or four fingers, should be held by two persons at the two ends. After a short time, the parts will approach each other gradually, and at length they will be united and the bough will be intact again! The 'scientific' explanation of this phenomenon, 'wonderful beyond all that I have seen and heard', is given by Pliny, whose views Bacon accepts: certain things are mutually attracted although they are locally separated. This explanation is based upon belief in sympathetic magic, namely, that like attracts like. Had anyone told Bacon that this was magic, he would have been astonished, for he ends his report thus: 'This is a wonderful thing. Magicians perform the experiment, repeating all sorts of incantations. I have disregarded these incantations and have discovered the wonderful action of nature, which is similar to that of the magnet of iron.' Thus, in Bacon's opinion, magicians are charlatans, reciting magical formulas though they know that the phenomenon is a natural one – 'as anyone can see'! We frequently find similar 'observations' in Bacon's manuscripts: he condemns magic, being a magician himself.

Bacon's writings have a vivacity which we do not often find in the heyday of scholasticism, and his impatience, mingled with an enigmatic clairvoyance, compels him at times to make truly astounding predictions. 'First, I will tell you,' he says in his letters,

about the admirable works of art and nature. Afterwards, I shall describe their causes and their form. *There is no magic connected with this*, for magic is inferior to such things and unworthy of them. Namely: machines of navigation can be made, huge ships for rivers and the seas. They move without oars; a single man can manoeuvre them better than if they were manned fully.

Then there are also cars, moving without horses and at a colossal speed; and we believe that such were the battle wagons of old furnished with sickles.

Flying machines can be made also. A man sitting in the centre controls something which makes the machine's artificial wings flap like those of birds.

A device, small in size, for lowering heavy weights can be made, most useful in emergencies. For by a machine, three fingers high and wide, and less in bulk, a man could free himself and his friends from all dangers of prison, and could rise and descend.

Another instrument can be made with which a single man can pull a thousand men violently and against their will; and it attracts other things similarly.

A machine can be constructed for submarine journeys, for seas and rivers. It dives to the bottom without danger to man. Alexander the Great has made use of such a device, as we know from Ethicus the astronomer. Such things have been made long ago and they are still made in our days, except perhaps the flying machine. . . .

And infinite other such things can be produced; bridges that span rivers without pillars, or other supports and devices, ingenious and unheard of.'

No wonder that Bacon has been credited with numerous inventions and discoveries: gunpowder, eye glasses, the telescope, etc.

That magic existed, he no more doubted than did his contemporaries. He admitted also that there were difficulties in discerning between science and the black arts. He accepted natural magic, which is not evil; and if we divest his arguments of their subtleties and crudities, we find that the scholar's conceptions were not unlike those of the philosophers: magic aiming at the good is permissible and is called natural magic; the black arts, promoting what is evil, are to be rejected.

Alchemy, he says, is related to physics. It treats of colours and other substances, of burning bitumen, of salt and sulphur, of gold and other metals, and though nothing concerning the alchemical art is written by Aristotle, the latter is necessary for the study of natural philosophy and speculative medicine. Through alchemy, gold can be made, and thus the Hermetic art can provide for the expenses of the state. It prolongs man's life. But there are few who work alchemically, and still fewer are those who can produce works that will prolong life. The art is suited only to the wisest, who know the meaning of the eagle, the deer, the serpent, the phoenix, creatures who renew their lives through the virtues of herbs and stones.

Potable gold must be dissolved, according to Bacon, in a mysterious liquid, a water which only specially gifted scientists know how to prepare. Such gold is better than that found in nature or alchemical gold. It will produce a most wonderful action when dissolved correctly. Many things should be added to this solution: 'That which swims in the seas . . . and also the thing which grows in the air, a flower of sea dew.' To this there should be added the dianthos, a mixture of leaves and fragments of wood, with a small portion of flowers: and furthermore, that which is cast out by the sea: ambergris. And finally, a most important ingredient is the snake, mentioned by Aristotle. The Tyrians used to eat it, properly prepared with spices. A bone that grows in a stag's heart will give the final touch, because the stag is an animal of longevity. Here again Bacon uses medicine according to the magic principle that like produces like: the animal of longevity will give man long life! The friar considers his concoction an excellent remedy for curing one of old age and for all the corruptions of the body. He believed that one could prolong one's life with it for several hundred years. He knew a man 'who had a letter from the Pope, testifying to the truth of his patriarchal age'.

Bacon believes such incredible things to be proven adequately by this vague report. What he says about speculative alchemy is hardly encouraging to one who wants to explore its confused realms. He declares that very few know about this art and therefore they do not deign to communicate their knowledge or even to remain among those whom they call fools, for such people quibble about the law and cultivate sophisms. The alchemists reproach others for separating philosophy from theology. He adds that alchemical operations are difficult and expensive so that many acquainted with the art cannot operate it for lack of money. Also, the books are written in terms so obscure that one can hardly understand them. Bacon's exclusiveness is truly exasperating. He praises science, describing its insurmountable difficulties, and despises magic and every unscientific method. It would seem that he would have all knowledge controlled by a few supermen, perhaps only by one, himself.

Having declared that all human knowledge depends upon mathematics, he asserts that its noblest branch is astrology, which should be used in medicine, in alchemy and in predicting the future. It is specially useful in political matters: the recent wars could have been averted had the wise observed the stars more carefully. At man's birth the heavenly bodies determine his physical complexion and his change; with every hour the bodies are subject to the influence of another constellation and the works of man shift in character, according to the everlasting celestial movements. But they only dispose man towards his fate, and do not decide it, for his will is free. He says:

> In accordance with the fact that certain signs are fiery, hot and dry, some things partake also of this fiery nature. They are therefore called Martial, after the planet, and are of the nature of Aries, Leo and Sagittarius. The same principle is true concerning other characteristics of things, signs and planets. However, to name and mark things individually with regard to planets and signs, is a matter quite difficult to accomplish, and impossible except through the *Books of the Hebrews*.

Like Rabbi Moses Maimonides (1136–1204), Bacon believes that Holy Writ is the basic source of astrology, a fact which makes the study of the stars and their influence a legitimate occupation. Bacon's opinion in this matter was not shared by all, for in spite of the growing influence of astrology on medieval learning, the official attitude of the Church was rather adverse to it. At any rate, Bacon implies a belief that philosophy, which he identifies with astrology and mathematics, should ultimately lead to and confirm theology. He goes even further, asserting that without astrology or philosophy Church doctrine was not complete. In his *Opus Majus* he says: 'If the truth of philosophy is impaired, damage is inflicted upon theology whose function it is to use the power of philosophy, not absolutely but in controlling the Church, directing the commonwealth of believers and aiding the conversion of predestined unbelievers. . . .' And of the theologians who opposed such ideas, he says: 'But they err not only in this, that they ignorantly condemn knowledge of the future secured through mathematics, but because for the sake of a *part*, which they abhor as the result of their ignorance, they condemn the whole.' This again is one of Bacon's boasts, and quite a dangerous one.

Bacon believed in the power of the spoken word, which he explains thus:

> We must consider that it has great force; all miracles at the beginning of the world were made by the word. And the peculiar work of the rational soul is the word, in which the soul rejoices. Words have a great virtue when they are pronounced with concentration and deep desire, with the right intention and confidence. For when these four things are joined together, the substance of the rational soul is moved

more quickly to act according to its virtue and essence, upon itself and upon exterior things.

As he declared that experiments are the only sure test of certainty in science, we may conjecture that he explored suggestion or hypnosis. But this is only surmise, for we have seen before how seriously we may judge his experiments. Such things, he continues, can also be worked differently, without the help of a favourable constellation and without the enumerated virtues, but with magical formulas and foolish thought. It is then the unscientific work of old wives which cannot produce results unless aided by the devil.

Repeatedly he reveals the pride of the learned and his contempt for things which are not well expressed and coordinated. He accepts contradictions only in matters of theology. He mentions, for instance, a mystery which is contrary to reason: Christ is the angular stone, yet he is also the centre in which the twelve apostles converge. In religious matters he was absolutely orthodox, and his life and study were devoted to the Church. Whatever he discovered served the purpose of increasing the prestige of the Church and facilitating the realization of its plans and activities. In his book, *On Experimental Science*, he says about scientific inventions that the Church should consider their employment against unbelievers and rebels, in order to spare Christian blood, 'and specially it should do so because of future perils in the times of antichrist, which with the grace of God it would be easy to meet, if prelates and princes promoted study and investigated the secrets of nature'.

Seen as a whole, Bacon's teachings are not of the Faustian character which enthusiastic investigators claimed them to be. He was not the enlightened forerunner of a scientific time, whose voice was unheard in the scholastic desert. In his determination to unify all learning, wisdom and faith, he produced a unique work, the *Opus Majus*, which includes material already known to many in his time but which he has arranged and coordinated according to his own original views.[16]

The most interesting aspect of his books is that they have a more individual flavour than other contemporary works. From Bacon's passionate outbursts we glimpse his great sensibility against which, without doubt, he fought when he praised the dull methods of learning. His outstanding statements, which we believe were unique in his time, were marked by the prophetic air, so contrary to science (despite his assertion that all his discoveries are purely scientific). In these predictions, he articulates the deep desires of mankind which led finally to the great inventions.

THE DEVIL

The Principle of Evil

You have the devil underrated:
I cannot yet persuaded be,
A fellow who is all behated
Must something be!

Goethe

How can one measure the good without knowing the bad? How can one long for light without knowing the anguish of darkness? In what an unpleasant land of plenty would one live were there no bad. Evil causes suffering and from pain springs the desire for something better; deficiencies cause us to want improvement, evolution, and to set up ideals. It can safely be said, as it has often been, that God would cease to exist if there were no devil, or as a French theologian expressed it: 'God and the devil are the whole religion.'

Religions of antiquity conceive of evil as partaking of the divine. Among the early Mesopotamians, both principles are intermingled. In the Egyptian theogony the destructive Seth is the brother of beneficent Osiris; in Persia the dark Ahriman was believed to have sprung from a doubting thought of Ormazd, the light-god.

Monotheism arose from age-old dualism, but the monotheistic world equilibrium is more precarious than that of old. The Apocrypha of the Old Testament are hesitant about the power of evil. In the story of Tobit (150 B.C.) Asmodeus is God's opponent; in the book of Esdras, however, two abysmal beings – Enoch and Leviathan – do not produce evil. In the book of Enoch (110 B.C.) demons have a character similar to that of the Gentiles. The Book of Wisdom, a product of Alexandrian Judaism, reiterates that through Satan death came into the world and 'those who hold to the devil's side will find death'.[1]

The problem of evil has been taboo for centuries. The official dogma was to be the only valid explanation of the perennial strife of good and evil, and every unconventional interpretation was punishable. Even this rigour seemed to the European dualists proof of the partiality and vengeance of the Supreme. When the Albigenses witnessed the cruelties of their persecutors, when the Templars were confronted with their iniquitous judges, they may have really believed that the world was topsy-turvy, that the evil one was good and the good evil. But such a reversal would not lead to any solution of the problem. Good and evil would still exist in their antagonism, ever destroying and renewing themselves like the alchemical serpent: he devours his tail, but the tail is as immortal as the head.

Satan is an individualist. He upsets the commandments of heaven which enforce a definite moral conduct. He inspires us

56. *The torments of Hell*

with a longing for the unknown; he gives us dreams and hopes.
He endows us with bitterness and discontent, but in the end he
leads us to the better, and thus he mainly serves the good. He
is that 'force which strives for the evil yet causes the good'. The
messenger of knowledge cannot be ignorant. He is an idealist, a
Don Quixote. Blinded by fanatic conviction, he does not perceive that the giants are windmills and the warriors swine, and
his vast pride precludes recognition of his errors. Milton has
depicted him as a noble rebel who would rather suffer eternally
than accept humiliation. Yes, Satan's essence is his one-sided-
ness, for he is the antithesis.

Can we mould him and his opponent into a synthesis? The
Zoroastrians did not achieve this, but they made us believe it
possible. Ormazd and Ahriman will be reconciled at the end of
time. Side by side, they shall enter the new kingdom as brothers.
The Gnostics made it clear that the universe exists only through
this everlasting antagonism and, the universe being one, good
and evil are united in the divine. In his *History of the Devil* Paul
Carus comes to a similar conclusion: 'God being all in all, regarded as the ultimate authority for conduct, is neither evil itself
nor goodness; but nevertheless he is the good, and he is in the
evil. God is in growth and decay; he reveals himself in life and in
death. He lives also in the visitations that follow evil actions. . . .'
In most beautiful verses Victor Hugo reveals his dualistic bias.
When Satan was cast out, he says, a feather detached itself from

his wings and lay upon the rim of the abyss, gleaming and growing mysteriously. From this miraculous feather God created a beautiful angel, a woman whom he called Liberty. Both God and Satan may claim fatherhood, but actually she is the reconciler of good and evil.

Such voices, in defence of Satan, have been raised in liberal times. Abbé Constant, alias Eliphas Lévi, attempted to be just to Satan. His verdict, however, is confused. He distinguishes between Satan and Lucifer, whom he judges from his hobby-horse; the astral light. In his play, the *Nuptials of Satan*, published in 1890, Jules Bois depicts Satan as a 'beautiful athletic youth, whose crackling hair reflects the heavenly stars like a glistening sea'. Psyche is betrothed to him and 'amidst delicious thunderbolts' the ineffable voice announces reconciliation: 'My pure essence, according to the law, is to be *Love*. I love you both. Be united in suffering. Ultimate reward is promised to you. . . . You are the dear chosen of my wrath. The most glorified you are because the most foolish.' These verses reflect their time and environment, that of the satiated French bourgeoisie. Satan in fact was once represented on the stage of the Folies Bergères, when Monsieur Benglia appeared as Satan in *Sabbat et la Herse Infernal*. The Reverend Father Montague Summers, who did not expect to be reminded of the devil in so gay a place as the Folies Bergères, says in his *History of Witchcraft and Demonology* that this play does not 'call for more than passing mention'.

In Summers's chapter on the 'Witch in Dramatic Literature' we learn of the prodigious amount of 'devil plays' performed upon the stage since the Renaissance. The devil can be an actor. He can be whatever he chooses. He is everywhere, the demonologist Denis de Rougemont says. According to him, the evil one wants to pretend that he does not exist. 'I am nobody,' he says. But he is legion. By definition, he is an imperialist; he is a gangster on the lookout for a kidnapping; he makes us doubt the reality of the divine law; he is a liar, a tempter, a sophist and, though being nobody, he can impersonate as many beings as there are in this world. This is true indeed, for the devil is ever-changing in man's mind, unlike God, whose established image, that of a good and wise old man, has remained constant throughout the centuries. The devil likes to be modern.

He is everywhere. But he is not unique in this characteristic, for we can say the same thing about God. Both are manifest only to him who believes in them. Satan comes to the believer who is haunted by remorse. The diabolic apparition will either compel him to return to what he recognizes to be the good or to yield to Satan, in whose existence he also believes. However, such capitulation is rarely irretrievable, for the good welcomes the repentant.

Hercules struggled with the mythical hero, Antaeus, who regained his force when he was thrown to earth – the earth who was his mother. According to many old beliefs a divinity was hurled to earth in order to be resuscitated thereafter. Concerning the serpent the alchemists maintain that the great miracle is that the poisonous tail contains the healing medicine.

Believing in the good, we can say that an evil deed recognized and corrected is more important to man than the anxiously heeded good, saved from that painful fall to earth. Over-anxiety about one's actions will impede one's life, which in its very nature is subject to error.

This leads to two stories which demonstrate that the devil's claws are not as crooked as many connoisseurs say they are and that he often relinquishes his prey with the sportsmanship of a good loser. Theophilus, the Faust of the Middle Ages, being in need of 'silver and gold', conjured up Satan. The evil one appeared readily, for who could resist so attractive a conjuration:

> Bagabi laca bachabe
> Lamac cahi achababe
>   Karrelyos
> Lamac lamec Bachalyas
> Cabahagy sabalyos
>   Baryolas
> Lagoz atha cabyolas
> Samahac et famyolas
>   Harrahya.

Theophilus, somewhat hesitatingly, gives a sealed parchment to Satan in which he promises to renounce God, His Mother, and everything which is spoken or chanted in church. The document is signed and sealed: no power upon earth or in heaven can save Theophilus. He is rich and miserable. One day, he prostrates himself before the image of Mary. She descends from her pedestal, setting the child upon the floor. Mary begs the child for Theophilus's forgiveness, but Christ remains mute. Finally He says: 'Why, mother, dost thou beg so much for this stinking carrion?' Mary insists, and the infant yields. She calls Satan and orders that he restore the parchment. He hesitates; but threatened, he descends into hell and returns with the contract. 'I do this for the last time,' he says. The Virgin places the letter upon the sleeping Theophilus, takes her child and returns to the pedestal.

A knight who has wasted his whole estate sees himself abandoned by his friends. He rides into the dark forest where the devil is already waiting. This is his proposition: he will give him chests filled with glittering gold in exchange for his fair wife. They agree. Laden with treasures, the knight returns to the castle. 'O, lady dear,' he says, 'wilt thou ride with me through the green and pleasant forest?' In the forest stands a small chapel, where men worship Mary, our worthy mother and lady. The wife wants to stop here to pray. She falls asleep in the chapel and Mary, clad like the noblewoman, steps forth. Knight and Virgin mount their horses and at the crossroads meet the devil, who is confused: 'Thou hast cheated me, promising to bring thy lady fair, and bringing the lady of heaven.' But Mary is firm: 'The woman shall stay with me; she shall live in my son's kingdom, now and forever, Amen.'

It was in the thirteenth century that the devil throve. In that epoch he was hardly the nobody who wants people to believe that he does not exist. On the contrary, he gave daily proof of his bodily reality. It is sufficient to read Aquinas's *Summa Theologica*,

Caesarius of Heisterbach's *Dialogue on Miracles*, St Gregory's famous *Dialogues*, the writings of Thomas Cantimpré and others, to understand that Satan appeared as a tangible individual possessing the senses of man. Moreover, his scent was not agreeable. When disappearing, he left behind an odour of sulphur tainted with hellish putrefaction. In this way too he was the antithesis of good just as holy men and women were wont to emit that proverbial odour of sanctity. Satan's physiognomy was then most unpleasant. One could scarcely recognize in him the ancient promoter of science and the future handsome rebel. The tympanum of the church at Souillac represents Theophilus dealing with Satan as the eleventh century conceived him. Emaciated and clad only in the coat-of-mail apron of the medieval warrior, his features are those of a released mercenary who has exchanged his armour for food. His face, however, is depicted in several variations and is reminiscent of a nightmare. There is something unreal about his figure; his legs and arms are grooved, showing no joints or muscles. The devil of Souillac is unnatural, as if to show that evil is against nature. The Last Judgement at the cathedral of Bourges (thirteenth century) acquaints us with a different type of demon. The hordes of hell have become fearsome and real. They are made up of misshapen human beings, men and women wearing heads upon their bellies, wings on their thighs, and showing other abnormalities, whether appalling or ludicrous it is difficult to decide. Some of their faces are marked by the fantastic features of medieval monsters, others are human.

But let us allow their contemporaries to describe them. Caesarius of Heisterbach informs us that the devil can appear in the shape of horses, cats, dogs, oxen, toads, monkeys, bears; at times, however, he favours the features of a 'decently' clad man, a handsome soldier, a husky peasant, or a good-looking girl. Then again he assumes the form of a dragon, a Negro, or a fish. He is the ape of God, copying all forms with which the creator has endowed man. Being an imitator, however, he is never capable of completely assimilating the original; there is always something missing. In assuming human features, a devil explains concerning his colleagues, '*dorsa tamen non habemus*', 'we have no bottoms'. Such a banal thing as the buttocks devils are incapable of copying, and it is not clear whether this is more offensive to the demons or to man whose head or facial expression they copy perfectly. Instead of the missing part, they wear a second head on their back side.

What is unpleasant about devils is their power of seducing men and women, in assuming the shape of the incubus or succubus. So concrete have they become that they visit the credulous in their beds – but let us omit some of Caesarius's details. Briefly, the devil can procreate, and the ugly Huns are none other than the descendants of the incubi. A similar origin is ascribed to the great seer of Britain, Merlin.

Already in the twelfth century we find the evil one at the court of justice pleading his cause. He accuses mankind and Christ. Such 'legal' treatment of theological problems became popular during the Middle Ages. It attained its most perfect form in the book of Jacobus de Theramo, written in 1382. The infernal powers chose the demon Belial as official representative of the hellish interests, for Belial according to tradition is most expert in legal questions. He appears before God and demands that the deeds of Christ be investigated. God chooses King Solomon as judge, and the accused Christ demands that Moses be his defender. In *The Book Belial* (Augsburg, 1473) a woodcut shows the representative of hell discussing the matter with his uncanny companions. The jaws of hell are wide open and kept in this position by a heavy stick. The devils are sitting in the flaming gap, listening avidly to Belial's dissertations. His gesture is reminiscent of some contemporary preaching scholars; he moves his hands according to Lully's mnemotechnical method. Another

57. Belial before the gate of Hell

woodcut depicts the demon handing his credentials to the imperturbable Solomon in the presence of Moses. The Hebrew king is well suited for the role of judge, for he did have – as the legend reports – many dealings with the demons. In Belial's complaint, we read that *'quidam dictus Jesus* [a certain individual called Jesus] has unlawfully tampered with the infernal rights, and usurped the government of things that are not his, namely hell, sea, the earth and all beings that inhabit it'. Belial does all he can to influence the kingly judge favourably towards him. He dances before him agitatedly, while Solomon watches with obvious satisfaction. The verdict, however, favours Jesus, and Belial has recourse to an appeal of his case.

Another judge, Joseph, the Egyptian king's vicar, is to decide about the infernal appeal. Belial and Moses are pleading vehemently for their clients and finally arrive at a compromise: a committee shall be formed whose decision shall be final. Under the presidency of Joseph, Emperor Octavianus, Aristotle, Jeremiah and Isaiah ponder the problem. Christ is found not guilty. Satan, however, obtains the confirmation of his authority over all the iniquitous damned on judgement day.

Infernal Helpers

Being inhabitants of the inner earth, devils have more experience with earthly affairs than good angels, whose concern is more spiritual than material. The devil is a clever craftsman, a labourer who is usually cheated on pay day. In the dealings of the devil with virtuous men, evil often results in good. Bishop Olaf Magnussen, who signed his treatise on *The People of the North* with his Latinized name, Olaus Magnus, asserts that in Scandinavia devils work in the stables at night; they clean them and feed the animals, who find the stable devils as sympathetic as the stable-men. Devils work also in the mines, whose dark labyrinths are probably familiar, reminding them of their own hellish habitation. As a rule, the noise they make is greater in volume than the work they produce, but they are harmless so long as the miners do not molest them. In the Swiss village of Davos a silver miner mocked them, which resulted in evil consequences, for his head was turned around and it remained in this extremely uncomfortable position the rest of his life.

According to Olaus Magnus, devils are excellent navigators. Possessing power over the elements, they can induce favourable winds. A crude woodcut in the Basel edition of his work depicts a devil at the rudder, holding in his left hand the propitious cloud from which emerges the desired wind. In the same picture, men travel in the air, their heavy wagon pulled by a demon. Such demoniacal services cause us to be suspicious: we ask ourselves anxiously whether the devil's reward in these cases was perhaps not man's soul. First-hand witnesses, however, quiet this fear. The famous monastery at Citeaux was infested by joyous and benevolent devils. Fond of practical jokes, one of them appeared to a novice as the tail of a calf, which disappeared after having flicked across his face. Later he reappeared in the form of a distended eye. In 1221 an infernal visitor made himself useful to a serf. The monastery was famous for its wine, and the vineyard had to be guarded day and night. The serf on watch grew sleepy, so he called the devil to whom he promised a basket full of grapes if he would take his place, and the good devil, overcome by the boy's ingenuity, sat up all night for this modest reward.

In 1130 a devil visited Hildesheim, in Saxony. He would still be there had not the wickedness of men aroused his truly devilish wrath. The devil gained admittance into the episcopal palace and soon gained the confidence of its inmates by making himself useful with his good advice and by his excellent cooking. In those days no true bishop was indifferent to juicy steaks; and the devil lived peacefully between kitchen and council hall, until a rebellious kitchen drudge insulted and beat him. Having complained about this unworthy treatment to no avail, the devil returned to the kitchen, killed half a dozen kitchen drudges, and disappeared.

Being a patron of travellers, the devil appeared to a scholar who was journeying from Guadalupe to Granada. The scholar was met by a black rider who bade him mount his black mare.

They travelled all night with the speed of the wind and at dawn
reached Granada, having completed overnight a journey that
usually took days. The fiendish horseman departed without
harming his fellow traveller and without leaving behind the
usual stench upon which most demonologists agree. That the
devil is not insensible to human candour, we learn from the
Acts of the Saints by Bollandus. A young girl named Agnes was
obliged one day to pass a house of ill repute. When she appeared
before the open door, Satan and a group of his companions flew
down disguised as ravens, blocking the entrance and driving
Agnes away. The unchaste inhabitants of the house as well as
Agnes were greatly astonished, and the latter understood immediately that this was a sign from – heaven. Later she purchased
the house and founded there a nunnery, of which she was the
first inhabitant.

Though intending evil, the devil produces good when treated
justly by saintly or good men. He has built many bridges when
human wit was exhausted, and regularly he has received as a
reward a cat or a dog or a goat, instead of the expected human
being – the first farer across the devil's bridge. A popular print
of the last century depicts the imposing figure of St Cado handing

*58. St Cado and the
devil*

a cat to the disconcerted devil. Below is the bridge, a monument of masonry betraying the true touch of a cunning engineer. Similar bridges exist all over Europe. In many instances men have nearly forgotten to whom they are indebted for this or that particular bridge. They are indeed very forgetful of the helpfulness of others and attribute the talents of outsiders to themselves. Often they behave as wickedly to the devil as malicious artists do to their colleagues. Not only do they steal their ideas and call them their own, but they treat the bereft ones with contempt.

Thus men would have forgotten completely that the bridge of St Cloud in Paris was built by the devil, had not Grillot de Givry reminded them of the undeniable fact. 'Who would believe,' he says, 'that this bridge which leads to the famous park and to the gay Parisian Fair and upon which electric trolley-cars cross, the honest Pont de St Cloud, is the work of Satan?' But the people of St Cloud gave the devil no better a reward than that which he has received from others: he had to be content with a meagre black cat which would have died soon at any rate. A similar reward was given to the devil who built that famous bridge in the Schöllenen gorge in Switzerland, which boldly spans the Reuss river. For modern engineering, the gorge would hold no serious problem, but in those days the site offered great obstacles. One side of the gap is formed by nearly vertical rock formations, and the road had to be carved out from the granite and made secure by masonry. The legend states that a shepherd promised to the devil the first living creature that would cross the bridge if he could span the vital spot which linked the south and north of Europe. When the work was completed, the shepherd drove a chamois over the bridge which the devil had to accept as his reward.

As might be expected, the evil one is also expert at building walls and fortifications. On one occasion he nearly captured a French nobleman, the High Constable of Lesdiguières, whose castle he had girdled. It was agreed that the castellan's soul would be the devil's reward if the former were unable to escape before dawn. The devil thought that he could finish the wall in time to trap the nobleman in his castle, but the latter fled on his horse at the very moment when the wall ends were being joined together. So narrow was his escape that the horse's tail got caught in the joint, but the rider freed himself in cutting it off with his sword and then galloped a hundred miles before he dared to stop. And thus the devil got nothing, not even a cat! Bits of horsetail are still to be seen in the castle's wall.

England and Scotland in the days of old were separated by a huge wall, fragments of which still exist. So solid was its cement and so perfect its joints that from time immemorial it was called the devil's wall. Many more examples could be cited to prove that the devil is not as formidable and black as he has often been depicted and that he has been approached from time to time by good and energetic people who returned from their ordeal with not even a hair of their heads harmed.

Unholy Images

It has been noted above that devils can borrow any shape they choose. Such an opinion has been expressed by many demonologists; others, tarring all things with the same brush, have tended to standardize the devil, saying that he and all his fellow devils are horned and hoofed and possess tails. There are authorities, however, who assign to certain infernal inhabitants a corporeal personality which is not a disguise of the nobody but their characteristic form. John Wier held this belief. He was a great traveller, and when entering a new country, his first question was concerning its devils. In this way he collected an impressive number of infernal beings among whom we will mention a few, depicted by Louis Breton, the master engraver, 'according to formal documents'.

Bael is the greatest king below; his lands are in the East. He has three heads, that of a toad, that of a man and that of a cat. His voice is hoarse. He is a law expert and his hobby is fencing. He brings wisdom to man, but can also render him invisible. Sixty-six legions of devils obey his command. Forras, or Forcas, is a renowned president in hell. He looks like a strong man. His wisdom is great; and more than others, he knows the marvellous virtues of herbs and stones. He too can render man invisible. But he can even do better than that, for he teaches rhetoric, logic and mathematics. With his help, the magician will detect treasures and find lost objects. Forras renders man vivacious and ingenious. Buer, also a president as well as an expert in ethics and logic, is concerned mainly with healing juices found in plants. He bestows familiar spirits and this power makes him very desirable to man. He commands fifty devil-legions. Wier says that Buer is as visible as a five-branch star, a form which Louis Breton interprets in an original way.

59. *Bael*

60. *Forcas*

61. *Buer*

62. *Marchocias*

Marchocias is a great marquis in hell. He appears with a
griffin's wings and a snake's tail. 'His mouth vomits out something,' Wier says, 'I do not know what.' When Marchocias
adopts a human shape, he resembles a courageous soldier. When
you ask him questions, he will answer truthfully. Before Satan's
fall Marchocias belonged to the dominations. Now he commands
thirty legions. He hopes to be reinstalled upon the seventh
heavenly throne after twelve hundred years, but this, Wier says,
is a vain hope. Astaroth, a mighty lord, looks like an ugly angel.
He sits upon a dragon of hell and holds a viper in his fangs.
Astaroth knows the past, the present and the future – everything that is concealed. He speaks freely of the creation of all
spirits, of their fall, in what way they have sinned and how they
were precipitated into hell. He claims not to have fallen voluntarily, which betrays that he has not yet overcome his grief. He
is the patron of the liberal arts. Though not included in Wier's
pseudo-monarchy, we mention finally the heavy Behemoth
whom Louis Breton has depicted so dramatically. Wier mentions
him in another section of his voluminous work, recalling that the
Creator spoke to Satan: 'Here is Behemoth, whom I have made
together with you. He devours grass like the oxen, and his
strength resides in his loins. His virtue is upon the navel of his
belly.' Besides this uncanny fellow, who seems to symbolize
brute force and whom Wier has wisely omitted from his infernal
government, the rulers below are endowed with great wisdom
and manifold knowledge, according to the tradition of antiquity
with which Wier must have been acquainted. His demons are
repulsive scholars, sophisticated city devils.

The peasantry, however, clung to their old images. In the
country the evil one does not teach philosophy. There he offers
more practical advice and instead of the treasures of wisdom, he
gives money. To the peasant he appeared and still appears in
the beastly shape of old, with horns, hoofs and tail. Thus he is
depicted in the black books of the last century, wearing occasion-

63. *Astaroth*   64. *Behemoth*

ally a fringed jacket, as if to pay tribute to progressing civilization. His three horns he has donned like a fool's cap, and his goat's feet are those of his ancestor, Pan. He carries money, and for this reason many people have found him sympathetic. But devil's money does not bring lasting wealth, for after a while it changes into horse dung or ashes. Wizards are therefore always eager to get rid of such ephemeral currency. It was literally 'hot money' which burst into flames when thrown upon the earth. Sometimes he borrows the shape of an ox, as we learn from the conjuring book, *The Black Hen*, where he is seen wearing an old-fashioned embroidered frock-coat and frills. But all this does not render him any more amiable. In velvet and lace he is still the old fiend, a redoubtable monster.

The discrepancy between the country and city devil was observed by Francis Barrett, professor of chemistry, natural and occult philosophy at London, who published in 1801 his famous book *The Magus*. In this he undertakes to restore to the rulers of hell their true shape, in an epoch highly conscious of the changes which history has wrought. Thus Barrett despoiled the devils of all the embellishments with which they had been adorned by various eras. For this reformatory enterprise Barrett went to the trouble of drawing the correct outlines of certain demons who had attracted his interest. He depicts Asmodeus as a short-nosed and sharp-toothed fellow and Theutus as a singularly good-natured Anglo-Saxon who hides his small chin behind a voluminous beard. The lascivious Incubus, however, has a keen and rather disconcerting grin which might have deeply impressed Barrett's female students, to whom he used to lecture on the Cabala and ceremonial magic. In Barrett's book there are more of these hellish portraits, inspired perhaps by some fountainheads or architectural ornaments in the good city of London.

Collin de Plancy, to whom the devil appeared in the first quarter of the nineteenth century, confirms the views of the country people. The tempter has in truth the traditional attributes, horns and a tail, but no hoofs. He is eight feet tall but well proportioned. Unfortunately, he encountered St Dunstan who pinched his nose with red-hot tongs and did not release his hold until the nose was longer than a foot! St Dunstan, archbishop of Canterbury, lived in the tenth century, but the memory of such an extraordinary deed has not yet vanished among the English country people. The devil, Collin de Plancy explains, claims to have received most of his deformities from man. They are not in his nature; God has decided that whatever men attribute to him, he must retain. 'Thus at the beginning of my exile, I had no tail,' says the devil, 'until popular belief gave it to me.' The horns were set upon his forehead by ladies and nurses 'who wished to terrify their little charges'. Thus he was laden with gifts which he did not request. His ears are swollen, Plancy says, because every box on the ear, which the exorcizers inflict upon the possessed, must be accepted by the devil who sums up his state by saying: 'I am disfigured so as not to recognize myself. They give me every name and every shape.'

The belief that he is a nobody is erroneous. For from the irrefutable first-hand account concerning him, we learn that Satan has a well defined primary form, in which he appeared to Plancy, saying that at various times he transforms himself into various shapes, merely for a pastime. He is corporeal, material, and sensible, as Psellus claimed in the eleventh century. And since he is, he can walk, write, sleep, speak and strangle; on devil's contracts he places his seal, real wax upon which his hand has impressed his sign or crest, as substantial as that of the mayor. He inscribes bizarre signatures on the title pages of the black books, to show his approval of their devilish contents. Yes, the devil is a concrete being, a somebody. Only those who dislike plastic expression, who proscribe the veneration of images, would have the evil one vanish into limbo. Such iconoclasts do not look at themselves in a mirror without fearing that Satan may appear in it. But those concerned with artistic creation are in some way connected with the Inferno.

To Victor Hugo, Satan appeared as an intellectual athlete, the projection of the poet's desire to have his power of thought combined with physical prowess. When an old man, Hugo was still haunted by the symbols of youth. Adelbert von Chamisso conceived of the devil as an orderly, sad-looking citizen, wearing a top hat and a tidily buttoned jacket. Yet he endowed this banal type with the power to produce marvels. Chamisso wanted the mediocre bourgeois to be an artist, because he was torn between the desire to live independently and to have his income assured. From such a dilemma he could never free himself, and he ended his days as a professor at the University of Berlin. Collin de Plancy's life story clarifies his views on the devil. A child of the revolution, he had early been taught to believe in reason alone. He repressed his longing for religion and wrote many books on the devil, subconsciously seeking God at heaven's back door. He cites authorities who have stressed the devil's inoffensiveness: Jean Bodin had maintained that demons could

do good and angels evil; St Augustine that 'the devil is a chained dog; he can bark, but he cannot bite'; St Bernard that 'if the devil had the power to do evil, he has at any rate not the will to do it'. Plancy feared the beyond. He was converted to Catholicism soon after the publication of his book, *The Devil Painted by Himself*.

65. *The devil and the coquette*

WITCHCRAFT

Possessions

In his *Dialogues* Gregory the Great mentions the modest story
of a servant who swallowed a devil. She had eaten a few lettuce
leaves from the convent garden when she suddenly felt that a
devil inhabited her. An exorcist was called who admonished the
demon to be gone, but the unwelcome guest excused himself,
saying that he had been sitting quietly upon the lettuce when the
girl came and swallowed him. He was duly expelled. This
singular event was the forerunner of frightful epidemics of later
centuries, when entire nunneries were possessed by demons.
In the quietude of the convents, where life was regulated by unalterable rules, devils were always on the alert, precipitating
passions long repressed, awakening desires, and sowing
impatience among the inmates.

In the late twenties of the seventeenth century they found an
easy prey in the monastery of Loudun. One of the nuns was a
young woman whose curious ambitions had frequently alarmed
the others. But Joan of the Angels, as she was called, was the
daughter of Baron Louis Bécier – and the nunnery was poor. As
she knew that the superior of the convent was about to leave, and
her ambition was to occupy her place, Joan refrained from being
extravagant, giving unexpected proof of devotion and humility.
Her strategy was successful, but once she had assumed authority,
she found it no longer necessary to veil her old habits. At that
point, a priest made his appearance in Loudun, one Urbain
Grandier. He was handsome and brilliantly gifted and soon
became the parish priest of the town, being noticed of course within a short time by the ladies. He had ways of consoling widows
and of comforting maidens that were not quite in accord with
his profession.

The consequence of his vainglorious conduct was that several
redoubtable enemies rose against him in Loudun. He had seduced
the daughter of Trincant, the king's solicitor. Then Grandier
met Madeleine de Brou, daughter of the king's councillor,
for whom he composed a witty treatise against the celibacy of
priests. These scandals agitated Loudun. At the nunnery, Joan
of the Angels was strongly moved by all this gossip; she dreamed
of Grandier, whom she had never met. He appeared to her as a
radiant angel, but the words he addressed to her were not those
of a divine being. When Moussant, the old prior of the convent,
died, Joan of the Angels offered the position to Urbain Grandier,
who, however, refused it. Joan's psychic disturbance grew worse,

and her hysterical screams disrupted the nightly quiet of the convent. Ashamed of her weakness, she resorted to discipline, asking the nuns to whip her. The result was inauspicious: after a few days several nuns suffered hallucinations similar to those of Joan.

Incapable of appeasing the storm she had caused, Joan sought help from Canon Mignon, a relative of Trincant. They decided that Mignon should carefully investigate the details. Grandier's adversaries remembered the execution of a priest in Marseilles, Gaufridi, who was burned alive for having bewitched a girl; they hoped that a similar justice could be meted out to Grandier. Exorcists were sent to the nunnery, and the odd ceremonials, the extravagant rituals for summoning devils, which were carried on daily, gave the final blow to Joan's disturbed mind. Her convulsions terrorized the nuns, convinced now that devils infested her and everybody else. One after another, they fell into fits, and amidst their gibberish and shrieks the word 'Grandier' was frequently heard.

Accused by his enemies of having bewitched the nuns, Grandier suddenly became aware of the abyss into which they wanted to drive him. He appealed to the bailiff of Loudun, pleading to have the nuns isolated; but the bailiff's orders were not obeyed by the exorcists. Grandier made another appeal to the archbishop of Bordeaux. The prelate sent his doctor who declared, after having examined the afflicted, that they were not possessed. The archbishop forbade further exorcisms and ordered the nuns to confinement in their cells. Thus peace was re-established and the convulsions ceased. After a while, however, the hysteria began again, and Dr Sourdis had to report that 'the nuns were persecuted constantly by impure temptations'. Day and night they rushed about, calling loudly for Urbain Grandier.

This was the situation when in Loudun appeared the Councillor of State Laubardemont, whose character is depicted by his proverbial saying: 'Give me two lines written by a man – and I will hang him.' He was a relative of Joan of the Angels and the brother-in-law of two other nuns, the ladies Dampierre. Having witnessed the misery that had befallen the convent, he made a report to Cardinal Richelieu, who ordered Grandier's arrest. In 1618 Grandier had written a libellous discourse against the cardinal. Now an occasion for revenge offered itself.

The exorcists returned to the convent, and to the churches also, for now the affair was handled publicly. Father Gault succeeded in dislodging a few demons, and he was cautious enough to have them sign a promise:

I promise that when leaving this creature, I will make a slit below her heart as long as a pin, that this slit will pierce her shirt, bodice and cloth which will be bloody. And tomorrow, on the twentieth of May at five in the afternoon of Saturday, I promise that the demons Gresil and Amand will make their opening in the same way, but a little smaller – and I approve the promises made by Leviatam, Behemot, Beherie with their companions to sign, when leaving, the register of the church St Croix! Given the nineteenth of May, 1629.

Signed: Asmodeus

This strange document is preserved at the Bibliothèque Nationale in Paris. It is written by Joan of the Angels.

The expulsion of the devils proceeded very slowly. Father Gault was succeeded by Father Lactance and Father Surin. The demons signed several other documents. One is dated 30 June 1634. That same year Grandier was burned alive. Before his execution he was tortured by Father Lactance and the Capuchin Tranquille. His legs were broken and he had to be carried on a stretcher to the stake. At that moment he summoned Father Lactance to appear before the heavenly judge within thirty days. Father Lactance died at the appointed time. Others who were involved in this affair – for instance Tranquille – died under similarly strange circumstances. The scandal of Loudun continued until Richelieu cut the exorcists' salaries. The most tenaciously possessed was Joan of the Angels, whom the demon of lust, Isacaaron, tortured with fits, showing, according to the alienists Lègue and Tourette, the typical symptoms of a particular type of hysteria. In 1637 peace was restored. From this time on Joan was rewarded with heavenly consolations and died a holy death in 1665.

The convincing proof of Grandier's guilt was not only the accusations made by the demons through the mouth of Joan and the other nuns, but a pact with Lucifer, 'found' in Grandier's house. It is signed by the priest, and countersigned by the dignitaries of hell: Lucifer, Beelzebub, Satan, Elimi (?), Leviathan and Astaroth. Though the verdict stipulated that all such papers were to be burned together with Grandier, a last-moment decision saved them. One agreement signed by 'an enemy of the Virgin' is half burned as if it had been rescued from the pyre.

An affair at the Louviers convent, where the nuns were tormented by various appearances of Satan, ended no less tragically. There were, however, human apparitions mingled with those of the supernatural, for one nun attacked courageously one of the 'spirits' and was rather astonished when she held a man of flesh and bone in her arms. He escaped through the chimney, and as the nun held him tight, crying for help, he dragged her halfway up the chimney. She fell down, covered with that pomade with which sorcerers used to anoint their bodies.

Here, as in Loudun, the mask which Satan used to wear most successfully was that of a beautiful angel. In such a disguise he succeeded in inducing the nuns to commit grave theological errors. His conversations were full of heresies, so cleverly professed and clothed in such charming words that none could resist them. When objecting timidly that such things had not been taught them by their superiors, Satan answered that he was a messenger of heaven, an angel of divine truth, and that there were many errors in the established dogma. Father Bosroger was charged with the recording of the facts. His book, published in 1652, gives an astounding account of the devil's conversation with the exalted nuns. His style is baroque; a mystical glow emanates from these diabolic conversations, and the transport of sensuality is restrained by rule and reason. And yet what an

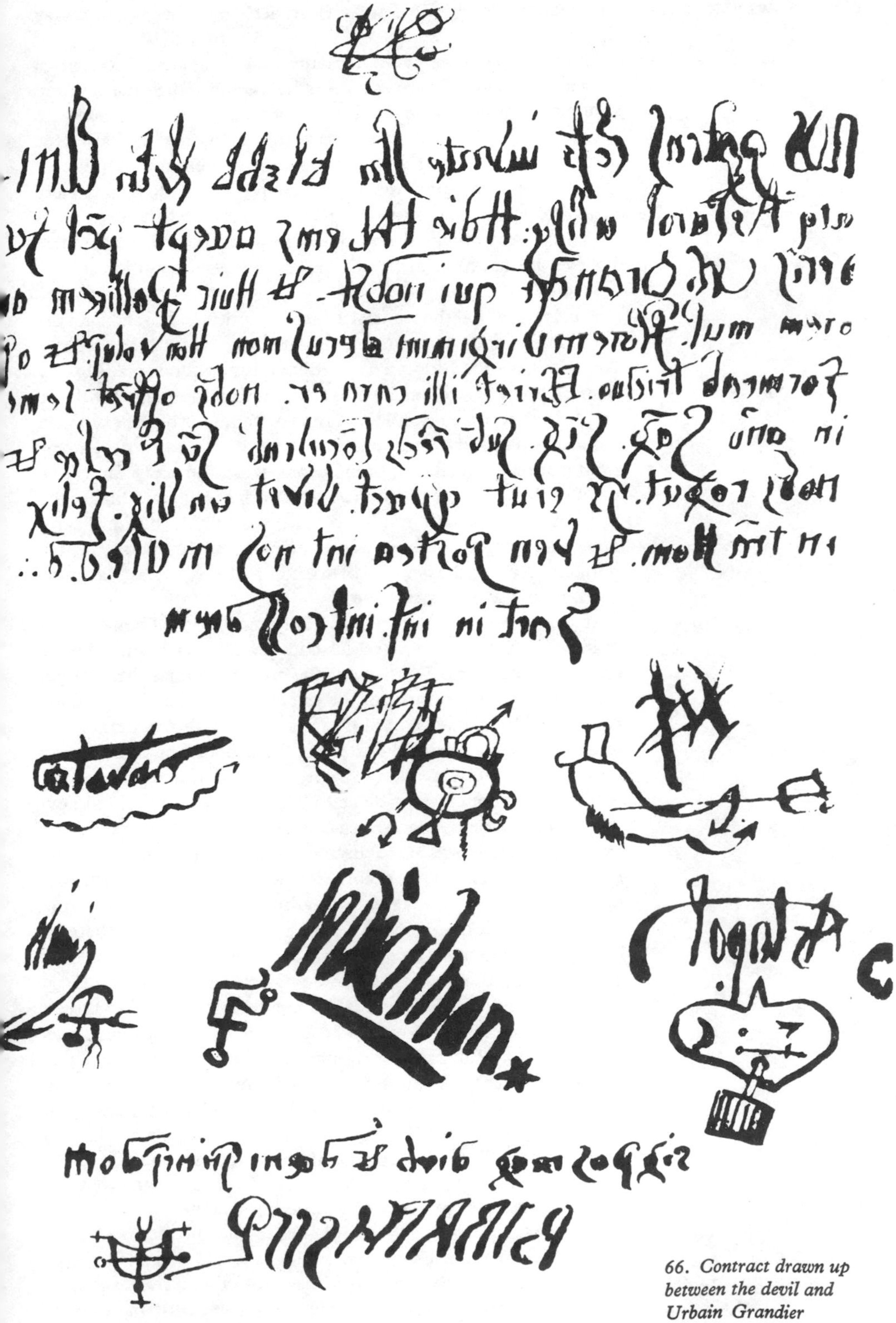

66. Contract drawn up between the devil and Urbain Grandier

abundance of folly did Father Bosroger's cultivated pen convey to paper!

The disturbances were fomented by Madeleine Bavent, a nun in attendance, Mathurin Picard, director of the nunnery, and Thomas Boullé, vicar at Louviers. Madeleine confessed to having been led by the two clerics to the witches' sabbath. She became married to Dagon, a devil, and committed horrible deeds with him upon the altar. There, she said, babies were strangled and eaten, and two men who attended the orgy from curiosity were crucified and disembowelled. One is tempted to believe her account, although her hysterical disposition invites one to be cautious.

During the trial the nuns of Louviers continued to show all the symptoms of possession – contortions, talking in strange languages, insults addressed to the exorcists, wounds made by the demons upon the women's bodies. Their shrieks mingled with the cries of the tortured Boullé and the vociferations of the exorcists. Almost everybody was molested by the inquisitors; cross-examinations, threats, apprehensions were the daily fare. The whole city was dragged into the general hysteria, and finally the parliament of Rouen rendered the verdict. Mathurin Picard, dead a short time before, was exhumed and his body burned publicly. Madeleine was imprisoned in the ecclesiastical dungeon. Boullé was burned alive.

It would be tedious to enumerate many cases of similar possessions. One, however, we do add because its heroines were children. Antoinette Bourignon, the only survivor of her family, wishing to make pious use of the estate she had inherited, founded a school for homeless children. In 1658, with the permission of the Bishop of Lisle in Flanders, the school was transformed into a cloister. The girls were kept, as she says, under strict discipline. No mention is made as to whether they were asked how they felt about being placed in a cloister. After three years, thirty-two of the pensioners were discovered to be witches. The treatment of the girls was, in accordance with the views of the time, rather rigorous. Madame Bourignon, responsible for this convent of minors, reports that every Friday they had to humiliate themselves by admitting their faults in the public hall. These pious exercises were followed by corrections, by whipping, or by confinement in a place called the prison. One girl of fifteen unlocked the prison door and returned to the class, which was considered by Madame Bourignon an act of witchcraft. The girl declared that she had been delivered from her imprisonment by a black man. Three pastors were called, and upon examining the culprit, discovered that she had a devil. Another girl who was to have been whipped declared that the 'crime' she had committed was accomplished with the help of somebody and that she would confess everything if she were not beaten.

'Taking her aside in my chamber, she told me that it was the devil. He was a handsome youth, a little taller than herself.' Such children-devils must have pleased the other girls, for shortly afterwards, thirty-two novices told about their little man-devils who were kind to them, caressing them day and night, escorting them to witches' festivals, etc. It seems quite clear that the girls, having experienced but little affection in Madame Bourignon's establishment, compensated their sad existence with day dreams of an adventurous life. They preferred to be exorcized to being penned in and fustigated. Madame Bourignon reports also that she lodged adults, such as a girl of twenty-two whose confessions were those of a disturbed adult. Having been subjected for eight months to exorcism and penance, she admitted to having attended regularly the nocturnal assemblies of the Sabbath, 'where every devil brought from day to day his love, whether male or female. . . '.

The exorcisms continued with admonitions, prayers, interrogations, punishments, until the devil appeared to Madame Bourignon in the form of a little wrinkled woman with a wry mouth. It is not reported whether this wealthy spinster endured now the same treatment she had found convenient for her pupils, and whether she was exorcized, admonished, and punished. The three pastors lost patience and the affair was brought to court. The judges were extremely lenient with these 'criminals'. Only one, an adult, was imprisoned – she had begged to be put to death. The little tract ends gracefully, that it 'was never known what since has become of her'.

The Sabbath

No mention shall be made of witches, who do not exist.

King Koloman of Hungary

Upon lonely roads on clear nights men and women could be seen walking in silence towards a well-known gathering place. Young and old marched on, attracted irresistibly by some magic force, a bleating voice summoning them from the forest or from the plain. Upon the crossing of some desolate tracks, the master awaited them. The women carried sticks and brooms, upon which they had fixed candles. When reaching the assembly, they straddled their besoms and entered the company's circle, hopping and shrieking. Cries coming from the midst of the crouching witches answered them. The sabbath was rarely disturbed by undesirable spectators. When the shouts and the music reached the pious, they closed the shutters and crossed themselves. The boldest witch persecutors turned a deaf ear, for they knew that Satan was present at the sabbath and weapons were of little avail against the master of darkness.

The gathering took place preferably near a rotten tree, a road sign or a gibbet. Under the pretext of magic rites, a carnival of lust unfolded its grotesque pomp. The sabbath became sinister when the old pagan rites were no longer considered the revival of a decayed past but evil activities born of heresy and witchcraft. Together with the devil, the witch made her entry into the Middle Ages. At the beginning of the eleventh century the historian John of Malmesbury tells the story of a witch who was carried away on the devil's horse garnished with iron pikes. He reports also that two old women on the highway of Rome transformed men into horses and mules whom they sold for pack animals. John of Salisbury also reports a witches' sabbath where the devil appears in the form of a goat or a cat. In the thirteenth century, when the devil lore had attained its definitive form, Vincent of Beauvais mentions 'wandering dames', witches who fly to gatherings: and William of Auvergne confirms these views, speaking of the canes and sticks upon which the sorceresses ride through mid-air.

Up to the eighteenth century the belief was common that witches could fly with the speed of the wind. Perhaps it was a demon who carried them in such a way, or a devil in the shape of a goat or a griffin, or the enchanted stick, broom, pitchfork, or magic wand. Guazzo, the famous demonologist, depicts in his book *Compendium Maleficarum* (Milan, 1608) a witch riding a supernatural winged goat; and Ulrich Molitor, the well-known legal authority from Constance, illustrates his report on the lamias (1498) with a crude yet striking woodcut: two witches and a wizard ride together upon a fork, having the heads of an ass, a hawk and a calf. It was generally accepted that witchea could transform themselves into animals. Sometimes, however,

67. Witch astride a diabolical goat
68. Departure for the Sabbath

they wore animals' masks and hides, as had been customary in the Bacchanalia. In fact, many activities of the sabbath remind us of the ancient cults of Diana, of Janus, the two-headed god who rules over the crossroads, of Priapus and Bacchus. The nightly gatherings in the open air, against which the defenders of the faith had fought so vigorously, were remnants of the *religio paganorum*, the religion of the country people. But the animals' hides and horns were now considered as the devil's attributes. Often the disguise was mistaken for the original and before long the fur-clad master or president of the sabbath was believed to be Satan in person.

What was the aim of these witches' gatherings and what ceremonies were performed on such occasions? The goodly people were certainly as frightened as they were curious to

know about the sabbath, to which the sorceresses made mysterious allusions. From the witches' confessions, we can re-create
many such details; it is, however, difficult to say whether any
of them correspond to the actual happenings for, under torture,
the witches confessed whatever the judges wanted them to.
Many among these wretched women, lacking imagination, were
only too pleased to have their answeres suggested to them, since
confession was the only way of ending the torture. The reports
varied, depending upon the particular country, but all demonologists and witches agreed that for the nightly flight through
the air, a pomade was necessary – a narcotic oil with which the
sorceresses themselves as well as their magic sticks had to be
anointed. Such witches' ointment was not an invention of the
Middle Ages. In his *Metamorphoses* the novelist Apuleius
(second century of the Christian era) already describes its use.
With specific salves witches could transform themselves into
various animals. The hero of Apuleius's novel, probably the
author himself, is peeping through a chink in the attic door
behind which the sorceress, Pamphila,

having unlocked a certain cabinet, took out of it several little boxes.
Removing the lid from one and pouring some ointment therefrom,
she rubbed herself for a considerable time with her hands, covering
herself with the oil all over from the tips of her toes to the crown of
her head. Then, after she had muttered a long while in a low voice,
over a lamp, she shook her limbs with tremulous and jerky motions,
then gently, until soft feathers emerged from her; strong wings grew,
the nose was hardened and curved into a beak; the nails were compressed and crooked. Thus did Pamphila become an owl.

When the time for the sabbath came, the witches felt uneasy,
they itched or felt pains. They interpreted these physical
symptoms as signs that the master was waiting and disliked
having his summons ignored. The witches on such an occasion
disappeared to a solitary place, in the attic or cellar or any room
having a fireplace, for it was through the chimney that they
ascended into the air. They oiled themselves with the witches'
pomade, murmuring all the while their incantations. Suddenly
they flew up – or thought they did. The poisonous pomade, it
has been said, affected their spines. A fit overcame them. In
such a state of trance, they thought themselves to be at the
sabbath. A modern demonologist has tried to explain their
ability to fly by some occult phenomenon such as levitation.
Citing the legends of saints, he professes that in a certain state
of exaltation human beings can rise into the air and transport
themselves from one place to another. To such a fantastic
assertion we oppose the older and better witnesses who have seen
witches lying rigidly in their trances, insensible to pain. When
they awoke, they related their flying experience, and talked of the
meals they had shared with their companions at the gatherings,
and so forth.

The witches' meal was an important part of the rites of the
sabbath, and such rites did without doubt occur. Witches used
to attend the sabbath in person, even though they had to go on
foot. In Guazzo's book an illustration depicts the banquet on the

69. *The Sorcerers' feast*

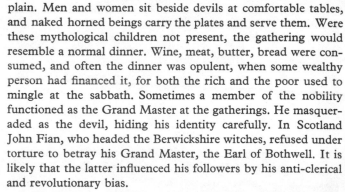

70. *The meal at the Sabbath*

plain. Men and women sit beside devils at comfortable tables, and naked horned beings carry the plates and serve them. Were these mythological children not present, the gathering would resemble a normal dinner. Wine, meat, butter, bread were consumed, and often the dinner was opulent, when some wealthy person had financed it, for both the rich and the poor used to mingle at the sabbath. Sometimes a member of the nobility functioned as the Grand Master at the gatherings. He masqueraded as the devil, hiding his identity carefully. In Scotland John Fian, who headed the Berwickshire witches, refused under torture to betray his Grand Master, the Earl of Bothwell. It is likely that the latter influenced his followers by his anti-clerical and revolutionary bias.

In Molitor's book, an illustration depicts the gathering of the three wives of wealthy burghers. Their dinner is very sober, as it takes place *in absentia diaboli*. No fantastic creatures attend them and without reading the text no one would suspect this to be a witches' gathering. But Molitor reminds us of fantastic happenings when evil spirits infested an inn. They had the features of the innkeeper's neighbours yet they were evil demons who disappeared when St Germanus exorcized them.

Considering the epoch in which Molitor published his work (1489), he appears to be rather sceptical. Most of the misdeeds attributed to the witches he believes to have been caused by demons. His book, though endowed with the beliefs of his time, restricts considerably the power of the devil and still more that of the witches. In his epilogue he sums up: 'Save the judgement of the doctors whose opinions are better than mine and to whom I am ready to submit, the devil cannot, by himself or with the help of man, stir up the elements or harm man and beast. He cannot render man inept to generation, if he does not receive such power from the most merciful God.' In other words, it is doubtful whether witches can be punished for activities sanctioned by God. Among other arguments, Molitor professes that the witches' sabbath actually takes place only in the imagination of some wretched woman, that the gatherings are mere illusions!

The voice of this early sceptic found few echoes among the learned. Molitor's book, it is true, was reprinted many times, but belief in the sabbath could not be so easily eradicated from the minds of the people. Artists depicted witches, for they were interested in fantastically grouped naked bodies. Dürer copied the striking engraving by Israel van Mechelen showing four witches ready for departure. Leonardo drew a witch who operated with the help of a magic mirror. Hans Baldung chose the witch as a preferred theme. One of his drawings, dated 1514, describes the sabbath ceremony as a frenzied occasion. A witch rides through the air on a billy goat. She carries a pole ending in a fork, which holds a pot containing an evil brew. Below, four women of different ages sit on the ground, which is littered with magic implements: a human skull and bone, a horse's skull, several pitchforks, etc. A cat is crouching against a middle-aged woman who holds the lid of an earthenware pot, from which

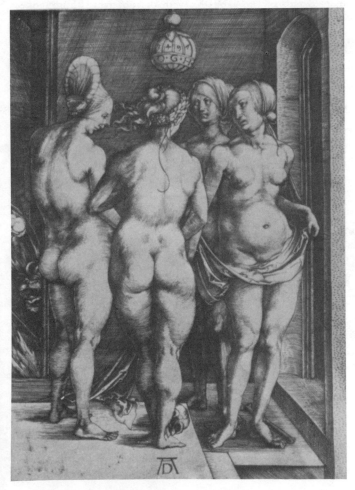

71. *The four witches
by Albrecht Dürer*

escapes a hellish steam, mingled with toads and other 'ingredients' stewed to conjure up hail storms. An old woman raises a metal plate upon which rests a cooked monster, half bird, half toad. She lifts her emaciated arms in a magic incantation. To the left, a younger woman raises her goblet. Behind her is a jug, and some sausages hanging over a witch's fork will be served at dinner, after the incantation has been performed. A gaily bleating goat surveys the improvised kitchen. The scene takes place near a rotten tree.

When the witches were inebriated, the fantastically shaped tree-trunk transformed itself into a huge devil moving his arms in the flickering light of the bonfire. At dawn he turned again into the old familiar tree, whose broken limbs emerged miserably from the morning mist. At the cock's crow, the witches disbanded silently, for the cock is the symbol of light and of pious vigilance. Since time immemorial, the cock was considered a defender against demons; the Hebrews believed that he had only to move his wings to drive away some uncanny visitor. But he was also used for magic operations.

In a less artistic but no less revealing image Guazzo gives us more details of the sabbath. With disconcerting thoroughness the eminent Brother of the Milanesian Order of the Ambrosiani uncovers every deed of iniquity performed at the sabbath. At the gathering, he says, parents bring their children to the demons, whether alive or dead, according to the witch's intention to have her baby either rebaptized or cooked and eaten by the unholy congregation. Newcomers, whether adults or children, have to endure the rites of baptism, Guazzo says. And this is the way Satan proceeds with them: first, they have to deny the Christian faith and withdraw their allegiance from God. According to St Hippolytus, they must say: 'I deny the creator of heaven and earth. I deny my baptism. I deny the worship I formerly paid to God. I cleave to thee, and in thee I believe.'

72. *Sorcerers presenting a child to the devil*
73. *Evocation of the devil*

The devil then marks them with his claw, preferably upon the eye-brow, 'and this mark destroys the one of baptism'. After such a horrible pact the devil rebaptizes his believers, sometimes with filthy water. Then he gives them new names, as in the case of Rovere de Cuneo whom he renamed Barbicapra, 'Goatbeard'. Fourth, he makes them deny again the sacraments of the Church, together with their godfathers and godmothers.

After this, he demands a piece of the initiates' clothing, 'something of their very own', and often, their children. Again, they must swear allegiance to him within a circle drawn upon the ground which according to Guazzo is the symbol of the earth, 'God's footstool' (apparently still thought to be a disc by the Ambrosian doctor). With this ceremony the devil wishes to persuade them that *he* is God.

Furthermore, he inscribes their names in a black book, also called the Book of Death, and they must promise to strangle a child for him every month or two weeks. Still this is not enough, for the devil seems to like thoroughness as much as did Brother Guazzo, who preferred being repetitious to being forgetful. The devil's followers have to offer a gift to their demons to avoid being beaten by them. Such bribes must be black in colour to be legitimate.

Tenth: 'He places his marks upon some part or other of their bodies, as fugitive slaves are branded. He does this not to all but only to those whom he thinks will prove inconstant, preferably to women. Neither does he always mark them upon the same place.' Such a practice, Guazzo explains, shall mock the rite of circumcision. As to the question of why women are included in the old rite, the ingenious Ambrosian has a ready answer: in the New Testament the sign of the holy cross substituted for the circumcision, and this sign is made over all babies of either sex.

The eleventh degree of the initiation sums up various insults and impieties which the devil-worshippers must commit, to the detriment of the Church. They will abstain from using the sign of the cross, holy water, blessed salt and bread, and other consecrated things. On certain days they shall fly, if they can, to the witches' sabbaths. In the meantime no one shall be inactive: evil deeds will be credited by the devil, proselytes should be made, which is difficult as the witch must also promise to be silent about her pact and about the gathering. If they attempt to send misfortune to their neighbours and fail, the evil shall return to the evil-doer, and so on.

The devil's obligations are formulated vaguely. He will always sustain them, fulfil their prayers, and give them happiness after death. One cannot but be astonished that for such little assurance the witches would fulfil these promises. Was it not known from the never-ending witch executions that the master of hell was absolutely unable to assist his flock? It was a very common belief that Satan feared the judges and that he rarely ventured into a prison, if it was not for the purpose of enticing the accused witch to commit suicide. Even the most unintelligent people must have grasped that he never keeps faith nor thinks himself bound by any promise.

Similarly the judges made false promises to the accused. Alleging that they would grant them freedom, they meant, tacitly, to free them from their earthly miseries, or when promising to build them a new house, they meant the pyre. Such false commitments believed to partake of the good were recommended by highly-trained and well-known legal experts. Jean

Bodin, who wrote an excellent book, *The Republic*, professes in his *Daemonomania* that 'it is a virtuous thing, necessary and praiseworthy, to lie in order to save the lives of innocents, and it is condemnable to tell the truth which might destroy them'.

The Devil's Share

Giving up witchcraft is in effect giving up the Bible

John Wesley, 1768

So long as devils retained their debased Neo-Platonic character, they were not dangerous to the Church. But with the advent of the medieval Satan, everything was changed. He also was one. In conceiving Satan, the one devil, theologians disposed the creed towards the old dualism. The devil grew ever more powerful; he demanded his share, that which according to the heavenly decision had been alloted to him. He established himself upon earth and dwelled everywhere in nature. The things of this world became suspect, if not fearful. Satan had become a personality, which whether ugly or beautiful, formidable or beneficent, was of less importance than was his actual existence or his power. With this power, many were willing to compromise.

When the Black Death annihilated whole populations, Satan's rule upon earth appeared unchallenged, and his power undermined the authority of the Church. Theology wanted to rule alone, but had found a redoubtable challenger in its own creation. Many serfs perceived this, not without satisfaction. True, the Church united the higher classes with the humble ones. Master and servant together sang their pious chants in the chapel of the castle; together they bowed their heads when the host was raised. But the peasants were driven to despair by the increasing disorder and growing oppression which dominated Europe.[1] They had to toil for the monks and the noblemen; and their misery is inconceivable today. In the Middle Ages, they learned that there was no hope in open revolts. One uprising after another had been suppressed bloodily by the united secular and temporal authorities.

Despairing, the serf took refuge in dreams. He clamoured for the old deities, who had been driven into shelter but who continued their mysterious life, many living as gnomes under the good earth. These had grown very small and very ugly, but they were full of beneficent activities, and they were fond of the humble man, whose skin was as brown and as wrinkled as their own. Fairies lived in trees and springs – beautiful ladies of the supernatural, far more powerful and fairer than the haughty chatelaines, who exploded with laughter when the lord of the castle related the cruelties and vexations the village women had to endure from his own men.[2]

The early revolts had shown that large masses were so profoundly dissatisfied with the Church that they were ready to sacrifice their lives in the struggle for transformation. State and Church united in the defence of established society, and revolts were suppressed. But the desire for a thorough change continued to haunt the humble. In fairy tales, transformation is the main

element of the marvellous: a pumpkin transmutes itself into a
carriage, shabby clothes become shining garments, coarse food
an exquisite meal.³ An old witch fond of human flesh lives in a
house made of sweetmeats. Who else is she but the druidess of
old, living in her forest temple where she performs the rites of
human sacrifice, and where the devotees come to offer their
food?

In the fairy tale, the ancient faith survived. The country
people clung to these images despite assertion by the priest that
they were delusions sent by the devil. The old gods suited the
humble people better than the new one, whose representatives
were their severe masters and whose symbol was that of bloodshed and suffering. A witch confessed to de Lancre that her devil
had one face in front, the other at the back of the head. 'Just as
the god Janus is represented,' the learned judge adds, and he was
perfectly right. Another witch said that her devilish paramour
looked exactly like a billy goat with a human face. It was none
other than old Pan.

With the devil's establishment of his power, the ancient
survivals, the amusements of serfs, the most innocent stories,
were henceforth Satanic, and the women who knew about the
old legends and magic traditions were transformed into witches,
or evil fairies, as the old stories call them. The traditional
gatherings, the Druids' festival on the eve of May day, the
Bacchanals, the Diana feasts, became the witches' sabbath; and
the broom, symbol of the sacred hearth, though retaining its
sexual significance, became an evil tool. The sexual rites of old,
destined to stimulate the fertility of nature, were now the
manifestations of a forbidden carnal lust.⁴ Mating at random, a
survival of communal customs more ancient than the Old
Testament, the judges now decided to be an infringement of the
most sacred laws. The peasants felt differently about these old
traditions. They had been taught by their lords not to be
jealous; their wives and daughters were at the nobleman's mercy
if he desired them. For the peasant, the people of the nightly
gatherings were equals with whom he was willing to share everything; he had the same feeling about this as the primitives of
the South Sea islands do, or did. It was not a perversion, but a
primitive and innocent custom. At the sabbath he was free to do
as he pleased. He was feared also; and in his lifelong oppression,
this gave him some dignity, some sense of freedom. Here he
could give himself to excitement without the interference of the
Church, that wanted to regulate even human emotions. If this
was Satanic, the peasant thought, I shall cling to Satan.

The sabbath and the witch existed because there were non-
conformist people in Europe who, oppressed though they were,
clung to the defeated gods of the past, their brethren in oppression. Today we tend to overlook the fact that the new religion
was alien to Europe, whereas the old peasant customs were
rooted in the very soil where they had always lived. Most of the
resentment which religion was earning had sprung from the
feeling that it was something foreign and that it had come from a
remote land, from the East. The old aversion was still alive in

our epoch, when a nation, Christianized for a thousand years, reinstalled her pagan customs, reminding the citizen of his bond with the soil upon which his ancestors had lived.

Persecution produced resistance and also leaders for such resistance; and Satan, who represented nature, freedom, hatred of the established order, became a political figure. Witchcraft was considered a penal offence in legislation ordained by Catholics and Protestants alike, and by the leaders of the state. Wherever the voice of freedom was heard or an original idea was expressed the authorities detected the activities of Satan.

In the Middle Ages, when an ideal of order and unity still seemed attainable, witch persecutions were clad in a relatively mild form. With the increasingly disturbed social order of later times, the desperation of rulers was demonstrated in their means of defending religion and the state, and the witch burnings degenerated into the most horrible orgies. The authority of the old Church was tottering, but the reformed faith brought no respite to the sorceress. Calvinism denounced all happiness as sin.[5] In Calvinistic Scotland the judges proceeded with ever-growing eagerness, but these rigorous ideals fought a losing battle against the growing attraction which banished nature exerted upon men's minds. Although timidly at first and under haphazard leadership, investigation into the things of nature produced a new world, of which the sorceress with her healing herbs and simple remedies could be called a forerunner.

The Witch

In his book on the inconstancy of evil angels and demons, Pierre de Lancre (died 1630) gives a detailed description of all the activities at the witches' sabbath. He had gathered his material from accused sorceresses. In 1603 a complaint was filed at the parliament of Bordeaux describing the disquieting increase of witches in the districts of Bayonne and Labourd. Pierre de Lancre was charged with the inquiry and he acquitted himself well of so delicate a task. During the years 1609–10 the prisons were not spacious enough to hold the multitude of witches indicted by the king's councillor. De Lancre, a scholar and patron of the fine arts, reported on all these activities in his elegantly written work, for which Jean d'Espagnet, his friend and occasional collaborator, had made a beautiful Latin introductory poem.

The aim of the treatise was above all to prove that the witch-trials were held 'more juridically and more ceremoniously than in other empires, kingdoms, republics and states'. The form of the procedures was apparently of greater concern to de Lancre than the crimes which he judged. But this was only in appearance, for the king's councillor was fascinated by the accounts of these evil women, who embellished their confessions in order to please the over-curious magistrate. Such obliging ways, however, did not save them from the stake but only delayed their condemn-

ation, for de Lancre decided that the simple fact of having assisted at the sabbath sufficed for the verdict, punishment by death. He adorned his book with a large etching, depicting in an impressive panorama the entire ceremonial of the nightly gatherings. The centre is occupied by the cauldron in which the evil women brew their poison. In its nauseating vapours evolve witches, demons and obnoxious insects. To the right a banquet is being held: women of different social rank sit together with the devils with whom they share the horrible repast – a cooked baby. To the left children watch the toads that will serve to poison the cauldron.

Such venom was used, de Lancre says, for various purposes. It was a greenish water, or an unguent strong enough to kill when brought into contact with the victim's clothes. In their earliest years children were taught to concoct such mixtures, active also in powder form. A sorceress, Rivasseau, revealed its composition: 'They make it with a flayed cat, a toad, a lizard and a viper, which they lay upon live coals until they are reduced to ashes.' When stinging worms appeared, the poison was ready for use. Witches' unguent, according to the confession of a girl, Androgina, could be used for the oiling of door latches. She alleged that every inhabitant of the house was killed by this crime, perpetrated at Geneva in 1563, as reported by Jean Bodin. But the most common use of the evil powder was made for the poisoning of crops, of fruit and wheat. 'In Labourd,' de Lancre says, 'they sow it, saying in the Basque tongue: "This is for

74. The witches' Sabbath, after Ziarnko

wheat, this for apples." To the grapes they say: "You will come in as flowers and not as fruit." '

In de Lancre's etching the spectators grouped behind the children are all people of wealth and social position, men and women accompanied by devils. In the background six nude witches perform a backward *sardana* to the music of a female orchestra. At the right, behind the feasting anthropophagites, another dance is performed by women and demons around a young tree, not far from the devil enthroned, a four-horned billy goat mounted by a will-o'-the-wisp. The master is flanked by the queen and the princess of the sabbath. A child is presented to him by a kneeling sorceress and a butterfly-winged devil. These were the details which de Lancre learned from the Labourd witches. They reported this freely without being tortured, he assures us. No doubt they preferred the voluntary confession to the excruciating procedures prescribed by the sixteenth-century laws for the extortion of the truth. These wenches surpassed each other in fantastic accounts, of which many are of a nature that forbids repetition.

A few of the councillor's remarks, however, will outline the atmosphere of phantasy and sadism in which the trials and executions took place. De Lancre reports with astonishment that a witch called Detsail refused to be kissed by the hangman, 'a handsome youth' who tried vainly to extort the 'kiss of pardon' from the girl tied to the stake. 'She did not wish to profane her lovely lips which yet had so often kissed the devil's back.' Elsewhere, de Lancre tells us that a young witch of fifteen or sixteen was forgiven after full confession and a declaration that she was able to detect all witches and wizards by their devil's marks. She was appointed to examine men and women, and this vicious girl brought numerous goodly people to the stake. With obvious pleasure, de Lancre reports also a Spanish mass execution, an *auto-da-fé*, which he describes in great detail. The imposing pomp of the Spanish Inquisition impressed him greatly, and he did all he could to 'improve' the Labourd district.

It would be a mistake to suppose that de Lancre was an exception in his time. The witch problem had induced a science that occupied large groups of scholars. They were not lawless and ignorant but on the contrary represented the flower of learning. Jean Bodin, for instance, who finds no method too vile to be applied in witch trials, was a great authority on law. It is rather unexpected to find that he revealed throughout his life a tolerance which proved nearly fatal to him during the Night of St Bartholomew. After the Parisian massacre of the Protestants he had to leave the capital because he was suspected of having defended them and of having recommended tolerance.

Henri Boguet (died 1619), an eminent and humane legal expert, judge of the province of Burgundy and president of the tribunal of St Claude, was implacable in witch questions. In his *Discourse on Sorcerers* he shows fanaticism and a disconcerting cruelty. This book, which ran into at least eleven editions, was for a long time an authoritative work for French parliaments and bailiwicks; it is a collection of horrid, ridiculous, indecent details.

Ein erschröckliche geschicht/ so zu Derneburg in der Graff-
schafft Reinstepn am Hartz gelegen von dreyen Zauberin vnnd zwapen
Mafien/ In ettlichen tagen des Monats Octobris Im 1 5 5 5. Jare ergangen ist.

75. *Three witches burned alive*

Boguet pronounced or ratified about six hundred capital sentences against witches.

Nicholas Rémy (1530–1612), after having filled several important legal positions, was appointed secretary to Duke Charles III of Lorraine, and one year later became a member of the supreme court at Nancy. He wrote several valuable works, such as a *History of Lorraine*. Yet his most famous, or infamous, treatise is the *Demonolatry*, a voluminous collection of witch-trial examinations and their results, representing his knowledge of magic charms, incantations, spells, the sabbath, and hundreds of details concerning witches, gathered from the confessions of indicted persons. This learned man is credited with the condemnation to death of some nine hundred sorceresses, an impressive number which, when divided by his fifteen years of public service, averages more than one witch a week.

These examples may suffice to illustrate the problem of reconciling the apparent inconsistency of the learnedness and integrity of these scholars with their cruelty and prejudices. Two possible solutions present themselves: that there were no witches, and that the judges were fools and ogres; or that witches existed and these men performed their horrible duty. Both explanations are fallacious.

There were no witches, as the persecutors understood them. They could not fly upon a broomstick, they could not conjure up hailstorms, and their snake and toad stews contained hardly any poison. Yet, actually, witches did exist, and the sabbath likewise existed, attended by men as important as the Earl of Bothwell. No more did the judges pronounce their verdicts against public opinion. On the contrary, they were to a great extent in agreement with popular views. Moreover, the belief in witches and the conviction that they must be destroyed were the few ties which united all classes in the sixteenth century –

the rebellious peasants as well as the conservative burghers, Catholics and Protestants, the clerical and the secular judges.

A modern philosopher, Ian Ferguson, has attempted to show the good contained in the reckless witch persecutions. He declares that without bloodshed and persecutions resulting from a spiritual effort, there is no human progress. 'Out of bloodshed comes bloodshed,' he says, 'but out of lethargy comes extinction.' Having witnessed in our day persecutions far more terrible than any imagined in the past, we have become cautious about bloody experiments. It will take a long time to prove again that oppression and the annihilation of minorities will produce any – even minor – good for the oppressors.

The Pursuit of an Ideal

Attendance at the sabbath by the members of the upper classes, encouragement of these mock-revolts by men of politics, was of evil consequence to the witch. Divergent ideas found a common expression in her gatherings. Most of the wealthy spectators were persons eager to witness something forbidden, and their curiosity indicated that established authority was losing ground among all classes. No wonder that rulers agreed upon the uprooting of witches, without regard for those of higher standing involved in this hoax. Those who were not willing to keep things in their proper place and who mingled with these treacherous wenches must be eradicated as well. To a certain degree, envy, hatred and greed may have contributed to the spreading of the persecution, but these motives are not an adequate explanation for the terrible storm that devastated Europe for centuries. An abridged list of persons executed in the bishopric of Würzburg may serve to illustrate this.

The Sixth Burning, six persons:
    The steward of the senate, named Gering
    Old Mrs Canzler
    The tailor's fat wife
    The woman cook of Mr Mengerdorf
    A stranger
    A strange woman

The Eighth Burning, seven persons:
    Baunach, a senator, the fattest citizen in Würzburg
    The steward of the dean of the Cathedral
    A stranger
    A knife grinder
    The gauger's wife
    Two strange women

The Eleventh Burning, four persons:
    Schwerdt, a vicar-choral in the Cathedral
    Rensacker's housekeeper
    Stiecher's wife
    Silberhans, a minstrel

The Thirteenth Burning, four persons:
    The old smith of the court
    An old woman
    A little girl, nine or ten years old
    A younger girl, her little sister

The Fourteenth Burning, two persons:
    The mother of the two little girls before-mentioned
    Liebler's daughter

The Twentieth Burning, six persons:
    Goebel's child, the most beautiful girl in Würzburg
    A student who knew many languages, an excellent musician
    Two boys from the Minster, each twelve years old
    Stepper's little daughter
    The woman who kept the bridge gate

The Twenty-Fifth Burning, seven persons:
    David Hans, a canon in the New Minster
    Weydenbusch, a senator
    The wife of the innkeeper at the Baumgarten
    An old woman
    The little daughter of Valkenberger was privately executed
        and burnt on her bier
    The little son of the town council bailiff
    Wagner, vicar in the Cathedral, was burnt alive

The Twenty-Eighth Burning, six persons:
    The wife of Knertz, the butcher
    The infant daughter of Dr Schultz
    A blind girl
    Schwartz, canon at Hach
    Ehling, a vicar
    Bernhard Mark, vicar in the Cathedral

The Twenty-Ninth Burning, five persons:
    Viertel, the baker
    The innkeeper at Klingen
    The bailiff of Mergelsheim
    The wife of the baker at the Ox Tower
    The fat noblewoman

From this excerpt we may gather that the victims met with death for one reason alone: they were believed to be wizards and witches. Greed could not have condemned poor strangers, envy could not have destroyed the blind girl of the twenty-eighth burning. Indeed, what horrible hatred would have brought innocent children to the stake, except such as was born from the fear of a social and moral catastrophe threatening the very traditions upon which the past had been built?

A schism took place within the classes. One group clung to the spiritual ideal of old, seeing hope and salvation only in the pursuit of the most rigorous religious ideal: fasting, chastity, purity, self-punishment, concentration upon that which comes from above, the renunciation of pleasure, the rejection of every material good which the fruitful earth offers its inhabitants, discipline, preparation for the hereafter. By such superhuman efforts, a turning of the tide was attempted in order to avert pest, strife, catastrophes, in order to reconcile the irate Father by coordinating all activities for the sole glory of God.[6]

The other group turned towards what could roughly be called materialism. The earth offered pleasures which were no sins, relaxations necessary for man's well-being. From discoveries and inventions emerged new necessities. Capital began to expand, industries were started on a modest scale. Diseases were not unanimously called the work of the devil. Scientists, as readily condemned as witches, initiated their investigation into the true nature of man. The days were past when popes forbade every surgical intervention accompanied by bloodshed. In the revolutionary sixteenth century, the voices of common humanity asserting its right to pleasure grew ever louder, and well-being was no longer considered the privilege of the few.[7] The rigid hierarchy of feudalism had collapsed; cities acquired liberties; the lower classes started to think and to question the legitimacy of knight's privileges.

Peasants posted a couplet at the Emperor Maximilian's palace:

When Adam toiled and Eve spun,
Where was then the nobleman?

To which the Emperor answered honestly, and according to his firm belief:

I am a man like every man,
My honour came from God alone.

In the midst of this turmoil stood the witch, something more than an evil woman capable of destroying her neighbours. She incorporated in its awesome extreme that which Christian idealists were fighting with all their resources. Yet the incensed crusaders themselves could not avoid being driven by the swelling tide. When Calvin burned the scientist Servet, who had dared declare that the blood in man's veins was circulating, he had still acted according to his ideal.

But witch persecution soon became an industry. It employed judges, jailers, torturers, exorcists, wood-choppers, scribes and experts, and the abolition of the trials would have caused an economic crisis. All those who found their livelihood within the orbit of persecution were interested in its continuation. There was no escape: the witches had to confess. They were driven to such despair that they preferred a most dreadful death to the pleading of their cause. One of the most sensible opponents of these trials, the Jesuit Friedrich von Spee (1591–1635), declared: 'Often I have thought that the only reason why we are not all wizards is due to the fact that we have not all been tortured. And there is truth in what an inquisitor dared to boast lately, that if he could reach the Pope, he would make him confess that he was a wizard.' Canon Loos claimed that the war waged in the name of idealism was controlled by material interests. He called the witch trials a newly invented alchemy, by which human blood is transmuted into silver and gold.

The defence of an ideal cannot be a profession; it must be a vocation. Witch persecutors, however, were craftsmen, with a professional pride. A hangman grew melancholic when a witch resisted him unduly. That was akin to a personal offence. In order to save face he let the accused die under the torture, and thus his honour was not impaired, for the blame for killing would then rest on the devil. The cultivation of such professionals produced a harvest contrary to the noble aspirations which these trials primarily symbolized. The business became so prosperous that the hangmen's wives arrayed themselves in silk robes, rode upon beautifully harnessed horses or in painted carriages – and of course nobody dared reprove them! During witch hunts considerable amounts of wine and beer and food were consumed by the hangmen's assistants. Innkeepers' bills which have come to us bear testimony to this. For every burned witch the hangman received an honorarium. He was not allowed to follow any other profession, therefore he had to make the best of his craft. Soon the torturers had discovered an infallible method for perpetuating their business. Under torture, the witch was constrained to name her accomplices. Thus one trial gave birth to a hundred. It was a Satanic *perpetuum mobile*.

Merry-making was a sin. Popular amusements not ordained by the Church led to hell. With the execution of witches, however, a new kind of macabre merry-making was introduced which could not be found in the old ecclesiastical calendar. The place of execution was no longer the gallows' field, or other uncanny places. Any public square spacious enough to hold the curious was suitable for the purpose, and not far from the pyre were food stalls and other improvised shops where the out-of-town spectators could purchase souvenirs, rosaries, holy images, and pamphlets printed for the occasion.

Sometimes several witches, sometimes a hundred, were burned in one day. Masses, driven by Satan into an obsessional anxiety, projected it upon the condemned who could hardly find one expression of compassion in the crowd. Such executions combined, as Schiller said, the horrible and the comic. They revived the sacrifices of antiquity in their debased form: the circus. The Spanish Inquisition clothed the condemned with a sulphur shirt and a cardboard tiara, on which were painted devils, flames and a human head resting upon burning faggots. The procession moving towards the place of execution resembled those early heathen festivals when mock kings were sacrificed. In Germanic countries, the custom still exists at the carnival to burn an effigy symbolizing winter. Such remnants of the pagan past found a parallel in the *auto-da-fé*, the burning of humans by the Inquisition, as well as the burning of stuffed effigies of indicted persons who had died before judgements had been rendered against them. Such puppets were carried on poles in these pageantries and burned on the pyre with the coffins of the deceased. Judgement was passed in the market place. Scaffolds were erected with special loges for the king, the queen, the nobility, the councillors and all the functionaries of the Inquisition. The ceremony lasted all day. The judgements were proclaimed from special platforms, and the condemned had to stand in a cylindrical cage in the middle of the square, to hear the announcement of their condemnation. A hugh awning was stretched across the square as protection against the sun and the heat, as had been customary in the Circus of ancient Rome, and the sacred fury which animated the crows was restrained by a pompous ceremonial performed amidst comfort. This sacred carnival was further embellished by the varied costumes the condemned had to wear: the sanbenitoes, the samanas, the carrochas. All this was contrived in order to impress the masses.

The results were manifold. Temporary satiation was succeeded by a desire for more; anxiety was not abated; the devil himself could not be brought to trial – only the devil's friend. There were always more witches to be hunted. The spectacle witnessed by young and old was of a nature to affect dangerously the psyche of the people. So long as the procedure rested in ecclesiastical hands, its legitimacy could not be questioned by the believers. But now lay judges showed more fanaticism and rigour than the clerics, who had inherited experience in psychological matters. The conduct of the lay judges was open to criticism and among sober-minded spectators must have awakened a doubt about the rightness of all these procedures.

The spreading of these persecutions was so serious that ignorant or inexpert lay judges in remote parts of the country were now faced with the difficult problem of knowing how to conduct these trials. In England the invention of 'witch-pricking' helped them to solve their perplexity temporarily. By this device, bleeding or not bleeding was used to establish the proof of innocence or guilt. Tedious procedures were no longer necessary for the conviction of the witch. The custom was not new. Previously, however, it had been considered only as a means for the establishment of suspicion, not of guilt. English judges, encouraged by King James's book, *Daemonologie* (1599), did not shrink from even the most primitive means in their search for the guilty.

C. L'Estrange Ewen describes scenes of witch-pricking in the town of Newcastle-on-Tyne, which meant merry-making to its inhabitants, but not to the unhappy indicted women: 'As soon as the witch-finder arrived, the magistrates sent their crier through the town, ringing the bell, and shouting that anyone wishing to lodge a complaint against a woman for being a witch should bring the complaint to the person appointed. Thirty women were brought into the Town Hall and stripped, and pins were then publicly thrust into their bodies. Most of them were found guilty.' The witch-finder was paid twenty shillings for every convicted woman, and Ewen adds that the bluebeard was hanged finally after confessing that he had caused the death of two hundred and twenty women.

Lieutenant-Colonel Hobson, present during the above-mentioned procedure, tried to save one of the suspects. During the examination of 'a personable and good' woman Hobson observed that she was of good repute and did not need to be tried. The examiner, offended in his professional pride, 'said, she was [a

witch], for the town said she was (!) . . . and presently, in the sight of all people, exposed her body, naked to the waist, with her clothes over her head. . . .' As the pin pricks caused no bleeding, he decided she was guilty. Fortunately for this woman, Hobson remarked that 'through fright and shame all her blood had become clotted in one part of her body' which, he thought, had prevented the bleeding. He requested that she be brought in again, 'and required the Scot to stick the pin into the same place, and then blood gushed out, and the Scot cleared her, saying she was not a child of the devil'. Hobson's energetic intervention, which intimidated the witch-finder, saved this woman. Now this experiment could have been attempted with regard to the others condemned, but no one had such a notion. Even the brave Lieutenant-Colonel did not dare insist. To show too great a compassion for these wenches might have caused his own end at the stake or gallows.

Another instance reported by Ian Ferguson is in the same vein, showing to what perversion the pursuit of an ideal may lead:

There came then to Inverness one Mr Paterson, who travelled all over the kingdom trying witches, and was usually called the Pricker. Stripping them nude, he alleged that the spell spot was discovered and could be seen. . . . He first polled all their heads and collected their hair in the stone dick, and then proceeded to pricking the women with pins. . . . This villain gained a great deal of money and had two servants; at last he was discovered to be a woman disguised in men's clothes. Such cruelty and rigour was sustained by a vile varlet's fraud.

The procedures at the trials became as arbitrary, anarchical and chaotic as the alleged activities at the sabbath. In fact, many of the imagined horrors of the witches' gatherings were repeated

76. *An execution of witches in England*

by the persecutors themselves. The pin-pricking resembled strangely the devil's marking of the witches. The magic broth which the accused had to consume before the torture was a mockery of the sabbath meal. The stripping and shaving of the witch were not less licentious than the dancing before Satan.

When at the behest of Pope Innocent VIII the Dominicans Sprenger and Kramer published their guide book for witch-trials, the famous *Witch Hammer,* they understood that the evil activities of sorcerers were to be classified under heresy. They continued the tradition initiated by the inquisitor-general of Aragon, Nicolas Eymeric, who had in 1376 compiled his voluminous *Directory for Inquisitors.* The *Witch Hammer* pronounces that these matters should be judged *in foro ecclesiastico,* by clerical courts. But Sprenger's book did not follow the injunction of Pope Boniface VIII (1294–1303) who had recommended wisely that heretics and witches be judged 'without noise'. Eymeric's work was a manuscript circulated only among a select group of law experts within the Church. But the *Witch Hammer,* originally published in 1485, was reprinted in numerous editions. It made much noise and fell naturally into many non-ecclesiastical hands. In using the printing press as a modern means of distribution, Sprenger thought perhaps that a wide circulation of his carefully written work would open the eyes of many, still unaware of the imminent danger which sorcery had conjured up against the Christian commonwealth. But he himself was not conscious that heresy and witchcraft had both changed their meaning since Eymeric's time and that no pressure was able to avert the danger of a general religious revolt. Trying to strangle in one large embrace every opposition to the Church, he did very little or nothing for his cause. Thirty years after his publication, half the population of Europe became 'heretic', and there would not have been sufficient wood in Christian lands to burn all the Protestants. That the Reformation and witchcraft could not be tossed into the same sack became evident very soon when the Protestants accepted the *Witch Hammer* as the standard work for their own witch persecutions. Even a more farsighted theologian than Sprenger could not have forseen this turn of events.

The witch-trials continued unabated in both Protestant and Catholic countries for a considerable time. In the Swedish village of Mohra a witch epidemic broke out in 1669. The sorceresses took about three hundred children with them to the sabbath upon the imaginary Blokula mountain. At a crossroads, they called out: 'Antecessor, come and carry us to Blokula,' whereupon 'he' appeared, in a grey coat and red and blue stockings. 'He had a red beard, a high-crowned hat, with linen of divers colours wrapped around it, and long garters upon his stockings.' In short, it was a typically Swedish devil. He set them upon a huge beast and carried them over churches and high walls. Twenty-three witches who confessed freely were burned, and fifteen children suffered the same fate. Thirty-six children between nine and sixteen were forced to run the gauntlet, twenty more had their hands beaten with rods on three successive

Sundays, and the 'aforesaid six and thirty were also deemed to be lashed this way once a week for a whole year'. The execution occurred on 25 August 1670. Pastor Antony Horneck who published the account adds: 'The day was bright and glorious, and the sun was shining, and some thousand people were present at the spectacle.'

In Arendsee, Germany, three witches were executed in 1687. They were Susanna, Ilse and their mother Catharine. This Protestant execution was accompanied by an unpleasant religious unction: 'On the way, prayers alternated with exhortations and the singing of hymns. Before Seehausen Gate a circle was made, and Susanna was led round until the public had finished singing the hymn, "God, Our Father, dwell within us". When she was decapitated, the people sang: "To Thee we pray, O Holy Ghost". Next came Ilse, who was killed in the same way, accompanied by the singing of the same hymn. While the singing continued, Catharine was placed upon the faggots and her neck fastened with an iron chain, which was drawn so tight that her face swelled and became suffused with a brown colour. The faggots were lit and all present – clergy, schoolchildren and spectators – sang until her body was consumed in the fire.'

In France things were somewhat better. In 1669 two brothers, Ernoul and Charles Barneville, lodged a complaint at the Rouen parliament about the disquieting increase of witches in the districts of Coutance, Carentan and Haye du Puits. Five hundred persons were suspected, among whom there were a hundred priests. The affair was ready to degenerate into a large-scale persecution. After six months of witch-hunting, twelve were condemned to immediate execution. The burning of thirty-four more was decided upon, and a few had already perished at the stake, when Louis XIV stopped the orgy, commuting the death sentences to lifelong exile. The good parliament of Rouen dispatched its vigorous protest to the king, pleading that the old tradition should be maintained. The king's answer was a stern refusal, accompanied by an injunction that the prosecutions be suspended immediately, which was obeyed.

In England the persecutions reached a new level in 1638. They differed from those of the continent and were on the whole less cruel. Women were not tortured with special instruments but were watched and submitted to the 'water ordeal': when they swam, they were found guilty; when they sank, it meant they were innocent. Excessive and incredible cruelty was, however, not infrequent. In 1608 the Earl of Mar made the following revealing report to the Privy Council: 'Albeit they persevered constant in their denial to the end, yet they were burned quick after sic and cruel manner that some of them died in despair, renounced and blasphemed, and others, half burned, broke out of the fire and were cast quick into it again until they were burned to death.'[8] Many of the English witches were hung, but a large number perished at the stake; and a few were condemned to the pot, i.e., they were boiled alive.

The Scottish trials were worse. In 1678 two old women of Prestonpans were executed, having accused seventeen others before their death. Nine of them, victims of this denunciation, were condemned. In 1679 a group of witches was discovered at Borrowstowness. They confessed to having attended the sabbath, to their intercourse with devils and to similar crimes. Annaple Thompson, Margaret Pringle, Margaret Hamilton, Bessie Vickar and others were found guilty of 'the abominable crime of witchcraft'. They were burned to ashes, after having been 'wirried at the stake till they were dead'.

In 1696 a girl of eleven years saw the maidservant Katherine Campbell drink milk from the can, and threatened that she would report this to her mother. The maid answered angrily that 'the devil might harl the soul through hell'. The child was beset by fits, crying out against the maid. Soon a large number of people became involved, of whom five were burned in 1697. One of the indicted, John Read, hanged himself in prison. The executed were a seventeen-year-old beggar girl, her cousins aged fourteen and twelve, their grandmother, and Jean Fulton. Twenty others were condemned to less drastic punishment. Thus a drink of milk proved sinister in effect. The possessed girl whose name was Christiana Shaw grew up and became an expert in spinning yarn. With the help of a friend, she introduced the famous Renfrishware products. She married a minister and died in 1725, greatly lamented by her husband's flock.

In Italy, where Guazzo had revived the tradition so well, a full-scale trial in 1646 brought misery to many. It took a full year to convict all the culprits. Domenica Camelli, Lucia Caveden, Domenica Gratiadei, Caterina Baroni, Zinevra Chemola, Isabella and Polonia Gratiadei and Valentina Andrei were condemned to death by the assizes of Nogaredo. The sentence was carried out by Leonard Oberdorfer, an Austrian hangman.

Of the trial of Penn, the Quaker who was acquitted in London in 1670, the recorder, Sir John Howell, said: 'Till now I never understood the reason of the policy and the prudence of the Spaniards in enduring the Inquisition; and certainly it will not be well with us, till something like the Spanish Inquisition is in England.' Of the Magna Carta, this man of justice spoke publicly in gross terms. The Inquisition was, however, an institution opposed diametrically to the interests of an expanding England, a trading country relying upon international relations, and a future colonial empire.

The distinction between heresy and witchcraft, religious rebellion and the creed of foreigners, science and magic, was never made by the prejudiced judges of Lisbon and Madrid. Until their demise, they clung to medieval concepts. Protestants, Calvinists, Zwinglians and Huguenots alike were considered heretics, and everything uncatholic was combated. Witches, polygamists, Jews, blasphemers, English tradesmen, astrologers, were thrown into the prisons of the Holy Office. In the seventeenth century the inquisitors condemned to the stake a horse, whom his owner, an Englishman, had taught some tricks. Such retrogressive mentality signified the end of the Spanish empire. In his *History of the Inquisition* Philip van Limborch (1633–1712) says quite rightly: 'This monstrous tribunal of human opinions

is aimed at the sovereignty of the intellectual world, *without*
intellect. It may be restored again, to keep Spain stationary in the
Middle Ages.' As he had foreseen, it was in fact restored and
continued its policy until Napoleon abolished it.

In New England, finally, the witch persecutions appeared late
and in the mildest form possible. The American settlers were
too scattered and too preoccupied with the immediate necessities
of life to spend much time on merry-making. The cruelties also
lacked the refinements which were so highly developed on the
old continent. The total number of witches executed in New
England is inconsiderable and the executions lacked that pomp
displayed particularly in the southern countries of Europe. The
Salem witches were hanged, according to the former practice of
the country, not burned as is generally believed.

Shortly after the happenings in Salem in 1692, people spoke
of them as a calamity A truly astounding and unique fact in the
history of witch-trials is the recantation and public repentance
made by the judge and the jury in Massachusetts. Some passages
of this extraordinary document read as follows:

We confess that we ourselves were not capable to understand, nor
able to withstand, the mysterious delusions of the powers of darkness. . . . On further consideration and better information, we justly
fear we have been instrumental, with others, though ignorantly and
unwittingly, to bring upon ourselves and these people of the Lord, the
guilt of innocent blood. . . . We do, therefore, hereby signify to all in
general (and to the surviving sufferers in special) our deep sense of, and
sorrow for, our errors . . . for which we are much distressed and dis-
quieted in our minds. . . . We do heartily ask forgiveness of you all,
whom we have unjustly offended, and do declare, according to our
present minds, we would none of us do such things again, on such
grounds, for the whole world; praying you to accept this, in way of
satisfaction for our offence, and that you would bless the inheritance
of the Lord, that may be entreated for the land.

Foreman: Thomas Fisk	Thomas Pearly, sen.
William Fisk	John Peabody
John Bachelor	Thomas Perkins
Thos. Fisk, jun.	Samuel Sayer
John Dane	Andrew Eliot
Joseph Evelith	H. Herrick, sen.

We have enumerated all the undersigned, not with the intention to divulge once more the names of those responsible, but in
order to honour these men. They have by their insight, honesty
and modesty rendered a service to humanity. Their repentance
and recantation came, as Kittredge has remarked, at a time
when they proved to be singularly effective arguments in the hands
of the opponents of the witch-dogma in England. And for this
reason, the declaration is not only a great document of American
history but a promoter of the good for all.

The Witch Controversy in English Literature

> How much more natural that our understanding should be carried from its place by the volubility of our disordered mind than that one of us should be carried by a strange spirit upon a broom staff, flesh and blood as we are, up the shaft of a chimney.
>
> Montaigne

A good interpretation of the official belief in matters concerning witches at the end of the sixteenth century is given in the book *Daemonologie*, published in London in 1597. Its author is none other than His Majesty King James I of England. In this short treatise, written in the form of a dialogue between Philomathes who asks the questions and the wise Epistemon who gives the answers, the kingly demonologist sums up the most important problems that witchcraft and magic brought to that epoch. The book attacks the facts directly, and the author unlike others does not get lost in the details, but adheres to the principles of the forbidden arts, their operations and their punishment.

The *Daemonologie* has been severely criticized and has marred the memory of its author, whom Grillot de Givry calls a sinister figure. Mrs Lunn E. Linton wrote in 1861 that his name 'stands accursed for vice and cruel cowardice and the utmost selfishness and fear'. In 1904 Trevelyan blames the king for the enactment of the new 'death law', and Robert Steele's criticisms are similar: 'In the first Parliament of James, the more merciful act of Elizabeth was repealed.' Under the new act seventy thousand persons, Steele says, were executed.

George Lyman Kittredge, to whom we owe these notes, undertakes to rehabilitate the royal witch expert. In his book, *Witchcraft in Old and New England* (Cambridge, Mass., 1928), he proves that according to available records (which might be incomplete) only forty or even less executions took place during the reign of King James – an average of two a year. According to Kittredge, James was sceptical, and a good influence upon the judges. He protected the occultist Dr John Dee and tolerated scoundrels like Forman and Lamb, notorious wizards. Kittredge asserts further that James did not make the Scottish law of witchcraft, which was enacted before the king was born; nor did he teach it to the Scottish nation; such beliefs were the heritage of the human race, and they survived for more than a hundred years after the death of James. The worst period of Scottish witch persecution did not come within his reign.

James was involved in a famous trial that took place in 1590, in which his cousin, the Earl of Bothwell, was denounced by Agnes Sampson as a wizard. The king was then seventeen years old. He was present during the questioning of the witches and also, it is said, during the torture. In reading his work, it appears that James could not champion anything but the traditional, as befits a king. Original ideas are not his strong point; he wrote his *Daemonologie* in refutation of new ideas, namely those of John Wier and Reginald Scot. Wherever James is sceptical, it is upon religious grounds, and he does not miss an occasion to brand the superstitions of the Papists.

He does not believe in werewolves, but assumes that lycanthropy is a disease of people who *think* they are wolves. He declares that the papists' beliefs in the power of the cross to expel devils and in the power of God's name are both superstitions. The rite of exorcism produces good effects, but the conception that created the rite is false. Such subtleties are not convincing. His suggestion that only people of good repute should be accepted as witnesses, however, is an improvement over the French methods of the sixteenth and the beginning of the seventeenth centuries. Moreover, James rejects the bodily or spectral existence of the nightmare, which he claims is a natural sickness. Devils appeared more frequently in papist times; now they had become rare. 'Because before we erred grossly and that mist of error overshadowed the devil to walk more familiarly among them.' And, finally, Satan, Beelzebub and Lucifer are one and the same. These are about all the reformatory suggestions that James made – and they are not his own invention. In the fifth chapter of the *Daemonologie* he gives a clue as to his leniency with Dr Dee and other magicians: to Philomathes's question as to why princes and kings frequently retain magicians, Epistemon answers that evil customs cannot be interpreted as good laws.

James's first book of the *Daemonologie* is devoted to magic and to necromancy, that is, prophecy by the dead. The magicians command the devil, according to their pact signed with blood. After the magician's death, the devil assumes the command. The evil one entices man to forbidden practices through three passions: curiosity, hunger for revenge and greed. Astronomy is permissible, even necessary. Astrology, concerned with seasons, weather forecasts and simple remedies, when exerted moderately is not unlawful. But all astrological calculations regarding governments, wars, and the like, all prophecy which places too much trust in the stars is utterly illegal and forbidden, together with geomancy, hydromancy, arithmetic, physiognomy and chiromancy. Study and knowledge of such arts are not against the law, but their practice is.

In the second book James deals with witchcraft. Sorceresses do not command the devil; they are merely his slaves, whom he brands with a devil's mark. James refutes Wier's thesis that witches are melancholics. Melancholics, says the king, are lean, pale and seek solitude, whereas witches are corpulent, rich and worldly-wise, and devoted to the pleasures of the flesh. They like company and merriment, lawful or unlawful. They fly, in reality and in imagination. They counterfeit the divine service. There are twenty women to one man, because women are more frail and thus caught more easily by the serpent, as the story of Eve teaches. They make wax images, James continues, for evil purposes. The devil gives them stones that cause diseases. Witch poison is not a natural poison but is made with the power of evil.

Sorceresses can make men and women love or hate one another; they can raise storms, in the measure that God will permit it. They can render man maniacal; they can dispatch spirits to haunt men and houses; they can cause people to be possessed. The witches' evil is inflicted upon sinners as a punishment, upon godly people who are guilty of a great sin or exhibit weakness in faith, and also upon the best, in order to try their patience. Although the pious is most protected, no one is safe. Every evil occurs by the will of God, for whom the devil serves as executioner. The devil visits the captured witch in prison; he clothes himself with dead bodies and appears thus as incubus or succubus, mingling with man and woman. To Philomathes's question as to why the devil can make use of the cadavers of good men for evil ends, Epistemon answers with Mark 7:15: 'It is not anything that enters man that defiles him but that which proceeds and cometh out of him.'

In the third and last book, James gives new proof of his learning in expounding the different species of spirits, spectres, lemures, Ziim and Iim, fairies, etc. He dwells on the evil deeds of the incubi and succubi, who, according to the king, are much more frequent among barbaric peoples such as the Finns, the Laplanders and the inhabitants of the Orkney and Shetland Islands.

Conviction of sorceresses can be obtained by 'pricking' and 'fleeting', i.e., diving. The bleeding of the murdered is also a proof of guilt, as well as the witch's not shedding tears. In the sixth chapter of the third book Philomathes asks about the punishment that witches deserve:

'EPISTEMON: They ought to be put to death according to the law of God, the civil and the imperial law, and the municipal law of all Christian nations.
PHILOMATHES: What kind of death, I pray you?
EPI.: It is done commonly by fire, but that is arbitrary, to be decided in every country according to the law and the custom thereof.
PHIL.: But is there no sex, age, or rank that may be made exceptions?
EPI.: None at all. . . .
PHIL.: Then bairnes [youth] may not be spared?
EPI.: Yea, not a hair less of my conclusion, for they are not that capable of reason as to practise such things. And for any being in company and not reviling thereof, their lesser and ignorant age will excuse them no doubt.
PHIL.: I see ye condemn them all who are of the council of such crafts?
EPI.: No doubt.'

And the amiable conversation ends thus: '. . . the consummation of the world and our deliverance drawing near makes Satan rage all the more through his instruments, knowing his kingdom to be so near the end.'

James's opinions are typical of his epoch. His timid attempt to restrain the judges should, however, be noted in his favour. One should also recall the fact that in 1597 he revoked all indictments which had been piling up throughout Scotland, generating a social catastrophe. But this apparent progressiveness was contradicted by the *Daemonologie* published in the years of the Scottish affair. One might have expected that James would at

least have cautioned his over-zealous magistrates more energetically. But the book seems rather a recantation than a justification
of his leniency. One reads between the lines that James feared
that public opinion might interpret his stand in Scotland as a
signal for a new course to be taken in the English jurisdiction of
witches. The king's opinion in a controversial matter must have
carried decisive weight, and the matter was already open to
dispute, as we learn from the sceptical questions James makes
Philomathes ask, and still more from Reginald Scot's book,
Discoverie of Witchcraft, which appeared eleven years before the
Daemonologie. Scot was a student of Wier, who in his turn had
acquired his scepticism from Agrippa von Nettesheim. In the
latter's *Vanity of the Arts and Sciences*, with its superficial and
sweeping statements, a controversy which he had with Savini,
the inquisitor of Metz, is reproduced.

We learn about his defence of an accused witch in that city.
The inquisitor 'had hail'd a poor country woman into his
slaughter house'; his chief argument was that the suspected
woman's mother had been burned as a witch. Agrippa contested
this opinion, alleging the grace of baptism. Satan is cast out of us
and we are made new 'creatures of Christ from whom man can
be separated only by his *own* sin, for it is far from truth that he
should suffer for another man's sin'. The inquisitor had nothing
to answer, 'and the bloody monk stood rebuk'd and shamed
before them all, and ever after was infamous for his cruelty. And
the accusers of the poor woman in the Capitol of the Church of
Metz whose subjects they were, were very considerably fined.'
Agrippa was never forgiven by the judges for this courageous
stand. After his death his name remained stained with the
suspicion of witchcraft, though Wier did all he could to clear his
master's reputation.

John Wier advocated the existence of the hellish monarchy
because the devil was, and still is, inseparable from theological
dogma. But the Brabantian doctor, though admitting the existence of witches who use vain words and operate with the devil's
help, stresses rather the ineffectiveness of such operations. They
are not based upon any true knowledge. Fantasy is the witches'
only teacher. They cannot heal, but may harm the cattle by some
poison. They have lost all understanding, thinking as they do
that they have executed the devil's command. They believe
foolishly that they can cause disturbances in the air and other
impossible things. Their operations are as ridiculous as they are
strange. They are not heretics but fools. Even their evil designs
should not be punished, for a child's or a melancholic's bad and
ineffectual intentions are not punishable. All those who repent
and recognize their folly should be forgiven at any rate, and in
case of obstinacy a fine, as ordained by the Pope, is sufficient
punishment. By no means should they be executed cruelly. Such
ideas, uttered as early as 1576, are very different from James's
compromises. They come from a physician who could report
with legitimate satisfaction that he had cured many witches, in
an epoch when judges boasted of having burned hundreds of
helpless women.

In Germany the cleansing process was initiated by three Jesuits. Adam Tanner (1572–1632) and Paul Laymann (1575–1635) strongly advised the judges to be careful in lawsuits against witches. Friedrich von Spee (1591–1631) published anonymously in 1631 his *Cautio Criminalis*. Scarcely thirty years old, he was asked by the Bishop of Würzburg why his hair had turned grey. 'Through grief,' he replied, 'over the many witches whom I have prepared for death; not one was guilty.' In Holland witch prosecution was abolished in 1610; in Geneva it ceased in 1632. From this we can gather that James's scepticism and leniency should not be overrated. His sanction of fleeting and pricking gave the signal for further monstrosities.

But let us turn to Reginald Scot, whose suggestions had injected some scepticism in James. The titles of a few chapters in Scot's *Discoverie* will illustrate the writer's enlightenment:

That incubus is a natural disease, with remedies for the same (besides magical cures) expressed herewith.

Of four capital crimes brought against witches, all answered fully and refuted as frivolous.

A confutation of witches' confessions, concerning especially their league (with the devil).

A conclusion of the first book, wherein is foreshown the tyrannical cruelty of witch-mongers and inquisitors, with a request to the reader to peruse the same.

Of vain apparitions: how people have been influenced to fear bogies, which is partly reformed by the preaching of the Gospel; the true effect of Christian miracles.

Scot's ideas fell apparently upon barren ground, and the controversial literature concerning witches continued unabated into the seventeenth century. James's *Daemonologie* was reprinted in 1603. In 1616 John Cotta published his *Trial of Witchcraft*, in which he cautions the judges, as Wier had done before, although he accepts the entire witch-dogma. In 1617 Thomas Cooper presented to the public his *Mystery of Witchcraft*. He agrees essentially with the famous William Perkins, a Calvinist minister whose *Discourse of the Damned Art of Witchcraft* appeared in 1608. Equally conservative was Alexander Robert's *Treatise of Witchcraft* (1616). Robert was 'minister of God's word at King's Lynn'. Richard Bernard's *Guide to Grand Jurymen* (1627) shows the Anglican views on the matter, full of reservations. Then follows *Antidote against Atheism* (1653) by Henry More the Platonist, who believes that witchcraft is evidence for the reality of the unseen world.

Many more writers on this controversial theme could be cited. They are, however, overshadowed by Joseph Glanvil, the last 'great' defender of the belief in witches on the British Isles. As a member of the newly founded Royal Society and Rector of the Abbey Church in Bath since 1666, Glanvil's opinion carried considerable weight. He published three books on witchcraft. His *Blow at Modern Sadduceeism* ran into four editions (1668–9). It was reprinted in 1681 as *Sadducismus Triumphatus*.

Glanvil's book contributed the last glamorous touch to the decaying art of extorting proof for learned theories from ignorant women. It is divided into two parts: the first deals with the possibility of the real existence of witches, and the second proves it. An artless yet revealing frontispiece in the second part of the book depicts various manifestations of the evil one. The engraving is divided into six small pictures. The first shows the devil, accompanied by some uncanny companions, drumming on the top of the house of one Mr Montpesson. Then follow scenes of the devil as a black clergyman, of a man flying through the air, of the devil in his natural apparel marking a witch upon her eyebrow, of Mr Montpesson's little son being held by infernal powers in the air, and finally of an angel (or is it the devil?) appearing to a sleeping woman. From Glanvil's preface we learn with satisfaction that there are people who 'have unalterably fixed and determined the point, that witches and apparitions are things ridiculous, incredible, foppish, impossible'. And he is 'assured beforehand that no evidence of fact is possibly sufficient

77. *Diverse manifestations of the devil*

to remove the obstinate prejudice of divers resolved men, and therefore I know I must fall under their heavy censures'.

These expected censures did not prevent Glanvil's book from being reprinted in 1683, 1689, 1700 and 1726, whereas John Wagstaffe's sceptical *Questions of Witchcraft Debated* (1669), as far as we know, was never reprinted. Webster, in his *Displaying of Supposed Witchcraft* (1677), clings still to the belief that there is a corporeal league between the devil and the witch, but otherwise he is absolutely sceptical. He attributes manifestations of the witches' evil activities to deceit and imposture, to melancholy and fancy. He denies utterly that devils or imps suck witches' bodies, that there is any carnal copulation among mortals and spirits, that witches can tranform themselves into dogs and cats, that they can raise tempests and the like. Since Scot, no other book dealing so brilliantly with the theme had appeared in England.

At the beginning of the eighteenth century, probably encouraged by Glanvil's success, the defenders of witchcraft published a few treatises. Richard Boulton's *Complete History of Magic* is an incomplete narrative of witch-trials, ghostly apparitions and the like. John Beaumont's *Treatise on Spirits* (1705) is called by Montague Summers a sound work, exhibiting a reasonably conservative tendency. One should rather call it the work of a psychopath, who was constantly tormented by ringing in his ears. He thinks that this denotes a presage: 'that it be no natural thing, but something different from the natural. As it was in that ringing, wherewith I was admonished for many years, of any fame and rumour concerning me. For this was not like a morbid effect, which now I have sometimes experiences of. . . .'

The final chapter in the witch controversy is Francis Hutchinson's *Historical Essay on Witchcraft* (1718). Hutchinson was Chaplain-in-Ordinary to His Majesty and minister of St James's parish in Bury St Edmunds. The Bible furnished him the proofs of the vanity of the witch belief. 'I have hated them who hold superstitious vanities: But I trust the Lord [Psalm xxxi, 6]. . . . Refuse profane and old wives' fables, and exercise thyself rather unto godliness' (1 Tim. 4:7). Hutchinson deals extensively with the trial of Jane Wenham, indicted in 1712 as a witch. Against the convictions of the judge, Justice Powell, she was formally condemned. However, she was soon pardoned and placed under the protection of Colonel Plummer. After his death, a small pension was allowed her by the Earl and Countess of Cowper. She died in 1730. An extensive 'Wenham literature' flooded England after the trial. Hutchinson took the trouble of visiting this last English witch, of whom he says: 'I have very great assurance that she is a pious and sober woman. . . . I verily believe that there is no one who reads this but may think that such a storm as she met with might have fallen upon them, if it had been their misfortune to have been poor and to have met with such accidents as she did, in such a barbarous parish as she lived in.'

In the conclusion of his book, he says: 'I have shown plainly that accusing and prosecuting and hanging in that case does not cure but increases the evil; and that when a nation of people are in such a state, they are under a very great calamity.'

DIABOLIC RITES

. . . that by magical mutterings rapid
rivers can be made to run backwards,
the ocean be congealed, the winds
robbed of breath, the sun stopped in
his course, the moon made to drop her
foam, the stars plucked from their
spheres, the day annihilated, and the
night indefinitely prolonged.

Black Magic

Apuleius, *Metamorphoses, Book 1*

Turning from the witch to the 'black' magician, we may now
uncover the latter's secret ritual, the means by which he conjures
up the infernal powers, and holds them in servitude. For unlike
the witch, who is the slave of the devil, the magician *commands*.
He has the knowledge and sells his soul at a high price; he knows
how to control the spirits, whose strange names he has learned
in secret books, the *grimoires* or black books. 'O men, feeble
mortals, tremble at your own temerity,' starts the famous
instruction to the magician which is recorded in the *Great
Grimoire*. 'Do not heed blindly such profound wisdom. Raise
your spirit beyond your sphere and learn from me that before
undertaking anything, one should be firm in all decisions.'

The infernal powers are to be controlled craftily. They are
like a horse, aware of the horseman's timidity. They will try by
every means to dismount him. People who are impressed easily,
who fear horrible apparitions and infernal noise, should abstain
from summoning the forces below, for these will manifest themselves at first in terrifying images. When called, the devil will
appear in the most bizarre forms, before condescending to that of
man, and if the conjuror cannot stand quietly in his protective
circle, if he allows only a finger to trespass across the magic line,
he will be torn to shreds. For devils hate to serve magicians, and
it is only for the reward of the costly human soul that they accept
servitude. They rejoice in catching unaware the conjuror who
has infringed upon the rules.

'If you wish to make a contract with hell,' it is written in the
book *Sanctum Regum*, 'you must first decide whom you want to
call.' It is not necessary to disturb Satan in person, when an
inferior hellish prince can fulfil your wishes.

Two days before the conjuration, you must cut a bough from a wild
hazel tree with a new knife, that has never before been used. It must
be a bough which has never carried fruit, and it must be cut at the
very moment when the sun rises over the horizon.

After this, take a bloodstone, as it is known by the druggists who sell
it, and two blessed wax candles and select a lonely place where the
conjuration may proceed undisturbed. Old ruined castles are excellent, for spirits like decayed buildings; a remote room in your house

may do equally well. With your bloodstone, trace a triangle upon the floor, and set the candles at the sides of the triangle. At the bottom of the triangle, write the holy letters I H S, flanked by two crosses.

Take your stand within the triangle with your hazel wand and the papers containing the conjuration and your demands, and summon the spirit with hope and firmness:

'Emperor Lucifer, master of the rebellious spirits, I beg you to be favourable to me, when now I call for your minister, the great Lucifuge Rofocale, as I desire to sign a contract with him. I beg also that Prince Beelzebub may protect my enterprise. O Astaroth, great count, be favourable likewise, and make it possible for the great Lucifuge to appear to me in human form and force, without bad odour, and that he grant me, by the agreement which I am ready to sign with him, all the riches which I need. O great Lucifuge, I pray that you leave your dwelling wherever it may be to come here and speak to me. If you are not willing to come, I will compel you to do so by the power of the great living God, of the Son and the Spirit. Come promptly, otherwise I will torment you eternally by the power of my mighty words and by the great Key of Solomon, which he used when compelling the rebellious spirits to accept a pact. Thus appear as quickly as possible, or else I will torment you continuously by the powerful words of the Key: "Aglon Tetagram Vaycheon Stimulamathon Erohares Retragsammathon Clyoran Icion Esition Existien Eryona Onera Erasyn Moyn Meffias Soter Emmanuel Sabaoth Adomai, I call you, Amen."'

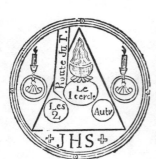

78. Magic circle

This incantation is irresistible. Before you have finished it, Lucifuge will appear and will speak thus: 'Here I am, what do you want, why do you disturb my repose? Answer!' The conjuror: 'I wish to make a contract with you to the end that you give me wealth as quickly as possible; otherwise I will torment you with the powerful words of the Key.' Lucifuge will answer with an established ceremonial, according to the rules of diplomacy: 'I cannot obey your command if you do not surrender your soul and body, after twenty years, agreeing that at such date I may do with you whatever I wish.'

This is the crucial point. The magician has to be on his guard and not commit himself in any way. He must try to force Lucifuge into obedience without promising anything. But such artifices are of little avail. For hell will not give without reward. This is the way in which one should, according to the black book, circumnavigate the dangerous reef: throw your pact out of the circle. The script must be set upon virgin parchment and it must be signed with your blood. It shall read: 'I promise to the great Lucifuge to reward him after twenty years for all the treasures which he will have given me.' This devious document Lucifuge will not accept at first. The magician will insist; in reading the grand appellation and the fiend-smiting words of the Key, he will force Lucifuge to appear again:

Why do you torment me still more? If you will leave me alone. I will give you a treasure not far from here. My condition is that you will consecrate a piece of money to me every first Monday of every month; and that you will call for me once every week between ten at night up to two in the morning. Take up your pact which I have signed. And if you do not keep your promise, you will belong to me after twenty years.

There is some doubt as to whether our black book reports the whole truth, for it is strange that Lucifuge gives his signature, a thing which devils keep ordinarily for themselves. The conditions set down are unfavourable to hell, and Lucifuge does not even demand a copy of the foul agreement. The magician will answer thus: 'I agree with your suggestion, provided that you show me now the treasure you promised me, as I wish to take possession of it immediately.' Lucifuge: 'Follow me and take up the treasure which I will show you.' Now the conjuror will step out of the magic triangle and follow the evil spirit to the riches, which he will touch with the magic wand. He will also place the agreement upon the treasure, and after having taken as much money as he can carry, he will return to the magic triangle, walking backwards. Then he will dismiss the spirit with these words: 'O great Lucifuge, I am satisfied with you; for now I will leave you, go in peace, and I permit you to retire wherever you desire, but without noise or stench.'

This is a simple way of conjuring up the evil powers – and to become rich quickly. Other black books prescribe far more complicated rites. The *Black Pullet*, however, also has the virtue of simplicity. According to the author, the magician must carry a black hen that has never laid an egg to the crossing of two roads; there, at midnight, cut the fowl in half and pronounce the words: '*Eloim, Essaim, frugativi et appellavi.*' Then he must turn his face towards the east, kneel down, and pronounce the great appellation, holding a cypress staff before him – and 'he' will rise immediately.

79. *The devil pointing out hidden treasures*

King Solomon was considered the master of all dealings with the underworld, and many 'original' texts of his conjuration circulated among the magicians. The wording was Hebrew, written in Roman characters. Solomon's seal was considered a most efficacious magic design, recommended by Peter of Abano for the summoning of an air spirit. It should take place when the moon is expanding. Another magic design, four concentric circles, Abano recommends for the invocation of good spirits in the first hour of the Lord's day in springtime. It is a circle of white magic in appearance, the name of Varcan being that of the Lord's king-angel of the air; Tus, Andas and Cynabel are his holy ministers. The highest angels of the Lord's day, Abano says, are Michael, Dardiel and Huratapal. The wind which carries them is the north wind. These angels may be invoked in magical ceremonies which should be rendered efficacious with incense made of red sanders.

Other magic circles and signs may be found in the rare black books wrongly attributed to Pope Honorius, in the *Little Albert* and in the *Red Dragon*. Especially suggestive symbols illustrate a series of works attributed to the arch-wizard, Dr Johann Faust, who lived in the sixteenth century. There are several versions of the Faustian *Höllenzwang* (*Hell's Coercion*), like that said to have been printed in Rome during the pontificate of Alexander VI (1492–1503). It is known, however, that Faust did not start his occult career before 1525, or even 1530, a fact which makes the little treatise somewhat suspicious. At any rate, the magic

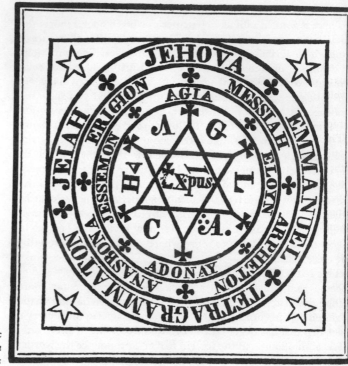

80. *The great magic circle for the evocation of demons*

81. *Magician's circle and wand*

82. *Magic circle*

drawings which it presents are very fine. Another, undated, *Höllenzwang* was found in the collection of a nineteenth-century occultist and bears on its title page a striking fantasy portrait of the famous sorcerer, the Magus Maximus from Kundlingen, or Knittlingen. A third black book attributed to Dr Faust is that printed in Passau, carrying the date 1407, i.e., before the invention of printing with movable type, and about a hundred years before Faust was born. It contains a curious circle, in which the cross is a part of a wholly unreligious design, perhaps composed in this way for the deception of the devil.

Dr Faust's *Great and Powerful Sea Ghost* is the title of a black book printed in Amsterdam in 1692, to be obtained from Holbeck Boecker, salesman at the Cabbage Bridge. In its introduction Faust gives a summary account of his dealings with Beelzebub, who sent him a servant spirit, Mephistopheles. 'Such a thing,' he says, 'will only be doubted by people who have entrenched themselves in prejudice and who deny that such compacts can be made.' The making of the circle is rather difficult: it has to be cut out in sheet metal. With every stroke of the hammer, one has to pronounce: 'Made strong against all evil spirits and devils.' The triangle in the centre has to be formed by three chains taken from gibbets and nailed down with those nails that have gone through the forehead of executed criminals, who were broken upon the wheel, and other such horrors. Then the magician addresses himself to God with holy prayers, which have to be said in great devotion, but are intermingled with exclamations: 'yn ge tu y ge sy San mim ta chu'.

After an unctuous amen, a curse must be pronounced over Satan: 'Hound of hell, Spirit, precipitated in the abyss of eternal damnation; see me standing courageously amidst the hordes of devilish furies', and more of such boasts. Three times Satan must be cursed before he fulfils the magician's wishes. With horrid expressions he is sent away. And the booklet ends thus: 'When you have taken possession of the money and the jewels, and Lucifer is gone, then thank God with a psalm. With all your possessions, go to another country. Remain pious. Do not forget the poor and the converts.'

83. *Magic circle and character*

The *Red Dragon* and the *Grimoire of Pope Honorius* tell us about the principal spirits of hell and their signatures. Lucifer is the emperor; his sign is a four-horned head. Prince Beelzebub recognizes himself in an unpleasant profile. Grand Duke Astaroth thrusts his tongue out, as if to rail at such useless things as signatures. Lucifuge, chief of the cabinet, shows some resemblance to the American Indian. Satanachia, chief of the armies, signs with an insect-like image. Agagliarept, a general, uses two heads for his seal. Fleurety, lieutenant-general, is characterized by a clumsily drawn horse hoof and by a sharp profile that does not fit his lyrical name. Brigadier Sargatanas's signature is a butterfly of hell, and Nebiros, the field marshal, has adopted as his seal a leaf and a being which is half insect, half baby. These quasi-official effigies are not very frightening. Are they caricatures drawn by some fearless humorist?

LUCIFER, Empereur.

BELZÉBUT, Prince.

ASTAROT, Grand-duc.

LUCIFUGÉ, prem. Ministr.

SATANACHIA, grand général.

AGALIAREPT., aussi général.

FLEURETY, lieutenantgén.

SARGATANAS, brigadier.

NEBIROS, mar. de camp.

84. *A few authoritative portraits of demons*

Related closely to the conjuration of devils by the magician is the old necromantic art, the evocation of the dead. At the operator's demand, they rise from the tomb to reveal the future and to tell of treasures which they had hidden during their lifetime. The deceased walking by night appear often without being summoned; at times, they form weird processions, marching silently through the terrified city. In Mediterranean countries, this belief is still alive, and in many towns the inhabitants barricade themselves in their homes at nightfall, in fear of the wandering dead. Sometimes these ghosts are garrulous, adding thus to the terror of their appearance. So in Shakespeare's *Hamlet* 'the sheeted dead did squeak and gibber in the Roman streets'.

Ghosts do not find peace in their graves because they have committed evil, have neglected to accomplish something important during their lifetime, or have taken a secret with them to the grave. They return but, having been separated from life, they behave in unnatural and incomprehensible ways. They guard their money chests yet are unable to reveal the place where these are buried. They stare, mumble, remain immobile. They walk without moving their legs, they haunt the places which they used to like, unable to forget the delights of life which have now become alien to them. They sit in their rocking chairs at the fireplace and attempt with their half-decayed hands to seize the old pipe still lying there. At times they seem completely insane, re-enacting their former deeds or simply frightening their beloved ones with their unearthly behaviour. The necromancer has found means by which he can call them to order. They must answer his questions truthfully, and disappear into their graves when he dismisses them. Through his magic words, the dust in

85. *John Dee and Edward Kelly summoning the dead*

the decayed coffin takes shape again, and rises from a long forgotten past.

The notorious Edward Kelly, alias Talbot, was a necromancer who exerted so great an influence upon Dr John Dee that this scholar left England with him in search of occult and alchemical adventures. Kelly died in 1597, when trying to escape from prison. Dr Dee returned to his native country and wrote his memoirs, which were published in 1659 under the title: *A True and Faithful Relation of What Passed for Many Years between*

Dr Dee and Some Spirits. Though in this work he does not speak of any necromantic experiments, it was nevertheless known that he and Kelly had, before their departure from England, evoked the dead in a lonely cemetery. And an early engraving, whose dryness does not attenuate its macabre effect, depicts the two men huddled together within the magic circle. Kelly holds the magic wand, reading the black book, while the frightened Dr Dee raises the weirdly burning torch. Upright before them stands the deceased in her shroud. Upon the circle we read distinctly the words *Raphael, Rael, Miraton, Tarmiel, Rex,* showing once more that holy angels of white magic could be misused for the blackest kind of sorcery.

In the *Red Dragon* we learn a most curious way of summoning the dead. In the chapter, *The Great Art of Speaking with the Defunct,* it is said that it is indispensable for a true necromancer to assist at Christmas Mass, at midnight precisely. As the host is raised, he must bow down and say in a low voice. '*Exurgent mortui et ad me veniunt*' (the dead rise and come to me). After this the necromancer must leave the church and go to the nearest graveyard. At the first tomb, he shall say: 'Infernal powers, you who carry disturbance into the universe, leave your sombre habitation and render yourself to the place beyond the river Styx.' After a few moments of silence, he adds: 'If you hold in your power him whom I call, I conjure you, in the name of the King of Kings, to let this person appear at the hour which I will indicate.' Next, the conjuror takes a handful of earth and spreads it like grain, murmuring all the while: 'May he who is dust wake from his sleep. May he step out of his dust and answer to my demands which I will make in the name of the Father of all men.'

Bending his knee, he turns his eyes to the east. Thus he must remain until the 'gates of the sun open', whereupon he gathers two human bones and holds them in the form of a St Andrew's cross. Then, leaving the yard, the magician shall toss the two bones into the first church he encounters. Afterwards, walking towards the north and having made exactly four thousand and nineteen hundred steps, he lies down upon the ground, outstretched, his hand on his legs, his eyes raised to heaven in the direction of the moon. In this position, he summons the deceased, saying: '*Ego sum, te peto et videre queo.*' The spectre will appear readily. It is dismissed with the words: 'Return to the kingdom of the chosen. I am happy about your being here.' Leaving the spot, the necromancer returns to the grave where his experiment began, and with his left hand he traces a cross upon the stone. The instructions in the black book end like this: 'Do not forget the slightest detail of the ceremonial as it is prescribed. Otherwise, you would risk falling into the snares of hell.'

The Magus

We think of the magus as the possessor of occult secrets, a master of esoteric wisdom, who makes use of this knowledge for his own good as well as for that of his fellow men. He is a 'white' magician, less fond of prodigies than of the contemplation of nature, in which he discovers marvellous active forces where others only see familiar things. For him the power of God is not concentrated in the One, but permeates every being of the universe.

The three wise men of the Orient were magi. Through the centuries, they have preoccupied the theologians. Some believed that they were astrologers who abandoned their defective knowledge after having recognized the Saviour; but others affirmed that they were true sages who followed that heavenly sign which led them to the crib of Bethlehem. They conjectured that it was not a real star moving on the heaven's vault, but a light attracting their inner light or enlightenment.

The monarchs of the Eastern empires used to have such magi at court. They were the councillors, and during times of epidemics, famine and war, a sage's word could halt the course of adverse events. The magi of old were the spiritual leaders of the community, as opposed to the sorcerers whose evil works undermined the foundations of society; they were forerunners of the prophets. But their power ultimately vanished, and their light was given to the saints of the new faith. Theology, in the belief that nothing good can spring from unorthodox theories and practices, subsequently made no distinction between magi, sorcerers and witches.

Although the magus now found himself without official status, yet it was not his wisdom which was condemned by the sages of Christianity, but rather his pagan creed. The precious fragments of ancient lore were collected and incorporated into the mosaic of the new world image. During the Renaissance the influence of ancient magic gained new strength. Profane learning, though led by religion, ventured into the most recondite compartments of human thought. Many inquired eagerly into wisdom formerly forbidden. The printing press was already working at full speed, and before 1500 more than eight million books had flooded Europe. Among these were not only the Bible and the accepted Greeks, but also works strongly tinted with magical elements. The divinatory arts were held in high esteem; palmistry, astrology, physiognomy, and similar occult arts were in vogue. Even magic incantations and the summoning of good and evil spirits were accepted by some writers who expressed boldly their ban.

More than ever the Orient fascinated people. The Crusades had brought the East closer to the West; its mysteries now seemed less impenetrable, as expanding trade reached across the Mediterranean. Also, with the discovery of America, the equilibrium of Europe was disturbed. The social revolution implicit in the Peasants' War in Germany, the Reformation, the political expansion by the House of Hapsburg, the economic marasmus aggravated by inflation, caused partly by the abundance of gold imported from America, and the constant threat of Turkish invasions, created an atmosphere of instability. These things weakened the social structure and were favourable to new or long repressed ideas.

Magic became a distinct branch of learning. The magus, though despoiled of his antique splendour, made his official entry into Christian society. But simultaneously arose the critics, who railed at those who believed in magical wonders. Scepticism found its expression in the praise of folly. All is vanity; men are sinners, but still more, they are fools. Those who bought magical books and could not understand them laughed at themselves. In his *Ship of Fools* Sebastian Brant declares that in the fool's dance the first round is his own, for he possesses countless books which he neither reads nor understands. Magic also carried men of the clergy into the occult whirlpool. Trithemius (1462–1516), a Benedictine, encouraged Agrippa to write on magic, after having himself written on the names of angels and their government, on cabalistic cryptic alphabets and the like.

In Agrippa's revealing treatise, *Three Books on Occult Philosophy*, we find instructions for the magician and the worker of miracles. He recommends purity and 'dignification'. The faculty of the soul is the only producer of wonders, 'which when it is overwhelmed by too much commerce with the flesh and occupied with the sensible soul of the body is not worthy to command the divine substances'. Such moral commandments do not let us forget that miracles have become a secular affair.

The Renaissance magus has in common with the wise men of old the belief that magical forces dwell in the visible and the invisible world, forces which can be controlled for good as well as for evil. Such ambivalence makes it impossible to define clearly the Western magus. Faust, the black wizard, made use of that same force which enlightened Paracelsus, the white magician. The distinction is slight between the charlatan and the scholar, both promoters of magic. However, even the worst of them exerted in some way a beneficent influence. Their enchantment awakened interest in nature's mysteries and challenged the critical attitude of the sceptic. They levelled social differences, showing the value of the individual who could, unassisted, accomplish great things by the power of his intelligence and knowledge. If 'purity and dignification' are more important than piety and submission, then rank, race and faith are no longer the criteria. Preoccupation with ancient magic, moreover, encouraged the study of languages, of ancient learning; and, finally, it stimulated experimental science in general. Seen in this light, magic cannot be called a false or sinful practice but an important promoter of intellectual activity in the West.

The characteristics of the magus can best be described by giving a few short biographies of some of the well-known defenders of the occult.

Pico della Mirandola (1463–94)

The woodcut reproduced from Porta's *Celestial Physiognomy* is accompanied by a description of Pico's features: his skin was of a yellow cast, subtle in colouring; his body was well proportioned. He had small eyes, the whites of which were also yellow; his face was attenuated and so was his nose. His lips were refined, his face youthful, very beautiful and angelic. '*Fu di tanta altezza d'ingenio*,' Porta says in his full-sounding Italian, which we may translate to mean that Pico was high-spirited. 'His memory was that of a phoenix, his speech and writings incomparably prolific; he was a philosopher, a mathematician, and he explored the secrets of theology. He wore the most elegant clothes, ate and drank little. Exhausted by study and insufficient rest, he died in his youth.'

Pico, Count of Mirandola, was born in 1463 in Mirandola castle, near Modena. His precocity was considered a marvel, comparable to that of the painter Masaccio who died at twenty-seven after having given a decisive impetus to the plastic arts. At twenty-four Pico went to Rome, where he posted his nine hundred theses for public debate. Among these, many were concerned with magic and the Cabala, a secret doctrine which will be discussed in later chapters. These occult systems were to prove the divinity of Christ. Pico's plan did not win the approval of the Church. Pope Innocent VIII, whose rigorous attitude towards matters of witchcraft has already been noted, appointed a commission to examine the whole of Pico's theories. The verdict was unfavourable: four theses were judged to be rash and heretical; six others were also condemned, though less severely; three were called false, heretical, erroneous.

In his work Pico favours the prediction of the future by dreams, sibyls, spirits, portents and also by birds and the intestines. The two latter methods, being irretrievably pagan, certainly could not be tolerated by the Roman theologians. His leanings towards Chaldean oracles, Orphic hymns and the like were no more acceptable to them. Some of his propositions have a Neo-Platonic flavour: with Proclus, he speaks of the junior gods.

But Pico's ultimate goal went beyond that of reviving old, more or less known magical ideas and of introducing new ones. His ambition was to reconcile the officially sanctioned Aristotelianism and Platonism which the Renaissance scholars were studying again. This he strove to accomplish with the help of the Cabala, which he had studied on the recommendation of his Hebrew teachers.

With the condemnation of Rome, Pico's troubles were only beginning. He offered an apology, published in 1487, in which he defended the thirteen rejected propositions and accused the judges of being heretics, implying, moreover, in his preface that they were unable to express themselves in good Latin. This was too much for the 'stammering barbarians'. Two bishops with inquisitorial power brought the rebel to submission. A papal bull interdicted the printing of the theses. Pico fled to France where he was arrested by the Roman nuncios and confined in a dungeon at Vincennes. Through the intervention of Lorenzo de' Medici and others, he was allowed to return to Florence. Pope Innocent VIII remained mute and hostile. It was only from Alexander VI that he was able to obtain forgiveness and safety from the Inquisition. This happened one year before his death, which occurred in 1494, his thirty-first year.[1]

Trithemius (1462–1516)

During the time that Trithemius was a student in Heidelberg, he met a mysterious teacher who instructed him in the secret sciences. When in 1482 Trithemius decided to return to his native town, Tritenheim, in the district of Trier, the teacher informed him that on his journey he would find the key to his life. As Trithemius reached Sponheim snow was falling heavily and he sought shelter in the Benedictine monastery. Life there appeared so attractive that he decided to become a monk – and this was the famous key of which the master had spoken. At twenty-two he succeeded the old abbot, who had died in 1483. Trithemius found the monastery in a state of complete disintegration. Parts of the building had fallen to ruin. Debts, chaos, laziness and ignorance were the obstacles which he had to fight. But he brought order into neglected affairs and soon the Benedictines of Sponheim became famous.

He taught the monks many crafts and kept them occupied constantly, preparing parchment, writing books which they adorned with gilded initials, and gardening. The debts were paid and more money was earned with which Trithemius bought rare manuscripts. In 1503 his library consisted of two thousand volumes, a rarity in that time. People from France, Italy and Germany came to see the collection, and to meet the famous abbot whose erudition had become proverbial. Princes and kings sent their emissaries to Sponheim; Emperor Maximilian asked the cleric's advice on political questions. It is said that as early as 1482 Trithemius was summoned to the emperor's court to give his counsel upon a matrimonial question. The Empress Mary of Burgundy had died as a result of an accident. Maximilian wished to marry again. According to the legend, Trithemius advised the emperor to evoke the spirit of the deceased queen and to have her decide whom he should choose for a spouse. The conjuration took place and Mary appeared in all her beauty. Maximilian left the magic circle to embrace her. He fell to the ground, thunderstruck, at which moment the apparition vanished. But before disappearing, she had revealed many future events and also named her successor, Bianca Sforza, Galeazzo's daughter.

In 1505 Trithemius was summoned to the court of Philip, Count Palatine. He travelled to Heidelberg where he became dangerously ill. In the meantime the monks at Sponheim revolted, hoping to gain more leisure and freedom by ridding the convent of the over-zealous abbot. Utterly disappointed, Trithemius did not return to Sponheim, though it caused him unhappiness to abandon the monks and especially the marvellous library. At Würzburg he was offered direction of the abbey of St James, which he entered in 1506 and where he remained to the end of his life, writing and sending out his admonitions. He is buried in St James.

Though most of his works are ecclesiastical treatises, Trithemius wrote also on magic. Alchemy attracted him greatly and he declares in his books that transmutations can be made and that the philosophers' stone can be attained by certain methods. This stone, he says, is the soul of the world, or *spiritus mundi*, rendered visible. One might call it the petrification of God's breath, as the abbot affirms that the world soul is the breath emanating from its divine source. In this sense, we may understand his saying that God permeates everything, a belief which became widespread after Trithemius, for in the midst of the sixteenth century Copernicus discovered a new world, that of the planets circulating together with the earth around their central star, the sun, a discovery which demolished the old Christian dogmatic hierarchy. God could not be above, as there was no above and no below, and there was nothing outside the world. Therefore a new dwelling had to be found for Him. The belief then became prevalent that God's residence was everywhere.

Trithemius was very modest and timid and, as a man of the clergy, he did not wish to do or say anything that was contrary to the established tradition. He invented all sorts of secret methods of writing by which profound thoughts could be disguised in apparently harmless texts. The fact that he influenced Paracelsus and Agrippa suffices as an indication that he was sympathetic to magic learning. He speaks often in dissembling terms, saying, for instance, that the golden age would arrive when the lion and the lamb would dwell together. In this Biblical symbol he clothed the thought that the philosophers' stone was attained when the fire of God, the lion, and the divine light, i.e., Christ, are joined mystically.

His fondness for the occult is revealed in the advice which he sent to Agrippa after having read the latter's book *On Occult Philosophy*: 'I have only one more admonition to give you. Never forget it: to the vulgar, speak only of vulgar things: keep for your friends every secret of a higher order; give hay to the oxen and sugar to the parrot. Understand my meaning, lest you be trod under the oxen's feet, as oftentimes happens.'

Trithemius's book on the *Seven Second Causes* is certainly not for the oxen, and the parrot will find little in it about which he can chatter. The seven second causes are the seven highest angels, whom Trithemius correlates with the seven planets. God is the first cause. The second causes are his ministers in charge of the government of the world. The spirit or angel of Saturn, for instance, is Orifiel, who governed the universe immediately after the creation. His rule started on the fifteenth of March, in the first year of the world, and he governed for 345 years and four months. Under his reign men were rude and savage, like beasts, as the Genesis reports. Orifiel was succeeded by Anael, spirit of Venus, who ruled from 345 to 705. Trithemius draws the dynastic data of the heavenly spirits up to the year 1879, when the rule of Gabriel ends. The seven angels govern in turn, and from the order of the past one can prophesy that of the future, because heavenly institutions are unchangeable.

According to modern occultists, these apparent trifles contain an enormous amount of magic wisdom. It is expressed in a code, they say, each word having a double meaning, but the key to this mystical work Trithemius carried to the grave. Since the words should be read according to certain combinations, the book loses its sense completely when translated from its original Latin.

Agrippa von Nettesheim (1486–1535)

In the whirlpool of the Renaissance, Henry Cornelius Agrippa von Nettesheim, perhaps the most important figure among the occultists of that age, was driven from one position to the other, from country to country, from high favour to prison, from silent study to the battlefield, from wealth to poverty. As a man of erudition, he corresponded with the great Humanists of his time, such as Melanchthon, Erasmus and Cardinal Campegius. Agrippa was encouraged by Abbot Trithemius to commit to writing his knowledge of the occult, towards which he was by nature greatly inclined. His acceptance of Neo-Platonism, which at that time had truly burst into flower, was championed by the Humanists in place of the Aristotelianism of the Middle Ages. In his study of the Neo-Platonists such as Plotinus, Iamblichus and Porphyry, Agrippa became immersed in the supernatural and the occult, and his enthusiasm for these philosophers overwhelmed his scholar's sense of criticism. With a mind open to every current of occult thought, he strove, like Mirandola, to conciliate various magical doctrines and to unite philosophy with Cabala. In his later years however, Agrippa, probably under the influence of the Counter Reformation, recanted his magical writings. Now, as incredulous as he had been credulous before, he professed that nothing was certain either in the arts or in the sciences, and that the only reliable thing in the world was religious faith. In order to find an interpretation of this astonishing development from credulity to utter distrust in the competence of man, it may be interesting to follow the magus through various episodes of his life.

When still a young man, he went to Paris on a perilous mission for the Emperor Maximilian. There he met some young scholars, noblemen, with whom he founded a secret society. They formed a mystical plan for a reformed world, and promised each other mutual assistance. One of their members, a young nobleman from Gerona in Catalonia, learned that the peasants of his domain had dispossessed his family and had assumed power. Under the leadership of Agrippa and assisted by a detachment of soldiers, these noble 'Freemasons' met with the revolting peasants. However, their effort to reinstate the lord of Gerona into his rights proved a failure, and the group disbanded.

In 1509 Agrippa arrived at Dole, of which Margaret of Austria, Maximilian's daughter, was mistress, together with Burgundy. With the aid of a friend, Agrippa obtained permission to lecture at the university, where he expounded Reuchlin's Cabalistic treatise, *The Mirific Word*. Wishing also to win Margaret's patronage, he composed *The Nobility of the Female Sex* and *The Superiority of Women*. With arguments borrowed from the Bible, the Church fathers, and philosophy, he praises the fair sex in exalted phrases. The work was dedicated to the 'divine Margaret, the august and very clement princess'. Margaret's favours were slow in coming, but Agrippa's enemies were quick to appear, especially the clerics who detected in his sympathy for the Jewish Cabala a dangerous heresy. At Ghent in the Netherlands, where Margaret resided, a Franciscan friar, Catilinet, preached before her against this impious Cabalist, and he was prevented by his adversaries from publishing his praise of women. He relinquished his cause and went to England and later to Cologne where he lectured publicly. His clumsiness in financial matters became notorious, and various blunders estranged him from his admirers and sponsors. In 1515 he followed Maximilian's army to Italy and was knighted on the battlefield. The Cardinal of St Croix sent him to Pisa as representative to the Council. This was his last chance to right himself with the Church and to please Pope Leo X, from whom he had received a friendly letter. But the Council was disbanded and the assemblies were discontinued.

Leaving behind his military and ecclesiastical career, Agrippa taught at Turin and Pavia, where he lectured on Hermes Trismegistus, earning more fame than money. In 1518 the lords of Metz chose him as Advocate, Syndic and Orator of the city. Two years later he left this post, after his quarrel with the inquisitor Savini from whom he had rescued an innocent country woman, unjustly accused of witchcraft, an episode which has been related in a previous chapter. Subsequently he lectured in Cologne, also in Geneva and Fribourg, where he practised medicine. Then in 1524 he was finally granted a pension by Francis I, and appointed physician to the Duchesse Louise of Savoy, the king's mother. She wanted Agrippa to predict the future from the stars, but he replied that his talents should be used for more important matters. When the duchess left Lyons, Agrippa did not follow her, and his name was removed from the pension list.

In 1529 fickle fortune once again seemed to smile. He was

summoned by four different sponsors: Henry VIII of England; the German Emperor's Chancellor; an Italian marquis; and Margaret of Austria, Governor of the Netherlands. Twenty years after the composition of *The Superiority of Women*, Margaret seemed finally to have been won over, and Agrippa was made historiographer.

It was at this time that he published his famous work, *On the Vanity of Arts and Sciences*, in which he declared human thought and activity is vain. Once more, his enemies were exasperated. The Pope's legate, Cardinal Campegius, and the Cardinal de la Mark tried in vain to defend him. His pension as an imperial historiographer was cancelled and, being unable to pay his debts, he was imprisoned at Brussels. He was released after one year. Now finally appeared his *Occult Philosophy*, which he had written in his early days but which had remained unpublished. The belated publication created incredible confusion because its contents had already been recanted by his work *On the Vanity of Arts and Sciences*. The *Occult Philosophy*, on the contrary, indulged in the optimistic belief that men were able to work miracles by the power of their wisdom. Once more Agrippa decided to leave Germany, and ultimately sought shelter at Grenoble in the house of a M. Allard, Receiver General of Provence, where he died in 1535.

The *Occult Philosophy*, having so greatly influenced Western occultism, deserves a brief résumé. Magic, says Agrippa, is a powerful faculty, full of mystery and comprising a profound knowledge of the most secret things, their nature, power, quality, substance and effects, as well as their relationships and antagonisms. It is a philosophical science; it is physics, mathematics and theology. Through physics we learn the nature of things; through mathematics we comprehend their dimensions and extent, and the movement of heavenly bodies can be calculated; through theology we come to know God, angels and demons, intelligence, soul and thought. Physics is terrestrial; mathematics, celestial; theology concerned with the archetypal world.

The magus, in his study of nature, will increase his wisdom by degrees: through the study of stones, he will learn the essence of the stars; from the planets his knowledge will be led to the sublime. Agrippa starts with the four elements: fire, water, earth and air. These elements occur in three types: here below they are mixed, impure; in the stars, they are pure; thirdly, there are composite elements which can change and which are the vehicle of all transformations. He affirms the opinion of the Neo-Platonists that the elements are found here below, in the whole universe, in spirits and angels, and even in God.

From the elements are born natural virtues of things, but not occult virtues. The latter are infused into things through ideas by means of the world-soul. In order to ascertain occult virtues, we should explore the world by means of resemblances. For instance, fire here below excites celestial fire, the eye cures the eye, sterility produces sterility. Therefore sacrificial fire reacts upon the divine fire or light; frogs' eyes cure man's blindness; mules' urine renders women sterile. As there is accord between things akin, there is discord between things hostile. Experience has shown, for instance, that between the sunflower and the sun there is accord; whereas between the lion and the cock there is hostility, just as between the elephant and the mouse. It is the task of the magus to recognize these sympathies and antipathies in order to operate magically through nature.

Similar dispositions are to be found in the planets, whether friendly or hostile to one another. Such relations, when made use of, yield magical results, for all things inferior submit to those above. Not only single objects depend upon the stars, but whole provinces and kingdoms, to which planetary and zodiacal signs have been allotted. In tracing such celestial signs, the magus propitiates virtues from above. The sign of Sagittarius brings down the virtues of that constellation and, in attaching such a talisman to a horse's neck, the animal's well-being is guaranteed, since the horse and Sagittarius are akin. Thus, through various contrivances, well prepared and coordinated, favourable influences are attracted, not only from the stars, but also from good demons, and even from God.

Agrippa enumerates these marvellous contrivances. They are fire and smoke, pomades, plants, animals, metals, gestures and words. Explaining at length the essence of divination and augury, he states that such mysterious predictions are brought forth through the knowledge of sympathies and antipathies. Knowing relationships between things on earth and their masters above, the inspired will discover signs of events to come which are hidden from the profane.

Mathematical sciences are indispensable to the magus as natural virtues are governed by numbers, weights and measures. Moreover, light, movement, even the world's harmony, take their origin from mathematics. In order to know the plan of the world's architecture, it is necessary to comprehend the proportions upon which it is built. Numbers conceal virtues having marvellous capacities in either world. Thus the number one, the base of all numbers, expresses also the one God, the cause of all creation. According to the Pythagoreans, says Agrippa, there are sacred numbers dedicated to the elements and the planetarian gods. These numbers should be used in magical diagrams. Knowledge of mathematics is necessary for musical harmony, which is a reflection of the harmony of the universe.

In the third book Agrippa asserts the necessity of religion in every magical venture. 'Religion is the most mysterious thing,' he says, 'and one about which one should keep silent, for Trismegistus says that it would be an offence to religion to confide it to the profane multitude.' Religion is the accomplishment and key of magic, a discipline leading to the dignifying of man. Agrippa's conception of religion is far from being orthodox; it is rather a mixture of Christianity, Neo-Platonism and Cabala. He speaks of planetarian spirits, of demons, good and bad, of conjurations and sacred pentacles, of the ten sacred names of God, to which he attributes magical power. He knows the language of the angels and their names as well as those of the star spirits, those of the elements, and those of the four corners of the world. He exposes the secret of sacred Cabalistic hieroglyphs, and all this with the intention of instructing the magus in the manner of conjuring the supernatural, for, in his words, 'though man is not an immortal animal, like the universe, he is nonetheless reasonable, and with his intelligence, his imagination and his soul, he can act upon and transform the whole world'.

Theophrastus Paracelsus (1493–1541)

His device was: 'Be not another if thou canst be thyself.' There is no one comparable to Paracelsus, physician, astrologer, anthroposophist, theologian, mystic and magus. At a time when knowledge was assuming many ramifications, when faith was divided into opposing dogmas, when the earth was about to lose its proud position as the centre of the universe, in short, when the old unified world structure collapsed, Paracelsus achieved what had seemed impossible: he wove his knowledge, practice and faith into one. In pursuing this magic ideal he betrays himself as being solidly tied to the bygone Middle Ages, an epoch in which such unification of every branch of thought was still possible. But in contrast to his fondness for the past is his empiricism. When he publicly burned the works of Galen, denouncing the sterility of his fellow physicians, he made it clear

86. *Theophrastus Paracelsus*

that his own world was to be welded into one by other means than those offered by conventions. He wanted to know the true nature of things through investigation and not through the study of dusty volumes.

These bold views guided his critical attitude towards the classical authorities to whom the past had clung with unshaken faith. Paracelsus believed that nature was the highest authority, because nature, unlike man, does not commit errors. Everything in nature partakes of the *machina mundi*, the world machine, built according to a divine plan. And the various forms and events of the corporeal world have their profound meaning and are just so many manifestations of the divine.

Man's first doctor is God, the maker of health, Paracelsus says, for the body is not a thing apart but a house for the soul. The physician, therefore, must treat the two simultaneously and strive at bringing them into harmony, which is the only true health. Such inner accord harmoniously unites in man the things of the world with the divine. Religion is derived from the Latin *re-ligare*, i.e., to unite again. The curative process shares this characteristic. Religion is the basis of medicine. In his prophecies, Paracelsus predicts an evil end for people who fail to achieve self-recognition, for they do not know the true nature with which they are endowed. Living rightly and healthily is the attainment of harmony with one's true self. Therefore the physician must be an astrologer as well; he should know about the harmony of the spheres and their influence. Moreover, he must be a theologian to comprehend the needs of the soul. He must be an anthropologist in order to understand the needs of the body. He must be an alchemist to perceive the universal substances which are found in harmonious mixtures everywhere in the material world. Also, he should be conscious of the primary creative cosmic forces because they are universal and are in man himself. And he must be a mystic, to recognize that there exists something beyond logic, as the ancients have demonstrated; thus mysticism will complete the system.

Paracelsus affirms that God has given various qualities to things at their creation, forces which enable them to exist independently. The divine intervention is, therefore, not constantly to be sought, for man has the capacity to help himself, like the stars which move by their own initiative. The heavenly bodies influence man. They are inhabited by the Greco-Roman divinities who emit a mortal light – for everything in creation is mortal. God alone sends forth a divine light which is immortal and which is received by that which is immortal in man. These two kinds of light are the essence of all. The astrologer inquires into the mortal light of the stars, by whose contemplation he gains knowledge. Man is moulded from the dust of the stars, his older brothers, whence emanate reason, art and science. All these are mortal. The astrologers do not investigate Christ, the apostles and the prophets – religion and mysticism fulfil this high function.

Man is receptive to the radiance of the stars, and to be attracted to their light is godly, but mortal at the same time. It existed before the coming of Christ; it still exists and grows even stronger. During Christ's earthly life astronomers, magi and diviners quite understandingly abandoned their art to follow the eternal light. Paracelsus reminds us of Dionysius the Areopagite of Athens who relinquished astrology to follow St Paul, for he wished to rise from the lesser to the greater; and so should we all strive for the greater, each according to the essence bestowed upon him by the stars.

But man, unfortunately, is blind to his essence and to the two-fold light that is in him. When it becomes completely disunited, he must fall sick, his body being severed from the current which animates it. Most men are neither truly pious nor truly scientific. 'Were Christ to descend from heaven, he would find no one with whom he could converse; were Jupiter to come down from his planet, he would encounter here below no inquirers but only *schools* of men who repeat the wisdom gathered by their fore-fathers from the stars. These schools of old are dead and their followers remain blind to the mortal light.'

How few raise their eyes to the starry heaven, from which flows a constant enlightenment guiding mankind to new sciences and arts. Music, for instance, is offered by the planet Venus. If any musicians were open to receive her light, they would create a music more beautiful, more celestial, than the tunes of the past which are still repeated mechanically.

Such poetic images uttered by a physician were too much for his colleagues, who based all their knowledge upon the herb medicine of Galen. Their recipes were complicated and expensive. Their Philistine minds abhorred the ways of Paracelsus, his negligence about clothes, his rude language, his writing in German rather than in Latin. These good bourgeois detected the vagabond in him. They considered his magic signs and talismans as objects of heresy. In vain Paracelsus explained that in this physical world all things were related, that the sign of a specific planet engraved upon a talisman was endowed with astral forces; that such ore as was used for the magic medal was related to that same planet, enforcing thus the power of the talisman; that these signs were the marks imprinted by the stars like signatures upon earthly bodies.

Paracelsus clothes his theories in concrete forms derived from medieval realism, where ideas are not abstractions, but entities. His will to render everything visible and palpable induces him to make at times fantastic assertions which would provoke a smile in the most indulgent critic. He professes, for instance, that mythological beings like fauns and nereids actually exist, that it is possible to produce an artificial man, the homunculus. Viewed in detail, these assertions do not make sense, yet, seen as a part of the Paracelsian system, they group themselves logically into the whole.

What is more important, in spite of such errors, Paracelsus performed miraculous cures with his fantastic methods, whereas the patients of the reasonable Galenians died. It was this fact, rather than mythological stories, which aroused the scholars against Paracelsus, who was driven from town to town. His rugged character and irascibility forbade him to compromise, and he became a tramp haunting the highways in search of wisdom. In his writings on surgery he enumerates the many countries through which he travelled. 'Everywhere,' he says, 'I inquired diligently and gathered experience of the true medical art, not alone from doctors but also from barbers, women, sorcerers, alchemists, in convents, from the low ranks and from those of the nobility, from the intelligent and the simple-minded.' Many of the simple ways of the country people he recognized as being better than the intricate compounds of the learned. His prescriptions are simple and, given by a man whose strong conviction produced confidence and optimism, they worked wonders. The fear of disease, he said, is more dangerous than disease itself.

Through his alchemical studies begun in childhood, he was led to the idea of using minerals as medicaments. Thus he added a new branch to science: pharmaceutical chemistry. He treated syphilis successfully with mercury and recommended also guaiacum, which the Spaniards imported from San Domingo. Alchemy was transformed completely by Paracelsus and his followers, for he professed that the alchemical task is above all to separate the pure from the impure and to develop various species of primordial matter. What nature has left imperfect shall be perfected by alchemy, be it metals, minerals or other substances; thus the Hermetic art is liberated from its early bonds. Gold can be produced by alchemical methods, Paracelsus asserts; the physico-chemical procedure, however, is poor. The finest gold should be made by psycho-chemical means, an idea which led away from the gold-cooking to the consideration that the main object of the experiment is the perfection of man.

As a mystic and a magus, Paracelsus was very much concerned with prognostication. It is an uncertain art, he says, because man within himself is doubtful. He who is doubtful can accomplish nothing certain; he who hesitates can bring nothing to perfection. Prophecy requires imagination and faith in nature. In a similar way, medicine makes use of imagination, fixed strongly on the nature of herbs and upon healing. He who imagines, compels herbs to reveal their hidden nature. 'Imagination is like the Sun, the light of which is not tangible, but which can set a house on fire. Imagination leads man's life. If he thinks of fire, he is on fire; if he thinks of war, he will cause war. All depends only upon man's imagination to be Sun, i.e., that he imagines wholly that which he wills.'

About intelligence, Paracelsus professes that there are two kinds – that of the carnal man and that of the spiritual. Prophecy is caused by the spiritual, which he calls Gabalis: 'You should know that man can foresee the future from the books of the past and from those of the present.' Describing what today we would call clairvoyance, he says: 'Man also possesses the power by which he may see his friends and the circumstances by which they are surrounded, although such persons may be a thousand miles away from him at that time.' Elsewhere he speaks of the practice of divination, which can be caused by sortilege. But the customary ceremonies, he says, are mere superstition, invented to lend an air of solemnity to the operation. At any rate, those who practise the art are often ignorant of the laws that control it. He mentions several other preternatural capacities, having explored these dark realms with a thoroughness worthy of a man of science.

Nostradamus
(1503–66)

After my earthly death, my writ shall do more than when I was among the living.

Nostradamus

Nostradamus (Michel de Nostre-Dame), greatest of all seers and astrologers, was born in St Remy, France. Though his prophecies are styled in the scurrilous language of most predictions, the fact remains that many lent themselves to striking interpretations of happenings that have occurred centuries after the stargazer's death. Even names mentioned by the seer coincide at times with those connected with the predicted events. Here is an example:

> *Le part soluz mary sera mitré*
> *Retour : conflit passera sur la thuille*
> *Par cinq cens; un trahyr sera tiltré*
> *Narbon : et Saulce par couteaux avous d'huille.*

> The separated husband will be capped with a mitre
> Returned – conflict shall spread over the tile
> By five hundred – a traitor will be called Narbon
> And Saulce watchman over oil-barrels.

This apparent nonsense can well be interpreted as predicting certain events of the French Revolution: Louis XVI, *separated* from Marie-Antoinette (who underwent a similar treatment in another room) was *capped* by the Jacobins with the Phrygian bonnet (*mitre*) and the tricolor cockade. This was after his *return* from Varennes, where the fleeing royal family had been arrested. *Conflict* broke out two months later at the Tuileries (a palace built upon the site of a former *tile* manufactory, from which the name derives). It was caused by the resistance of the Swiss guard, *five hundred men*. The *traitor* Count *Narbonne-Lara* was the minister of war whom Louis dismissed abruptly under suspicion of treason. *Saulce* owned a general merchandise store at Varennes. He had the royal family arrested. Marie-Antoinette was sitting between *oil cans* and candles in Saulce's store when the arrest took place. All this happened in the years 1791 and 1792, two and a quarter centuries after Nostradamus's death. The conflicting spellings of the names involved can be explained by the changes of French orthography. Many more such astounding predictions and their interpretations may be found in the works of Pierre Rigaud, in the English version of Theophilus de Garancières, in the books of L. Pissot, A. le Pelletier, Torné-Chavigny, P. Piobb, and in a recent book, *The Story of Prophecy*, by Henry James Forman.

A forgotten fact is that the great seer has written, besides his predictions, an often-reprinted work on cosmetics, on perfumes, on the art of making jam with sugar, honey and cooked wine. This indicates that Dr Nostradamus was also well-versed in the science of herbs and minerals, like his grandfather, Jacques de Nostre-Dame, physician at the court of King René of Provence. Michel was one of the greatest physicians of his epoch. When studying medicine at Montpellier University, he interrupted his studies and helped to stamp out an epidemic of the Black Death which appeared simultaneously in different provinces and countries. Nostradamus, apparently immune to the pest, travelled from city to city performing miraculous cures. In Aix the grateful citizens offered him a pension, which he distributed among orphans and widows, and after a most beneficent stay at Lyons, he settled in Salon, Provence. His prophecies, which he called *Centuries*, were published in 1555, long after his book on cosmetics. These predictions made an enormous impression, and people from all classes travelled to Salon seeking the seer's prophecy and advice. Salon, the modest town, became famous through him.

Catherine de' Medici, who was greatly attracted by occult science and magic, had attached to her court several astrologers and soothsayers, such as the questionable Ruggieri, more sorcerer than sage, and the mathematician Reignier for whom she had an astrological column built which is still to be seen in Paris. There was also the famous Luc Gauric, who had warned Catherine's husband, King Henry II, to avoid single combat, alleging that he was threatened by the stars with being wounded on the head, or with blindness.

The king, though rather sceptical, did not object to the summoning of Nostradamus, who arrived in Paris in 1556. The queen was eager to know the future of her three sons, who were living at Blois, and Michel was sent there to see them. When he returned to Paris, he predicted that all three would sit on a throne. He did not want to be more explicit, for he often said that it was harmful to know the whole truth. Catherine believed the prediction, but Michel may have meant that they were to ascend, subsequently, to the *same* throne, which actually happened.

Michel had enemies at court and he suffered especially from those who feared his influence upon the queen. A poet, perhaps Bèze or Jodelle, wrote an acid couplet against him, playing upon the seer's name:

> *Nostra damus cum falsa damus, nam fallere nostrum est.*
> *Sed cum falsa damus, nil nisi nostra damus.*

> We give what is ours in giving lies;
> For to deceive is our business.
> And measuring out the false
> We give nothing else, but our very own.

The carpers, however, were silenced when King Henry died in the following year under strange circumstances. He had been celebrating the wedding of his sister, Marguerite de France, to the Duke of Savoy, during which a tournament was held. Henry invited the young Earl of Montgomery to cross lances with him.

Having first modestly declined this honour, Montgomery yielded finally to the king's wish. An accident occurred; the Englishman's lance pierced the grille of Henry's golden helmet and entered the king's eye, wounding him cruelly. Luc Gauric's warning was remembered now, but also the thirty-fifth verse in the first book of Nostradamus's *Centuries*:

> Le lyon jeune le vieux surmontera,
> En champ bellique par singulière duelle,
> Dans cage d'or les yeux luy crevera.
> Deux playes une, pour mourir mort cruelle.

> The young lion will conquer the old
> In a single combat upon the lawn.
> He will pierce his eye in a cage of gold,
> Two wounds one, to die a cruel death.

And in the fifty-fifth verse of the third book one reads:

> In the year when the one eye rules in France,
> The court will be utterly disturbed,
> The lord of Blois will slay his friend,
> The kingdom will be treated ill and double doubt.

That there was trouble because of the dying 'one-eye', everybody at court knew. Henry died soon from his wound. But what did the other verses signify? The three young princes who were all to be kings, according to Nostradamus, knew a sad fate. The first, now Francis II, was only sixteen. He died a year later. The second, the ten-year-old Charles IX, ascended to the throne under his mother's regency. Catherine began to suspect that the predicted royal crowns were one and the same. In 1564 she journeyed with Charles to the plague-stricken and desolate Salon, seeking Nostradamus's advice. Little is known of what the seer told the aggrieved mother. The Huguenot storm arose in France, dividing the kingdom under the rule of an intriguing mother and of a child. Bloody St Bartholomew's Eve brought horror and hatred, and Charles died at twenty-two, leaving his land in disorder.

The last of the princes was crowned Henry III. He resided at Vincennes, and he loved sorcery and every occult practice. Sometimes he retired to the Tower of Paris at Vincennes, and people whispered horrible tales about his conjurations. After his death, they found there the tanned skin of a child and blasphemous implements of silver which his adversaries readily reproduced in a pamphlet. Henry III had summoned the États Généraux, the representatives of the state, to the city of Blois. There he had his friend, the Duke of Guise, treacherously murdered. 'The lord of Blois will slay his friend. . . .'

Civil war broke out and Paris revolted. Just as Henry was ready to besiege the city, in 1589, a monk named Jacques Clément murdered the most inept king of France, and Nostradamus's prophecy about Catherine's family was fulfilled. But the seer did not live to see it; he died in 1566 under circumstances which he had predicted in his *Centuries*. His last interview with any member of the royal family was with Charles IX, who gave him on that occasion the title of Councillor and Physician to His Majesty. Suffering from dropsy, he had lived 'between bed and bench' (the bench of his writing desk). On 1 July 1566, in the morning, they found him sitting dead at his desk. More than a decade before, the seer had written about himself:

> Back from embassy, gift of the king, confined to place,
> Nothing he will do with it, will have gone to God,
> Nearest family and friends of my blood,
> Find all dead, near the bed and the bench.

Guillaume Postel (1510–81)

The erudite magi were considered healers of both body and soul. They wanted to help their fellow man. To accomplish this, it was first necessary to establish a world system into which man could be harmoniously incorporated. For did not all the magi share the belief that man was the replica of everything that existed? Guillaume Postel was one of these architects of an idealistic world. Born in Dolerie, in Normandy, he learned early to face adversity. When he was eight he lost both his father and his mother during an epidemic. At thirteen he was a schoolteacher. Saving his modest earnings, he was able to go to Paris, where he entered the Collège St Barbe. By his own initiative he learned Hebrew and Greek, and he was soon considered a prodigy of his time.

The Emperor Charles V was at that time fighting in Tunisia, thus threatening France. The French king negotiated a treaty with the Osmans directed against the Germans. The ambassador of France took Postel to Constantinople where the latter could make use of his knowledge of oriental languages. Having successfully accomplished his task, Postel travelled in Greece, Asia Minor and Syria. On his journeys he learned the New Greek, Armenian and a Slavic tongue. When he returned to Paris he accepted the chair of a professor of mathematics and Oriental languages, which was offered him by Francis I. The life of this scholar seemed settled; he had many sponsors and admirers, among whom were the king and his sister.

But now his career of a seer and reformer began. He gave up his respectable post and travelled through Europe, hoping to mould society into a completely new form. Several times he was offered brilliant positions by European potentates, but he always declined. From the Orient he had brought back an extraordinary library of ancient Arabic and Hebrew works, which poverty compelled him now to sell.

A witness reports that he heard him preach in Venice that all religions, the Mohammedan, the Hebrew, and the Christian, should be fused into one. Postel wanted to unite the whole known world under the hegemony of the French king, with the pope ruling over spiritual matters, though elected by a secular assembly. He advocated one religion, one king, one pope, one government, one humanity, a scheme which attracted the interest of many scholars and statesmen. Naturally, the Germans were displeased with the planned French hegemony; yet, strangely enough, the emperor protected Postel and sent him to Vienna to supervise the printing of Arabic books. In consideration for his learnedness Postel's adversaries treated him leniently, for they saw in him the dreamer rather than the dangerous revolutionary. Postel, however, was very serious about his plans; although they were as impractical as they were ambitious, they testify to his unshakeable confidence in the power of man's intelligence.

Postel claimed that he had received his ideas by divine revelation. The Hebrew scholar read the will of God in the stars. In archaic Hebrew letters eternal laws were written upon the heavenly vault. In drawing lines between the stars, one could form letters and words. This idea was later adopted by Richelieu's librarian, the Cabalist Gaffarel.

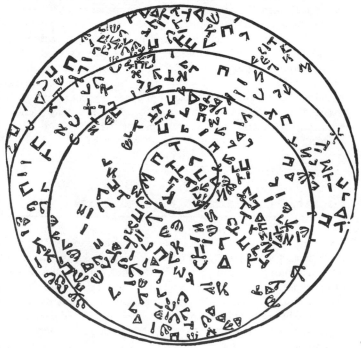

87. The celestial alphabet

Postel also concerned himself with the purification and completion of the Christian faith. Being a syncretist in the Gnostic sense, he shared the Gnostics' interest in the female sex. The soul is divided into the *animus* and the *anima*, the male and the female part, which have their separate residences in the brain and in the heart. Christ, he said, had redeemed the male element of the soul; redemption still awaits the lower, female part, which could be raised from sin only with the help of a woman. This chosen saviour-woman he had met in Venice. Her name was Joan; she was fifty years old and died before her mission was fulfilled; but her spirit penetrated Postel, who called himself male and female simultaneously.

Had Postel clung to his general Christian ideas and political plans, he probably would not have encountered open hostility.

But this idealist and magus was attracted to Loyola, the founder of the Jesuit order, whom he visited in Rome. The two men seemed to agree; Postel was accepted as a novice in the Society of Jesus, but after eleven months he had to be dismissed, Loyola being opposed to his reading of Oriental books and his plans for reform. The dismissal was followed by his incarceration. He seemed doomed to spend the rest of his life in the prisons of the Holy Inquisition. But there was a revolt in Rome; the prisons were opened, and Postel escaped. He travelled again and settled finally in Paris, where his position as professor of Oriental languages had been kept open for him.

His courses now became so successful that the rooms of the university were not large enough to hold his audience. The mystical allusions in his discourses were reported to the authorities, and Postel was compelled to recant some of his assertions. His recantation, however, was not a capitulation. With great dignity he defended his ideas, correcting only some of his views about Joan, the Venetian virgin. This document, written for Catherine de' Medici, was never printed. It is preserved at the Bibliothèque Nationale in Paris. He was ultimately granted a refuge in the Convent of St Martin des Champs where he remained the rest of his life. Not a prisoner there, as some have asserted, he continued his studies undisturbed, receiving friends, students, sponsors, and various people whom his brilliant rhetoric had converted to his faith and wisdom.

Giambattista della Porta (1538–1615)

From the Renaissance, Porta inherited imagination, elasticity of thought and a taste for intellectual adventure. He stood upon magical ground and interpreted the world alchemistically; a few of his experiments, however, were of a scientific nature. To the camera obscura he added the lens, for which reason he has been called the father of photography. He also invented and described other optical instruments. Modern ophthalmology is indebted to him for his study of the human eye. Porta in his later years collected rare specimens of the animal, the vegetable and the mineral world and grew exotic plants in his garden. Travellers used to go to Naples to visit this private museum, one of the first of its kind, and also his botanical station. It is likely that Porta's activity inspired the Jesuit Athanasius Kircher (1601–80) to start his famous collection in Rome.

Porta's master, we read, was Arnold of Villanova. But the latter died in 1311, two hundred and twenty-seven years before Porta was born. Arnold's works probably did influence Porta since they contain items which reappear in the latter's book on *Natural Magic*, and both stress the importance of experimentation. Upon one point, however, the two physicians disagree completely, namely on the influence of the stars upon the human body, on man's features, his complexion and his destiny.

An article by Casey A. Wood (New York, 1935) draws the conclusion from Porta's book, *The Celestial Physiognomy*, that the Neapolitan physician believed in astrology. Wood attributes this 'superstition' to the influence of the Church. But both assertions are erroneous. The Church by no means appointed herself a promoter of astrology, and in the book mentioned, Porta states repeatedly that neither complexion nor inclination derives from the stars but from man's humours: 'The ensemble of a constellation, the astrologers say, is like a painting whose force derives from the various colours. The heavenly aspect at man's birth will prescribe in him customs, habits and a disposition to certain diseases. Thus speak the astrologers; but things work differently, they do not derive from planets: we declare that they are caused by humours. . . .'

But how are such humours produced? People who work hard, like those in the country, become dry and hot and sweat out their aquosity. They consume coarse food, as their parents did. Such habits cause their humours to develop in a different way from the humours of people who live quietly, who eat succulent meals, who relax often, whose humour will be more even-tempered, more fluid, and whose skin is more tender. 'Man's form is a gift from heaven, not from the heaven of the planets but from God the creator who stamps and adorns the individual with his character. And this character or these features may be beautiful, splendid, majestic, because they are shaped in the image of paradise, of the angels, and finally of God himself in Whom resides the sum of beauty, splendour, and majesty. . . .' Porta defends free will and possible development from the lower degree to the higher, for he knows several people of mean ancestry who have achieved wisdom and honour.

There is no doubt that the Neapolitan physician was favoured by heaven. At six Porta wrote a composition in Latin and Italian. At fifteen he composed his three books on *Natural Magic*, a work which was reprinted many times and later amplified by him. In his youth he travelled with his brother in Italy, Spain and France, visiting the learned and conversing with them. Upon his return to Naples he founded, in 1560, the Academy of the Secrets of Nature, which Pope Paul V ordered to be closed. Porta was called to Rome to give an account of the society's activities. His explanations were accepted, for after this episode he was no longer molested. He wrote two tragedies and numerous comedies, of which one was still being performed on the stage in the eighteenth century, namely the *Astrologer*, presented in London in 1773. A work on *Curvilinear Elements* is his contribution to geometry, also an architectural treatise and a book on hydraulics, works which certainly cannot be classified as magic.

His world image was, however, a magical one, like that of Pico della Mirandola, who at times also rejected astrology, while accepting other magical beliefs. Porta's system is a magico-spiritualistic metaphysics, which leads him constantly to conclusions of analogies between plants, animals and men. Similar humours are found in various apparently unrelated organisms. Plants and animals that correspond in shape are interrelated. A

leaf formed like a stag horn shares the character of the deer. The horse is a noble animal, therefore it is a sign of nobility to walk erect with the head held high. Men who resemble a donkey are like that animal: timid, stupid, nervous. He who looks like an ostrich is akin to it in character: he is timid, elegant, vicious, stolid. A man who reminds us of a swine *is* a swine, eating greedily and having all the other characteristics, such as rudeness, irascibility, lack of discipline, sordidness, lack of intelligence and modesty. In a similar way, men who look like ravens are impudent; those who resemble oxen are stubborn, lazy, irascible; men who have lips shaped like those of a lion are hearty, magnanimous, courageous; others who make us think of a ram are timid, malicious and humble. When practising medicine, Porta had many occasions to observe his patients, and to study their character and complexion; the results of this studious inquiry are laid down in his book *Physiognomy*, presenting a striking and convincing system, not to be lightly dismissed.

Porta's early experiments in physiognomy influenced the eighteenth-century philosopher, Johann Kaspar Lavater (1741–1801), who wrote many volumes on the art of judging men by their features. His elaborate system includes morphological, anthropological, anatomical, histrionical and graphical studies. Lavater quotes excerpts from Porta's books and inserts illus-

89. *A man of bovine nature*

trations from the latter's work. About Porta's woodcut of a
bovine face, the amiable Lavater remarks indignantly, 'Among a
million men are there only two who approach the brute to such
a degree? And suppose there existed only one individual of this
type, how superior he would still be to the ox!'

Based upon the testimonies of antiquity, such as that of Pliny,
Porta introduced into his theory the idea that some beings are
mutually attracted, others repelled. Creation is built upon these
two principles, which balance and unite all things. In his *Natural
Magic* Porta, referring to these principles as disagreement and
accord, says that 'some things are joined together as if they were
in a mutual league, and others are at variance and discord among
themselves; or they have something in them which is a terror
and destructive to each other, whereof there can be rendered no
probable reason.' He offers many examples of such mutual
reaction. A wild bull tied to a fig tree will become tame through
a sympathy which pervades the two beings in their very essence
to such a degree that beef, boiled with fig leaves, will rapidly
become very tender, a fact which according to Porta was known
to Zoroaster. Such power can be used chemically, so that the
milky juice of figs, together with other ingredients, is a remedy
against the draught of the blood of bulls.

Many other wonderful things are described in Porta's book
on magic. He asserts the frequently described marvel of animals
being produced spontaneously from putrefaction. He describes
the dangerous art of making bread heavier by increasing the
weight of wheat and gives instruction for the counterfeiting
of precious stones and for similar arts which his honest readers
were undoubtedly most eager to learn. The chapter on physics
contains items such as how to make a man mad for a day, or how
to cause sleep with a mandrake. This chapter deals also with the
art of causing pleasant and troublesome dreams. They are

produced by making the subject consume beans, lentils, onions, leeks, garlic and the like. Special parts of Porta's work are devoted to distillation, fireworks, cookery, hunting and fishing, and other activities that render life agreeable.

For those having weak eyes, there are descriptions of convex and concave glasses and other optical wonders, and finally in a last chapter which he calls *Chaos*, he enumerates a few experiments 'which are set down without classical order'. One of them is the experiment with a lamp. We quote it in full so that the reader may test the incredibly marvellous virtue of a mare's excretion:

I much rejoiced when I found among the ancients that Anaxilaus the philosopher was wont to make sport with the snuff of a candle and the wick, and by such delusions would cause men's heads to look like monsters, if we may believe Pliny. But taking venomous matter that comes from mares newly having taken horse, and burning it in a new lamp, it will make men's heads seem like horse heads, and such like. I do not know whether this is true as I never tried it. But I take this for truth.

Thus ends Porta's book, and its conclusion contradicts somewhat its beginning, where he states: 'I shall observe what our ancestors have said. Then I shall show by my own experience whether they are true or false. . . .'

CABALA

Christian Cabalists and the Jews

The Humanists of the Renaissance rediscovered the beauty of art and learning of antiquity. Pagan literature was considered the ideal for good writing. The study of ancient languages became widespread. Pico della Mirandola, Reuchlin, Pistorius, Melanchthon, Erasmus were contemptuous of the half-educated who wrote and spoke a barbaric Latin or Greek. Agrippa uses as an argument against his opponents the fact that they ignore Latin grammar and write idolatry with a Y, implying that such men cannot possibly be the defenders of a good cause.

Trithemius considered the knowledge of languages more important than any other erudition. He alluded to a secret universal language, comprehensible to all mankind. Recalling the confusion of tongues at the time of the Babylonian tower, he suggests that through language a divine curse might be lifted from humanity. During the Middle Ages Hebrew had been utterly neglected. The great Christian scholars, with the possible exception of Raymond Lully, ignored it. A few magicians pretended to Hebrew knowledge, inserting in their incantations generally known words such as *Elohim* or *Adonai*, or borrowing from Jewish magical texts Cabalistic anagrams whose meaning was not always clear to them.

In the early Middle Ages the Jews had been propagators of Arabic wisdom. However, cultural exchange between Christians and Jews later became difficult. Persecution changed their intellectual course. They restricted themselves to the study of their holy scriptures and the Cabala. Moreover, the Jewish people indulged in numerous popular superstitions and magical customs, some adopted from their Christian neighbours, others preserved since time immemorial. Especially in the Germanic north, the Jews were regarded as sorcerers, poisoners, philtre-cooks; and in times of epidemics, they were accused of having attempted mass poisonings of their Gentile neighbours. In vain did the Jews plead that their community was just as plague-stricken as the rest of the city. Popular logic, shifting from superstition to religious ethics, saw in the Jews' disease a divine punishment of the criminals. Medieval science offered no tool for the systematic spreading of disease. The Jews, however, though unjustly accused of magic in this particular instance, did practice magical arts, and many magical customs had worked themselves into the Hebrew religion.

Like other Europeans, the Jews were powerfully affected by the Renaissance. Now the new spirit penetrated their seclusion and through the dismal lanes of the ghetto echoed the optimistic words of Hutten: 'It is a delight to live.' Erudite Gentiles must have been attracted by the secretiveness of the Jewish people whom they believed some superhuman knowledge had kept alive long after the other nations of antiquity had vanished. Curiosity overcame prejudice. Hebrew could be learned from the Jews, their neighbours, who recited their prayers in the language of their ancestors and wrote their books in the handsomely shaped characters of old.

This intellectual exchange was encouraged by Humanistic popes and prelates who needed translators of holy texts. In Italy a considerable number of Jews took part in public life, teaching at universities, like Lazaro de Frigeis, who lectured in Padua. Others were known as authorities in philosophical matters and more than once were they called upon as arbiters in learned controversies. It is also significant that in Mantua the first book-printer was the Jewish doctor Elia.

The rising interest in Jewish lore and wisdom was stimulated by the Humanists' search for a philosophical or metaphysical system that would free them from the medieval bonds of Aristotelianism. Such a system they discovered in an esoteric doctrine, the Cabala. Participating actively in the intellectual life of Europe, Jewish scholars were no longer able to withhold the Cabala from their Gentile colleagues. And soon Christian Cabalists arose, some of them challenging their teachers in subtlety and erudition.

Pico della Mirandola, having gained knowledge of Hebrew grammar, explored the scriptures of the Talmud as well as the Cabala. He surrounded himself with Jewish teachers, such as the famous Eliah del Medigo, Flavias Mithridates and Johanan Alemanno. In his *Heptaplus* Pico wrote Cabalistic terms on the seven days of creation; his book upon selected and obscure Cabalistic texts (*Cabalisticarum Selectiones*) was printed in Venice in 1569. Cabalistic ideas are also expressed in many of nine hundred theses (*Conclusiones Philosophicae Cabalisticae et Theologicae*, Rome, 1486). In Pico we meet with the first Gentile collector of Hebrew manuscripts.

He was succeeded by Johann Reuchlin (1455–1522), who signed his works with the Hellenized name 'Capnio'. Reuchlin's interest in Hebrew lore was awakened when he met Pico during a journey to Italy in 1490. Like Pico, Reuchlin sought knowledge of the Cabala from Jewish scholars. Among his teachers were the philosopher Obadja of Sforno and Emmanuel Provinciale, physician of the popes since Alexander VI. Reuchlin is the author of a Hebrew grammar, a Hebrew orthography, and two famous works, *On the Mirific Word* (1494) and *On the Cabalistic Art* (1517). He defended Hebrew scriptures against the accusations of a baptized Jew, Pfefferkorn, who, encouraged by the Dominicans, had demanded that all Hebrew manuscripts in Frankfurt and Cologne should be burned. Upon Reuchlin's favourable report, however, Emperor Maximilian rescinded his edict.

John Pistorius (1544–1607), a follower of Luther, compiled the most important works of Cabalism. His book *Artis Cabal-*

isticae. . . . Tomus I (1587) exerted a widespread influence. Sir Thomas Browne used it as a source, and other English scholars consulted it in the following century. Pistorius's anthology comprises works of Paulus Ricius, a converted Jew, of Rabbi Joseph, Reuchlin and Leone Ebreo, and commentaries on some of Pico's nine hundred theses. Not knowing the magnitude of the literature of Cabalism, Pistorius endeavoured to publish them all: 'Others will follow in the second volume,' he writes in his preface; but this project was never realized.

In his *Three Books on Occult Philosophy* Cornelius Agrippa expounds the Word-Cabala, the marvellous operations performed with Hebrew anagrams, magic squares and the names of angels, which are discovered through calculation. In his second book he speaks of the magical virtue immanent in numbers. Chapter I bears the suggestive title: 'Of the Necessity of Mathematical Learning and of the many Wonderful Works which are done by Mathematical Arts only'. Agrippa laid stress on the practice of Cabalistic operations, which he considered a hitherto neglected part of natural magic.

Guillaume Postel injected his knowledge of the secret doctrine into numerous writings. He published in 1538 a book on the origin of the Hebrew people and their language, and in 1547 *The Key of Hidden Things* (*Absconditorum Clavis*), in which he asserts that for the knowledge of God it is necessary that one's study be guided by the 'perscrutation' of sacred letters. He translated into Latin for the first time the *Book Yetzirah*, printed in Paris in 1552.

Among the English Cabalists the greatest and perhaps the only one who grasped the full range of the doctrine was Robert Fludd (1574–1637). In some respects akin to Pico, as he tried to reconcile Platonic and Aristotelian philosophy, Fludd attempted to identify the ten spheres of Aristotle with the ten Sefirots of the Cabala, which are the various manifestations of the divine being. Like his famous predecessors, Fludd was acquainted with Jewish scholars. Under their influence and that of Agrippa, he wrote his *Mosaical Philosophy* (1659) and *Summum Bonum* (1629), in apology of the Rosicrucian brotherhood, defending alchemy, magic and the Cabala. In agreement with the Jewish mystics, Fludd believed that illness is caused by demons; his work, *The Whole Mystery of Diseases* (*Integrum Morborum Mysterium*, 1631), is entirely based upon this conviction.

The impulse given by the early Christian Cabalists lasted throughout the seventeenth and eighteenth centuries. In 1642 Stephan Rittangel, professor at Königsberg, published his Latin version of the *Book Yetzirah*. Knorr von Rosenroth (1636–89) compiled with the help of a rabbi his *Cabala Unveiled* (*Kabbala Denudata*, 1677 and 1684). It includes in Latin translations three of the oldest fragments of the *Book Zohar* and an extensive commentary on the transcendental meaning of words occurring therein. The *Cabala Unveiled* contains in addition several treatises among which are *The Books Druschim* by Isaac Luria, founder of a Cabalistic sect in the sixteenth century, and the *Treatise on the Soul* by Moses Cordovero, who founded at that same period his own school. These two contemporaries are distinguished from one another by their approach to the sacred Cabala. Luria was a dreamer whose imagination led him away from the true tradition, while Cordovero followed the prescribed way; the fact that both of them appear in *Cabala Unveiled* is significant. Rosenroth compiled writings of varying quality and alongside precious scriptures he published also others of negligible value. In spite of this flaw, the *Cabala Unveiled* is one of the most important publications concerned with the old Hebrew doctrine, and is still used as a source by modern scholars.

Secrets of the Bible

The Cabala is a metaphysical or mystical system by which the elect shall know God and the Universe. It will raise him above common knowledge and make him understand the profound meaning and the plan of creation. These secrets are immanent in Holy Writ, yet not to be grasped by him who understands the texts literally. The Old Testament is a book of symbols; its narratives are the mantle in which are clothed sublime revelations. 'Woe to him who takes the mantle for the law.' To such a one, these simple accounts are the whole truth. If this were so, Writ could not be called the Book of Books; if the wise men of today would meet and compose collectively a similar book, it would without doubt be more coherent, less obscure and less shocking.

The Hebrew letters in which the sacred texts are written are not just signs invented by man for the recording of things, events and thoughts. Letters and numbers are reservoirs of divine power. 'Immovable numbers and characters,' Agrippa says, 'breathe forth the harmony of the Godhead, being consecrated by divine assistance. Therefore, the creatures above fear them, those below tremble at them.'

The Cabalist's task is to unriddle this hidden meaning through methods handed down by tradition. The verities thus gathered are in accord with the principles established by the founders of the Cabala. But who were these founders? History and legend disagree on this point. In Cabalistic writings we read that God Himself revealed the Cabala to mankind in Biblical times: Adam received a Cabalistic book from the angel Raziel; and through this wisdom he was enabled to overcome the grief of his fall and to regain dignity. The *Book of Raziel* was handed down to Solomon, who by its power subdued earth and hell. In another account, the *Book Yetzirah* is attributed to Abraham; but the prevalent opinion is that on Sinai, Moses received the key of how to interpret the Scriptures mystically. No one before Esdras (fifth century B.C.) had set down such interpretations. Some fifty years after the destruction of Jerusalem, Rabbi Akiba wrote the *Book Yetzirah*, and his pupil, Rabbi Simon bar Yohai, composed the *Zohar*. So much for legend, ever fond of the marvellous, and yet not entirely mistaken in placing the origin of the Cabala in the pre-Christian epoch. A cosmogony based upon letters existed in Israel one hundred and fifty years before our era. It is also likely that the Hebrew priesthood heeded oral traditions, as did the priests of other nations. That such empirical lore lived beside the scriptures we may gather from Esdras, who refers to the revelation made to Moses: 'These words,' speaks God, 'thou shalt declare and these thou shalt hide' (II, 14:5, 6).

Remnants of so venerable an age are not evident in the numerous works of the Cabala, but many of its ideas are latent in the apocalyptic texts written in the first and second century of our era. Yet the origin of a well-defined Cabalistic doctrine must be placed in still more recent times. During the Gaonic period which lasted from A.D. 591–1038, Neo-Platonic and Pythagorean influences transformed the bulk of learning into a metaphysical system of a speculative character. This change took place, not in Palestine, but in Babylon, where the Geonim, presidents of the Jewish Academy, decided religious matters. The worthy to whom the secrets were revealed were called Mekkubalim. The oldest Cabalistic book, the *Book Yetzirah* (formation) originated in the Gaonic period. The word Cabala, however, does not appear in literature before the eleventh century, and the *Book Zohar* (light) seems to be a product of the late thirteenth century, an epoch when the Cabala spread into a vast literature. The *Zohar* was and is considered the holy book, the pillar of Cabalistic wisdom. It owes its present shape to the famous Moses de Leon (1250–1305).

The Cabala betrays the influence of Gentile philosophy and esoterism in the fundamental ideas that the plan of the world architecture can be grasped by man and that the divine being can be comprehended (though not entirely) through speculation. From Greek philosophy sprang the Cabalistic idea that the world is constructed upon numbers and letters. In the *Timaeus* Plato deals with the proportions in which the universe is built. Neo-Pythagorean philosophers understood numbers and letters as divine beings endowed with supernatural powers. Alien to ancient Hebrew theology is also the Cabalistic idea of the Sefirot, manifestations of God's existence in creation. They are akin to the Neo-Platonic intelligences, intermediaries between the intelligible and the material world.

The ten Sefirot are contained in Adam Kadmon, the primordial man to whom Paul perhaps alludes when saying: 'God created a heavenly Adam in the spiritual world and an earthly Adam of clay for the material world' (I Cor. 15:45–50). And a Hebrew scripture, the *Midrash*, says that this first Adam is the Messiah whose spirit is ever-present. That things and beings exist as ideas before they are materially created has been expressed by Plato and also by Zoroaster. Moreover, akin to Zoroastrian teaching is the Cabalistic En Soph, the incomprehensible, limitless godhead from whom sprang the Sefirot by emanation, just as everything emanated from the Zoroastrian Zrvan Akaran, the deified space-time.

Other similarities exist between the teaching of the Cabala on the one hand, and the Gnostic doctrines, the doctrines of the

Alexandrian School, the philosophy of Philo and that of the Stoics, on the other. The earliest Cabalists, unwilling to ignore or unable to withstand these influences, were faced with the problem of how to accept them without doing violence to the existing Scriptures, which were inspired by God and could therefore not be altered. The solution which they found was to read into the ancient texts whatever they wished to discover in them, and to affirm that these ideas had been hidden in Writ from the beginning. In order to prove this, they resorted to such means as changing the value of letters, or substituting one letter for another, thus forming new words in accordance with the Cabalistic teaching. This procedure can serve the most diverse ideas equally well. And, in fact, it had been made use of before for the interpretation of the Talmud. From bibliomantic practices, moreover, there is only a short step to magical operations. The practical Cabala is nothing else but magic, endeavouring to induce marvellous effects through the power of the spoken word.

This apparent discrepancy between Cabalistic theory and practice is comparable to that existing in Neo-Platonism. Plotinus attacked the Gnostics because of their belief that the spoken word could expel demons; yet he could not prevent his followers from indulging in numerous magical customs. It is in the nature of theories that they call for practical application. And instead of decrying these practices we may rather ask ourselves to what extent they have been encouraged by the theories. In reading the Cabalistic texts, we will soon discover that they abound in magic, for the analogies which they establish between the real and the ideal are the products of the magical belief that the order of ideas is identical with that in nature. All that falls under our senses, the Cabalists affirm, can reveal divine thought; and everything that occurs in the world of intelligence will manifest itself in the world of matter.

Magic of Letters   Words do not fall into the void

Zohar

Whilst some learned investigators followed the Jewish scholars into the sublime realms of metaphysical speculation, others were attracted by the practical adaptations which the Cabalistic books seemed to suggest. Bibliomancy, i.e., divination from Scriptures, talismanic arts, and more generally thaumaturgy, still continued to haunt the magicians' minds when the true knowledge of the Cabala began to dwindle in the Christian West.

Fantastic reports about Jewish adepts who performed wonders with the Cabala consolidated confidence in the power of the word. The sixteenth-century master, Elijah of Chelm, had with the help of the *Book Yetzirah* made an artificial man, a Golem (literally: shapeless matter) who came to life when Elijah wrote the secret name of God upon the clay figure's forehead. A similar feat was later ascribed to Rabbi Judah Löw ben Bezalel of Prague who, frightened by the evergrowing monster, erased the secret word

on the Golem's forehead, whereupon the artificial man turned
back again into a lifeless mass. The latter fact proved clearly that
the marvel was done by the word alone, though Eleazar of Worms
had, in the thirteenth century, given a very complicated recipe
for the making of such monsters. The same Eleazar of Worms
is the supposed author of the Cabalistic book which legend
attributes to the angel Raziel.

This book is littered with strange names, surnames and aliases
of angels, formed upon known models like Gabriel, Michael,
Raphael, etc. Other such names were composed by the Cabalists
with a root term in accordance with the angel's specific activity
or function, to which was added the suffix 'el' (god). For
instance, the angel who revealed to Adam the Mysteries (Hebrew,
Raz) is Raziel; the angel of evil (Hebrew, Sam – poison) is
Samael, the angel of the Moon (Hebrew, Yerah) is Yarhiel, etc.
This simple rule, and others more complicated, were formulated
in the Talmudic period and elaborated during the Middle Ages.
Three of them will be considered here as the principal methods
of the symbolic Cabala, which discovers hidden meaning in
letters and words of the Hebraic Bible, forming new words,
anagrams and numbers for magical use.

Gematria was the name given to a process of discovering
relations between words through calculation of their numerical
values. Words with the same numerical value may replace one
another; or they may by their number indicate a new meaning.
In the Hebrew language, as in the Greek, numbers are equated
with letters. The numerical value of Jehovah (Yehova), יהוה is
10, 5, 6, 5, totalling 26. These numbers contained in the name of
God were interpreted mystically, and by similar calculations the
Cabalists discovered that the most mighty name of God must
contain seventy-two letters. The knowledge of this name was the
greatest power that man could assume. As an instance of Biblical
interpretation by Gematria the passage Gen. 14:14 may be
studied, where Abraham rescues the captive Lot with the help of
his three hundred and eighteen slaves. Did Abraham really need
so many men, inasmuch as God was on his side? To this
Gematria answers that the sum of the name of Abraham's
majordomus, Eliezer,

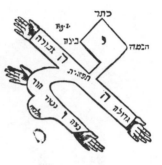

90. *Cabalistic ideogram
of the Hebrew letter
Aleph*

$$ר \quad ז \quad ע \quad י \quad ל \quad א$$
$$200 \quad 7 \quad 70 \quad 10 \quad 30 \quad 1$$

of Damascus, is three hundred and eighteen, and that Abraham
defeated the four kings and rescued Lot with the help of one
man. Gematria permitted the magician to melt together words
of the same numerical value, thus forming new obscure words
which were considered endowed with power.

The Notarikon's method was to consider the Hebrew words
as consisting of abbreviations, each letter of a word being the
initial of another word; or else the first and the last letters of
words were detached and arranged in new words. Famous
talismans and magical words were invented with the help of
Notarikon. The word *Agla*, occurring so often in magic circles,
is shaped from the first letters of the benediction: '*Athar Gibor*

*91. Cabalistic seal of
Agrippa*

Leolam Adonai' (Thou art mighty for ever, O Lord). The Genesis starts with the word *'Bereshit'* (at the beginning). According to Notarikon this word can be broken down into the initial letters of the sentence: 'He created the firmament, the earth, the heavens, the sea and the abyss.' Another example of Notarikon's procedures is the talisman which Agrippa reproduced in his *Occult Philosophy*. It reads *'Ararita'*, and it endows its owner with the power of solving all the riddles of the divine word. He will also be protected against evil spells, and all his desires shall be fulfilled. *'Ararita'* are the initial letters taken from the sentence: 'The One, principle of His unity, the principle of His Oneness, His changing form being One.' In Hebrew this reads (from right to left):

אחד ראש אחדותו ראש ייחודו תמורתו אחד

Temurah substitutes, transposes and alters letters of words. Any word may yield a hidden meaning by its anagram. In writing the twenty-two letters of the Hebrew alphabet in a special order and in two lines, the letters above and below placed in relationship may substitute for each other. The normal alphabetical sequence of the Hebrew letters is as follows: Arranged in two rows of eleven letters, A is related to L, B to T, G to Sh, etc. The result is an alphabet which reads AL BT GSH DR HK WTZ ZP CHI TS YN KM. This secret alphabet is called Albath, from the first two combinations.

כ	י	ט	ח	ז	ו	ה	ד	ג	ב	א
K	Y	T	CH	Z	W	H	D	G	B	A

מ	נ	ס	ע	פ	צ	ק	ר	ש	ת	ל
M	N	S	I	P	TZ	K	R	SH	T	L

There exist numerous different alphabetical combinations based on similar arrangements, which are called Abgath, Agdath, Adbag, Abbad, etc., according to their first two combinations. Using such alphabets, the Cabalists would discover hidden meanings everywhere in the Bible, and one word would produce another, especially when we remember that in the original Hebrew vowels are not clearly indicated. Even without mystical alphabets, one can in a scripture based on consonants read various meanings into words. Imagine that the English word 'boat' were written 'bt'! It could be read as bat, but, beat, bit, bait, bet. No wonder that the Cabalists, calculating words into numbers and numbers into words, discovered the entire world organization, the names of angels and those of God, and the number of the heavenly hosts, which is 301,655,172.

Such was the symbolical Cabala which extracted hidden things from the Scriptures and used words for magical operations. Before leaving its realms, a story from modern Palestine will demonstrate that today the Cabalists are still able to induce wonders with the help of the Temurah. When in the last war the German army occupied Greece, the Jews in Syria were in great fear that the Germanic invasion might extend into their country. As Allied strategy seemed powerless to stem the tide, the Jews sought help from the Mekkubalim, the Cabalists. The latter retired to meditation, and having sat up all night, they came

92. *Cabalistic allegory*

forth and declared to the waiting crowd that the danger was averted. They had transposed the letters of the word Syria, סוריה, into the word Russia, רוסיה, composed in Hebrew of the same letters, though differently arranged. 'And it came about just as they had provoked it by their magical art', for Hitler, instead of continuing his advance towards the Near East, attacked the Soviet Union shortly after.

By the power of words and numbers the Cabalists summoned spirits, extinguished fires, banished diseases. But a few Gentiles used their knowledge for another purpose. With arguments gathered from Cabalism, they sought to convert the Jewish scholars to Christianity. In the *Zohar* we learn that the highest manifestation of the supreme, Adam Kadmon, is shaped like man, as the form of man includes all that is in heaven and on earth. For this reason, God has chosen man's form as His own. To the Gentile Cabalist, God assuming the form of man could be no one else but Christ. Moreover, we read in *Zohar* that, having created this celestial man, God used him as a chariot for His descent.

In Heinrich Khunrath's Cabalistic scheme, the nucleus of the divine emanations, the En Soph, is occupied by the figure of the Saviour. He is standing on the phoenix, symbol of resurrection and immortality. From the luminous centre flash forth the ten appellations of God which correspond to the ten Sefirot, circularly arranged in this scheme. And the Sefirot throw their rays upon the Ten Commandments which form the outer circle of the scheme. The twenty-two letters of the Hebrew alphabet group themselves as mediators between the Sefirot and the Commandments. Scattered in the luminous centre are the five letters יהשוה (Yeshuah), Jesus. Though well imagined, this diagram would hardly have converted the Jews, for in placing Christ within the En Soph, the infinite and unlimited being, Khunrath has disregarded the dogma accepted by both Christian and Jewish Cabalists, namely that Adam Kadmon is contained in the Sefirot.

In Knorr von Rosenroth's *Cabala Unveiled* (Frankfurt, 1684) a curious dialogue between the Cabalist and the Christian philosopher serves also the purpose of converting the Jews. It enumerates all arguments produced as proof that Adam Kadmon is no one else but Christ. The short treatise is, according to its author, 'an application of the Hebrew doctrine of the Cabala to the dogmas of the new covenant, with the aim of forming an hypothesis, profitable to the conversion of the Jews'.

Is it necessary to say that in this dialogue the Christian philosopher wields the power? The half-converted Cabalist initiates the conversation, saying: 'Do you not know my friend, that there is nothing more urgent than our conversion?' Probably few such discussions had the desired effect, for Adam Kadmon was endowed with too many attributes which could only through far-fetched subtleties be identified with those of Christ. Did not the *Book Zohar* say about his traits:

He appears in the form of the old man *par excellence*, as the ancient among the ancients, that which is the most unknown among the unknown. But in the form in which he makes himself known to us, He remains still unknown. His garment is white and his mien brilliant. He is seated upon a throne of sparks which he commands at will. The white light of His head illuminates a hundred thousand worlds. . . . The length of His face is three hundred and seventy thousand worlds. He is called the Long-Face, for this is the name of the ancient of the ancients . . . .

Conscious of these difficulties, Athanasius Kircher reshaped the Cabala more energetically than his colleagues. He left little of its original form, replacing the famous ten Sefirot by twelve Christian appellations of the Eternal. The seventy-two hidden epithets of God, he says, are simply God's name pronounced in the various tongues: God, Dieu, Dio, Gott, etc. The anti-Cabalistic scheme suggests that, when God is summoned with fervent faith in any language of the earth, He will grant help more readily than when called with intricate magical formulas and bizarre appellations.

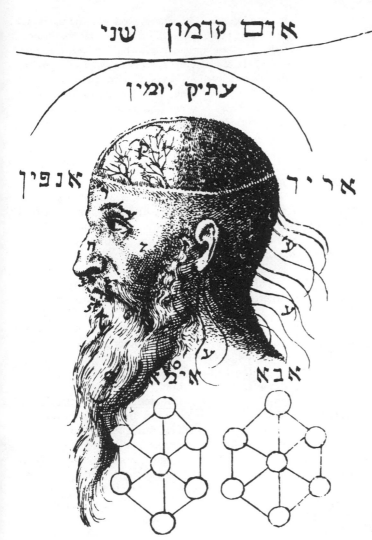

אום קדמון שני

עתיק יומין

אריך אנפין

אבא אימא

93. *The head of Adam Kadmon*

The 'Book Yetzirah'

A short résumé of the *Book Yetzirah*[1] may help to convey to the reader a general idea of the character of theoretical Cabala. 'This book,' says Juda Halevi, 'teaches us the existence of the One God, in showing us that amidst variety and multiplicity there exists harmony and unity which can only derive from the One Co-ordinator.' The *Sefer Yetzirah* reveals the formation of the universe, created by the One and sustained by Him, and everything has sprung from Him through emanation.

Unlike the Bible, the *Book Yetzirah* tells us that God shaped the universe, not out of nothing but from Himself. God is the matter and form of the universe. Everything exists in Him; He is at the bottom of all things and all beings, which carry the symbols of His intelligence. The whole, God and the universe, is a perfect unity. The uniting bond in creation are the twenty-two letters of the Hebrew alphabet and the first ten numbers (expressed by the first ten letters). These two types of signs are called the thirty-two marvellous ways of wisdom, upon which God has founded His name. They are identified with thought rendered visible, and they are superior to bodies and substances. God's breath is in the Hebrew letters. They are equally of man and of God.

They must be distinguished in three different forms: the Sefar, i.e., the numbers which express proportions, weight, movement and harmony; the Sipur, the word and voice of the living God which are alluded to in the words: 'Let there be light; and there was light;' the Sefer, finally, meaning writing. God's writing is the creation, God's word is His writing; and His thought is His word. Thought, word and writ are one and the same in God, whereas in man they are three. The ten numbers are the essential form of all that is; the number ten is the basis of the world plan. Through them, intelligence perceives the world's existence and the divine action. These numbers are called the Sefirot.

Their names are: Kether (crown), the ideal principle of all entities, and which in itself embraces all other beings; Chochma (wisdom), the principle of all life; Binah (intelligence), the principle of everything that has understanding; Chesed (goodness), the model of all grace; Geburah (power), the principle of the distribution of reward or punishment; Tiferet (glory), the principle towards which converges all that is beautiful and perfect; Nisah (victory), to which conforms the permanent and the lasting; Hod (honour), the principle of all that belongs to the glory of superior beings; Yesod (foundation), the principle of all that flows down to inferior beings; Malchut (kingdom), the link which transmits all things from the superior to the inferior, and which helps the inferior to assimilate itself to the superior. In Paulus Ricius's book *Porta Lucis* (Augsburg, 1516) the fourth Sefira, Chesed, is replaced by Gedulah (magnificence). And in Kircher's *Cabala Haebraeorum* (Rome, 1652) Pachad (fear), figures instead of Geburah.

The Sefirot are godly emanations, aspects of the infinite. 'For them there is no end, in the future, in the past, in the present, nor in the good or bad.' The higher they are placed, the closer they are to the divine. Kether, the first emanation, is the spirit of God – Chochma is His breath, coming from the spirit. In Chochma are engraved the twenty-two letters. Three is the water that flows from the breath; four is the fire, born of the water. The succeeding six numbers express the four extremities of the world, and its height and depth. The elements issued from each other, and the more remote they were from the Highest, the more gross they became. Air is the highest and the most subtle element; earth (condensed water) is the least noble among them. Everything emerged from God's bosom, and this emanation is symbolized by radiation of light, or flames. God's word is identified with His spirit. It is the generating element, the sub-

94. *The Sefirotic tree*

stance of the universe, the absolute form. His holy spirit, His voice and His word are one and the same. *He is the Word that became World*. With such a conception, substance is resolved into one principle and brought under one law.

The letters partaking of the intelligible and physical world leave their imprint upon all things; they are signs by which we recognize the supreme intelligence in the universe. And through their mediation, the Holy Spirit reveals itself in nature. With letters, God has created the soul of every form, in mingling them and combining them in infinite ways. Upon letters, He has established His ineffable and sublime Name.

Through word and writ, man can penetrate the most hidden divine secrets, and with words and signs work wonders. Such a possibility is not expressed in the *Book Yetzirah*, but only in later writings and traditions. The Hebrew letters according to the *Sefer Yetzirah* are grouped into three types: the mother letters, which are Aleph – A, Mem – M, Shin – Sh; the seven double letters, which have two sounds; and the twelve single letters. Aleph is air, because the letter is pronounced with a slight aspiration. Mem is water, being 'mute'. Shin is fire, because of its

Final Letters.	Figure.	Names.	Corresponding Letters.	Numerical Power.
Mother	א 1	Aleph	- - -	1
Double	ב } 2	Baith	B	2
		Vaith	V	- -
	ג 3	Gimmel	G	3
	ד 4	Daleth	D	4
	ה 5	Hay	H	5
	ו 6	Wav	W	6
Single	ז 7	Zayin	Z	7
	ח 8	Cheth	Ch	8
	ט 9	Teth	T	9
	י 10	Yood	Y	10
Double	כ } 11	Caph	C	20
		Chaph	Ch	- -
Single	ל 12	Lamed	L	30
Mother	מ 13	Mem	M	40
	נ 14	Noon	N	50
Single	ס 15	Samech	S	60
	ע 16	Ayin	- - -	70
Double	פ } 17	Pay	P	80
		Phay	Ph	- -
Single	צ 18	Tzadè	Tz	90
	ק 19	Koof	K	100
Double	ר 20	Raish	R	200
Mother	ש } 21	Sheen	Sh	300
		Seen	S	- -
Double	ת } 22	Tav	T	400
		Thav	Th	- -

95. Hebrew alphabet.

hissing sound. Thus the Cabala knows only three elements, instead of the familiar four.

Three, seven and twelve are the numbers with which the world is built. They recur in the three realms of nature: in the general composition of the world; in the division of time; in man. Fire is the substance of heaven, water the substance of earth; air is the mediator between the two, the dominator and also reconciler,

God's breath or word. Fire is summer; water, winter; and air, spring and autumn. For either time or season contains the same number arrangement as Man and World. In man, the number three is head, heart and stomach. The seven double letters are twofold in their essence, their effect being ambivalent, either good or bad. The Cabalist knows of the seven planets whose influence changes according to their position, exactly like the star gods of Chaldea. In the realm of time, seven are the days and nights of the week, in man they are the openings of his head: the eyes, the nostrils, the ears and the mouth. In the universe there are twelve signs of the zodiac; in time, twelve months of the year; in man, twelve capacities: sight, smell, speech, hearing, nutrition, generation, touch, locomotion, wrath, laughter, thought and sleep.

Summing up: the material form of intelligence, represented by the twenty-two letters of the alphabet, is also the form of all that exists; for, outside man, time and the universe, only the infinite is conceivable. Therefore, the three realms are called the faithful witnesses of truth. The world of letters and words is built in steps. One dominates three, three governs seven, and seven is superior to twelve, yet each part of the system is inseparable from the others. They are *one*, although many of their elements are in opposition, arrayed against one another. Finally, above man, above the universe, beyond time, above the letters and numbers, or Sefirot, is the Lord, who tolerates no duality or any definition, as He is the infinite, yet partaking of everything. But He does not submit to the law, which He embodies: He *is* the law. The closer things and beings are to Him, the more they are bathed in His light. To the Cabalist, evil is not a separate force, but rather the scarcity or absence of light.

As in Genesis, the beginning of the world is His Word; and similarly to the Gospel of St John, the Word became flesh. But to the Cabalist the Word is not *with* God, but *is* God, or a part of the threefold Jehovah. The Egyptians, as we have seen, have given a similar importance to the word, without which nothing exists. They attributed its invention to Thoth, the god of wisdom, magic and writing. The Cabalists attribute still greater power to the Word. To them, words are the principles and laws which we distinguish in the universe. In the Word they discover the invariable signs of thought which repeat themselves in every sphere of existence, and by which all that exists can be reduced to one plan. The number one, finally, is the most sublime and the most absolute manifestation of God: His thought and intelligence.

MAGICAL ARTS

The Wonder Cave

Architect de mes féeries
Je faisais, à ma volonté,
Sous un tunnel de pierreries
Passer un océan dompté.

Charles Baudelaire

The secret science was an entity, unalterable, neither to be expanded nor improved. It had existed in its totality since its inception, and could be reached by one path alone. The doctrine did not teach one how to study phenomena; it simply pointed the way which the adept was to follow.

An illustration in Khunrath's *Amphitheatre of Eternal Wisdom* shows the cave of wisdom hewn into the rock, and becoming narrower as the student approaches enlightenment. Six rays illuminate the cavern to console the subterranean traveller. It is inscribed with admonitions: 'Cleanse yourself, be pure; to the One give praise and offerings, and hymns to the inferior,' etc. There is no scientific inscription, no secret is revealed. They are simply ethical commandments, the foundation of all progress. Another of Khunrath's illustrations represents the secret doctrine in the form of the dragon of Hermes, who lives in an impregnable fortress. It has twenty-one entrances, which seem to invite the seeker to enter the sanctum, yet twenty of the ways lead him to closed compartments. The bewildered student of the occult may wander from one to the other, without ever reaching the drawbridge, of which Hermes is the watchman. But once the right track has been found, the adept advances from the humble to the high.

96. *The proportions of man, and their occult numbers*

Agrippa shows man's various attitudes, enclosed in circles and triangles. Since the world is built to human proportions, he explains, man moving in harmonious gestures means that he is expressing the world's harmony. He is in relation with the All. When his body moves according to these ideal figures, then he has captured the magical meaning of the earliest sacred dances that are performed in mystical rites. Such movements cause the gods to rejoice, and echoes to haunt the planets, like stringed instruments that vibrate when their harmonies are sung. The dance creates curative forces. When a person is sick, he is in discord with the universe. He may again find harmony and regain health, when he tunes his movements to those of the stars.

Who would believe that song and music are real magic! Yet there can be no doubt of it when we accept traditions that are most venerable. That the planets whirling in their orbs produce sounds is a discovery of the legendary Pythagoras. We cannot hear this celestial music, the Pythagoreans say, for our ears are not attuned to it, just as our eyes cannot look into the sun without being blinded. In *Scipio's Dream*, a fragment of Cicero's *Republic*, the younger Scipio Africanus is dreaming that his grandfather leads him to the stars which vibrate with a wonderful symphony. 'You hear,' Scipio the Elder says,

the Harmony. It is formed by unequal intervals, calculated according to perfect proportions, and reproduced by the movement of the spheres. The deep sounds are mingled with the shrill ones, united in ever-changing accords. For these huge movements cannot be accomplished in silence, and nature wants shrill sounds to re-echo at one extremity, and deep ones to emerge from the other. Thus the stelliferous world whose revolution is more rapid circulates with a precipitated shrill sound whereas the inferior course of the moon utters a slow and hollow sound. . . . Thus the spheres . . . produce seven distinct tones; the septenary number is the nucleus of all that exists. And men, who know how to imitate this celestial harmony with the lyre, have traced their way back to this sublime realm; in the same way as others who have by their genius raised themselves to the knowledge of the divine. . . .

Music is harmony; and harmony is the mystery of the universe.

Music will magically cure a sick person. Kircher and Caspar Schott (1608–66) explained this, although the belief is much older. Aesculapius ordained that fever shall be cured with songs. Damon cured drunkards with music. Chants and the playing of flutes and harps cure the soul as well. Had not Empedocles by his music caused a murderer to forego his abominable crime? Did not the divine Terpander pacify the revolting people of Lesbos with songs? Mecorna the Roman was sick at heart because the Emperor Augustus had taken Terentia from him. He endured insomnia for three years, until finally music cured him of his sorrow.

The proportions upon which the universe is built are those of the musical intervals; Robert Fludd says that the whole world, together with God's heaven, is like an instrument, and its keyboard is composed of the intervals between the angelic hosts, the fixed stars, the planets and the elements. God tunes the instrument, whose cord is fastened to the earth. The first diapason swings from God to the sun, the second spans the sun and the earth. The world being built upon the laws of music, man who is the world's replica must as well contain this mysterious keyboard. Fludd did not forget this. In his beautiful treatise *On the Music of the Soul* he offers an image depicting man, the microcosm, tuned to the harmony above, built in musical intervals, reaching from the head to the hips and comprising his soul and mind as well as his physical being. Above there is the *diapason spiritualis*, extending from the head to the heart, which marks the separation from the *diapason corporealis*. This dividing line is not arbitrary: as in the greater world the sun is the giver of life, so in the lesser universe the heart takes the place of the sun. Day and night, sunrise and sunset, are contained in Fludd's ingenious scheme.

Fludd had built these poetic images upon Agrippa's conceptions of the all-uniting power which music exerts in nature. 'Musical harmony,' Agrippa says,

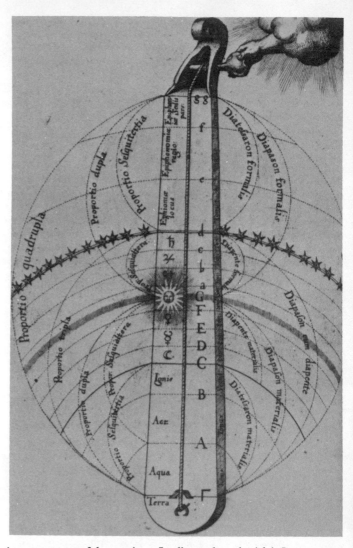

*97. The universe
conceived as a monochord*

is a most powerful conceiver. It allures the celestial influences and
changes affections, intentions, gestures, notions, actions and dispositions. . . . It lures beasts, serpents, birds, to hear pleasant tunes. . . .
Fish in the lake of Alexandria are delighted with harmonious sounds;
music has caused friendship between dolphins and men. The playing
of the harp affects the Hyperborean swans. Melodious voices tame the
Indian elephants. The elements themselves delight in music! The Hule-
sian fountain, otherwise calm, rises, rejoicing at the trumpet's sound,
and overflows its banks. And in Lydia, the nymphs' islands leave the
shore when music is played and travel to the middle of the sea where
they dance, and when the trumpet is mute they float back to the
mainland and attach themselves to the shore.

Dancing, singing, making music are the operations of white
magic; and similarly writing and reading are magical activities,
as we have learned from the Cabala. In the *Book Zohar* we read:

Throughout the expansion of the sky which encircles the world,
there are figures, signs by which we may know the secrets and the most

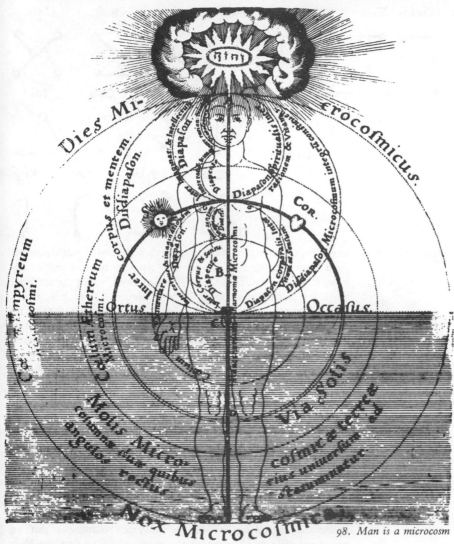

98. *Man is a microcosm*

profound mysteries. These signs are formed by the constellations which
are to the sage a subject for contemplation and delight. . . .

He who travels in the early morning shall look carefully to the
east. He will see there something like letters marching in the sky, some
rising, others descending. These brilliant characters are the letters with
which God has formed heaven and earth. . . .

Following the ancient sages' advice, many magi have scrutin-
ized the starry sky. Postel had read predictions from above and
Cabalistic mysteries; Agrippa had set down the secret alphabet
of heaven; Jacques Gaffarel had added to his book, *Unheard-of
Curiosities*, a celestial chart summing up the results gathered
during his nightly vigils. 'Since time immemorial,' he says,
'people in the Orient have read the prophetic words of the
wandering stars. We Europeans have utterly neglected this
marvellous art. Reuchlin was the first who called our attention
to it, and he was followed by Pico della Mirandola. . . . Talismans,

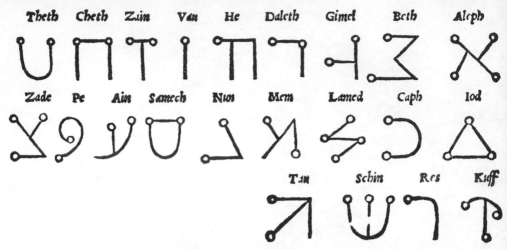

Theth Cheth Zain Vau He Daleth Gimel Beth Aleph

Zade Pe Ain Samech Nun Mem Lamed Caph Iod

Tau Schin Res Kuff

99. Celestial Scripture

engraved stones and metal plates are endowed with magic power.' And how can we explain the fact that people are moved by beautiful paintings, that they smile and weep before the artificial work of a painter or sculptor, if there were not something like a magical sympathy between the depicted scene and nature? The magi of Gaffarel's time clung to the idea of the Chaldeans and Egyptians that artistic activities were magical operations, based upon the principle which J. G. Frazer has called the law of sympathy. It is possible that the Hebrew legislators of old shared such conceptions with neighbouring nations, and that they forbade every representation of reality as being contrary to religion and magical in its very essence.

Astrology

To understand the wonderful order that rules the world and the ever-changing position of man in relation to it, we have to discover the means by which the heavenly influences can be measured. We must examine the world clock to find the laws that govern its wheels. From the dial plate, we must be able to know when the clock is going to strike.

Mathematical knowledge of the heavenly movements is as old as civilization. We have seen that Chaldeans, Egyptians, Assyrians, Greeks and Persians were masters of astrology, cunning mathematicians who without our telescopes or our delicate instruments discovered many important astronomical facts. Let us remember that spyglasses were first made at the beginning of the seventeenth century, and that the first telescope was not in use before 1663. Throughout the Renaissance, the stargazers used in their observations a stick or ruler whose function it was to guide the eye. Copernicus and Tycho Brahe worked with such aids.

To later generations, scrutiny of the sky without the telescope was unimaginable. The early astrologers were represented surrounded by fantastic instruments, among which a clumsy spyglass is usually included. The 'portrait' of Nostradamus, published in Plancy's *Infernal Dictionary*, is of this type. The seer's pointed hat and the magician's robe are purely imaginary, for astrologers never dressed pretentiously. They were clothed simply, like the learned men of their time. Guillaume Postel's portrait is that of a sixteenth-century scholar; William Lilly's effigy shows an English savant of the mid seventeenth century; and in Robert Fludd's *History of Both Worlds* (1617) an etching depicts an astrologer conservatively clad, wearing a fur-lined cap that protects his head against the draughts in his outdoor study. Significantly, in all three pictures, the spyglass is missing, though Fludd's work was published in 1619, after Galileo had already used the newly invented instrument. The scarcity of instruments is in fact noticeable; besides armillary spheres, there is little to remind us of astrology: a desk, a pair of spectacles, a compass, inkwell and pen constituting the sole equipment. Astrologers were scholars, not charlatans, and astrological wisdom required a knowledge of languages for the study of original texts, as well as considerable mathematical skill.

The stars either are favourable or bode ill to man's health and activities, and to those of the state. Nothing depends upon chance; everything is regulated and guided in a world built upon order. When a man is born, the aspect of heaven impresses its seal upon his future. But this is not its only influence; after this original impetus, the stars continue to exert their power. Rulers used to retain astrologers at court for their own benefit as well as for that of the commonwealth. No war was declared, no building begun, no financial transaction made until the stars were consulted. The astrologer then made a horoscope, a scheme that showed the ensemble of the stars exerting their supposed influence at the hour for which the action was planned. Such horoscopes were elaborated according to the following principles and methods.

The planets and the signs of the zodiac are always present in the heavenly vault, but not all are visible, some being above, others below the horizon. It was necessary for the astrologers to establish rules by which the quality of the visible heavenly bodies could be judged in order to know their influence, their strength and weakness: their exaltation and dejection. At particular points or regions of the heavens, certain planets or stars were supposed to be powerful; at others, their influence was considered negligible. The basis of the method was therefore to define these areas, to establish a system for the starry globe.

The planets were considered the most important heavenly bodies, since they exhibit initiative by their individual course, acting accordingly to their own laws and moving in a direction contrary to that of the fixed stars, which travel collectively. The circuit of the different planets covers varying spans. The orb described by the moon is much smaller in diameter than that of Saturn. The moon achieves its journey around the earth in one month, whereas Saturn requires thirty years for the same circuit.

Each planet has its own way. Their signs, established by astrology, were:

♄ Saturn   ☉ Sun
♃ Jupiter   ♀ Venus
♂ Mars   ☿ Mercury
          ☽ Moon

Their journeys, though unlike in length, carry them through the same areas, the signs of the zodiac, which mark the twelve compartments of heaven. The zodiac's inner ring is the ecliptic, i.e., the circle described by the Sun in its yearly circuit around the earth.

The northern signs of the zodiac are:

♈ Aries   ♋ Cancer
♉ Taurus   ♌ Leo
♊ Gemini   ♍ Virgo

The southern signs are:

♎ Libra   ♑ Capricornus
♏ Scorpio   ♒ Aquarius
♐ Sagittarius   ♓ Pisces

To every planet the astrologers attributed two houses, or headquarters: one of the night, the other of the day. Sun and Moon, being the heavenly bodies of day and night *par excellence*, have only one house each; the Sun resides in Leo, the Moon in Cancer. The zodiac was partitioned into the halves of Sun and Moon. Each half contains six signs. Those of the Moon, or night, are Aquarius, Pisces, Aries, Taurus, Gemini, Cancer; those of the Sun, or day, are: Leo, Virgo, Libra, Scorpio, Sagittarius, Capricornus.

This is the primary partition made by astrology. The important thing is now that each planet gains power or influence when entering his house. At night, he is most powerful in his night house; by day, in his day house. But things are more complicated, for the greatest power of each planet is not in his headquarters, but upon another degree. The Sun, for instance, has according to tradition his greatest influence upon the nineteenth degree of Aries, and his weakest spot is exactly opposite to his exaltation, upon the nineteenth degree of Libra. This position of extreme weakness is called dejection or fall. Why these mark the rise and fall of the Sun's power is not known. The other planets have their exaltations and dejections too.

There exists a third demarcation of the power of the planets, one which played an important role in ancient astrology. The whole heavenly globe being marked by 360 degrees, each sign of the zodiac is thirty degrees. Ten degrees of each sign are consecrated to a planet which becomes influential when passing through this so-called decan. There are thirty-six such decans at ten degrees, in which the planets alternate, Sun and Moon being

Planets	Houses		Exaltation	Dejection
	Day Houses	Night Houses		
☉	♌		♈ 19°	♎ 19°
☽		♋	♉ 3°	♏ 3°
♄	♑	♒	♎ 21°	♈ 21°
♃	♐	♓	♋ 15°	♑ 15°
♂	♏	♈	♑ 28°	♋ 28°
♀	♎	♉	♓ 27°	♍ 15°
☿	♍	♊	♍ 15°	♓ 15°

100. The houses of the planets, their exaltation and dejection

excluded. With the day and night houses, exaltation and dejection, and the decans, the astrologers established a system of correspondence between the zodiacal signs and the planets. By these means they will be able to judge various good or bad influences, according to the favourable or unfavourable position of the planets. Their individual qualities, little changed since the time of Chaldea, are stressed or modified according to their position.

But now, it is necessary to know from which point of the heaven the astrologer will receive the answers to his questions. The most important spot is the degree of the ecliptic or Sun trajectory which rises on the eastern horizon at the very moment of the birth or enterprise of which the horoscope is to be drawn. Originally, it was not the mathematical point but some important star rising in the east which was considered.

The rising degree of the ecliptic was called ascendant. The rising sign of the zodiac in which this degree lay was called horoscope. The name was given later to the entire constellation, the theme which was to be examined. Two other points are of importance: the degree in the west (that is, the disappearing point of the ecliptic), and the centre between these extremes in the middle of the way of the Sun. Starting from the rising degree in the east, twelve partitions of *loci* are made, which contain the answers to twelve questions. They concerned: 1. life; 2. wealth; 3. inheritance; 4. land and ancestral tombs; 5. wife or city, children, brothers and parents; 6. health and disease; 7. marriage; 8. death; 9. gods, religion, travels; 10. habitation, state, honours, art, character, etc.; 11. friends, charity; and 12. enemies and captivity. The twelve *loci* are divisions which contain the questions and correspond to twelve strips in the visible heaven, and are inscribed in a scheme which is commonly quadrangular.

The interpretation of the stars is guided by radiation or aspects. In this scheme, Aries is opposed to Libra. This is called opposition and is marked ☍. If we draw in the same scheme lines between Aries, Sagittarius, Leo and back to Aries, we obtain a triangle, called trine, whose sign is △. If we draw lines between Aries, Cancer, Libra and Capricornus we obtain the

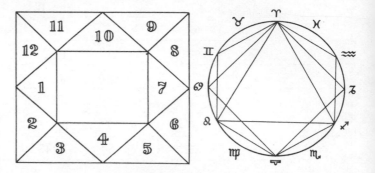

tetragonum or quartile which is marked □ Lines drawn between every second zodiacal sign produce a hexagon, or sextile, marked ✶. When a planet, for instance, is in Aries, another planet in Libra, they are in opposition, which is judged to be unfavourable. When three planets face each other in Aries, Sagittarius and Leo, they are trine, which is favourable, and similarly lucky is the sextile. The quartile is unfavourable. Finally, there is the conjunction whose sign is ☌. It signifies that two planets are in one and the same degree of a zodiacal sign, and this, according to the astrologers, is either good or bad as the planets are either friends or enemies.

Not only do the planets have their personal character: each sign of the zodiac is also endowed with particular virtues. Taurus is a feminine, nocturnal, melancholy, bestial, furious sign, cold and dry. Gemini is a masculine sign, hot and moist, diurnal, aerial, double-bodied, etc. Cancer is feminine, nocturnal, phlegmatic, cold and moist. Leo is diurnal, hot and dry, bestial, choleric, barren, etc. With all these combinations, astrology has developed a subtle means of star interpretations. Friendly and contradictory forces combat each other with ever-changing strength. Indifferent stars stand by; others, in the stage of dejection, try in vain to change the course of things. Here the planets dwell in propitious houses, grouped in a friendly trigon or sextile, promising the newly born a most brilliant career.[1]

Astrology has endowed the stars with the virtues of man; and the stars in turn impose upon man these earthly gifts. As the solar ecliptic swings up in the east and descends in the setting west, so do man's ideas rise to the stars and descend again, in an all-embracing, never-ending movement.

Divination by Moles

In the *Zohar* we read: '. . . all happens here below as it does above . . . on the firmament which envelops the universe, we see many figures formed by the stars and planets. They reveal hidden things and profound mysteries. Similarly, upon our skin which encircles the human being there exist forms and traits that are the stars of our bodies.' Magi who interpreted this saying literally examined the skin in their search for prophetic signs. They chose the legendary Melampus of ancient Greece for their patron. His brief treatise interprets the moles according to their position in the anatomy: 'A mole on a man's forehead,' Melampus says,

signifies wealth and happiness; on a woman's forehead, it denotes that she will be powerful, perhaps a ruler. Close to the eyebrow of a man, the mole predicts a happy marriage with a pretty and virtuous woman; and it foretells similar fortune to girls. Moles on the bridge of the nose mean lust and extravagance, for both sexes. When appearing on the nostrils, the mole signifies constant travel. Moles upon the lips of men and women betray gluttony, and on the chin – that they will possess gold and silver! Moles in the ear and on the neck are lucky omens; they predict wealth and fame. When upon the nape of the neck, however, the beauty spot carries an ill omen, that of being beheaded! Moles upon the loins are unfortunate, signifying mendacity, and ill luck for the descendants. When appearing on the shoulders, they predict captivity and unhappiness; on the chest, poverty. Moles on the hands announce many children; and under the arm-pits, they bring luck as they promise a wealthy and handsome husband or wife. Ominous are moles when found upon the heart and bosom and belly, as they signify voracity. They are a good omen when seen on the upper leg, announcing wealth; when upon the lower part of the stomach, they presage intemperance for men but the contrary for women . . .

Melampus concludes this miniature essay by implying that a still more elaborate method of mole interpretation exists, adding that one should observe whether the mole is on the right or the left side of the body, as left carries a sinister and morbid meaning, and right predicts general wealth and probity. Moreover, according to Melampus, moles have their correspondents; spots upon certain features of the face have their counterpart on the body.

The diviners of the occident, dissatisfied with these inadequate indications, have built a more elaborate system upon the theories of the Greek occultists. Jerome Cardan gave more precision to the doctrine by adding it to the signs of the zodiac. Moles upon the forehead, he says, need interpretation according to exact position, to determine whether they denote the signs of Aries, Taurus, Gemini, Cancer, Virgo or Leo. When appearing on the bridge of the nose, moles are correlated to Libra; on the cheekbones, to Scorpio and Sagittarius; on the jaw, to Capricornus; between the nose and upper lip, to Aquarius; on the chin, to Pisces. Accepting Melampus's views that a mole on the nape of the neck predicts decapitation, Cardan assigns to it the sign of the planet Saturn, the great misfortune, as the Babylonians used to call it. Jean Belot, vicar of Mil-Montant and professor of celestial sciences, disagrees with Cardan and Melampus, placing the planet Saturn upon the left ear [124]. Mars, Belot says, rules the forehead; the sun, the right eye, and Venus, the left one. The moon influences the nose; Jupiter, the right ear; and Mercury, the chin.

103. The relations between moles and signs of the Zodiac

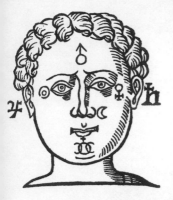

104. *Position of the planets in the human head*

The art of predicting the future and character from moles made little progress until the end of the seventeenth century when Richard Saunders published his treatise, 'resolving the Nature and Significance hereof largely, in more than three hundred particulars'. Having investigated carefully the correlation between facial spots and those on the body, he published the results of his inquiry together with an engraved copper plate. Besides this, he shows on a female figure some hundred and fifty moles that are scattered over the body, resembling a chart of the starry heavens. All these spots are interpreted according to the varying character and destiny of their owner. Saunders went further and reproduced a most curious face in an engraving made entirely by circular lines, as if to imply that the circular movement of the heavenly orbs has its counterpart in man. The face is covered with moles that bear numbers, to which his text refers extensively. Concerning number one, for instance, which is on the right side of the upper forehead, Saunders remarks:

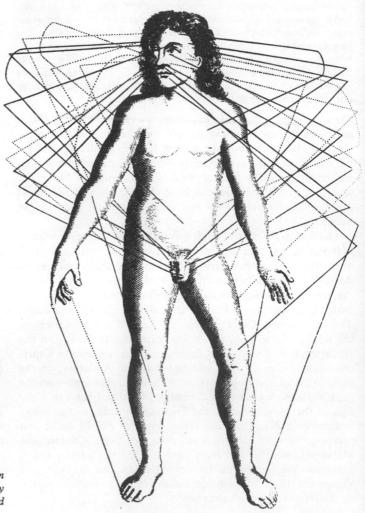

105. *The relation between moles on the body and those on the head*

106. The distribution of the principal moles on the human body

That man and woman who hath a mole on the right side of the forehead under the line of Saturn [the planets are also marked in Saunders's scheme] but not touching this line, in the first figure, they shall have another on the right side of the breast; this party may claim good fortune in building, in sowing, planting and tilling of the earth. And this mole, if it shall shine with a honey or ruby color, he and she shall have good fortune during the whole course of their lives; if black, his condition shall be mutable; if like a lentil, he shall be advanced and the first and chief person in a family. For a woman, it denotes the fortune of inheritance and gifts from the dead. This mole is of the nature of Venus, Mercury and Mars, and receives its denomination from Lyra, a star of the first magnitude.

Following the tradition of Melampus, Saunders predicts evil for him who has a mole on the left part of the hind neck. On the figure, it bears the number eight, which is opposed to number one upon the forehead, though that is bad luck as well, extremely bad, for Saunders says that it denotes imprisonment; if it is of a honey colour, he is imprisoned for frivolous causes: many enemies and contentions oppose him. If the mole is red, he shall be discharged quickly; when black, however, he shall end his life

*107. Head used in the
interpretation of moles on
the face*

in prison. To a woman, destiny seems to be somewhat more lenient, for if she has a similar mole, it means affliction, leaving the country, or two husbands, which does not necessarily imply a change from the good to the bad. Saunders's work on moles was the apotheosis of this divinatory art, which has been lost entirely if we except those picture postcards depicting attractive young ladies covered with the most flatteringly interpreted beauty spots.

Metoposcopy

She is going to offer her hand and
brow to the diviner's scrutiny.

Juvenal

The doctrine of moles was overshadowed by another related occult science, metoposcopy, which judges man's character and his destiny from the lines engraved upon his forehead. The discovery of this divinatory art is attributed to Jerome Cardan in spite of the fact that his metoposcopic treatise appeared later than other works on the subject. Metoposcopy is a mixture of astrological calculation and empirically collected knowledge. Astrology teaches that every part of the body is influenced by the stars; the study of the lines in the forehead gains special importance since it is closer to heaven than any other part of man. Once this idea was accepted, it became necessary to control the results obtained through astrological mathematics with observations gathered from nature. Cardan searched and compared hundreds of human foreheads, a painstaking and tedious task. His work is illustrated by some eight hundred woodcuts depicting heads and their frontal celestial demarcations.

One of these shows the location of the planets upon man's forehead, which is divided by horizontal lines into seven compartments. The order of the planets corresponds to that in astrology. Saturn is the 'highest'; then follow in turn Jupiter, Mars, the Sun, Venus, Mercury and the Moon. Having thus established theoretically the planets' spheres of influence, the practising metoposcopist will, when examining his patient, mark the latter's forehead with seven equidistant and parallel strips, with the purpose of recognizing his subject's planetary zones that are narrow or wide according to the measurements of the forehead. A wrinkle in the zone of Jupiter is endowed with the characteristics attributed to the planet; magnanimity, nobility, pride, etc. If the line crosses from one zone to another, it signifies that the two planets are in conjunction; their characteristics act upon and reinforce each other. Metoposcopy is nothing more than the astrology of the microcosm whose existence had been accepted long before, though it had never been controlled systematically.

108. The position of the planets on the human forehead

Let us consider a few of the instances offered by Cardan. A man whose forehead is marked by three parallel lines on its higher parts denotes, Cardan says, 'pacific and quiet character. He will possess a farm which he will manage with varying success. His fortune will be unstable. Moreover, he is in danger of being wounded on his head.' 'When the three lines are placed in lower compartments,' Cardan says, 'they reveal the man's irascible character. He will be a murderer.' When more distant from each other, the three lines predict clerical charges and good

109. The forehead of a peaceful and successful man

110. The forehead of a quarrelsome and murderous man

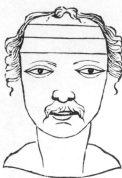

111. The forehead of an exalted man with a predilection for the priesthood

112. The forehead of a man destined to die a violent death

113. The forehead of an infirm man

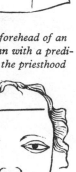

114. The forehead of a man successful in war

115. The forehead of a poisoner

116. The forehead of a man destined to be wounded in the head

fortune, intelligence and goodness. A short diagonal touching the left eyebrow foretells a violent death. And a straight line curved at one end means disease, infirmity, and other afflictions. A slightly tilted line predicts victory over various enemies, luck in war; to women it announces felicity, and superiority over the husband. There are, however, more complicated designs imprinted by the planets. For instance one that indicates death by fire, by witchcraft or incantations. Other signs predict violent death from a head wound or death inflicted by a member of one's own family.

In 1648 Philip Phinella published his treatise on metoposcopy. The work has become rare, and the two volumes are hardly ever found complete with all their roughly cut images. One of these shows the meek face of a man who is, according to Phinella, predestined to perish at sea. His curved wrinkles are like the rolling waves of the ocean, and it is more upon this magical similitude than upon calculations that the metoposcopist has pronounced his foreboding.

He who has a single line, Phinella says, is destined to travel from the Sun to the Moon. He partakes also of the Venereal and the Mercurial. Such a man will never be stable and settled. To a

117. The forehead of a man destined to be drowned

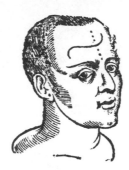

118. The forehead of an unstable man

119. The forehead of a happy and fortunate woman

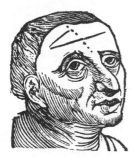

120. The forehead of a loving man

121. The forehead of an upright, intelligent man

122. The forehead of a vicious woman

woman, this line denotes even greater evil, for she will be heavy with laziness, light in her morals and volatile in temperament. The author seems to have depicted his own character by the image of a woman on whom he has commented thus: 'She will be held in high esteem by princes who seek her advice. And it is her natural inclination and disposition to predict the future.

Small dots traverse all foreheads, illustrating Phinella's theory, and are evidently the demarcations of the planetary regions. The author seems, however, to set his wandering stars in an order not acceptable to tradition. Cardan rightly places Jupiter second from above, but Phinella occasionally assigns this house to Venus. Such disagreement is even more confusing since Phinella does not explain or justify the innovation. One image shows a man whose features seem to express doubt, uncertainty. These lines, however, are good omens, Phinella says. He will be famous, a scientist establishing a well-founded doctrine. Also, his morals are excellent; such a man is trustworthy. Finally, Phinella's lady with the toothache is an ominously marked and ill-behaved person. In spite of her hypocritical piety and sad mien, she is a monster, libidinous and terrifying,

123. *The position of the planets on the human forehead*

124. *The forehead of an immoderate and sick man*

125. *The forehead of an unintelligent man*

126. *The forehead of an imbecile and long-lived man*

127. *The forehead of an adventurer*

128. *The forehead of a poet and musician*

a betrayer of her best friends, and the author of manifold ignominious deeds.

After the Dutch baroque of Phinella's figures, we shall now turn to those of the Signor Cavaliere Spontini. They have the detached air and the impassibility of old French playing cards. Ciro Spontini's booklet was published in Venice in 1637. His first image, depicting the order of the planets upon the forehead, awakens doubt as to whether metoposcopy can rightly be called a science, for he assigns to it zones that differ from those of Cardan and of Phinella. According to Spontini, the planets descend right to the middle of the nose; and the lowest heavenly body is not the Moon, as is generally accepted, but Venus; whereas the nightly companion of Mother Earth has found new headquarters upon the temples of the forehead. It is difficult to understand why he has changed the planetary order so arbitrarily unless we consider Spontini's desire to be original, a reprehensible trait in this case.

One of his images denotes an individual predestined to die from excessive indulgences through his physiognomy seems to betray a rather sober and stable character. Another signifies imbecility and a short life, marked paradoxically upon the forehead of an old man. If these lines were not intersected, Spontini says, they would designate every imaginable good: courage, Jovian wisdom, Solarian moderation and continence, Martial accuracy and promptitude, Mercurial memory and imagination, and Venereal playfulness.

A configuration with horizontal lines intersected by a vertical one predicts a variable life, spiced with dangers, impediments and permutations. A defiant mien in a victim of these signs, however, betrays his indifference to such accidents that he may overcome successfully.

A further image shows a young man who will be a vagabond, obstreperous; he will possess little faith and energy and will err in many ways. Yet he should be grateful to destiny that his lines are not intersected or slightly oblique, for then greater evil would befall him: he would be inclined to murder, be threatened by exile, and very probably, Spontini says, he would be killed.

Let us mention also one of the metoposcopist's good omens so that we may leave him with a more pleasant impression. A full-faced youth will profit from a propitious conjunction of Venus and Mercury. This means that he is inventive, a famous poet, a still greater musician. He will charm his fellow men. Beloved by beautiful women, a lucky gambler, he shall know every pleasure of life. And he may thank God that his lines are not tilted, as that would signify viciousness, dilettantism, and stupidity.

Physiognomy

Less certain in its principles but more artistic in its consideration was the physiognomic art which judges the character of an individual by his facial expressions and traits. The promoters of this were John of Indagine, or Jaeger, of Nuremberg, Bartolommeo Cocle or della Rocca (1467–1504), of Bologna, and the Frenchman Michel Lescot. Cocle, who was also a famous metoposcopist, published in 1523 his textbook on physiognomy, which contains a list of famous people and the great dangers that await them. Such an enterprise meant above all danger to himself. Jovius, the historian (1483–1552), admits that many of Cocle's predictions came true. Little is known of Lescot, whose *Physionomie* was printed in Paris in 1540. Indagine's book on divinatory arts was published in Strassburg in 1531. Its title page shows a striking physiognomic study: the author's portrait by the painter Hans Baldung. Clad in brocade, capped by the doctor's beret, the proud Indagine glances disdainfully through a handsomely decorated Renaissance window, fully aware of his own importance.

Other woodcuts in Indagine's book with their primitive and

Autore ꜰ ☉. INDAGINE. 1531.

129. John of Indagine,
by Hans Baldung Grien

lapidary execution are charged with life. One shows two audacious and impudent men. They are imposters, liars, debauched,
for their mouths are open and their lips wide. A well-shaped
dentition betrays an upright character and honesty. When the
teeth are close together and sharp, they denote a healthy complexion and predict a long life. When they protrude they reveal
a garrulous and insolent, pompous and unstable individual. Of
noses, Indagine has made a series of curious observations. Those
whose noses are curved betray by such facial deformation that
they are choleric, audacious and tyrannical. If their chin is
pointed, it means that their body is mutilated. Similar characteristics are inherent in those with a snub nose. People with strongly
curved noses laugh often at others. They, like the rhinoceros of
the proverb, are amused by the snouts of others. In ancient
Persia, a large nose was a mark of beauty – and Xerxes was a
most beautiful man. Such people as a rule are magnanimous,
courageous and good fellows.

Hair is a most important physiognomic element. Hirsute
people are choleric, their hair being coarse and dry because
of their hot humours; whereas soft, silky and smooth hair denotes a pacific, timid and meek character. Indagine begins his
observations concerning eyes with Matthew 6:22 'If your eye is
sound, your whole body will be light. . . .' And sound
eyes should be wide open, clear, shining and round. Such

130. *Lips of a mendacious and lustful man and of a modest and temperate man*

131. *Teeth of a choleric man and of a timid man*

132. *Chin of a bold man and of an impotent man*

133. *Nose of an arrogant woman and of a magnanimous man*

134. *Hair of an arrogant character and of a weak character*

135. *Eyes of a malicious man and of a lustful man*

136. *Ears of an unreliable man and of an ignorant man*

137. *Hair of an arrogant character and of a weak character*

138. *Hair of a homely man, beard of a ruthless man*

139. *Forehead of a liberal man and of an irascible man*

140. *Foreheads of vain and lustful men*

141. *Eyelashes of a malicious and mendacious man, and of an audacious and conceited man*

proportions reveal integrity and health. But sunken and small eyes are the signs of envy, malice, wrath and suspicion.

The two examples of ears offered by Indagine are both unfavourable, reflecting their bearers' capacities and characters. Large ears he calls asinine, an expression which already suggests the physiognomist's judgement: ignorance and stupid behaviour. Small ears, like those of monkeys, are simian, that is, they betray their owner's instability and fallaciousness.

Bartolommeo Cocle's *Compendium of Physiognomy* (Strassburg, 1533) is enhanced with masterly engraved plates. The artist's name is unknown; it seems, however, that he was inspired by the flamboyant Gothic of Strassburg Cathedral. Like Indagine, Cocle depicts two individuals who reveal their contrasting temperaments by their hair. If Cocle copied them from Indagine's book, he added two new types of hirsuteness of his own discovery. Men whose temples are covered by a dense growth of hair are simple, vain, credulous, stubborn, of mediocre intelligence and somewhat boorish in manners and language. Bearded fellows are brutal, vengeful, have poor memories, are unfortunate and covetous.

People with high and rounded foreheads are liberal, gay and possess a good intellect. They excel in many crafts and are manageable. Their counter-images, those whose foreheads are short and covered with hair, are quarrelsome and simple rather than refined. Others whose foreheads are too small in every way are simple, irascible, cruel, covetous and fond of beauty, especially of stately buildings. Men with well-rounded foreheads that have humps and little hair are intelligent and

142. Eyes of a crafty man and of a guileless man

143. Nose of a peaceable man and of a man of great intellect

144. Noses of vain and lustful men

145. Man and woman of excellent disposition

enterprising, high-minded even in adversity. They appreciate beauty, honours, responsibility and worldly pleasures. Eyelashes may also reveal man's disposition. Men having curling eyelashes are vainglorious, haughty, heinous and the like, whereas lashes that curve downwards denote malice, fallaciousness, dishonesty, laziness, secretiveness.

Cocle judges eyes differently from Indagine: large and round eyes, he says, signify a fickle and lazy fellow. At times he is bold, at others, meek; often he may speak the truth, then he lies; in short, he is like most men, whether they have large or small eyes. Little, sunken eyes belong to those of an obviously bad character: suspicious, malicious, bad tempered, deceitful, lewd, vain, etc. There is, however, another type of small eyes which denote very different things. If they are round, they signify the owner's timidity, weakness and sluggishness, as well as his credulity. Tilted eyes betray wisdom, dishonesty and malice.

Big noses, Cocle says, are a good sign, whether they are curved or straight. Such people are peaceful though not shy, and very intelligent. They may at times have an outburst of temper, but such reactions disappear quickly and are succeeded by long periods of generosity. Snub-nosed and flat-nosed people lack intelligence and indulge in lies, vanities and extravagance. They are fickle and, though acquainted with the technique of lying, believe other people's lies.

One image shows the ideal features of young people who are in good physical and mental health. In it the man is gifted in many ways. He is fond of normal pleasures and of healthful food, of which he partakes at the proper hours. His digestion is good, his blood of the right temperature; the modest young lady in the same image shares these qualities.

Chiromancy

> Nature has made the hand of man the principal organ and instrument of man's body.
>
> Aristotle

Why should the hand more than the other parts of the body reflect the forces from above? To this, the magus answers that since the world is a hierarchy, then the miniature world – i.e., man – must necessarily be organized similarly. In the system of man, the hand fulfils a unique function, that of the mediator between the above and the below, between the intellectual microcosm, residing in the head, and the material microcosm, which dwells in the body. If the brain is comparable to the unmoved mover, the magi say, then the hand may be called the active force through which the mover manifests himself. For this reason, the hand occupies the second rank in the microcosmic hierarchy and is, after the head, the most worthy of investigation. In the eighteenth century, when many magical traditions had been lost, over-zealous chiromancers believed it useful to investigate the plants of the feet, a ludicrous misconception. The feet are the most remote from the planets. Turned towards the earth, they receive the weakest light from above. They dwell, according to Fludd, in the microcosmic night, which is not tuned to the music of the spheres.

Chiromancy gathers from the heavenly imprints upon the hand two verities; character and destiny; a conclusion which all divinatory methods share. This is deductive as well as prophetic, rational and irrational. When reading his patient's hand, the chiromancer uses his reason and his divinatory gift. The lines whose significance was established by tradition are the scaffold upon which the magus sets his imagination. Imagination is the force which performs the marvel, as Agrippa, Paracelsus and others have affirmed. The chiromancers searched the Bible for verses that might prove the legitimacy of their art, for religion was believed to sanction magic, as in our days the occultist rashly relates his wisdom to true science. Thus, in the book of Job 37:7, we read: 'He seals up the hand of every man, that all men may know his work.' And in Proverbs 3:16: 'Long life is given in her right hand. In her left are riches and honour.'

It is not within the scope of this book to explain the method of hand reading, on which there exists an extensive literature, but rather to give a few of the most striking illustrations of the periods when chiromancy was at the height of its popularity, i.e., the sixteenth and seventeenth centuries. It is useful, however, to compare these early schemes with that of modern palmistry. Far more importance is given to the fingers today. They confirm the marks in the palm and add many interesting details to

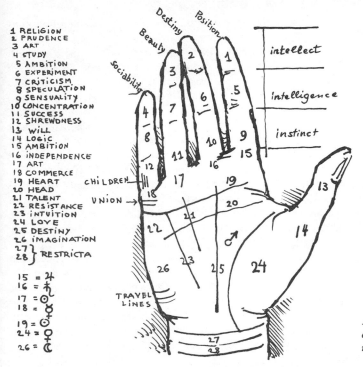

1 RELIGION
2 PRUDENCE
3 ART
4 STUDY
5 AMBITION
6 EXPERIMENT
7 CRITICISM
8 SPECULATION
9 SENSUALITY
10 CONCENTRATION
11 SUCCESS
12 SHREWDNESS
13 WILL
14 LOGIC
15 AMBITION
16 INDEPENDENCE
17 ART
18 COMMERCE
19 HEART
20 HEAD
21 TALENT
22 RESISTANCE
23 INTUITION
24 LOVE
25 DESTINY
26 IMAGINATION
27
28 } RESTRICTA

15 = ♃
16 = ♄
17 = ⊙
18 = ☿
19 = ☉
24 = ♀
26 = ☾

146. Meaning of the lines
of the hand, according to
modern chiromancy

the more general information gathered from the palm. The upper phalanx of the thumb expresses will, the lower, logic. In the three phalanxes of the index finger reside religion, ambition and sensuality. The middle finger contains prudence, the tendency to experiment and concentration. The ring finger informs us of the individual's artistic gifts, his critical sense and his successes. The little finger belongs to sociability; it is marked with the signs of study, speculation and shrewdness. All the upper phalanxes give information concerning the subject's intellect; the middle phalanxes, of his intelligence; and the lowest phalanxes, of his instincts.

The most important lines of the palm are those of life, of destiny, of the heart, of the head and of intuition. A shorter line that descends from the art or ring finger reveals artistic talents; and several parallel lines upon the wrist give supplementary information about the length of life. Besides the lines of the hand, its 'mounts' are important to the palmist. The hump of the thumb, called the mount of Venus, informs us about the individual's love; the mount of Jupiter, below the index finger, is marked by ambition; the mount of Saturn, below the middle finger, reveals man's independence; the mount of the Sun, below the annular finger, is that of Apollo, or art. And below the little finger, the mount of Mercury reveals commercial aptitudes. At the edge of the palm, opposed to the thumb, there are the mounts of Mars, denoting steadiness and resistance, and of the Moon containing the marks of imagination and melancholy. Close by are the lines of travel, and above, in the mount of Mercury, those of union. Distant from the mount of love, in the realm of shrewdness (lowest phalanx of the little finger), is

147. The principal lines of the right hand, after Indagine

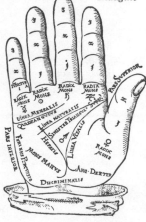

148. The principal lines of the right hand, after Tricasso

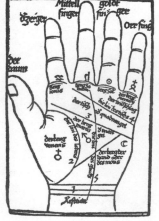

149. Chiromantic hand, after Cocle

marked the number of children the person will beget or conceive.

To the question of whether the right or left hand or both should be inspected, no definite answer can be offered. From tradition, it has been accepted that in the left hand, which does not work as much as the right, the signs are preserved better and not distorted. Others say that in the left is inscribed the primitive destiny given by the stars at man's birth, whereas in the right hand are marked those changes which man causes daily by his will and work. This argument cannot be accepted lightly. If man's will is free, why should one inspect his left hand? If he modifies his destiny, the stars' original marks offer no valuable information. But if the stars are omnipotent, then there is no point in inspecting the right hand, for will, labour and intelligence cannot overcome that which has been decided by the horoscope. This perennial strife as to whether man is free or not can certainly not be ended by the chiromancer. In his defence, one could say, however, that in the left hand he reads man's natural disposition, whereas the right hand reveals to him what he has made of his gifts. Thus one may recognize whether the subject is living according to his inclinations, if his activities are in accord with the gifts bestowed upon him at birth, and the like. Accepting this, we can say that the stars influence but do not irretrievably decide our destiny.

The palmists or chiromancers render their judgement according to the various lengths of the lines, the depth of their engraving, their colour, their continuity. They also consider whether the lines are doubled, like those in Indagine's woodcut. Indagine considers as the main lines the *linea mensalis*, identical with our line of the heart, the *linea media*, or middle line, the *linea vitae*, or life line, which he calls also line of the heart, and the *linea hepatis*, or liver line which reveals according to a few experts disturbances of the lower functions. The four mounts below the fingers correspond to those of modern palmistry.

The Dominican Tricasso de Cerasari (died 1550) shows a similar disposition of the principal lines in his treatise on chiromancy. 'Four grooves,' he says,

regulate and command the whole art of palmistry, and all the others depend on them. The lifeline must be divided into three parts – youth, maturity and old age. From its length, we can recognize how long its owner has to live. When the heart line is short, without ramifications, it denotes mortal danger, conjured up by negligence. When the head line is stopped below the middle finger, this means that the individual will wound himself dangerously. When the liver line is very distant from the one of life, it denotes a vain or an insane being . . .

Neither Indagine nor Tricasso count the line of Saturn, or destiny, among the important marks of the hand. The *linea Saturni* is, however, not a later invention for it is plainly marked in Bartolommeo Cocle's handsome woodcut. Agrippa's chiromantic hand [170] shows the locations of the planets; they are not different from those of modern palmistry, with the exception of the headquarters of Mars which occupy the centre of the palm.

In the seventeenth century the number of principal lines was increased. The Parisian Ronphyle adds to the older schemes the line of Saturn, which he also calls arbitrarily the liver line, and the line of Apollo, that of artistic talents. As late as 1676, however, an English edition of Indagine's book clings still to the four lines of old. To stress its conservatism, this book is printed in obsolete Gothic characters. The line of life, it says, has already been rightly judged by Pliny. Its length marks the boundaries of life. The middle line (E) reveals health and disease, the table line (A) informs us of our physical constitution and strength, of our temperament and mind. The wrist line (C, D) promises riches and felicity, when it is well coloured. But when it reaches into the hill of the Moon, it signifies betrayal by women, and many storms in fortune. Special attention is given in this little treatise to the conformation of the thumb. 'If there be about the first joint of the thumb a crest like a ring going round about, and dividing the thumb, many do sternly judge and say, that this man shall be hanged. The which thing I have proved true in one man. But because I have seen many hanged who have lacked that mark, I leave it as uncertain.'

A very instructive woodcut illustrates Jean Belot's treatise on chiromancy. It shows a synthesis of many lines and districts. Moreover, Belot added to his scheme a novelty, introducing the signs of the zodiac into the four fingers. The index contains Ram, Bull and Twins, the middle finger, Goat, Water Bearer and Fishes, etc. Upon the thumb is marked the lost virginity: and the

150. The position of the planets on the right hand, after Agrippa

151. The principal lines of the hand, after Ronphyle

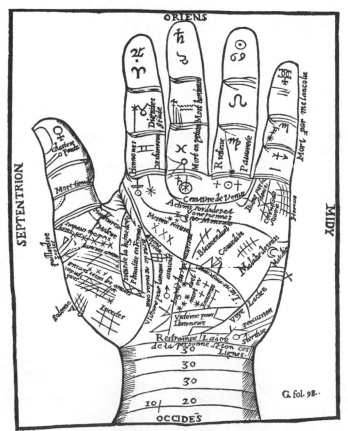

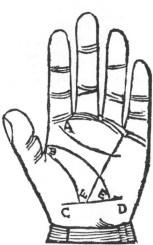

152. The principal lines of the left hand, after Indagine

153. Comprehensive diagram of the left hand, after Belot

mount of Venus contains other items which apparently interested the abbot's contemporaries. In the hollow of the hand, in the region of Mars, we read; 'wounded in a duel', which shows that the occult sciences, like the true ones, adapt themselves to their epoch. Further down, in the triangle formed by the middle line, that of the liver and the line of Saturn, we read about similar yet greater misfortunes: 'killed in a duel'. Such sad predictions are separated only by a few millimetres from good news: close to the wrist, we read; 'victory in defence of honour'. Below the mounts of the Sun and of Saturn reside sordid actions, and close by, upon the mount of Mercury, the good things brought to science. Between thumb and life line, finally, are the marks of polygamy; in the table of Mars, close to the life line, dwell success in love affairs, assassination and insults received.

Belot's illustration suggests an ensemble of one hand. Innumerable other combinations are possible. They are as inexhaustible as those of human physiognomies. But this recognition should not discourage us from showing a few more instances of manual conformations, if only to give the reader an idea of the prodigious richness of the chiromantic literature.

An early treatise, signed by Andreas Corvus of Mirandola, another pseudonym for Cocle, reproduced numerous types of hands upon everchanging backgrounds, in a rustic Renaissance style. One image represents an extended line of Saturn which is interpreted thus: 'When you see this line of prosperity, going through the hand down to the wrist and being deeply engraven, it denotes prosperity and good business. If you find the contrary, it signifies an inventive man or woman, an innovator of science, yet shabby, greedy, etc.' A little triangle at the wrist predicts a quiet life, the peace of the soul, honour, force of the mind and of the hand. If there are restricted lines at the root of the hand they denote inventiveness, specially in evil matters; bad fortune, disobedience to one's father and contempt. If such lines diminish in strength towards the arm they predict increase up to the middle of life of wealth and honour, and afterwards a decrease in both.

154. Hand of an avaricious and thoughtless man, after Cocle

It is remarkable how many of these combinations of lines are unfavourable omens, how little the palmists of old objected to communicating to others their inveterate pessimism, unlike the amiable disposition of modern palmists who predict when paid well the good things to come, mingling with their ingratiating talk a few friendly warnings. In these old books, we read nothing about fatal dark-haired persons and favourable blondes, or of a letter that will change the course of our fate.

155. Hand of a stubborn and iniquitous man, after Cocle

Palmistry of old was considered a science; the inspection of the hand was as grave as a doctor's visit is today; and the chiromancers were very serious about their craft. In his preface, Indagine describes the painstaking procedure necessary for efficacious investigation:

I look upon the hand and therewithal behold the whole body, with the lineament and proportions of the same, which is called his physiognomy. Then I focus my mind upon the hour of nativity, month, day or year, which I refer to the rules of natural astrology; I judge none of these by themselves sufficient, and think it better not to be rash or foolish in passing sentence. I gather all things and select those which I consider useful. Only then do I utter judgement, believing it madness to examine the hand and hastily interpret a life, and a body.

The chiromancer's verdict, pronounced with such strong conviction, was certainly endowed with a suggestive power. Sometimes it may have been based upon a general knowledge of man, on logical deductions and the like, things which did not require much astrological calculation and chiromantic inspection. Indagine's statement that he can read the palm like a physiognomy is revealing: experience can produce a routine which may have, in serious cases, been more than idle fancy.

156. *Hand of an irascible and evil man, after Cocle*

A Greek chiromancer predicted to Alessandro de' Medici that he was soon to suffer a violent death, which happened when he was assassinated by his cousin Lorenzo. In the last century, the physician Bruhier reported the true story of a young man in whose hand a lady had read an evil future. 'What a pity,' she exclaimed, 'that you have only one more month to live.' Some time after the youth went hunting, caught a fever, and died at the appointed date, as the amateur palmist had predicted. A famous case of a chiromantic prophecy which came true is that of a M. Raillois who had been warned by a gypsy to beware of the scaffold. His whole life seemed to disprove this prediction, made when Raillois was a boy. He would often mention in jest that he would suffer an ignominious death. He had a new house built on one of the fashionable Parisian boulevards. While inspecting the progress of the work, he stepped from a window upon the scaffold which, being fastened carelessly, collapsed. Raillois died from his fall. Cocle read in the hand of Bentivoglio, ruler of Bologna, that he was to be exiled and would die in a battle. The angry Bentivoglio decided to have Cocle killed. He chose for this task a Bolognese nobleman to whom the palmist had predicted that he was going to commit an ignominious murder. He railed at the dying Cocle, saying that his prediction had now come true.

157. *Wrist of a woman physically unsuited for motherhood, after Cocle*

The earliest chiromancer of the Renaissance, Antioco Tiberto of Cesena, was stabbed by the tyrant of Rimini, Pandolfo Malatesta, to whom he had prophesied death in exile and poverty. Tiberto was a lively and intelligent scholar held in high esteem, even by those intellectuals who thought little of the chiromantic art.

The Tarot

No calculation or scientific observation is necessary for the Tarot game. Its entire magic theory rests upon the belief that in nature there is no accident – that every happening in the universe is caused by a pre-established law. The most insignificant event is subject to this fundamental rule: cards mixed at random do not yield haphazard results but a suit of figures bound magically to the diviner and to the inquirer.

The practice of the Tarot is based upon a prophetic gift of man which manifests itself through a special condition, called clairvoyance by the occultists, and hyperaesthesia by the scientist. No doubt this state arises more frequently than we care to admit. Who has not, even if only once in his life, had that sensation called foreknowledge? Some future event is witnessed so clearly, so plastically, that its beholder knows immediately and with absolute certainty this *will* happen. And it does! There are people specially gifted with such prescience or premonition, the born diviners. They stimulate their abnormal sensibility in many ways. Gazing at the crystal produces an autohypnotic condition; in fact, any glistening or colourful object, when stared at for a time, may become equally stimulating to the imagination. Some clairvoyant people are able to tell where the stone which they press against their forehead was found. They can describe the landscape in which the stone lay, as well as the person who picked it up, and so on.

The primary function of the Tarot cards seems to be this sort of stimulation. In scrutinizing the vividly coloured images, the diviner will provoke a kind of autohypnosis, or if he is less gifted, a concentration of the mind resulting in a profound mental absorption. The Tarot's virtue is thus to induce that psychic or mental state favourable to divination. The striking Tarot figures, specially the trumps or major arcana, appeal mysteriously and waken in us the images of our subconscious. Many of the Tarot figures are medieval allegories: the eighth trump card, Temperance, the allegory of Force of trump eleven, are no mystery to the iconologist. The Wheel of Fortune, trump ten, is a theme used in Romanesque rose-windows. Other similar affiliations can be detected without too much difficulty. Most if not all of these figures belong to the orbit of Christian civilization.

The Tarot experts have, however, insisted that the trump cards and pip cards are of a more venerable age, that they date back to antiquity. Impetus was given to this theory by the French scholar, Court de Gébelin (1728–84), who says in the eighth volume of his *Primitive World*: 'If one were to know that in our days there existed a work of ancient Egypt, one of their books that escaped malicious destruction . . . a book about their most pure and interesting doctrines, everybody would be eager no doubt to know such an extraordinary and precious work.' This Egyptian book, according to Gébelin, is the Tarot. The ancient wisdom survived, he says, because it was clothed shrewdly in the garment of a game. Its frivolous character saved it from barbarism, ignorance and every destruction.

In Gébelin's time much interest centred on Egypt, whose literature was still undeciphered and whose relics were unexplored. Egypt was the land of mysteries. For a knowledge of its civilization one had to rely upon the ancient authors, Plutarch, Herodotus, Iamblichus. Lack of proof gave rise to conjecture, and Gébelin, carried away by his imagination, convinced himself that the Tarot was nothing more than the unbound leaves of the book of Thoth.

Thoth-Hermes, the presumed author of the earliest Hermetic

books, whom the alchemists claim as their Grand Master, was credited by Gébelin with the invention of the Tarot leaves. He was the inventor of magic, of languages, writing and figuration, and had according to the myth painted likenesses of all the gods. His mystical sketch book was called *A-Rosh*, '*a*' meaning 'doctrine', '*rosh*', 'beginning'. *A-Rosh* had inspired the Tarot with its images, and the word Tarot itself, Gébelin says, is derived from '*Tar*' (way) and '*Ro*', or '*rog*' (royal, kingly). Thus Tarot would mean the Kingly Way.

Gébelin's theories are based on shifting sand, but he promoted interest in the civilization of Egypt, and only eleven years after the publication of his *Primitive World* a discovery brought a shaft of light into the dark realms of conjecture. In 1799 a fragment of basalt was found in the town of Rosetta on the Nile. It contained two inscriptions, one in Greek and one in hieroglyphics. By comparing the two texts, which were obviously identical, it was possible after many centuries of complete mystery to establish the first scientific contact with the ancient Egyptian hieroglyphic characters.

Influenced by Gébelin, most of the writers on magic declared that the Tarot was of Egyptian origin. The wig-maker Alliette (*ca.* 1750–1810) published a series of essays on the famous game under the pseudonym Etteilla. He undertook to restore the original form to the Tarot figures which had been mistreated by Gébelin's engraver. Alliette, more artistically than scientifically, embellished them according to the taste of his epoch, but he also gave them some new and rather unorthodox attributes, and added astrology and the Cabala to the game. It is curious how many occultists believe and profess that an original secret wisdom has perpetuated itself through millennia, preserving traditions which they then readily distort or destroy. They seem to forget that their bad habits must have existed before them and that for this very reason no doctrine could have come to us in its original form. If any esoteric wisdom of old were still extant, it would be so thoroughly transformed that its inventors would not recognize it as their own child. Alliette, the vainglorious hairdresser, decided that the Tarot game should be rectified, and reinstated to its original glory. He changed the sequence of the leaves, discarding some and adding new ones which he declared were the oldest images, lost during the peregrinations of the game from Egypt to Europe – in brief, he confused everything completely.

During the nineteenth century Alliette's reforms were discarded and the old game was adopted again, yet none of the occultists could refrain from adding a few curlicues to the Tarot figures. Oswald Wirth, a pupil of the famous magus Stanislas de Guaita (1860–97), like Gébelin reversed his Tarot images, in the belief that he was correcting a mistake of the early engravers. Wirth made numerous additions in his designs, which are based on his own presumptions. Comparing his Temperance with the original figure, we see that in keeping with the lavish taste of his time he found it useful to place the allegory against a golden background, and to add a flower where the old image has only a

158. Tarot trump: Temperance, after Court de Gébelin

159. Tarot trump: Temperance, after Etteilla

*160. Tarot trump:
Temperance, after
Oswald Wirth*

*161. Tarot trump:
Temperance, French,
XIX century*

little shrub. Wirth represents the two jugs, which in the original are similar, as being made of different metals, the one of gold and the other of silver. The original colours – brilliant and transparent – are in this new suit of trumps subdued to saccharine pastel effects: salmon pink, pale ochre, moss green and chalky blue. At least two of the nineteenth-century magi sanctioned this modified Tarot game: Guaita and Papus, who published it in their works. Wirth's cards are numbered with Arabic instead of the traditional Roman numerals, and Hebrew letters are added, whose numerical values correspond to the cards' numeration.

Gérard Encausse, whose pen name is Papus (1865–1917), considered it necessary to start his book on the Tarot with an introduction on the Cabala of his own. Stanislas de Guaita organized his extensive treatise on occultism, the *Serpent of Genesis*, according to Cabalistic numbers and images of the Tarot. His fourteenth section deals with Temperance. It is illustrated by the fourteenth leaf of the trumps – Temperance – and the design betrays the talent of his secretary, Oswald Wirth. Alphonse Louis Constant, alias Eliphas Lévi (1816–75), likewise accepted the Cabalistic interpretation of the Tarot. In his colourful work on dogmatic and ritualistic magic, he uses the Hebrew letters and the Arabic numbers for the numeration of his chapters.

Still more marvels were added to the Tarot pack in the twentieth century. Mrs John King van Rensselaer published in 1911 her definitive book on *Prophetical, Educational and Playing Cards*, which is devoted largely to the 'Kingly Way'. She states that the Egyptian Thoth, the Greek Hermes, the Babylonian Nebo are of an identical character, and that the Tarot was consecrated to all three, united in a syncretistic godhead. The game, Mrs van Rensselaer says, is derived from the old practice of seeking knowledge of the future by divining rods, tablets or arrows, a practice common to Egypt, Greece and Babylonia. In the ancient Egyptian temple halls the images, now appearing on the Tarot cards, were painted on the four walls. The priest tossed the sticks upon the altar. 'As these rods fell, they naturally pointed towards the pictures on the walls, and since they represented nearly every event of life, the commands of the gods were interpreted readily by the priests who thus proved that Thoth was the god of speech. . . .' The four figures of the pip cards, the King, the Queen, the Cavalier and the Knave, may be connected with the four signs on the divining rods. These symbols represented the father, the mother, the child or children, and the servants, people about whom the inquirer wished to obtain the god's oracle. Mrs van Rensselaer concludes that in times of decadence and persecution the priests left their temples and carried secretly with them the temple wall images in the form of the Tarot pack, with which they continued to render oracles to the faithful. From Egypt, these priests travelled to Italy on the famous corn route between Alexandria and Baiae, near Naples.

The experts of the Tarot wanted at any cost, even by forcing some of their arguments, to connect the game with the divinatory art of antiquity. They rationalized this desire by believing that such noble antecedents would make the Tarot more venerable.

To us, such preoccupations seem unnecessary; the Tarot cards with or without this famous ancestry have attracted many and still fascinate those who ignore their assumed history.

The twenty-two trump cards were called Man, and it is with him they are concerned – with his desires and fears, his wisdom and activities, his goodness and badness, and his physical constitution. The whole world simmers down to man; in two cards only is the human element missing: in the Wheel of Fortune, number X, where animals caricature the human, and in figure XVIII, the Moon, in which two stargazers of the sixteenth century have been replaced by a dog and a wolf barking at the Moon. They too are caricatures of man. In this quality the Tarot cards resemble the images of other arts: the paintings, sculpture and stained-glass windows of the cathedrals, which also clothed ideas in human form. Their world, however, is the one above, while the world of the Tarot is below. The trumps depict the relation of the powers and the virtues to man; the cathedrals on the other hand embody man's relation to the divine. But both images impress themselves upon the mind. They are mnemonic. They contain a wide complex of ideas that would fill volumes were they written down. They can be 'read' by the illiterate and the literate alike, and they are destined for both. The Middle Ages were concerned with techniques that would enable man to remember and to compare many such areas of ideas. Under this impulse, Raymond Lully wrote his *Ars Memoria*, the Art of Memory. Similar preoccupations also resulted in the early block print, *Ars Memorandi*, printed about 1470. The author undertook the difficult task of making concrete the themes contained in the Four Gospels. For each Gospel he created a few images, angels, bulls, lions and eagles, emblems of the four Evangelists, upon which he imposed objects that were to suggest the stories treated in each chapter. The angel (Matthew), contains eight smaller emblems that were to recall Matthew's eight first chapters. In visualizing every figure of *Ars Memorandi* with all their emblems, one would remember the stories of the entire Gospel. To us, such visual memorizing would seem prodigious, but it was surely not unusual in times when only a few could read and write, and when images played the role of writing.

The Tarot cards by their mnemonic character are related to the images of *Ars Memorandi*, and if we accept the tradition that every detail in the Tarot trumps with their ornaments, implements, colours, etc., are just so many symbols, the cards contain a considerable number of elements to be remembered. But what exactly is there to remember? The difference consists in this, that *Ars Memorandi* refers to the well-known Biblical texts, whereas the Tarot confronts us with riddles. The Kingly Way leads us into an enclosure, where we are faced with our own subconscious.

The Tarot is both the generator and the battery. It gives birth to one's thoughts, and also nurses them. In studying the cards, one is stimulated to visualize images of our intellectual and psychic experiences; and returning again to them later, we will

162. Mnemonic Figure of Matthew

recall these images, which would have 'fallen into the void' without this mnemonic help. The Tarot produces for us an independent and self-sufficient world, and our psyche is made objective, and detached for contemplation. The Tarot figures are stereotypes; but what they suggest is in constant flux. They do not express or lead to an established doctrine. On the contrary, they liberate us from such bonds. This liberation may have a psychotherapeutic effect, as modern scientists have suggested, but above all, they free faculties in us which are suppressed by conventions and daily routine. They stimulate a creative power which appeals to the artist. They are the 'poetry made by all' of the surrealist postulate.

There is no key to the Tarot, but there are as many interpretations as there are individuals who consult the cards. The cards, we repeat, are not manipulated by means of theories and doctrines; they are interpreted through a natural gift, found among the learned and the profane. The nineteenth-century magi sought to introduce into the game an esoteric doctrine, resembling Hermetism. Their ideals might be justified as a reaction against the shallowness and the extravagant optimism of their contemporaries. But their rigid self-assurance is, so to speak, 'antitarotic', and they lack a virtue found in some Tarot cards, namely humour and irony. What they believe to be the truth they profess with a prophetic vigour which does not tolerate contradiction. They call sublime secrets inherited from the sages of antiquity, what we would describe as perennial human traits.

If the desire to establish an infallible dogma of the Tarot is a mistake, it is also wrong to change or 'correct' the figures of the game which are timeless prototypes. The beautiful trumps have risen from nowhere, and this is precisely one of the attractions of the game. To reform them to fit dogmatic expressions of a vanished civilization is to deprive them of their *constant* values. Such corrections are not sought by those who have accepted the images for centuries and still discover marvels in them now.

Like astrology, the Tarot proposes a method for predicting future events and man's character. But the Tarot abhors the scientific aspect of astrology. The future, the cartomancers say, cannot be explored by mathematics; the stargazers wish to discover the world order by calculations and abstractions, and are like dogs howling helplessly at the indifferent Moon. The Tarot diviners, on the other hand, discover futurity by intuition, prophetic images drawn from the vaults of the subconscious.

Neither does their strife have much in common with Hermetism. Their social element, in fact, is diametrically opposed to it. Hermetism isolates the adept; the Tarot is a means of communication. The Hermetic is concerned with his own felicity or improvement, the cartomancer is preoccupied mainly with his patients' disquietudes. The Hermetic master grows more indifferent to the accidents of life, the higher he ascends the degrees of self-initiation; the Tarot diviner wants to know what will happen here below, how the supernatural will act upon man. He is earthbound.

The fifty-six pip cards are divided into four groups, rods, swords, money and cups, numbered from one to ten. Each suit is ruled by four court cards, King, Queen, Cavalier and Knave. One could identify the four groups as those of medieval society: the peasantry is symbolized by the rod; nobility, by the sword; the tradesman by the coin; and the clergy by the chalice or cup. In their organization the pip cards recall modern card games. They were originally, without doubt, separated from the trumps which form an independent set. The two do not mingle well.

We give here the full list of the direct significance of the pip cards, according to Papus:

Pip cards

RODS

King, dark-haired man, married, having family; a friend.
Queen, dark lady, serious, good counsellor, mother.
Cavalier, young man, dark-haired, a friend.
Knave, child, dark-haired, friendly, sent by near relation.
Ace, beginning of an enterprise.
Two, difficulty, obstacle to the enterprise, unforeseen.
Three, initial success, the base is laid out, encouragement.
Four, renewed difficulty.
Five, obstacle overcome by assiduity, victory.
Six, failure, the obstacles overcome the enterprise.
Seven, success, one part of enterprise achieved.
Eight, opposition to final achievement.
Nine, final success, the task is performed.
Ten, uncertainty in the conduct of the enterprise.

CUPS

King, blond man, friend, judge, clergyman, bachelor.
Queen, blonde woman, friend, mistress, sweetheart, fiancée.
Cavalier, young man, blond, lover, beloved.
Knave, blond child, arrival, birth.
Ace, beginning of love.
Two, obstacles deriving from one of the couple.
Three, both have fallen in love.
Four, a third person provokes opposition.
Five, the obstacle is overcome.
Six, destroyed love, widowhood.
Seven, triumph of love.
Eight, deception.
Nine, pregnancy.
Ten, uncertainty.

SWORDS

King, dark-haired, evil man.
Queen, calumnious, dark-haired woman, evil action.
Cavalier, spy, young man, dark-haired, enemy.
Knave, bad news, delay, bad child.

Ace, beginning of tense relation. (*This and the following card indicate that the opposition comes from outside.*)

Two, opposition which will not last.

Three, hatred.

Four, success against the enemy.

Five, having been overcome, the enemy is now triumphant.

Six, overcoming the opposition, the enemy is rendered harmless.

Seven, the enemy has been able to achieve his evil plans.

Eight, but he is only partly successful.

Nine, persistent hatred.

Ten, insecurity in matters of friendship.

MONEY

King, blond man, enemy or also indifferent.

Queen, blonde woman, enemy or indifferent.

Cavalier, young man, foreigner, blond, arrival.

Knave, letter, envoy, blond child.

Ace, heritage, gifts, economy.

Two, difficulties concerning the establishment of wealth.

Three, moderate gain.

Four, loss.

Five, another transaction restores the equilibrium.

Six, heavy loss.

Seven, fortune.

Eight, the established wealth is again reduced by losses.

Nine, durable fortune.

Ten, changeable luck, gains and losses.

(The money cards indicate things that come from uphill, the country, the exterior.)

The Trump Cards

The twenty-two trumps depict the following figures:

    I   The Juggler or Pagad; executing some legerdemain behind his table.

   II   The Popess: a woman crowned with a tiara, enthroned.

  III   The Empress: a woman with sceptre and coat of arms.

  IV   The Emperor: a crowned and enthroned man, seen in profile.

   V   The Pope, blessing two kneeling people.

  VI   The Lovers: a youth between two women; above, Cupid with his bow.

 VII   The Chariot, pulled by two horses carrying a king or hero.

VIII   Justice: its allegory, a woman with scales and sword.

  IX   The Hermit: an old man with lantern and staff.

   X   The Wheel of Fortune, whirling around three animals.

  XI   Strength: a female figure forcing open a lion's mouth.

 XII   The Hanged Man: a person suspended by one foot from a gibbet.

XIII   Death, cutting off with his scythe the heads and members of man.

XIV Temperance: a female figure pouring a liquid from one jug into another.

XV The Devil and two satellites.

XVI The Tower: men precipitated from a tower struck by fire or lightning.

XVII The Stars: a woman kneeling in the water, pouring out two liquids from two jugs. Above are eight stars.

XVIII The Moon: two dogs bark at the Moon; in a pool is the cancer of the zodiac; the Moon's house.

XIX The Sun: two children in front of a wall, above, the luminary.

XX The Judgement: an angel blowing the trumpet, which summons the resuscitated.

XXI The World: a nude woman in the mandorla; at the four corners, the emblems of the four Apostles.

One trump is not numbered: the Fool. Dressed like a king's jester, carrying his bundle on a stick or spoon, he walks dreamily, unaware that a dog is biting his thigh.

For these higher Arcanes, we give only the immediate meaning:

I The Juggler: the inquirer; all cards lying close to the juggler are important for the inquirer's destiny.

II The Popess: the female inquirer; this trump has the same qualities as the Juggler, but for inquiring women.

III The Empress: initiative, action.

IV The Emperor: will.

V The Pope: inspiration.

VI The Lovers: passion.

VII The Chariot: triumph, protection by providence.

VIII Justice: justice.

IX The Hermit: wisdom, prudence.

X The Wheel of Fortune: destiny.

XI Strength: force.

XII The Hanged Man: sacrifice, ordeal.

XIII Death: death.

XIV Temperance: economy, moderation.

XV The Devil: disease, great strength.

XVI The Tower: ruin, deception.

XVII The Stars: hope.

XVIII The Moon: danger, enemies, false friends.

XIX The Sun: marriage, happiness.

XX Judgement: transmutation, change.

XXI The World: Success, harmony, attainment.

— The Fool: folly, inspiration.

For minor inquiries, Oswald Wirth recommends consulting only five cards of the twenty-two trumps. These are mixed and the inquirer is asked by the cartomancer to name a number lower than twenty-two. If he chooses seventeen, the seventeenth card is taken from the pack and set out. Its meaning is affirmative. The cards are shuffled again, and by the same process another card is selected whose meaning is negative. In this way, five cards are exposed and arranged according to the scheme below. One means affirmation, two negation, three discussion, four solution, and five determination or synthesis.

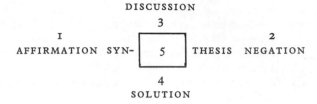

The synthesis is gained by the study of the whole 'conjunction'. The arrangement of the great game for the consultation of an important decision is indicated below. Pip cards and trumps are mixed together and laid out in the order indicated by numbers. The cards lying in the upper part of the arrangement, i.e., the farthest away from the cartomancer, express the present, the cards to the left, the future; and the cards to the right, the past. One leading card is placed in the middle.

It is clear that the more cards are chosen, the more difficult it is to bring their meaning to a synthesis, and greater lucidity is demanded from the diviner. It is therefore advisable to begin with a small game, and not to unfold the cards too often, or for frivolous reasons; a moment of concentration should be expected, or a feeling that 'it will work'. According to most Tarot experts, the trumps change their meaning when they are turned upside down. An ill-boding image like the Tower may be interpreted as ambivalent in this case. Moreover, it should be remembered that the trumps' numbers are interpreted prophetically as well. If the inquirer wishes to know *when* the prediction

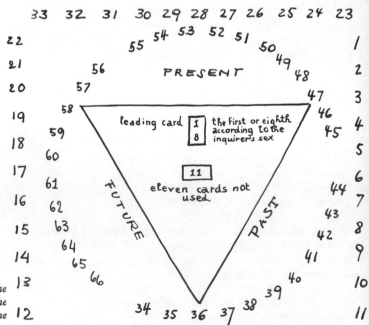

163. *The layout of the tarot cards for the Great Game*

will come true, numbers may be counted as days, months, years, according to the diviner's premonitions. The numbers of the cards are also interpreted Cabalistically by some experts.

Additional information cannot be given here; specialized books, the most important of which are those by Papus, Wirth, Marc Haven, Odoucet, Vaillant, Pelladan, de Sivry, Mathers, and Waite, contain further references. Unfortunately, most of these works have become rare, and the recent books on the Tarot are not all worthy of recommendation. Valuable scientific views on the Tarot have been expressed in the books and essays of Tassin, Foster Case, MacMonnies Hazard, Elizabeth Whitney and others.

The Juggler

Poetic licence may be forgiven to the tellers of unusual stories.

Eliphas Lévi

It is difficult to leave the Tarot without offering more details of at least one trump card, for which purpose is chosen the first leaf, the Juggler. His number is One, to which in modern cards the Hebrew aleph has been added. Why should a legerdemainist be placed at the head of this marvellous game? Was it to indicate that despite every effort to read order into the world one remains the victim of illusion? Aleph in the Cabala expresses the spirit of the living God. To attribute the number one to a juggler might seem blasphemy, the juggler being the magician's and the cleric's enemy, because he mimicked wonders by his dexterity, and was a promoter of scepticism. Yet certain diviners identified the figure Cabalistically with the spirit of God. The letter aleph א they said, underlies the figure of the Juggler; his torso bends backward, one arm is raised, the other bent downwards. He is the aleph, the master-spirit of the universe, which stretches before him like the Juggler's table. All things of creation are tossed about by him as if they were the Juggler's objects. He is pointing at the above and the below, confirming the teaching of Hermes Trismegistus that here below all is like that which is in heaven, that the little world, man, contains all the elements of the universe, and that the study of man will make us understand the wonders of the whole creation.

Court de Gébelin's interpretation of the Juggler is very sober, expressing the pessimism of the pre-Revolution savant. The game, he says, starts with a deceiver and ends with a fool. Man, in the middle, deserves their company. Who was the fool and who the juggler in Gébelin's time? The French king, whose politics was half jugglery and half sentimentality, allowed things to drift; and the learned and the philanthropic, who believed they were chosen to lead the people to better times, forgot that their dreams and theories could not feed the hungry masses, who were ready to assault them like enraged beasts. The Juggler upholds the people's staff or rod, which will sweep from the table the coins of the traders, the chalices of the clergy, and the swords of the nobility!

The Egyptians, Gébelin says, counted their Tarot cards from the highest number to the lowest. The Juggler to them was an allegory of the world here below. 'He is at the head of the worldly government; he indicates that this life is but a dream, a leger-demain, a perpetual game of hazard, dependent upon a thousand sets of circumstances.' The Juggler of a Tarot game printed in Paris in 1500 is of a political character. Dressed like a shepherd or magus, he is depicted giving advice to the king who is pondering over a chart spread out upon a table. The ruler's gesture expresses both confusion and meditation, as he tries to solve a dilemma. A third figure, the king's jester, listens with intense interest, following the Juggler's hands which point at two different places on the chart. Is it the above and the below, or does it signify that the Juggler can by his intellectual faculties coordinate contradictory elements? King, fool and Juggler are discussing the destiny of the commonwealth. They will not suc-ceed, as their endeavour is caricatured in a monkey searching for fleas on the hide of a sleeping dog.

Alliette held this trump in low esteem. He thought that such an undignified figure could not have been the one to open the Kingly Way. He placed the Juggler on number XV, where according to the Tarot tradition the devil resides. 'The Juggler,' he says, 'signifies disease, though he had been unjustly con-sidered as the symbol of Health.' Such simplified methods of interpretation did not please the famous magi of the nineteenth century. Eliphas Lévi, though calling Alliette an inspired hair-dresser, denounced these trivialities. The meaning of a card has to be discovered in many realms, in the divine world, in the world of nature, in that of man, in that of the intellect, and in the world of darkness! For Lévi, the Tarot is a monumental sum-mary of all ancient revelations, the key to the Egyptian hiero-glyphs, to Solomon, to the primeval scriptures of Enoch and Hermes. Such an implication opened new horizons for the cartomancers. Under Lévi's influence, Papus pronounced his pompous interpretation of the Juggler: 'He is Man as the collec-tive unity, the principle of mastership and domination over the earth. From this hieroglyphic meaning are derived the ideas of *unity* and of that principle which *determines* unity. Men or the microcosm, unity and principle: this is the sense of the Juggler.

'But an attentive consideration of this first trump,' he contin-ues, 'will enlighten us still more.' According to Papus, the Juggler's hat is shaped like the symbol of Eternal Life ∞ or the infinite, according to mathematics. The lower part of the figure signifies Earth adorned with the symbols of nature. The middle shows man's body placed behind a table, upon which lie chalices, swords and money. The fourth emblem of the pip cards, namely the rod, he holds in his raised hand. The meaning of these four emblems is explained by Papus Cabalistically. They conceal the four letters of *Jehovah* יהוה the tetragrammaton. י is identical with the rod, signifying the active principle of God; ה the chalice or cup symbolizing the passive principle of the universe; ו the spade or sword, is the symbol of the equilibrating principle – or of man. The second ה (the last letter) is 'the cyclic symbol of eternity uniting the three other principles'. These symbols, Papus says, correspond to the four great human castes: the men of י are the inventors, the nobility of the intelligence; the men of ה are the keepers of the great verities discovered by the inventors. The third caste is that of the sword men, the defenders of the acquisitions of the thinkers. They are warriors, the nobility of the sword. The last caste is that of the masses, the multitude·from which the three nobilities emerge.

These symbols are placed on the Juggler's card at random, whereas in the twenty-first trump, the World, they are ordered, set in the card's four corners. The four emblems of the Apostles are nothing more than the tetragrammaton. The two cards complete one another; numbers one and twenty-one added produce twenty-two, the whole suit of trumps. Summing up, Papus declares that 'above in the figure are hidden the number of letters, below the "vulgar names" of the card. At the right of the figure reside the three worlds: that of God, of Man and of Nature. Below is found the absolute key according to the image of the revolutions of the word YHVH.'

How can we use these occult hints for the interpretation of the Juggler's card? This is another question which Papus does not answer plainly. Eliphas Lévi declared that 'the truth must be veiled, yet not hidden from the people'. We believe that Papus added to the Juggler just *one* veil too many. Let us therefore resort to the amiable Oswald Wirth, who declares that this figure alludes in a positive sense to the following qualities of man: initiative, spontaneity of intelligence, acuity of discernment and comprehension, ready wit, self-control, autonomy, rejection of other people's suggestions, emancipation from all prejudice. In an ambivalent or negative sense, the Juggler may be interpreted as dexterity, cleverness, refinement, diplomacy, persuasiveness, lawyer, shrewdness, cunning, agitation, lacking in scruples, aggressive, intriguer, liar, rogue, charlatan and exploiter of human candour.

Thus we have finally a complete interpretation of the first trump's ambivalent qualities, upon which the cartomancer must decide according to the other cards laid out for the oracle. It is clear that those cards which lie closest to the trump are more influential than others. Ill-boding figures surrounding the Juggler will decide the inquirer's unlucky destiny, as well as the fact whether the card is lying reversed or upright, the first position having a negative meaning and the second a positive one.

In his metaphysical interpretation of the figure, Wirth relies mostly upon Papus's interpretations. The four Hebrew letters of God, the four emblems of the Evangelists are also identified by him. The synthesis is enriched by Wirth, who added the four elements to this mystical tetrad. His chart reads like this:

Money	Sword	Cup	Rod
Diamond	Spade	Heart	Clubs
Earth	Air	Water	Fire
Bull	Eagle	Angel	Lion
ה	ו	ה	י

In order to possess the four mystical instruments, one must have endured the ordeal of the elements. One has to triumph over the air, which for the Cabalist is achieved through the word. This victory will yield the sword, the symbol of the word which drives away the phantoms of terror. The conquest over water signifies the acquisition of the Holy Grail, the cup of wisdom. The fire ordeal, the highest initiation, will be rewarded with the commander's staff, which is the king's sceptre and signifies that the wise man rules by his own power and embodies sovereign will.

Wirth does not show the inquirer's dispositions only; he offers also ethical hints concerning self-improvement. The first condition is always to be active, even fruitlessly so, rather than to be indolent. Indeed the Juggler's trump expresses the everlasting motion that exists in the world and in man's body and mind. 'The individual,' Wirth says, 'must accomplish his mission which is to create himself, to become an entire man, a *homo totus*.' Such self-development modern scientists would call the process of individuation. The entire man is, according to Wirth, the refraction of the first cause, the principal unity in the self. This idea is not wholly alien to the psychological theories of C. G. Jung, of whom we are reminded when the Tarot experts allude to Hermetism as a means of accomplishing this task. The fact that only three legs of the Juggler's table are visible is not a coincidence. According to Wirth they signify sulphur, salt and mercury, the three pillars of the material world, 'the supports of the elementary substance which falls under our senses'.

Mrs John King van Rensselaer adds a few interesting observations. Convinced that the divining arrows or rods are the ancestors of the Tarot, she dwells upon the fact that the Juggler is manipulating his staff before the table. This is the magician's wand, 'readily recognized as such by the shrewd Frenchman' (Gébelin). 'It is one of the pip devices that has been reproduced in the ace of Rods, Staves or Sceptres . . . and by placing it in the hand of the inquirer, it denotes that he has been given the power to consult the oracle.' The table, Mrs van Rensselaer believes, was used in an ancient cult.

In antiquity, a custom existed of asking the godhead about the future profession of a child. Among the Greeks and Egyptians it was customary to conduct boys who had reached manhood to the temple where they had to take from the altar an object of their choice. If the boy grasped the sword, it meant that he was to be a soldier. The cup signified priesthood or love. This would explain that the Juggler, or the inquirer of the Tarot cards, is at the decisive point of questioning the oracle about his future, that all possibilities are latent, and that the Tarot game will now give its verdict. Good and bad lay ahead, as the gestures of the arms indicate. Papus had remarked already that 'man with one hand seeks God, and with the other he plunges below to summon the demon, and thus unites the divine and the diabolic in humanity'.

The cartomancer must decide whether his consultant will choose that which he considers desirable, the good or the bad, that which is befitting to him or alien to his essence. It is a most dangerous moment for the inquirer, who is abandoning himself to the Tarot player's cunning. His feelings may be similar to that of the patient who is led to the operating room, not knowing whether his surgeon is capable. Eliphas Lévi warns his readers, saying that 'cartomancy in its proper understanding is a literal consultation of spirits'. A good medium, he says, is a necessary condition, 'otherwise the Tarot is dangerous and we do not recommend it to anyone'. If one falls into the hands of a charlatan, the latter may offer him the wrong alternatives, like the cobbler who replaces the Juggler in a disfigured Italian game. The first Tarot trump is also called Pagad, a mysterious word derived, according to Parravicinio, from Paghead, meaning fortune. The Italians have interpreted the word as *bagatto*, cobbler, upon whose table are lying awls and the like: a bad choice for the inquirer! Others called the Juggler *Il Bagatel*, i.e., the trifle. But as we learn from all experts, there is nothing trifling about the Tarot and its figures.

IL BAGATTEL.

164. The Juggler

REFORMERS

| The Rosicrucians | Learn to know all, but keep thyself unknown. |

Gnostic device

In the sixteenth century Paracelsus had prophesied that the world was soon to be reformed. In his treatise on metals, he prognosticates that 'God will permit a discovery of the highest importance to be made; it must be hidden until the advent of the artist Elias'. The learned world, and especially the Paracelsians, conjectured about this coming world-transformation and its initiator. No one doubted that such a fundamental change, which everyone desired, was possible. Had not the Reformation been one of the great turning points in man's history? Paracelsus's attitude towards this religious revolt, however, was enigmatic. Accepting Luther as a great reformer, still he remained a Catholic, declaring that he wanted to be a reformer in his own field; Brother Martin was not sufficiently devoted to magic or to the Cabala. Though he had uncovered the evils of his epoch, he was unable to eliminate them. The magi hoped that in the days to come another reformation would take place whereby, unlike the one initiated by the temperamental monk, the sages of the world would unite for the good of mankind. This brotherhood of the chosen should be animated by the most noble aspirations: their aims were to be the perfection of the self and of nature.

This ideal gave birth to secret societies, such as the Brothers of the Golden Cross, founded by Agrippa, the Cross-bearing Evangelic Militia of Lüneburg, and several groups of Hermetics who identified the philosopher's stone with the Absolute, believing that transmutation was just one and a minor sign of the attained mastership. Paracelsus had declared that the comet of 1572 was 'the sign and harbinger of the approaching revolution'.[1] Many magi and intellectuals were eager to join forces in order to face the future collectively; and not a few offered their plans for the spiritual content and the organization of this society of sages.

In 1614 there appeared a pamphlet written in German, entitled *The Reformation of the World*. No one seemed to know how it had originated. The brief satirical treatise used the god Apollo as spokesman, assisted by the wise men of antiquity and of the modern world, and proposed an attempt to reform the universe; or rather, it maintained that Apollo had made such an attempt in vain. It has been debated whether this little tract is a Rosicrucian product. At any rate, it appealed to many intelligent people of various countries and was reprinted and translated many times. It is safe to say that the originator of this text was an Italian, Trajano Boccalini, whose book had appeared two years earlier in Venice, and who was murdered in the following year. *The Reformation of the World* in the German version is a translation of a chapter of Boccalini's book, but contained in addition a manifesto: *Fama Fraternitatis, or a Discovery of the Fraternity of the Most Laudable Order of the Rosy Cross.* A résumé of its contents is given in the following paragraphs.

The new discoveries, such as that of America, have increased man's knowledge and raised the hope that all arts and sciences might be perfected to a degree hitherto unheard of. Man will finally appreciate his own nobility and capacities, and the true meaning of himself as a microcosm. If agreement rather than ridicule existed among the good and the learned, mankind would be able to discover the greatest secrets of nature. The reactionaries with their Galen, Porphyry and Aristotle should be brought to reason. Such an attempt was once made by the Illuminated Father and Brother C.R.C. (Christian Rosencreutz), the most venerable ancestor of the Fraternity. At sixteen this great man travelled to the Holy Land, to Turkey and Arabia, where he learned a sacred and secret wisdom, which he translated into Latin, in the book '*M*'. Then he travelled to Fez in Morocco, in accordance with the recommendation of the sages. Whoever he met imparted to him his wisdom under the seal of secrecy.

In Fez, Rosencreutz acquired mastery of all secret wisdom. Man must be attuned to God, heaven and earth. His religion, his policy, health, nature, language, words and works must be in accord with the All. Diseases come only from the devil. From Fez Rosencreutz went to Spain, rejoicing at the good things he was carrying to Europe. There he conferred with the sages, showing them the new and marvellous fruits that were growing on the old tree of philosophy. But they ridiculed him. Unwilling to learn new things, they merely said: 'He who loves disquietude, let him be reformed!', and Rosencreutz heard the same refrain in the other parts of Europe. What great gifts were thus refused by the intelligentsia of the occidental nations!

Yet the world in those days was already big with commotion. And in painful labour did the world beget only a few sages, such as Paracelsus who, although he was not of the Fraternity, still was not one of those shallow, chattering philosophers and physicians who were enemies of the Cabala, magic and secrecy. Paracelsus read the book '*M*' by Rosencreutz, and his genius was exalted thereby.

Rosencreutz returned to Germany and, seeing that the world was not yet ripe for his reform, built himself a house where he lived peacefully, devoted to his studies. He possessed the philosophers' stone, i.e., he could produce gold and jewels, although he refrained from doing so, as he had no use for treasures which he could not share with the unworthy. He accepted only three disciples to whom he taught all that he knew, and who had to record his doctrine for the future members of the Brotherhood. In this way, the Fraternity was begun by four persons in all. Later when there were eight, they agreed on the following points:

They would not profess anything but curing the sick without reward.

They should wear no special habit.

They were to meet every year in the House of the Sainted Spirit.

The brothers were to choose their successors.

The letters R.C. should be their only seal and character.

The Fraternity should remain secret for a hundred years.

Five brethren were selected to carry out the philanthropic mission. They travelled through many countries, accomplishing wonderful charitable deeds. A few books were written which contained their ideology. In 1484, when Christian Rosencreutz died at the age of one hundred and six years, he was buried in secrecy, so that the location of his tomb was unknown. Not long afterwards, however, a Brother by chance discovered a concealed door that led to the burial chamber. Above the entrance were engraved the words, 'POST CXX ANNOS PATEBO' (After one hundred and twenty years I will appear).

The discovery gave impetus to the Rosicrucian movement. According to the Master's prophecy, the Fraternity was now to break its silence, and more Brothers were to be initiated and received among the chosen. The conclusion of the manifesto contains a profession of the Christian faith of the Brothers, and the announcement that another pamphlet would be issued to the learned men of Europe. Every opinion will reach the Brothers though they have not yet made public their names. Those who want earnestly to join them and are worthy shall be accepted.[2]

This first manifesto made a tremendous impression, and there was universal response to it. The curious wanted to know more about this mysterious brotherhood. Artistically minded people were fascinated by its attractive presentation. Scientists wished to grasp the superhuman wisdom of which the pamphlet spoke in such convincing terms. Mystics and magicians, men of high morality, were attracted by the proposed noble goal. Politicians hoped to learn from it the fine art of restoring peace, order, financial equilibrium and international understanding. The greedy (and there must have been quite a few of them) scented treasures. The sick longed now for the universal medicine that would restore the harmony of their bodies. And everyone wanted to live, like Rosencreutz, to be a hundred and six years old and more.

As promised, the second pamphlet, *Confession*, was distributed in the following year; and this promptitude confirmed the expectations of the learned world. Indeed, these Rosicrucians were not men addicted to vain words! The second publication was printed in Cassel in 1615 by Wesselius. It soberly cautioned the reader against making hasty judgements either of believing or of doubting. After these wise preliminaries, it was necessary to face the facts, some of which were disappointing.

East and West (Mohammed and the Pope) were condemned by the Brothers for their blasphemies. The *Confession* violently attacks the pope, 'who will be torn to pieces with nails'. The Fraternity offered its help to the Roman empire, and it meant *material* help: gold and jewels as well as advice. The second chapter of the Rosicrucian *Confession* attacked philosophy, which was 'fetching its last breath'. It was to be renovated in a rejuvenated world, 'if some of the more orderly among the learned respond to our fraternal invitation, they shall find among us far more and greater wonders than those they did heretofore believe, marvel at, and profess'.

Such boasts were followed, in the third chapter, by a greater caution: the secrets are not esteemed lightly by the Brothers, because they do not wish to influence the vulgar. Again, the succeeding chapter is full of extravagances. Whatever wisdom has come to man, through God's grace, by the angels and spirits, through sagacity and observation – all has been known by our Father, C.R.! If every book in the world were destroyed, it would not matter, for with their wisdom, they can teach everything in one volume. Then again the voice is lowered modestly: their wisdom is not so much for the princes as for the common people. But their arcana will not move gross wits, and every newcomer will be judged by the inspired Brothers.

The *Confession* continues in this cleverly modulated tone which, if not attuned to the world's harmony, is certainly so to the reactions of men, awakening hopes and doubts. But the latter are counteracted ingeniously by sober remarks and other signs of modesty, by alleging that all they possess has come to them without their having deserved such gifts; and they promise not to disappoint or deceive their followers.

In the remaining chapters the reader is acquainted with more of their ideas, of which we select the following as the most important. The Lord has inscribed great characters upon the world's mechanism; the wise can read them and thus comprehend creation. The end of the world is near; the catastrophe, however, shall be enlightened by the new reform to be initiated by goodness. The Brotherhood does not arrogate to itself the merits of other highly intelligent minds. God has sent messengers: new stars have appeared in the constellations of Cygnus and Serpentarius. The tongue shall come into honour when wise men with an open heart, bare heads and feet shall go merrily forth at the sun's rising. The stars predict an eclipse of the Church and how long it will last. Written letters and characters, placed by God in the universe, comprise the heavens, the earth and all beasts. From this secret code has been borrowed our magical writing, whence has come this new language. Ever since the beginning of the world, there has been a book more excellent than the Bible. Blessed is he who possesses it, more blessed he who reads it, most blessed he who understands it.

Transmutation is a natural miracle, and the universal medicine can be made by natural means; but one must not abuse these marvels. Throw away the books of the pseudo-chemists, deceivers of man. Destroy their monstrous symbols. They jest by applying the most Holy Trinity to vain things! The Fraternity offers money, it does not wish to receive any. The curious and the greedy may be led by knowledge into idleness, luxury, a pompous life. They shall not disturb us and our sacred silence. They are chastised by the will of God, and though we possess the means of helping them, we must obey God's decrees.

To the reader acquainted with some of the ideas of Paracelsus, it will be apparent that nothing new has been announced by the Fraternity beyond summoning the people to make a more unified application of the knowledge of isolated masters of the preceding century. The tract, however, betrayed the strong minds of writers and leaders gifted with suggestive power. How many there were, it is difficult to ascertain. The *Confession* indicates that the movement was already in full swing. One did not have to endure the difficulties implicit in the building of such societies; everything had been prepared for those who wanted to join, and the secrecy of the movement encouraged also those who feared to expose themselves, to be ridiculed or persecuted. The mystery in which the whole affair was clothed was the very kernel of its success.

Ever since, secret societies have exerted their attraction upon man. The Rosicrucian Fraternity became the object of the most violent controversies. Famous scholars like Robert Fludd, Michael Majer, John Heydon and the Hermetic Philalethes wrote apologies for the Brotherhood. Others spattered forth their invectives. The defenders, however, were on a higher level. Admittance into the society was sought, but nobody knew where the sages lived, nor where to find the House of the Sainted Spirit. Applicants vainly deposited their letters at the town halls of their cities, hoping that a mysterious traveller would gather them at a chosen time. But the Rosicrucians never appeared. In this manner the controversy about the invisible society continued among the learned. As impatience grew, a few charlatans took advantage of the Rosicrucian name, claiming that they were the delegates of the Fraternity, and succeeding in extorting high sums from a few, but ending in jail or on the gibbet.

In Paris, where the Brothers had announced themselves by a poster, opinion was divided, as in Germany. Officials detected a political plot fomented by the governments across the Rhine. Descartes had the affair investigated carefully and dispatched spies to Germany, but no Rosicrucian Brother could be found. In France the good people believed them to be sorcerers, working for the devil, possessing the gift of rendering themselves invisible, and paying with gold which changes after a while into leather or horn. They were supposed to be recognizable by huge sapphire rings on their fingers. The clergy warned their flocks to beware of these wizards. Sailors claimed to have seen, near the English coast, a Rosicrucian flying through the air upon a demon who disappeared suddenly into the waves; pamphlets were issued in considerable numbers – but the Brothers still remained invisible.

Valentine Andreae

165. The Rosicrucian emblem

The German name Rosencreutz signifies Rose Cross, or Cross of Roses. The name of the Fraternity was derived from its presumed founder. Its emblem was a dark cross and a light rose, combined in various ways. The dark cross symbolized sacrifice and hardship; and the light rose, delectation and reward. A contemporary of these Rosicrucians, Andreas Libavius, mentions that Luther's seal resembles strangely some Rosicrucian signs, and he concludes that the Fraternity had formed itself under the spiritual ascendency of Martin Luther. However, despite some intolerance in their programme, the Rosicrucians followed a higher ideal than that of combating the Pope. Their ideal was not Luther alone, but also Theophrastus Paracelsus, on whom was based their idealism, earthbound and irrational simultaneously. Their marvels, the homonculus, the mediatory and the elementary spirits, the signature with which nature has signed every being, all this is derived from the great Paracelsus.

166. *The seal of Martin Luther*

But Paracelsus had been dead for many years, and so had Rosencreutz. The manifestos must have been written by someone, a being of flesh and bone, though people began to suspect that their authors were ghosts or devils. Among the apologists for the Fraternity was a Lutheran pastor, Valentine Andreae, or Andreas (1586–1654). He published several treatises, printed in Strassburg in 1619 and 1620. These little works, *The Tower of Babel*, *The Christianopolitan Republic* and others, propose a general transformation of European society, implying the necessity of gathering energetic reformers and people of good will.

Andreae was a brilliant scholar; he knew five languages, and in his youth travelled to several European countries. Rising through various clerical charges to the position of a chaplain at the court of Württemberg, he resigned because of ill health, the hostility he had encountered, and most of all on account of the misery into which his German fatherland had been plunged by the Thirty Years' War. Embitterment and despair shortened the pastor's life and he died from apoplexy.

Andreae's coat of arms shows a St Andrew's cross and four roses. It is believed by many that he is the founder of the Fraternity; his armorial bearings resemble too closely those of the Rosicross not to arouse suspicion. Moreover, Andreae was the author of a Rosicrucian novel; *The Hermetic Romance*, or *The Chemical Wedding, written in high Dutch by Christian Rosencreutz*. Andreae admitted that this supposed allegorical autobiography of Rosencreutz, printed in 1616, was his own creation. The novel contains the following passage: 'Hereupon, I prepared myself for the way, donned my linen coat, girded my loins with a blood-red ribbon that reached over my shoulders. In my hat, I stuck four roses.'[3] This means that Christian Rosencreutz adorned himself with the armorial bearings of the Andreae family. From this we may surmise that Rosencreutz and Andreae are one and the same person; however a complete elucidation of the Rosicrucian origin has not been possible, and a few modern writers believe that the society originated in the Middle Ages.

The Chemical Wedding has been termed 'a comic romance of extraordinary talent'. This furtive appreciation is the only one which we could find among the critical writings on the Rosicross, a rather astonishing fact, for *The Chemical Wedding* is a unique piece of writing. In it, we travel through a Hermetic wonderland. Most, if not all, alchemical treatises contain a multitude of symbols, incongruously piled up and interrelated by dry and doctrinary elucidations, or rather occultations, so that even the mysterious becomes boring through monotony and pomp. The reading of Hermetic treatises, especially those of the baroque period, is tedious because none of the writers or poets was able to bring into plastic form so many stereotyped symbols. Andreae, however, overcame this tradition in a congenial way. He relates the most profound arcana in a light, at times jesting, manner. The alchemical allegories come to life and partake of the action as mythological beings, human beings, animals and implements. Unlike the slow pace of other alchemical treatises, Andreae's novel is full of action.

The hero, Rosencreutz, is eating his paschal lamb when an angel delivers a golden letter to him:

> Today, today, today
> The royal wedding is.
> Was this why you were born,
> Destined for joy by God.
> And unto joy of God designed?

The royal wedding is itself the alchemistic process, the seven stages, during which the female and the male principles are joined together, the King and the Princess. The angelic letter carrier departs by moving her eye-covered wings. 'But in mounting upward, she gave so mighty a blast on her gallant trumpet that the whole hill echoed thereof, and for a full quarter of an hour, I could hardly hear my own words.' Rosencreutz, on reading the letter, perceives that this is the appointed wedding of which seven years before he was told in a corporeal vision. He faints with fear.

In a dream, he sees himself with other sufferers who in the darkness climb upon each other, rattling their heavy chains. He and a few others are rescued by a cord lowered into the dungeon. Having adorned himself with the Rosicrucian emblems he starts out on his adventurous journey to the wedding of Silver and Gold. His emblematic provisions are bread, salt and water. He encounters marvellous trees and birds, day and night, symbolic castles, a venerable doorkeeper, beautiful maidens, strange inscriptions upon golden tablets, glowing lanterns, mysterious gates engraved with secrets and images; hills, rocks and plains unfold themselves, until he reaches the Palace, where one can wander for years without coming to the end of all its marvellous rooms, cellars, staircases, clocks, astronomical instruments, doors, paintings, lights and torches, invisible angels, musicians, warriors in armour, pages, and beautiful virgins, crowned with laurel and draped in sky-blue velvet.

In a huge banquet hall he meets the other adepts, both the invited and uninvited, witnesses of the Marriage. His modesty arouses laughter. At the meal, the unworthy are the noisiest, until a holy maiden declares that all are to be judged the following day. On a scale they are weighed against seven stones, and most of them are dismissed according to their merits. Charlatans who could not even move the scale are stripped and driven away with scourges. Kingly adepts who were unable to attain mastery are dismissed honourably and a drink of forgetfulness is given them to save them from undue torment. A few scoffers are beheaded.

The worthy are conducted into the garden where they behold still greater marvels. Alchemistical animals appear; a lion is swinging his shining sword, and amidst awe and admiration, a unicorn, white and majestic, emerges from the cluster of dark trees, jangles its golden necklace, and kneels reverently. 'The lion, who stood motionless like a statue of brass, broke his naked sword in two; the pieces sank to the bottom of the fountain; and he reared until a white dove brought a branch of olive in her bill, which the lion devoured instantly, and grew quiet. The unicorn returned to its place joyously, while our virgin led us down the winding stairs.' They descend 365 steps. They are crowned with laurel, and wear garments embroidered with the Golden Sun and the Silvery Moon. And afterwards the thing for which they had awaited anxiously happens – they are presented to the King, who was there all the while, concealed behind a curtain. A wonderful comedy is now enacted, describing the seven stages of the arcanum. The happenings are despoiled of their symbolic conventional garments, and the adventures of the King and the Queen are portrayed cleverly, revealing the author's psychological insight.

Putrefaction is the king of the Moors who leads the Princess away into his dark kingdom. She is rescued, but surrenders voluntarily to her tormentor. Again, the young King frees her from the Moor, and once more she falls prey to the monster, who has her scourged. She is condemned to die by poison, which does not kill her but afflicts her with leprosy. The imprisoned wench refuses to see the good King's ambassadors. Defiled, ill, and robbed of her royal honours, she submits to the tormentor. After a decisive battle, she is rescued against her will. The seventh stage of the process is approaching, the mystical wedding: 'The good parents are now invited. Long enough has she been kept; so in honour increase, till thousands rise, and spring from your own blood.' The wedding is celebrated with baroque pomp and from the stage the action moves imperceptibly to the real. But reality is stranger than fiction. It turns into a nightmare: every-body seated at the banqueting table is overcome by a fearful premonition. A little crystal fountain is brought in, together with a very small crystal glass from which the royal family drink. Afterwards, it is offered to all, and this is called the *draught of silence*.

'Music was heard, and if we demanded anything, we were fain given short answers. All things had so strange a face that the sweat began to trickle down over my body.' The whole royal family is beheaded in the banquet hall, quickly darkened with black velvet. A day of despair and mourning follows, trans-figured by unheard-of events. Deep in the dungeon, Venus is lying naked on a fantastic couch, Cupid is perambulating in the silent passageways, a tree is melting, tossing its shiny fruits into a basin, 'sirens, nymphs and sea-goddesses attend us', the princes and princesses are buried with dream rites; golden globes, mirrors 'forced to look out at windows', and fantastic barges appear on the nearby lake.

The alchemists are confined by the virgins in a tower where they work at the resurrection of the King and Queen. They produce a phoenix whose egg is cut with a diamond. The bird is nourished with the blood of the executed. His blood, in turn, resuscitates the murdered who appear first as homunculi, little beings not taller than four inches. They grow miraculously, and the reborn man and wife are wrapped together in velvet carpets, 'neatly laid by each other', and carried gently to bed where behind closed curtains and under Cupid's surveillance the mystical wedding is consummated. The novel continues with ever-changing images, figures and events. 'The King and Queen for the sake of recreation began to play together. It resembled chess, only the game had other laws, for it was the virtues and vices against each other, where it might be observed ingeniously with what plots the vices lay in wait for the virtues, and how to re-encounter them again. This was so properly and artificially performed that it was to be wished that we had a similar game too.' Then, after a few more pages, the novel ends abruptly: 'for two pages are wanting', and the reader is left in a state of uncertainty about the hero's fate and the further adventures of the royal couple.

The Chemical Wedding satisfied men's longing for the marvellous, for the continuation of childhood dreams, and for a refuge from the banalities of daily life. In every man there is a child that yearns to play, and the most attractive game is occulation, mystery. The underground of the human psyche finds its counterpart in the meanderings of a mythical labyrinth, subterranean meetings by candlelight, secret passages hidden within the double walls of castles, treasures concealed in gullies.

Secret Societies

It was through Andreae that Freemasonry, which probably originated in the eighth or ninth century, gained a new impetus. In 1645 a few English Rosicrucians met for the purpose of organizing their efforts, among them William Lilly, the famous astrologer, Elias Ashmole, the antiquary and alchemist, John Parson, Robert Moray and others. They justified their secrecy with the claim that the general intolerance of that wicked epoch would not otherwise endure them, and they had to find ways of gaining new members despite their concealment. Elias Ashmole found the solution. As every Londoner was obliged by custom to be a member of a corporation, Ashmole registered himself as a stonemason; the others followed his example and under the sign of the masons they now met freely in the assembly hall of ceremonial of the Freemasons.

The Rosicrucian game was, like the ancient initiation rites, a serious one. Its motive was true magic, not make-believe. Magic symbolized man's power over the material world, the belief that through thought and action he could ascend into realms where all men were brothers. Such an achievement was magic on a level higher than that of making a broomstick walk. All the brotherhoods agreed on the dignity of man, his infinite power, his rights, his duty to unite all men within the circle of the 'Sainted Spirit'. But before this gigantic task could be fulfilled, before humanity could attain so universal a bond, the Rosicrucians met their fellow men not on elevated intellectual planes but in the mysterious hall of the common human psyche. Andreae calls it the King's Palace; the magus Saint-Martin (1743–1803) describes it as the temple which men of peace and spiritual yearning shall some day enter.

The Chemical Wedding is a guidebook to this rendezvous. In his wanderings, Rosencreutz is directed by the magnetic needle and with its help he finds the way to the Palace. It is the compass of the sage that fathoms man, 'that compact which man has to renew constantly with himself'. Being one's better self is the highest morality and good deeds are the discipline that counteracts the evil pride which might arise in the brother conscious of his mission. The practice of charity transmutes man's intentions into reality, suggesting that whatever is in the mind can be realized. 'For every physical fact,' Saint-Martin says, 'is a neighbour of an intellectual truth.'

The Chemical Wedding, a lonely flower in the arid German baroque literature, links Paracelsian magic to the Romanticism of the nineteenth century. Does not Novalis evoke the mysterious travels of Rosencreutz when saying 'World becomes Dream, and Dream the World'? In like manner, Hölderlin recalls to man his identity with the macrocosm: 'O Sun, O Air, with you alone lives my heart, as with brothers.' Heinrich von Kleist expresses grief in the terms of an alchemist: 'Now, I descend into the depths of my heart; into the subterranean mine; and I dig up a deadly feeling, cold like ore; this ore, I purify in the crucible of my pain. . . .' That the philosophers' gold could be made by children was not ignored by Jean Paul: 'If the remembrances of infancy charm so much, this is not because they are merely memories. . . . The attraction must derive from their magical obscurity, and the reminiscence of that early expectation in which we were then living, of a felicity without an end.'

*

During the Thirty Years' War, interest in the invisible philosophers was kept alive by anonymous men who brought help here and there, and disappeared without leaving any traces. Were they the Brothers of the Rosicross, or candidates who desired to make themselves worthy of the fraternity by good deeds? Or were they men who, despairing of ever meeting the true brothers, began their charitable work independently? In later years also the appearance and disappearance of the Hermetic philosophers betrayed a Masonic character. The reader will remember the adventure that befell Helvetius in 1666, and the strange travels of Alexander Sethon, who left behind wherever he journeyed his projecting powder or alchemical gold.

But at the same time men existed, as they always have, who had no wish to play the game of mystery. Fervent nationalists were displeased with these societies, whose ultimate goal it was to destroy the fences that separated nations. A novel, published in Paris in 1670, seems to imply such convictions. Its title was *The Count of Gabalis, or Extravagant Mysteries of the Cabalists and Rosicrucians.* Its author, Montfaucon de Villars, says in the first chapter:

> Since common sense has always made me suspect that there was a great deal of emptiness in all that they call secret sciences, I never ventured to turn over a leaf of such books. And yet, not finding it reasonable to condemn without knowing why, I took the resolution of feigning myself to be a great devotee of these sciences. I decided, therefore, to make the acquaintance of these wise men, very learned for the most part, and eminent in gown and sword, people from whom I could learn about that clan.

The booklet was obviously written to amuse the Parisians; nevertheless, it is interesting because it reveals that in Villars's time there were still Paracelsians who sustained the old theories of elementary spirits, Cabalistic signs, talismans, and the whole apparatus of the sixteenth-century magi. Moreover, we learn that these secret societies had a spiritual leader, the German Count of Gabalis so-called, who went to France with the specific intention of initiating Villars.

Villars's book was dear to the defenders of common sense and reason, words now increasingly used in attacks on the idealists. Dull arguments were often introduced under the guise of common sense. True, there were also intelligent and even excellent writers who opposed and suspected the occult wisdom. The members of the French Academy were no magicians, but among them were men whose sentiment on the question is not well-defined. Even its founder, Richelieu, was not very definite in his opinions. He had been the dupe of the false alchemist, Dubois, who promised him mountains of gold that would increase France's wealth; and he had protected Jacques Gaffarel and the famous Thomas Campanella, both occultists.

Villars's betrayal of Rosicrucian secrets had another effect. In spite of its satirical character *The Count of Gabalis* awoke an interest in the occult, so much so that it is believed by some that Villars intended rather to promote Paracelsian magic than to destroy it. Only a few years after the appearance of the book, however, its author was murdered by the Rosicrucians, it is said, to avenge his indiscretion and mockery.

Although science was still in its swaddling clothes, the champions of common sense were rejoicing over the progress of knowledge. They were inadvertently using the same arguments as the authors of the Rosicrucian manifestos. Science was soon to solve all problems and mysteries. The golden age seemed to be approaching; the gold-cooks and Brothers were to become bogies to frighten children and the laughing stock of adults. The greater the failure of economics and politics, with the consequent corollary that science cannot solve all problems, the louder grew the mockery of the advocates of common sense.

The Classical Ideal

The lack of common sense in France in Villars's time may be illustrated by a few trials which took place during that period. A beautiful noblewoman, the Marquise of Brinvilliers, was said to have poisoned her parents, her friends and her servants without any motive. It was alleged that, searching for new victims, she went to the hospital, where she administered deadly potions to the poor. Convicted as a witch, she was judged to have been enticed by the devil, and was burned at the stake in 1676. In 1663, one Saint-Simon, a native of Aumale in Normandy, preached that he was Christ incarnate. The 'reasonable' Parisian judges, overlooking insanity, condemned this man to the stake. About the same time, a wealthy widow confessed that she had had intercourse with the devil. The parliament of Paris had her exiled, but not until she had been branded with a hot iron.

The famous trial of Catherine Deshayes, called la Voisin, began in 1679. The tribunal assembled in the 'Fiery Chamber', where mortal crimes were tried. Investigation revealed that ranking members of the nobility were involved. La Voisin told fortunes with coffee grounds and a magical crystal; but this divinatory trade was only a façade for larger enterprises. She evoked the dead and the devil, and solemnized magical rites in her back-chambers. She had many assistants, among them the two hangmen of Paris who brought her horrible gifts from the gibbet. Abbé Guibourg, a priest of noble descent, then sixty years old, performed black masses. Madame de Montespan offered herself as 'altar cloth'. She lay naked on the altar; the chalice was placed upon her belly; Guibourg slit an infant's throat and let the blood run down into the chalice. Many other equally dreadful acts were committed.

La Voisin was burned at the stake in 1680. Several who were indicted died in prison; others committed suicide. Thirty-six were executed; five were sent to the galleys; one hundred and forty-seven were sentenced to prison. Among the indicted were the flower of the French nobility – two nieces of Cardinal Mazarin, the Duchesses of Bouillon, Lusignan, Vivonne and Vitry; the Countesses of Soissons, Polignac and Montmorency; the Princess of Tingry; the Chevalier de Varnens; the Count de Longueval; the Marquis de Feuquières and, probably, the Duke of Buckingham! However, the nobility were spared, and many documents vanished. To the counts and duchesses, the whole indictment seemed a bad joke. When the Councillor of State asked the Duchess of Bouillon whether she had seen the devil during these evocations, she answered: 'I see him right now; he

is disguised as a Councillor of State, and he looks rather ugly!'
Everybody laughed. Yet during the black masses these witty
people had witnessed the slaughter of two thousand five hundred
babies.

The position of Louis XIV was rather difficult. Having interdicted witch prosecutions, he was now compelled to provide
new laws against crimes of magic. But he had the word magician
replaced by the phrase, 'people who call themselves magicians'.
The punishment was not death but hard labour. Murder was
judged as such and not as sorcery.

Connected with the Voisin affair was the scandal of the Maréchal de Luxembourg, a famous and capable military leader. He
had committed 'only' one murder, that of a woman blackmailer,
la Dupin, whom he and his helpers had cut to pieces. Among his
papers was found a pact with the devil. The investigation showed
that he was affiliated with la Voisin; perhaps the responsibility
was shifted to her in order to protect Luxembourg. The confused
judges deliberated for fourteen months, but no judgement was
rendered; the Maréchal went to the country for a few days and
then returned to his duties.

Ten years later a new affair flared up. This time the indicted
were shepherds, and the judges were less embarrassed in giving
their verdict. In the Brie region, the cattle died from an epidemic,
and peasants believed that a spell had been cast over the animals.
The malefactors were discovered and sent to the capital. The
chief sorcerer, Bras-de-Fer (Iron Arm), and many of his accomplices were condemned to death.

The incredible confusion which ruled over this epoch, supposedly devoted to 'classical ideals', is illustrated by a series of
demonological books published simultaneously with such
masterpieces of French literature as those of Corneille, Racine,
Molière and La Fontaine. François Placet, in his *Superstition of
Our Time*, attacked the belief in talismans and magical healing
which had been defended by an anonymous writer a short time
before. He was reasonable enough to leave out the usual devil
lore, and his little treatise is factual and interesting. In his *Pagan
Theology* Benjamin Binet passionately defends the existence of
demons and attacks the Dutch parson, Balthasar Bekker, who in
1691 had published his *Enchanted World (De Betoverde Weereld)*,
a formidable assault on the Inquisition and an indictment of the
whole devil lore. Jean Baptiste Thiers declares in his treatise that
magic is mere superstition, but that it ruins faith and the Church,
and must be severely combated. His enumeration of magical rites
and customs is interesting.

But the most curious of these publications is that of the
Capuchin Chevannes. Its title, significantly, is *Learned Disbelief
and Ignorant Credulity*. This scholar attempted to bring order
into the discordant views of the Church, of jurisprudence, of the
nobility, of the people, and of the demonologists. Such a task
kept him moving constantly among the various camps. In endless discourses, he proves that the existence of demons is in
accord with the Church. His description of the sabbath occupies
seven chapters. Then follows his struggle with astrology, which

he attempts to reduce *ad absurdum*. His verdict, heard often both before his time and since, is that it is enough for a mathematician to tell the truth once to make him famous, whereas he may lie a thousand times without discrediting himself.

Having thus demonstrated his 'reason', he is again ensnared by 'ignorant credulity' in a subsequent chapter, saying that sorcerers can heal with the aid of the devil. Whatever effects they produce, their simple remedies are ridiculous. Figures and characters are signs of witchcraft, and sorcery too can heal by the practitioner laying his hands upon the sick. Yet, he continues, with a bow to the throne, by the grace of God French kings can accomplish such marvels, for everybody knows that their touch will cure the scrofulous.

Having thus humoured the court, Chevannes returns hastily to the Church: witches are marked by the devil. This is not a fairy tale, but, continues Chevannes, casting a malignant look towards the other shore of the Channel, witches should not be 'fleeted'. This is a barbaric custom. The treatise goes on gropingly until he speaks of Agrippa, dead now for a hundred and forty years. He calls him and Paracelsus incarnate demons. Agrippa, he claims, pretended that he had derived his diabolic art from the Holy Ghost. Chevannes knows that in attacking the great magi he is also attacking the secret societies which continued to pursue their magical ideal in the midst of this turmoil. Chevannes's book, reprinted several times, had considerable success at an epoch when, according to a modern history of French literature, 'Boileau had definitely overcome the enemies of Reason and Truth'.

THE EIGHTEENTH CENTURY

Revolt Against Reason

A religious movement, Jansenism, was spreading rapidly in France. Its originator was Cornelis Jansen (1585–1638), Bishop of Ypres. In his work on Augustine, this peaceful and humble cleric had expressed an idea neither new nor voiced by him alone. Man, he said, has not the capacity of loving God purely, as he is constantly under the influence of sinful desires. Only by heavenly grace can he free himself from cupidity and attain purity and felicity. The man upon whom God confers grace will be saved, whereas he who is without this grace will remain in the bondage of original sin. The eternal question as to whether man's will is free or bound to a higher power was introduced once more, arousing a commotion that lasted until the second half of the eighteenth century. Without the resistance of those defenders of free will who caused the tempest, few people would have read Jansen's learned treatise.

But now France was divided into two camps: the Jesuits, who had official support, and the Jansenists. This passionate controversy would not be included in a book on magic had not miraculous happenings occurred in the Jansenists' camp which many failed to recognize as miracles. In the first quarter of the eighteenth century a young man, the deacon François de Pâris (1690–1727), a Jansenist, lived in the capital in piety and seclusion. After his death strange events took place at his tomb in the St Médard cemetery. Sick people who went there to pray were freed from their bodily afflictions. Crowds gathered, praying and trembling with nervous convulsions. Many fell into a state of ecstasy or trance. Paralytics were carried to the gravestone; the insane, the blind, the cancerous, the dropsical rubbed themselves against the deacon's tomb and were cured. Rich and poor made their pilgrimage to the cemetery and many returned home cured.

St Médard resembled a witches' sabbath. The aspect of the frenzied crowd, the display of hideous diseases, the howls and the macabre surroundings bore little resemblance to that elegance and refinement which we ordinarily associate with the eighteenth century. But these scenes were enhanced by the aura of the marvellous. The ten-year-old niece of the great Pascal (1623–62) had suddenly been cured there of a painful eye disease, a marvel which converted Pascal to Jansenism. The little daughter of the painter, Philippe de Champaigne (1602–74), had been cured of her complete paralysis in the same way, and her grateful father had painted the portraits of several of the holy women at Port Royal. Philippe, of course, had also been converted to Jansenism.

At a time when medical science was hardly developed, these marvellous healings must have exerted a formidable attraction; moreover, the disregard of the rigid, classic, Apollonian ideal, and the acceptance of the Dionysian frenzy, the uncontrolled, is significant in the epoch following the death of the dominating Louis XIV, who believed that he was the state, and who called himself the Sun King (Apollo). Voltaire did not exhaust the Jansenist problem when he said: 'There is apparently little advantage in believing what Jansen believed, namely that God demands the impossible of man. This is neither consoling nor philosophical. The secret pleasure, however, of belonging to any party, the hatred of the Jesuits, the wish to excel, and the general spiritual unrest, all this leads quickly to the formation of a sect.'

When finally a decree ordered the St Médard cemetery to be closed, a witty Parisian posted a couplet at its gate:

> In the name of the king 'tis forbidden to God
> To let miracles happen upon this spot.

The righteous and the stubborn did not want to accept defeat. A councillor at Parliament who had seen the miracles, Carré de Montgeron (1686–1754), published a compilation of proven facts from among the happenings at St Médard. His *Verity of the Miracles*, printed in Holland, is adorned with numerous fine copperplates. One hour after the appearance of the work in the windows of bookshops, in 1737, Montgeron was arrested and confined to the Bastille. He died in prison at Valence, after seventeen years of captivity. But other influential people carried on his efforts, such as the Chevalier Folard, and Fontaine, Secretary of the King's Commandments. Moreover, the hysteria spread to several cities, a fact which is seldom mentioned. Valence in particular, where Montgeron was imprisoned, was the scene of convulsions.

St Médard being closed and guarded, the sectarians tried to revive their miracles at home. But Louis XV did not tolerate private assemblies of this kind. His police was constantly active and hundreds of believers were arrested. Despite this rigour, the movement survived. The miraculous cures, however, now happened infrequently, and in their place developed a tendency towards self-torture comparable to fakirism. An eyewitness, Condamine, describes one of these *séances* which took place in 1759 in the apartment of Sister Françoise, the eldest of the hysterical group. For twenty-seven years she had been subject to frenzy. She had been twice crucified, as explained by Condamine in his report. The day he went to visit Sister Françoise two crucifixions were to take place. Sister Mary, a woman of twenty, was kneeling in the centre of the room, awaiting her agony. About twenty devotees were present, among them de Mérinville, councillor at Parliament, de Latour-Dupin, brigadier of the king's armies, Janson, officer of the musketeers, and others of lower standing.

First, Françoise lay upon the floor and was beaten with chains. At seven o'clock she stretched herself out on a huge cross to which the leader of the ceremony nailed her hands and feet. At a quarter to eight, the cross was erected. Seeing it, Sister Mary was seized by a fit. Françoise remained on the cross until half past ten. Meanwhile, Mary was nailed to another cross, but after forty-five minutes she exclaimed: 'Take me down, quick, I am dying.' This was done readily by the frightened assistants. She was removed to the next room and washed with the 'miraculous water of blessed Pâris'. Soon she returned smiling to witness Françoise's unnailing. 'Both women,' Condamine adds, 'are workers and need their hands for their livelihood. Tomorrow they have to go to work with their bruised members.'[1]

Through what strange realms did Jansen's ideas travel before reaching Sister Françoise's apartment on the rue Philippeaux! But the glorious times of the frenzied were over. Instead of healing, the saint now spread suffering. Even the patient Françoise grew weary of her tormentors. When Father Timothée wanted to burn her clothes, assuring her that it would not hurt, she revolted. The priest insisted and she yielded, but when the fire began to spread, Françoise shrieked and a Brother threw water upon her. 'What are you doing!' Timothée exclaimed indignantly, 'you are destroying our miracle. A few more minutes and the thing would have been accomplished.'

The thing was accomplished, though without Father Timothée's miracle. The fire of Jansenism was burned out, extinguished with Françoise's shabby garments. It smouldered weakly until 1787, and vanished a year before the conflagration of Bastille Day.

Vampires

If there ever was in the world a warranted and proven history, it is that of vampires; nothing is lacking, official reports, testimonials of persons of standing, of surgeons, of clergymen, of judges; the judicial evidence is all-embracing.

J.–J. Rousseau

We have already gathered, from the happenings at St Médard, that the so-called sceptical period ushered in by the eighteenth century was less sceptical than has been supposed. The number of occult publications did not diminish but rather increased. The old prophecies were revived and reprinted along with new ones for an expanding public. Secret societies found leaders and grew quickly. Magi and seers attracted public interest; magical cures, alchemy, divining rods, physiognomy, mystical sects, were the talk of the town. The Baroness d'Oberkirch wrote in her memoirs: 'Never were the Rosicrucians, the adepts, the prophets more numerous than today; never were they listened to with more credulity. The conversation turns constantly to these matters; they preoccupy every mind, strike every imagination, even of the most serious people. . . .' Louis XV was fond of working in his alchemical laboratory; and the royal example encouraged many gentlemen at court, as well as the citizens of Paris.

Ancient magical texts were systematically compiled. That this was done exclusively in the interest of science is difficult to believe. The textual reproduction of magical verses, customs, incantations, and the extensive list of dream interpretations, attracted readers more than the authors' sceptical prefaces, and shrewd publishers certainly did not ignore this fact. Nicolas Lenglet Dufresnoy (1674–1755) published many of these old documents. The prelate refrained from exhibiting too much scepticism, and his works sold excellently. In his later days, however, this reserve grew more difficult for the scholar to maintain, and in his treatise on Joan of Arc, his true feelings exploded: 'That this girl,' he says, 'had any visions, apparitions, and revelations, I do not believe in the least.' Like Joan, he died in the fire: he was reading before the fireplace, became drowsy, and fell upon the burning logs.

The Benedictine, Dom Augustine Calmet (1672–1757), a famous Bible commentator, also turned towards the occult. He treated the unusual subject of vampires, those evil dead who leave their graves to suck the blood of the living; and he found abundant material and avid readers in his time. Vampires had never been as numerous as they were in the eighteenth century. As cases of vampires were seldom reported in France, tales concerning them came from Russia, Silesia, Moravia, Slovakia, Hungary. In Poland vampires were called Upirs; in Greece, Brucolacas; in Arabia, Ghouls. The following are some reported cases of vampires which were taken seriously. Peter Plogojowich, who lived in the Hungarian village of Kisilova, near Gradish, became a celebrated vampire. He haunted the people, with the result that the villagers opened the grave; and Peter was found lying peacefully therein, his skin still fresh, although he had lain buried for six weeks. His cheeks were pink, and his nails had grown; but his mouth was full of fresh blood sucked from his recent victims, all of whom perished within eight days. He was disinterred and burned to ashes, and not until the cadaver had been destroyed completely did the vampire relinquish his bloodsucking activities.

Vampires did not always suck the blood of their victims. In that same notorious village of Kisilova died a man sixty-two years old. Three days after his burial, he appeared to his son, demanding food. Having been served, he ate and returned to his grave; but two days later he again appeared, and once more asked to be fed. Perhaps he was not satisfied with the food, for the next day the son died, and at the same time five others in the town became seriously ill, and died shortly afterwards. The villagers disinterred the five victims with the father and son, and burned all of them, as they knew that he who dies of the vampire will become one himself. This story was printed in a newspaper, *The Gallant Mercury*, in 1732. That the dead experienced hunger was a common belief of that period. German professors investigated this matter with characteristic thoroughness, and one of them, Michel Ranfft, published his *Treatise Upon the Dead who Chew in Their Sepulchres*. He must have been morbidly attracted by this theme, and we may omit what he professed.

Another tale concerns two officers of the Belgrade Tribunal, assisted by men of the government, a doctor and the Count Cabreras, who journeyed to a certain village. They had been alarmed by the story told them by a soldier, who said he had been invited to dinner by a peasant. While they were eating, a stranger entered the room and without invitation joined them. Everyone showed signs of fright, but the soldier did not ask why, lest he seem indiscreet. The next day, the master was dead, and the people now related that the stranger was the grandfather who had been dead for ten years and was now a vampire. The rest of the tale is taken from the official protocol made by the examiners. The old man's tomb was opened by the officers, who found the vampire in a state of perfect preservation. The physician opened a vein and fresh blood gushed out. Count Cabreras ordered the cadaver's head to be severed and the body to be returned to the grave.

At this sight, several people stepped forward, declaring that this was an occasion to rid the village of other vampires. Cabreras had four more tombs opened, that of a villager who died thirty years earlier and those of his victims, members of his family and a valet, who had also become vampires after their deaths. Like the others, the thirty-year-old corpse was found in a state of perfect preservation, and the blood in all the corpses was fluid. They were nailed into their graves, which caused people to grumble at Cabreras's ignorance. The count then commanded that another vampire be burned to ashes. This man had been dead for sixteen years and two of his sons had been killed by his bloodsucking. The commissioner who recorded the happenings sent his report to the General Officers who ordered him to give a verbal account at the emperor's court. The emperor had a new commission investigate the case and several officers of the law, physicians, and some scholars were sent to the village.

A famous account of vampires is that of Arnold Paul of Medreiga at the Turco-Serbian border. During his lifetime, he had often complained of having been tormented by a Turkish vampire. He died when a hay wagon fell upon him, before he had had a chance to eat some earth covering a vampire's grave, supposedly the only medicine that kept the dead quiet in their graves. Arnold Paul developed into an arch-vampire. After forty days, he was exhumed. His blood, it was reported, bubbled in his veins and the whole body and shroud were covered with it. When the bailiff ordered his heart pierced, the vampire shrieked horribly, but this was his last protestation, as fire consumed him entirely. This occurred in 1730.

A terrible story is reported by Charles Ferdinand de Schertz in his *Magia Posthuma*, dedicated to Prince Charles of Lorraine. In the village of Blow, in Bohemia, a vampire killed people by summoning them. Many had heeded this sinister call, until finally the villagers opened the monster's grave and fastened him to the earth with a post. 'How friendly you are,' the vampire said, 'to give me a stick with which I can drive away the dogs.' That same night, he arose and suffocated five people. He was dug out the next day by the hangman, and pierced repeatedly.

Carried on a cart to the pyre, he was howling all the while and moving his arms and legs. After his execution, in 1706, the Bohemian village grew quiet. 'Thank God,' Dom Calmet adds, 'that we are not credulous. We must admit, however, that the light of physical science has been unable to cast its rays upon this case.'

Having termed this occurrence Epidemic Fanaticism, Dom Calmet shifts from the psychical to the physical, and tries to explain the phenomenon of the vampire scientifically. Chemical substances of the soil may conserve corpses indefinitely. By the influence of warmth, the nitre and sulphur in the earth may render liquid coagulated blood. The screams of the vampires are produced when air passing through their throats is stirred by the pressure which the stake causes in the body. Often people are buried alive, and certain dead, such as the excommunicated, can rise from their tombs; but it is not possible to leave the grave bodily without digging up the soil, and none of the stories about vampires mention that their tombs were disturbed.

Magic Unveiled

Salt, heat and motion is the whole secret of the vampire, according to the Abbé de Vallemont, Pierre de Lorraine (1649–1721). Anything which has been, can appear again: there is nothing alarming about this! The dead can return, just as plants and animals can be revived, at least temporarily. Take a flask and put into it the vital essence of the seed of a beautiful rose. Burn this to ashes, imbue it with the morning's dew, collecting enough for a modest distillation. Extract the salt from the ashes and mix it with the distilled dew; seal the bottle with pounded glass and borax. Lay the vessel on fresh horse manure and leave it there for a month. Then expose it alternately to the sunlight and to the moonlight. When the gelatinous matter at the bottom of the vessel swells, this shows that the experiment has been a success. Now, each time you expose your bottle to the sunlight, the spectre of the rose will appear in the glass in all the beauty of its leaves and petals. When cooled, it will disappear; when heated, it will appear again; this process can be repeated indefinitely.

167. The spectre of the rose

There has been no other age in which rose petals, vampires, steam engines, electricity, ghosts, horror and elegance, balloons and garlands, legerdemain and occult sciences, refined ceremonials and hysteria, are mingled so intimately as in the eighteenth century. In the glass retort of nascent science a fantastic past reappeared, just like the spectre of the rose.

Where the salts proved ineffectual, humours, vapours, exhalations, atoms and magnetism served as arguments in the explanation of occult phenomena. Everything had to be explained scientifically. The dark past was to be enlightened, and rendered agreeable. Since all research depended on the sponsorship of the nobility, things had to be expounded elegantly and harmlessly in order to humour the patrons. The explorers of the new and the hidden imply that there is no cause for fear; demonstrations can be held in any *salon*. Do not worry about soiling your embroidered velvet jackets; simply be amused.

Benjamin Franklin made known his discoveries during an 'electric evening', for the amusement of his guests. The rediscovered force which was to bring light and power to mankind was then used for fireworks and the like. The first balloon, a most dangerous engine for the man who rode in it, was embellished by the brothers Montgolfier with the initials of King Louis, showing garlands and other urbane decorations intended to pacify the frightened spectators. The fear of steam and electricity still haunted the men of the early nineteenth century. Adelbert von Chamisso, who had travelled around the world in a six-hundred-ton sailboat, says in his journal that steamships might be efficiently replaced by tamed whales which could pull the boats with greater speed than any engine.

Towards the end of the century Henri Descremps, a mathematician (1746–1826), published his books on *Amusing Physics* in which he explains magical phenomena rationally as legerdemain. One of his works, *White Magic Unveiled* (Paris, 1785),

168. Miraculous effects brought about by Montgolfier balloons

has as its frontispiece the 'professor and demonstrator of physics', an elegant prestidigitator performing his show against a background covered by Bourbon lilies. The frontispiece of the second volume illustrates Descremps's prescription for pacifying savage tribes. From a Montgolfier balloon, three paper divinities descend into the midst of the awed South Africans. The figures will ascend again after a while, when the burning sulphur has severed the string attached to the lead weight which made the figures descend. Then the governor of the island will offer to the native chief the gift which Pallas Athene has brought down from heaven, and the formerly dangerous people will become friendly. It is an amiable way of pacifying savages, whose reasoning is absurd, Descremps says, though not as shocking as that of civilized people.

The most amusing part of Descremps's book, however, is that many automata and the machinery with which marvels are to be performed are controlled, according to the author, by a concealed canary or a magnet. In reality, neither would be strong enough to overcome gravity and friction and produce such results. Descremps's mathematics have calculated more than one impossibility, as has been correctly pointed out by Jean Baptist Fiard (1736–1818). In 1803 this cleric published a venomous booklet: *France Deceived by Magicians and Demonolators*. Many of the eighteenth-century magicians and prophets are branded in Fiard's work, and Descremps does not escape the invective. 'These automata cannot be moved by any means but one, the devil.'

But let us return to the Abbé de Vallemont, whose palingenetic studies were preceded by those of the divining rod. This mysterious implement, by whose reactions metal, coal and water can be located in the earth, was then, and still is, a matter of conjecture. Some modern scientists are sceptical about the efficacy of the divining rod. An American geologist working in Brazil has discovered water in many places without any rod, entirely with modern methods, yet he still carries the traditional implement with him as a make-believe. Other moderns accept the workings of the *virgula divina*, or divining rod, as a matter of fact. Gérin-Ricard, whom we cannot rank among the credulous, is of the latter group. One is tempted to classify the famous rod among the 'damned' phenomena, as Charles Fort calls them, snubbed and ignored by modern science. That the divining rod was successfully used by sixteenth-century miners is known from an early standard work on mining, published in 1571 by George Agricola. A plate shows the preliminary exploration for a coal mine. Two prospectors manipulate the instrument, while another is cutting his rod from a willow tree. Two surveyors point to the spot indicated by the 'kicking' rod. Agricola's book deals only with technical matters and is in no way connected with the occult.

The practice was continued and in 1692 Pierre Garnier, a physician of Montpellier, published an astounding report: the rod could detect crimes! Aymar, a labourer in the Dauphiné district, discovered several thieves and murderers with the help

169. The divining rod

of his instrument. He was summoned to Lyons where a wine merchant and his wife had been assassinated. In the cellar where the murder had been committed, Aymar's rod swirled frantically. Guided by the rod, he followed the criminals' traces; he stopped at the inns where they had rested, designated the bottles which they had touched, travelled down to the south of France, and finally halted in front of the jail of Beaucaire, declaring that within it was the murderer. His verdict proved correct; one of the three assassins admitted the crime, declaring that the two others had fled across the border.

The Abbé de Vallemont attempted to explain this occult phenomenon by his never-failing science. In this case the wondrous natural causes were described as the action of corpuscles: 'They perspire in the hand of him who holds the divining rod; they are sent forth or exhaled by water beds and mines, or they emanate in columns from the perspiration of the fugitive assassin. These corpuscles cause the rod's reactions.'

Whether explained or not, the occult continued to manifest itself. How can we interpret the cures at St Médard? And even if science could show how the miracle worked, there still remains the marvel that such efficacy was discovered spontaneously and collectively by the populace. What blind man or paralytic today would refuse to endure the St Médard test on account of his scientific convictions? Magical healing is indeed one of the most startling phenomena of the occult.

Hildegard von Bingen, the medieval saint, cured her patients with the virtues of precious stones and bread upon which a cross was drawn. Diseases which demand surgical intervention like appendicitis could of course not be cured by these prescriptions, but many other ailments have been successfully combated by such irrational methods. To call it suggestion does not explain the degree to which these wonderful qualities exist in man, nor their effect upon his health. Among the primitives, anthropologists say, an infringement of a taboo may kill the culprit instantaneously. How else can this be explained if not as magic? If you prefer the word suggestion, go to a hypnotist and ask him *why* his power functions. Besides a few common places, you will learn little; he himself does not have the explanation. Concepts and convictions cure and kill. And this is as magical as any Cabala.

A wizard who believed that he knew how he cured his patients was Friedrich Anton Mesmer (1734–1815), the inventor of animal magnetism. Based upon older theories such as those of Van Helmont he professed that the human body and all living bodies emanate corporeal rays that are controlled by the soul. The vital spirit, known to the old magi, descends from heaven and can be captured in a receiver. From there, this force can be guided to enter the sick, and such a transfusion revives weakened spirits. People endowed with a powerful vital spirit can transmit their health to others if they know how to direct the rays that carry this force. They may lay their hands upon the sick, or direct the emanation with an iron stick, the conductor. The receiver was a huge bucket which Mesmer had installed in his beautiful apartment. The bucket had the shape of a gigantic circular box and was filled with converging bottles whose vital power was led towards the main bottle in the centre. They contained magnetized water, glass powder and iron filings. This accumulator was covered by a lid. A series of metal rods emerged from it.

The sick had to grasp these sticks or use them as support for their ailing limbs. Comfortable chairs surrounded the instrument and a small orchestra played during the *séances*, for music is a great healer. The influence of the stars, their sympathy and attraction, was also considered by Mesmer. Nothing in his private clinic was unpleasant or reminiscent of a hospital. People met there for coffee and held animated conversations. Beautiful paintings, precious clocks and crystal-ware created the impression of wealth and position. Mesmer was a charming conversationalist and at the same time was filled with delightful modesty. All Paris went to see him, including the poor, for whom this benefactor reserved special afternoons. His success was enormous, his cures miraculous. They continued despite the hostile reports of the Medical Academy. Mesmer was accustomed to such opposition. He had left Vienna for similar reasons. But Louis XVI was his defender; the king offered him a generous yearly pension, which Mesmer refused. He wanted to have a clinic built for him, but these grandiose plans were never realized. In the end Mesmer was no longer in fashion, and his adversaries increased in number. His most fervent patient and defender was Court de Gébelin, the great linguist. But Gébelin, apparently cured, died suddenly in front of the bucket. In our day, how many patients must die before an authority is discredited! But the eighteenth-century Parisians were different. They were like those monkeys painted on the panelling of elegant

Parisian interiors. They became passionate about something, let it drop, and turned to something new. Mesmer left France, and lived incognito in England and then in Germany, where he died.

Masonic Lodges

In the eighteenth century magic and philosophy, politics and religion, were so intimately mingled that it is difficult and perhaps impossible to define the true character of the secret societies that now flooded Europe. Philanthropy was a slogan used by everyone: by kings, nobles, citizens, workers and philosophers. Most of them, however, were content with the gesture. They considered equality established when the count and the worker sat together in the Mason's assembly hall, both wearing the white apron, singing the same hymns and expressing the same ideas. But when the meeting was over the count returned to his elegance and the worker to his misery.

The contrasting political ideas and clashing interests of the classes were reconciled by sentimental phrases and an ostentatious charity which was very different from that of the anonymous seventeenth-century Rosicrucian Brothers. Everything was arranged theatrically and calculated to arouse sympathy. An idea of these tear-jerking proceedings may be gained from the following description of a session of the lodge Candor in the year 1782. The event was a dinner given in honour of the Montgolfier brothers, inventors of the balloon. On this occasion a young war hero, Claude Thion, was to be crowned by the Masons. One hundred and seventy persons of both sexes were present. The president, the Marquis of Saisseval, made an impassioned speech on the discovery, emphasizing what an honour it was to have present one of the two inventors. The unassuming M. Montgolfier had to step forward to take his place on the stage, where he received a wreath from the Countess of Choiseul-Gouffier. At this moment the echo of drums could be heard; the sound came closer; the doors opened wide, and soldiers entered unfurling the white and golden flags of France.

In this troop marches the young and brave Thion who has lost an arm while carrying a grenade. He advances to the stage, where beautiful ladies crown him with a golden laurel wreath. Drums are beaten, and the blowing of the trumpet causes the windows to rattle. Amid general applause Madame la Comtesse presents a medal to the valiant youth. The trumpets sound again, and everyone rushes to tables heaped with delicacies. A member of the Lodge now reads the couplet he has prepared:

> Victim of fate and weapons,
> If their blows could not make me retreat
> At this moment full of charm
> Feeling can only speak in tears
> Tears I did not shed when suffering.

And what may we expect after such well calculated verses but that Thion should burst into tears – and everyone is happy and weeps.[2]

It would, however, be an error to attribute such nonsense to all secret societies. There were other lodges, not supported by the king. Some groups were led by their Masters to revolution, while others defended ultra-Catholic ideals. Most, if not all, of the brotherhoods worked zealously for the dissolution of the Inquisition, which was still powerful in those days. Opposition against the decaying organization of the state was advocated and fostered by Freemasons, Martinists, Rosicrucians and Sweden-borgians with more or less vigour. In many cases this opposition was no more than a gesture, a demonstration with no immediate consequence. At length, however, this mingling of the poor and the rich, of the noble and the humble, had its good effects, and the hollow phrases of a human brotherhood, of equality of rights and duties, bore fruit because they contained a truth. Seen in their totality, the lodges promoted political progress, democracy, and the honest defence of an ideal. For the most part the Brothers were peace-loving citizens and the fear they inspired was greater than the danger they actually embodied. Their resistance was passive – but it was resistance.

The fear they inspired in the authorities soon led to the persecution of the brotherhoods. Such a policy created martyrs, heroes, opponents. In 1738 Pope Clement XII excommunicated all the Freemasons of Europe; and Louis XV interdicted Masonry in France. Many members were imprisoned. A new prohibitory decree was issued in 1744, despite the fact that Louis de Bourbon Condé was the French Grand Master.

However, the lodges proved ineradicable, a fact which impress-ed the intelligent and cast doubts on the action of both spiritual and secular authorities. On the other hand, many leaders of Masonry were unworthy people, and interior strife impeded concerted action. The confusion and sectarianism prevalent in France before the Revolution is comparable to the chaos in the first centuries of our era. The Freemasons, and especially the Martinists, shared the ancient ideal of raising man from sin to felicity. Initiatory rites were reminiscent of paganism. The candidates' ordeal was inspired by Greek and Egyptian prece-dents. The Masons were to be regenerated, like the initiates of Eleusis, to ascend to higher realms and thus acquire knowledge, revelation, and secret wisdom.

However, the Masonic initiations were more than antiquated rites culled out of a dead past. The will to regeneration had its significance in an epoch of decay. The acquisition of wisdom for the good of the commonweal, the hope of better times, the trust in humanity, the renewal of bonds with the Eternal: all this contained genuine ethical values. The times were not ripe for a complete regeneration through science. Help was to be sought rather by faith. Nearly all of the Brothers were religious. But the official faith did not satisfy their longing, and on it they grafted marvels which had been discarded in times when the Church had been purged of oriental extravagances. The cleansing process had been too radical; precious wisdom had been tossed away, and had to be recovered. Not without reason was one lodge called the Great Orient.

Distrust in science is clear in the case of the Swedish savant, Emanuel Swedenborg (1688–1772). He is the moving spirit of all the secret societies of that time. He was devoted to the study of Greek, Latin, Oriental languages and several European tongues. He promoted metallurgy, anatomy, mathematics, geology; in short, he was the prototype of the scholar; methodical, sober and sceptical. But suddenly he experienced apparitions, travels into the marvellous beyond, apocalyptic revelations. The champion of science turned seer, and a true one, if we are to believe Immanuel Kant. The clairvoyant Swedenborg saw the great Stockholm fire at a distance of some three hundred miles. His Church, the New Jerusalem, still has some several hundred thousand adherents. But his influence went further. Pasqually, Saint-Martin, Pernety and Cagliostro borrowed ideas from Swedenborg.

Seeing the misuse of the slogan 'equality', some magi soon abandoned the idea of attracting the masses. Antoine Joseph Pernety (1716–1801) gathered mainly the nobles and princes. The former Benedictine and librarian of the Prussian king was an admirer of Swedenborg, whose Latin works he translated into French. Pernety had travelled around the world with Bougainville, and his wide knowledge of men and countries spurred him on to unite all mankind under the sign of the philosophers' stone. Under the influence of Plutarch, he wrote a fantastic work on the Greek and Egyptian fables, showing that all these allegories can be condensed into one magical kernel, the Hermetic process, or Great Arcanum.

Another Hermetic was the Rosicrucian Martines Pasqually, who founded in 1754 the new Masonic rite of the Chosen Cohen. His main ideas are likewise borrowed from Swedenborg. Man's creation, his disobedience and fall, his punishment and mental sufferings; these form the nucleus of Pasqually's initiatory rites. Man was to recover his 'primary dignity, and having approached his creator on the path of speculation, he will be animated by the divine breath. He will know the secrets of nature: alchemy, Cabala and divination.' Pasqually's Swedenborgian rites were modified by his friend Louis Claude de Saint-Martin (1743–1803) who spread the doctrine over all Europe, when Pasqually had retired to Port-au-Prince, in the Republic of San Domingo. The Martinists had their associates in Russia, especially among the nobles led by Prince Galitzin. The great attraction exerted by the Martinists were magic rites which resemble those of modern spiritualists. The dead were evoked, and hallucinations were stimulated by magic circles, aromatic herbs, beautiful black silk robes and diamond-studded insignia. The enlightened communicated with divine powers and gathered from them advice as to how to promote their humanitarian ideal.

Among these magi, the Zurich pastor Johann Kaspar Lavater (1741–1801) was foremost as a promoter of tolerance. This modest author of a famous work on physiognomy had his own views on religion: those who could not find peace in his Church, he sent over to the 'good mother', Catholicism. He observed his fellow men with deep insight, for the physiognomic art was the study of man's features as the signs and characters formed by nature to reveal the inner man. His urbanity often proved more effective than the tempestuousness of his fellow magicians. 'I have seen,' Mirabeau writes, 'letters which Lavater sent to sovereigns . . . I have seen monarchs answer him with expressions of the highest esteem. They obey him, they become his tributaries.'

One would think that such a learned and influential man would not need advice from a fellow magus. And yet in 1780 Lavater travelled to Strassburg where he hoped to gather more wisdom from the Count Cagliostro. The latter, however, refused to see him. They exchanged letters. To Lavater's question, 'In what precisely does your knowledge reside?' Cagliostro answered laconically; '*In verbis, herbis et lapidibus*' (in words, herbs and stones)[3] – alluding to his marvellous cures which he performed with simples concocted from minerals and vegetables, and with the suggestive power of his word. Such an answer was unusually modest, as the 'count' (whose real name was Giuseppe Balsamo) made little secret of his miraculous knowledge, his adventurous travels in the Orient and his most noble descent. Cagliostro was less talkative when referring to his stay in London, where he had committed several frauds. Nor did he mention the fact that he had been expelled from Russia for similar reasons. Goethe, in his *Voyage in Italy*, refers to Cagliostro in the following terms: 'I answered that indeed, in the eyes of the public, he posed as an aristocrat of high birth, but that to his friends he liked to acknowledge his humble origin.' In spite of Cagliostro's shady past, even his enemies did not deny the magician's astounding intelligence. And many friends and followers acknowledged their master's scandals and lies as extravagances to be weighed against his wisdom, his charity and truly superhuman talents as a seer, healer and Hermetic.

It was in Strassburg that Cagliostro produced alchemically a diamond which he offered to Cardinal Louis de Rohan. The gem was evaluated by the prelate's jeweller at twenty-five thousand livres. One day Cagliostro conjured up a dead lady whose memory the cardinal cherished. De Rohan's affection for the magician was boundless. In his study he placed Cagliostro's bust bearing the inscription: *To the Divine Cagliostro*. It was an irony of fate that this friendship was finally shattered through an affair in which Cagliostro was in no way involved: the scandal of the necklace which the Countess de la Motte had acquired for Louis de Rohan, who wanted to offer it to the Queen of France. Madame de la Motte had concealed the cardinal's money, set aside for the necklace – and the necklace as well. When questioned by the judges, she involved Cagliostro. At that time, his star was declining. He wanted now only to live quietly and honestly, a thing which proved more difficult for him than adventures and deceits.

Cagliostro was the founder of the Egyptian Lodge. The power

of his word attracted numerous adherents and whole groups of Freemasons abandoned their rites to follow those invented by the Grand Kophta, as Cagliostro called himself. Brothers of every creed were accepted. The only postulate was to believe in the immortality of the soul. During the *séances* magical ceremonies were performed with the intention of communicating with the seven 'pure spirits'. An innocent girl, the 'Dove', was led to a table where a glass bottle was flanked by two torches. The girl had to stare into the bottle, in which absent persons, future happenings, or angels would appear; or she was led behind a screen where she would experience a mystical union with an angel. Similar rites were performed in the Egyptian Lodge Isis, whose members were women. Their Grand Master was Lorenza Feliciani, Cagliostro's wife. Men were admitted in these *séances*, and the highest Parisian nobility was wont to gather there. But still greater was Cagliostro's influence upon the populace. When he was released from the Bastille, where he had been detained under false suspicion, ten thousand Parisians carried him triumphantly through the streets, and the following day the Boulevard Saint-Antoine where he resided was filled with a crowd cheering Cagliostro. Rioting was feared and the seer was ordered to leave Paris within eight days. When this decree became public a new crowd gathered around his house. From the balcony, Cagliostro appeased them by saying: 'The moment will come when I will let you hear my voice.'

The Count of Saint-Germain

Who was he and where did he come from? The riddle has never been solved. The dates of his birth and death are unknown. Incredible things are claimed of him. Frederick the Great called him the man who cannot die; and the count himself asserted that he had lived two thousand years as a result of the professed discovery of the liquid that could prolong human life. He would speak familiarly of a chat with the Queen of Sheba and of wonderful happenings at the marriage of Cana. He knew the gossip of the court of Babylon, tales thousands of years old, yet resembling so strangely the current Parisian gossip that he captivated everybody at court. His knowledge of European history was uncanny. He would mention various happenings in the reigns of Henry IV and Francis I. To an astounded lady, he would whisper family secrets, true things the lady said, which he had heard from her ancestor on the battlefield of Marignano.

The count was neither tall nor very handsome; he always appeared about forty, and dressed exquisitely. He was dark-haired, lively and smiling. His clothes were covered with precious jewels. He spoke and wrote Greek, Latin, Sanskrit, Arabic, Chinese, French, German, English, Italian, Portuguese and Spanish. His erudition verged on the supernatural; he was also a talented painter, a virtuoso on the harpsichord and violin, and his chemical knowledge far surpassed that of his contemporaries.

He knew how to remove flaws from diamonds, an art which has since been lost. In this way, he improved one of the diamonds of King Louis XV, increasing the value of the gem considerably. He could make gold and of course he also possessed the elixir of life. Besides this, he was extremely rich.

He composed little operas and folk songs and it was said that he collected paintings, in particular Murillo and Velasquez. He also spoke about his invention of the steamboat, which was to unite the people of the next century. He could render himself invisible, and reappear wherever he wished, a fact which was witnessed by several of his friends. He hypnotized others and could fall at will into a state of auto-hypnosis. His knowledge of pigments was also extraordinary, and the painters Latour and Van Loo begged him in vain to reveal this secret.

He was surrounded by servants and valets who told many astounding stories about their master. A sceptic said to Roger, Saint-Germain's butler: 'Your master is a liar,' to which Roger answered: 'I know this better than you: he tells everyone that he is four thousand years old. But I have been in his service only a hundred years, and when I came, the count told me that he was three thousand years old. Whether he has added nine hundred years by error, or whether he is lying, I do not know.' Such were the tales told by his valets; but the aristocracy told similar stories. When Saint-Germain arrived in Versailles he met the Countess of Gergy, who said to him: 'Fifty years ago I was ambassadress in Venice, where I remember having seen you. You looked exactly as you do now, though perhaps somewhat more mature, for you have grown younger!' The composer Rameau, who was then an old man, remembered having seen Saint-Germain in 1701, at which time the count appeared to him about fifty years old, a little older than in 1743. King Louis XV ordered Saint-Germain to be lodged at Chambord, and in later years he had free access to the king's private chambers.

Let us try to unravel the baffling mystery, and show the true character of this magus. The first suspicion arises from Frederick's statement that Saint-Germain could not die. Why should the sceptical Prussian king promote such a fantastic tale? The only explanation would be that he had an interest in doing so, that he followed some plan. Saint-Germain had come to France with the French Ambassador, Monsieur Belle-Isle; he was graciously received by Louis and lived like a nobleman of high rank. This implies that he was on a mission, and that he was on a secret mission, his person being intentionally surrounded by mystery. Frederick's statement is not the only proof of this. The ostentatious declaration of Countess Gergy is also suspect; she had been 'ambassadress', that is, on a diplomatic mission. Apparently, the shrewd old lady had been taken into the secret by the king. She was probably the only woman at court who could be trusted in so delicate an affair; and a court lady was needed to promote the fantastic tales. Old Rameau may have been mistaken, and have confounded Saint-Germain with someone else whom he had once met, or perhaps he too knew the secret.

Saint-Germain betrays himself as a diplomat, with his astounding tales of a political past. Having access to secret files, he studied European history methodically and with purpose, whereas his other talents, whatever the legend relates, were amateurish. His operas were inconsequential; his gift as a painter must have been unimportant, since none of his works remain. His chemical discoveries were anodyne, and have been lost. The painters Van Loo and Latour may have flattered him, for nothing is more common than a professional giving credit to a dilettante.

Saint-Germain's knowledge of languages must have been astounding; but here too we must make an abstraction of the accounts. A witness relates that no matter where the count journeyed, he invariably passed as a native, so that he is said to have had complete knowledge of the various languages. We wonder who substantiated such facts in China, which Saint-Germain, according to his own boasting, visited often. And what about his Sanskrit? If he knew all these languages so perfectly, how can we explain that the only tongue which he spoke constantly in France, his French, revealed a foreign accent, as many witnesses relate?

Extraordinary things about Saint-Germain were told with ever increasing exaggeration, and were sanctioned and promoted by the kings of Prussia and France. Regarding Saint-Germain's art of transmuting base metals into gold, it is doubtful that he knew the arcanum. There is a story recorded by the famous Casanova, who visited Saint-Germain at the Hague. The count transmuted a piece of silver into gold, but Casanova refused to believe in the transmutation, saying that it had been performed by legerdemain. The count politely ushered the guest out of his house and refused to see him again. Would it not have been wiser to give an irrefutable proof than to be offended at someone's not believing the unbelievable? Regarding the king's diamond, which Saint-Germain kept for more than a month, this could well have been dispatched to Amsterdam, where the count had many relatives, and exchanged for a similarly cut gem. Perhaps Saint-Germain wanted the king to believe that after all he was not entirely an invented prodigy, and the wealthy agent may have been willing to pay for this mystification whatever fee was necessary to exchange the old diamond for the new one. Even the count's collection of valuable paintings is somewhat suspicious. Famous art works have a history and a pedigree, and to our knowledge, there is no Velasquez or Murillo that can be traced back to a Saint-Germain collection.

The count was apparently preoccupied with matters that forbade him to waste time with collections and travels to China. He may have made frequent journeys east, but his trips went no further than Berlin, where Frederick awaited his report, or to Vienna, the Rosicrucian headquarters. It is certain that he was in Frederick's service, and it is also likely that he took orders from the Fraternity. But how could the interest of the Brothers and those of the Prussian king have been linked together in Saint-Germain? Here we enter the realms of pure conjecture, although nothing too fantastic emerges from such speculation. The more prominent groups of German Rosicrucians were conservative; they pursued Johann Valentine Andreae's political ideal, monarchy and German hegemony over Europe and the Pope. Why should this programme have displeased Frederick? He wanted to weaken France, and events indeed seemed favourable. Yet actually to destroy the monarchy was the aim neither of Frederick nor of the Brothers. Their common offer to the king was the preservation of the French monarchy; but they certainly demanded a counter-service!

In Louis XV's time the situation of France was grave but not desperate. The capable minister of foreign affairs, the Duke of Choiseul, was continuing the late Louis XIV's policy, which was to weaken Prussia. But it was a trait of Louis XV to handle certain matters alone, without consulting his ministers; and he conducted his negotiations with Saint-Germain in secrecy. The 'immortal' count was characterized as a wonder-man who had attracted the king's interest by his transmutations, and the two met often in Louis's alchemical laboratory. But Choiseul did not trust his master's Hermetic studies, and soon began to suspect the Count of Saint-Germain. The latter, as he discovered through discreet investigation, had never received funds from abroad. He collected great sums of money from a source within France, perhaps the German embassy or the Masons' treasury.

Saint-Germain's subversive activities were exposed when he suddenly appeared in Holland, through whose government he attempted to negotiate a peace with England. This must have been his own idea, as neither the French ambassador in the Netherlands, d'Affry, nor Choiseul knew of it. Both would have disapproved of this step. D'Affry complained about this to Casanova, and sent him to the count. Instead of taking Casanova's visit seriously, Saint-Germain played the juggler, and at Casanova's demand to know what he was doing in Holland, he answered that it was to negotiate a loan to France. The shrewd and seductive Casanova had found his master. He invited Saint-Germain to dinner, but the latter refused with the excuse that no one had ever seen him dine with unknown people and that he consumed only pills, bread, groats and the like (which was perfectly true).

Choiseul could not permit this evasion. He enjoined d'Affry to have Saint-Germain arrested. But the Netherlands refused to extradite the count. The king officially abandoned his agent, but only officially, for a few days later Madame d'Urfé encountered Saint-Germain in the Bois de Boulogne. She hastened excitedly to Choiseul, who told her calmly that Saint-Germain had been in his study all night. This meant that the secret could no longer be concealed, and that Louis had ordered Saint-Germain to report his plans to the foreign minister. Choiseul was aware that England was supporting Prussia and disapproved of the plans; he had Saint-Germain dismissed. However, Louis retained him as a spy, and in this capacity he travelled to Germany and Russia. Soon after his arrival in Russia, the emperor changed his Francophile policy and made an alliance with Frederick.

Shortly before leaving France, the count had been questioned by Louis XV about some mysterious crime, the details of which were known only to Saint-Germain. The latter had offered to reveal the facts under one condition: 'Sir,' he said, 'become a Rosicrucian, and I will tell you.' Had Louis accepted this proposition, he might have saved his dynasty. But time was growing short; it was too late for effective intervention, and Saint-Germain was becoming old despite his 'immortality'. Louis XVI ascended the throne, and the mysterious envoy of the Rosicross appeared once more in France. He tried desperately but unsuccessfully to win the new monarch over to his cause. He had been sent to save the throne and the royal family, but after a last effort to convince Marie Antoinette, Saint-Germain took his leave. He knew that such prolonged insistence was interpreted as the activity of an enemy agent. The minister Maurepas was after him, and a longer stay would end in prison. Every border was guarded, but he managed to escape to Germany, and lived at the court of the Landgrave of Hessen-Cassel, a fervent alchemist. Now he admitted to being eighty-eight years old, and during the Landgrave's absence, died suddenly in the arms of two chambermaids.

But in spite of his supposed death, many instances of his reappearance have been recorded. After the fall of the Bastille, Marie Antoinette received an anonymous letter: 'Oppose yourself energetically. No more manoeuvres. Destroy the rebels' pretext, by isolating yourself from people whom you do not love any longer. Abandon Polignac and his kind. They are all vowed to death and assigned to the assassins who have just killed the officers of the Bastille. . . .' At the same hour, Madame Adhemar, Marie Antoinette's confidante, received word: 'All is lost. You are a witness that I have done everything I could to give another trend to the events. One has disregarded me. Too late. I wanted to contemplate the work prepared by that demon Cagliostro. It is infernal . . . I promise to meet you; but do not demand anything. I can help neither the king nor the queen, nor the royal family. . . .' Both letters were written by Saint-Germain.

Madame Adhemar went to the rendezvous with the count, 'dead' now for five years. They met in a chapel. Saint-Germain, knowing that the court lady ignored his motives entirely, fell back upon his fantastic tales, though mainly to disguise his emotion. He had just arrived from Japan, and 'by Jove, how they have compromised Louis XIV's politics. You cannot know all this, Madame, but I have seen it from the beginning.' He showed himself many times. During the Revolution he appeared here and there in Paris, not infrequently at the Place de la Grève, where the guillotine stood. He said that he wanted to see the infernal work initiated by his pupil Cagliostro.

But this great magus, the anti-monarchist Cagliostro, was arrested in that same year in Rome and thrown into the prisons of the Holy Inquisition. Shortly before his imprisonment, he wrote to the National Assembly, begging to be admitted to France, he who 'had taken so much interest in the people's liberty'. His request remained unanswered. One did not have to be a seer to understand that the Holy Office was waiting patiently for its prey. Cagliostro could not escape. He was caught in Rome, for all the Italian states had expelled him from their territory.

Cagliostro had cured hundreds of people by magic. His house in Strassburg was filled with the crutches of cripples whom he had restored to health. He had spent a fortune in alms. He had established innumerable lodges that followed his rites and prescriptions. 'One million Europeans,' he said in his defence, 'believe in the Egyptian rite which I have founded.' But now he was alone, completely abandoned. His last effort to escape the Inquisition was a project in which he asked all Egyptian lodges to send delegates to Rome, instructing them to rescue him, in case he was arrested, and, if necessary, set fire to the Castello or any other prison where they might confine him. He entrusted the papers to two unworthy men, who delivered them readily to the Inquisitors.

Epilogue

In France, events moved on, and while the guillotine accomplished its bloody work, magic had not lost its influence. The famous Alliette gave Cabalistic lessons to the populace, and in Mademoiselle Lenormand's parlour the heroes of the Revolution met to have their fortunes told; Danton, Desmoulins, Marat, Saint-Just, and even Robespierre. Later, when her clients had perished under the axe, new customers arose in the Directoire and under the Empire. Napoleon, predisposed to magic, tolerated Mademoiselle Lenormand in Malmaison, where she predicted to Josephine that the emperor was to divorce her. Like Socrates, Napoleon had a demon – a red man who appeared at times in the passageways of the Tuileries. Just like the Roman emperors of old, he sanctioned his own magic and condemned that of others. Did he not persecute Fabre d'Olivet who had cured the sick with the methods of ancient Egyptian priests? Guided by his clairvoyant wife, d'Olivet attempted to revive Pythagoras's religion. He died at the foot of the altar he had built for his gods.

Fantastic apparitions continued to haunt the people of the West. Magicians were still at work in a period when science was moving forward with giant strides. Throughout the nineteenth century, seers and magi continued the lineage of the ancient wise men.

Hoene Wronski, former artillery officer in the Napoleonic armies, expounded theories based on Pythagorean mathematics and on the Cabala. Charles Fourier, a philosopher and sociologist, strove towards the complete reformation of society by semi-magical means. In 1814 Madame d'Eldir, a seductive lady of Oriental origin, revealed her visions to a group of wealthy Frenchmen. A vicar of Notre-Dame, William Oegger, having met Judas Iscariot in England, turned to occultism. Alphonse Cahagnet, a modest artisan, sent his revelations to Pope Pius IX.

The Baron du Potet believed that his hypnotic gift was related to magic. Eliphas Lévi, former deacon of St Sulpice in Paris, revived occult doctrines of antiquity which he wanted to fuse with science and religion. Louis Lucas wrote on 'transcendental' physics and chemistry. The Baron Guldenstubbe evoked spirits of illustrious dead. Plato, Caesar, Germanicus, Abélard and others were conjured up, and wrote their signatures and opinions upon the baron's tablets.[1] Albert Poisson abandoned his medical career and became a practising alchemist. St Yves d'Alveydre established a system of affinities between numbers, colours, odours, letters, planets, etc.; he had this system patented in 1909. Madame Helena Blavatsky and Annie Besant astounded the world with their esoteric writings and their prophecies. Stanislas de Guaita, Oswald Wirth and Gérard Encausse carried on Eliphas Lévi's work.

The epoch of positivistic science could not break the spell. Many savants suspected the occult forces to be some unknown power, like electricity, still undiscovered. They weighed and measured magical phenomena, photographed apparitions, and in darkened salons linked hands with more or less successful mediums. They witnessed cases of levitation, persons or objects being raised into the air without apparent mechanical help. They investigated table-rapping, ectoplasms, clairvoyance, premonition, haunted houses, etc. Some of them believed that they had discovered the reality of the occult. Others cautiously concluded that nothing should be denied, so long as it is not disproved.

Conclusion

Hegel says that magic has existed in all times and among all people. Our short cut through the occult history of the Old World has shown this to be no overstatement. Magic has exerted a powerful influence on the human intellect. Whether such influence was beneficent or nefarious to mankind has been discussed by several scientists. Eusèbe Salverte who published his *Essay on the Occult Sciences* in 1829 regards magic as a means of deception used by the leaders of ancient peoples. Science, he implies, has liberated man from superstition arising from the faulty observation of nature. At the end of the last century Sir James Frazer voiced a similar opinion. Magic was a lie, he says, but a lie which had beneficial results: social and scientific progress.

Modern anthropologists, such as Hubert and Mauss, assert that the primitive magician was no impostor; but that he and his contemporaries believed that he was endowed with supernatural power, and that his rank was given him by common consent. In the light of modern psychology this theory seems more acceptable than the idea that, through thousands of years, true knowledge of nature was deliberately concealed by a minority. The longevity of magic suggests that it is deeply rooted in the psyche of man. The psychologist Jean Piaget has shown that up to the age of six or seven every human being lives in a magical world, sharing beliefs and habits with the remote past no less than with the modern primitive.

Magic still is popular among all peoples. Hardly one among us can say that he is entirely free of magical thought or action: 'There is a desire in everyone of us,' says Malinowski, 'to escape from routine and certainty. . . . To most men nothing is more cheerless and oppressive than the rigidity and determination with which the world runs. Even the most sceptical at times rebel against the inevitable causal chain which excludes the supernatural and, with it, all the gifts of chance and good fortune.' Within our society astrologers, palmists, crystal-gazers and mediums prosper, as numerous perhaps as in ancient Rome. Mystic and esoteric sects, their publications swelling the book market, are ever on the increase. Magic, as Probst or Bachelard have revealed, still lurks behind scientific thinking.

Civilizations have vanished, together with their beliefs. But man's desires are constant, and whatever promises their fulfilment is apt to perpetuate itself, taking precedence over newly risen dogmas and often over reason. In the fairy tale the magician bids the poor man eat his fill, make his own the treasure in the marvellous cave. Through his courage the hero overwhelms his enemies, is chosen king, marries the beautiful princess, gains wealth, and so on. Such tales recount man's desires, and the repeating of them reveals his wish that they may be somehow marvellously realized. The witches or the village magicians promised tangible benefits. They hardly rationalized their operations: a certain ceremony, they knew, would produce such a certain effect. But the why was as dark to them as it was to their clients.

The best minds of the West were influenced by a higher type of magic. The investigators of nature followed for centuries the path trodden before them by the ancient philosophers and magi. They believed that in magical wisdom lay the secret of the world's harmony. The religions of the West have admitted that Satan's revolt split the universe, that he infests the world of matter, and that the ever-tempted believer may gain lasting felicity only after death. The magical systems of old did not admit disharmony. They encircled the totality of being, good and evil, life and death, the visible and the invisible. All is contained in All. And All is One. The supernatural is not separate from the world of matter but is infused in every object. Good and evil sprang from the same source; both obey the same law. The magical world is a huge wheelwork of which man forms the main pivot. Were he removed – were anything removed – the world clock would come to a standstill.

This figure, however, does not convey the entire magical man. Not only is he harmoniously integrated within the All, but he can act upon it. He strives for cognizance of the world mechanism. The wise, he believes, can penetrate this mystery, move the world of matter, and conjure the supernatural, angels and elementary spirits. In its purest form, magic in Christianity sprang from man's longing to partake of the divine through knowledge, from his will to attain felicity, not in the hereafter but here upon earth.

This type of magic was akin to mysticism, yet it contained a stimulus to scientific research, because to partake of the divine through the knowledge of creation meant an investigation of nature. Throughout the Middle Ages the sole counterweight to blind belief lay in clumsy and often faulty research into the real 'virtue of things' by magically minded scholars. Thorndike, in his *History of Magic and Experimental Science*, has established this fact, already stressed by Maury and others. Magic gave a stimulus to experimentation and, in a broader sense, to thinking, not only in Christianity, but in the ancient world as well. The ancient wise men, taking over primitive magical traditions, were faced with the task of transmuting apparent absurdities into a magico-religious system adequate to their more advanced civilization. The more absurd the belief, the more intense was their effort to weave around it a sparkling web of philosophy or transcendental doctrine.

And if we trace our way further back, into the eras of primitive mankind, here too we have reason to believe that magic was no vain observance. The early wizard was a benefactor of his tribesmen, promising assistance against the fearful unknown. Just as today there are many who feel the need to lay their guilt in the hands of a confessor or psychiatrist, so also did the so-called savage entrust his worries and anxieties to the magician. Magical operations constituted a discipline which permitted men to go about life's daily business, to overcome the oppression of hostile reality through regular intercourse with supernatural forces. Such were the real gifts which man was able to extract from magic, his own invention, the only system in its day that could achieve these goals. Of course, the magician's power could serve evil purposes too, for evil was ruled by the same laws as good, and the temptation was ever present to bridle the occult forces with destructive intent. This fact, however, is not inherent in magic alone. In every society, leaders may use their influence for various ends.

But a system that prevailed in society for thousands of years hardly needs an apology. The fact remains that magic upheld the great civilizations of the ancient world. Its predominance did not prevent man from leaving behind him works of continuing value, from tolerating his neighbour, cherishing his family, doing the adequate thing at the right time. Magic was a stimulus to thinking. It freed man from fears, endowed him with a feeling of his power to control the world, sharpened his capacity to imagine, and kept alive his dreams of higher achievement.

Notes

MESOPOTAMIA

1–5 The incantations are translations from François Lenormant,
    La Magie chez les Chaldéens, Paris, 1874.
  6 François Lenormant, *La divination . . . chez les Chaldéens*,
    Paris, 1875.
7–10 Franz J. Boll, *Sternglaube und Sterndeutung*, Leipzig, 1926.
11, 12 James G. Frazer, *Folklore in the Old Testament*, vol. I, London,
    1919.

PERSIA

  1 Boll, *op. cit.*
  2 A. V. William Jackson, *Zoroastrian Studies*, vol. 12, New York,
    1928.
3–5 James Darmesteter, *Sacred Books of the East: the Vendidad*,
    Oxford, 1880.

THE HEBREWS

  1 The interpretation of Dagon as a female divinity follows
    Athanasius Kircher (*Oedipus Aegyptiacus*, Rome, 1652),
    although Dagon was originally regarded as a male divinity.
2, 3 James G. Frazer, *The Golden Bough*, London, 1915.
  4 Gustav Rosskoff, *Geschichte des Teufels*, Leipzig, 1869.
  5 Frazer, *The Golden Bough*.

EGYPT

  1 E. A. T. Wallis Budge, *Egyptian Magic*, London, 1899.
  2 James H. Breasted, *A History of Egypt*.
  3 Amélineau, *Histoire de la superstition dans l'ancienne Égypte*,
    quoted by L. de Gérin-Ricard, *Histoire de l'occultisme*, Paris,
    1939.
  4 Breasted, *op. cit.*
  5 The content of this section in the main is based on E. A. T.
    Wallis Budge, *The Papyrus of Ani*, New York, 1913.
6–8 Lenormant, *La Magie chez les Chaldéens*.
  9 Alexandre Moret, *Du caractère religieux de la royauté pharaon-
    ique*, Paris, 1938.

GREECE

  1 Wilhelm Heinrich Roscher, *Ephialtes*, Leipzig, 1900.
2–6 Jacob Burckhardt, *Griechische Kulturgeschichte*, Leipzig (n.d.).
  7 Philostratus, *The Life of Apollonius of Tyana* (trans. F. C.
    Conybeare, London and New York, 1927). The story of
    Menippus is somewhat embellished with details from P.
    Christian, *Histoire de la magie*, Paris (n.d.).
8, 9 Burckhardt, *op. cit.*
 10 Conybeare, Introduction to Philostratus, *op. cit.*
11, 12 Burckhardt, *op. cit.*

GNOSTICISM

  1 The quoted passages are from G. Horner's translation of *Pistis
    Sophia* from the Coptic.
2, 3 C. W. King, *The Gnostics and their Remains*, London, 1887.

1, 2 Lynn Thorndike, *History of Magic and Experimental Science*, New York, 1923–34.
  3 King, *op. cit.*
4–5 W. C. (France) Wright, *Julian's Relation to the New Sophistic and Neo-Platonism*, London, 1896.
  6 Gaetano Negri, *Julian the Apostate*, London, 1905.
7, 8 King, *op. cit.*

ALCHEMY

  1 William Jerome Wilson, 'Historical Background of Greco-Egyptian Alchemy', *Ciba Symposia*, vol. 2, no. 7, Summit, New Jersey, 1941.
  2 Marcellin Berthelot, *Les Origines de l'alchimie*, Paris, 1885.
3, 4 William Jerome Wilson, 'The Greek Alchemical Papyri', *Ciba Symposia*, vol. 2, no. 7, Summit, New Jersey, 1941.
  5 Berthelot, *op. cit.*
  6 Wilson, 'Historical Background of Greco-Egyptian Alchemy', *op. cit.*
  7 Breasted, *op. cit.*
  8 Louis Ménard, *Étude sur l'origine des livres hermetiques.*
9–11 *Musaeum Hermeticum*, Frankfurt and Leipzig, 1749 (trans. Arthur E. Waite).
 12 Louis Figuier, *L'Alchimie et les alchimistes*, Paris, 1854.
13–17 *Musaeum Hermeticum*, *op. cit.*
 18 R. Allendy, *Le Symbolisme des nombres.*
 19 Arthur E. Waite, *Lives of Alchemistical Philosophers*, London, 1888. (Modern scientists like C. G. Jung accept Cremer as an historical figure.)
 20 *Musaeum Hermeticum*, *op. cit.*
 21 Aristotle, *On Generation and Corruption*, Book I.
 22 Passage quoted in Reginald Scot, *Discoverie of Witchcraft*, London, 1584.
23, 24 Figuier, *op. cit.*
 25 Waite, *op. cit.*
 26 Nicolas Flamel, *His Exposition of the Hieroglyphical Figures*, (reprint), London, 1898.
27, 28 Figuier, *op. cit.*
 29 Waite, *op. cit.*

MIDDLE AGES

  1 Grillot de Givry, *Le Musée des sorciers*, Paris, 1929.
2, 3 Montague Summers, *The Geography of Witchcraft*, London, 1927.
  4 This section follows roughly Thorndike, *op. cit.*
  5 Gérin-Ricard, *op. cit.*
6–8 Thorndike, *op. cit.*
  9 Jacob Burckhardt, *Die Kultur der Renaissance in Italien.*
 10 Thorndike, *op. cit.*
 11 D. M. Menendez Pelayo, *Arnaldo de Villanova.*
 12 Summers, *op. cit.*
 13 John H. Randall, Jr, *The Making of the Modern Mind*, Boston, 1940.
 14 Thorndike, *op. cit.*
 15 Albertus Magnus, *Libellus de Alchymia*, in *Theatrum Chemicum*, vol. 2, Strasbourg, 1618.
 16 Thorndike, *op. cit.*

1 Paul Carus, *The History of the Devil and the Idea of Evil*, Chicago, 1900.

WITCHCRAFT

1–7 Ian Ferguson, *The Philosophy of Witchcraft*, New York, 1925.
8 C. L'Estrange Ewen, *Witch Hunting and Witch Trials*, New York, 1925.

PORTRAITS

1 This treatment follows closely Thorndike's articles in his *History of Magic and Experimental Science*.

CABALA

1 This follows mainly Ad. Franck, *La Kabbale, ou la philosophie religieuse des Hébreux*, Paris, 1892.

MAGICAL ARTS

1 The explanation of the principles of astrology follows roughly Boll, *op. cit.*

REFORMERS

1, 2 Arthur E. Waite, *The Real History of the Rosicrucians*, New York, 1888.
3 The English version of *The Chemical Wedding* has been reprinted in Waite's *The Real History of the Rosicrucians, op. cit.*

THE EIGHTEENTH CENTURY

1 Louis Figuier, *Histoire du merveilleux*.
2 Henri d'Alméras, *Cagliostro, la franc-maçonnerie et l'occultisme au XVIIIe siècle*, Paris, 1904.
3 Cagliostro's answer recalls Johann Rudolph Glauber's treatise *Explicato, oder Auslegung über die Worte Salomonis : in herbis, verbis et lapidibus magna est virtus*, Amsterdam, 1664.

EPILOGUE

1 A description of the principal French magi of the nineteenth century is given by Auguste Viatte, *Victor Hugo et les illuminés de son temps*.

Bibliographic Résumé

SOME AUTHORS ON MAGIC AND WITCHCRAFT

Debay, A., *Histoire des sciences occultes*, Paris, 1883
du Prel, Carl, *Die Magie als Naturwissenschaft*, Jena, 1889
Ennemoser, J., *The History of Magic*, London, 1854
Ewen, L'Estrange C., *Witch Hunting and Witch Trials*, New York, 1925
Ferguson, Ian, *The Philosophy of Witchcraft*, New York, 1925
Fischer, Hans, *Magie und Mystik in Vergangenheit und Gegenwart*, Berlin, 1929
Frazer, James G., *The Golden Bough*, London, 1915
Garinet, Jules, *Histoire de la magie en France*, Paris, 1818
Gérin-Ricard, L. de, *Histoire de l'occultisme*, Paris, 1939
Gleadow, Rupert, *Magic and Divination*, London, 1941
Goerres, Johann Joseph, *La Mystique divine, naturelle et diabolique*, French trans. Paris, 1855
Grillot de Givry, *Le Musée des sorciers*, Paris, 1929
Gulat-Wellenberg, Carl, *Der physikalische Mediumismus*, Berlin, 1925
Hartmann, Franz, *Magic White and Black*, Chicago, 1910
Hauber, D. E. D., *Bibliotheca Acta et Scripta Magica. . . .* (n.p.), 1739–1741
Hubert, H., and M. Mauss, *Mélanges d'histoire des religions*, Paris (n.d.)
Kaplan, Leo, *Das Problem der Magie*, Heidelberg, 1927
Kittredge, George Lyman, *Witchcraft in Old and New England*, Cambridge, Mass., 1929
Lehmann, Alfred G. L., *Aberglaube und Zauberei*, Stuttgart, 1898
Lévy-Bruhl, L., *L'Âme primitive*, Paris, 1927
Maury, L. F. Alfred, *La Magie et l'astrologie dans l'antiquité et au moyen-âge*, Paris, 1860
Mayo, Herbert, *Popular Superstitions*, Philadelphia, 1852
Oesterreich, Konstantin, *Occultism and Modern Science*, New York, 1923
Piaget, Jean, *The Child's Conception of the World*, New York, 1929
Rivers, W. H. R., *Medicine, Magic, and Religion*, New York, 1923
Saintyves, P., *La Force magique*, Paris, 1914
Salverte, Eusèbe, *Des sciences occultes*, Paris, 1834
Summers, Montague, *The Geography of Witchcraft*, London, 1927
Thorndike, Lynn, *History of Magic and Experimental Science*, New York, 1923–34

THE MESOPOTAMIANS

Berosus, *Le antichità di Beroso Caldeo sacerdote*, Vinegia, 1583
Budge, E. A. T. Wallis, *Babylonian Life and History*, London, 1884
Fossey, C., *La Magie assyrienne . . .*, Paris, 1902
Gadd, C. J., *History and Monuments of Ur*, New York, 1929
Halévy, Joseph, *Documents religieux de l'Assyrie et de la Babylonie*, Paris, 1882
Jastrow, Joseph, *Religion of Babylonia and Assyria*, Boston, 1898
King, Leonard William, *Babylonian Magic and Sorcery*, London, 1896
Lenormant, François, *La Magie chez les Chaldéens*, Paris, 1874
 – *La Divination et la science des présages chez les Chaldéens*, Paris, 1875

PERSIA

Darmesteter, James, *Sacred Books of the East : the Zend-Avesta;
the Vendidad*, Oxford, 1880
Jackson, A. V. William, *Zoroastrian Studies*, vol. 12, New York,
1928
Scheftelowitz, Isidor, *Die altpersische Religion und das Judentum*,
Giessen, 1920

THE HEBREWS

Frazer, James G., *Folklore in the Old Testament*, London, 1919
Kircher, Athanasius, *Oedipus Aegyptiacus*, Rome, 1652
Margolis, Max L. and Marx, A., *Histoire du peuple juif*, Paris, 1927
Scholz, Paul, *Götzendienst und Zauberwesen bei den alten Hebräern*,
Regensburg, 1877
Trachtenberg, J., *Jewish Magic and Superstition* (thesis), New York,
1939

THE EGYPTIANS

Breasted, James H., *Development of Religion and Thought in Ancient
Egypt*, New York, 1912
Budge, E. A. T. Wallis, *Egyptian Magic*, London, 1899
– *The Papyrus of Ani*, New York, 1913
Erman, Adolph, *A Handbook of Egyptian Religion*, London, 1907
Lexa, F., *La Magie dans l'Égypte antique*, Paris, 1925
Maspéro, Gaston C. Ch., *Études de mythologie et d'archéologie
égyptienne*, Paris, 1916
Moret, Alexandre, *Du caractère religieux de la royauté pharaonique*,
Paris, 1938
Weigall, A., *Histoire de l'Égypte ancienne*, Paris, 1936

THE GREEKS

Apuleius, *Works* (trans.), London, 1888
Artemidorus Daldianus, *De Somniorum Interpretatione . . .* , Basel,
1539
Burckhardt, Jacob, *Griechische Kulturgeschichte*, Leipzig (n.d.)
Hero Alexandrinus, *Buch von Luft und Wasserkünsten*, Frankfurt,
1688
Kern, O., *Die Religion der Griechen* (n.p.), 1926
Nares, R., *An Essay on the Demon of Socrates*, London, 1782
Philostratus, *The Life of Apollonius of Tyana*, trans. F. C. Cony-
beare, London and New York, 1927.
Ptolemy, *Tetrabiblos* (trans.), London, 1822
Roscher, Wilhelm Heinrich, *Ephialtes*, Leipzig, 1900
Taylor, Thomas, *The Mystical Hymns of Orpheus*, Chiswick, 1824
Tillemont, Le Nain de, *An Account of the Life of Apollonius
Tyaneus*, London, 1702

GNOSTICISM

Amélineau, Emile, *Essai sur le gnosticisme égyptien*, Paris, 1887
– *Pistis Sophia*, Paris, 1895
Bidez, J., and Cumont, F., *Les Mages hellénisés*, Paris, 1938
Harnack, Adolf von, *Über das gnostische Buch Pistis Sophia*,
Leipzig, 1891
Hopfner, Theodor, *Griechisch-ägyptischer Offenbarungszauber*, in
Studien zur Palaeographie und Papyruskunde, Heft 23, Leipzig,
1937
King, C. W., *The Gnostics and their Remains*, London, 1887
Malone, Herbert, 'Ophites', 'Basilides', *Encyclopedia Britannica*,
1941

Reitzenstein, Rich., *Studien zum antiken Synkretismus aus Iran und Griechenland*, Leipzig, 1926

NEO-PLATONISM, ROME

Bidez, J., *La Liturgie des mystères chez les Néo-Platoniciens*, Bruxelles, 1919

Boissard, Jean Jacques, *De Divinatione et Magicis*, Oppenheim, ca. 1605

Henry, Paul, *Plotin et l'occident*, Louvain, 1934

Iamblichus, *The Egyptian Mysteries*, trans. A. Wilder, New York, 1909

Negri, Gaetano, *Julian the Apostate*, London, 1905

Porphyry, *Porphyre: L'antre des nymphes*, trans. J. Trabucco, followed by *Un Essai sur les grottes dans le culte magico-religieux et dans la symbolique primitive*, by P. Saintyves, Paris, 1918

– *Traité de Porphyre touchant l'abstinence de la chair . . .*, Paris, 1747

Proclus, *Divine Arithmetic*, trans. A. G. Ionides, London, 1917

– *The Commentaries on the* Timaeus *of Plato*, trans. T. Taylor, London, 1820

Wright, W. C., *Julian's Relation to the New Sophistic and Neo-Platonism*, London, 1896

DYING PAGANISM

Ammianus Marcellinus, *The Roman History . . . during the Reigns of the Emperors Constantius, Julian, Jovian, Valentinian, and Valens . . .*, H. G. Bone, London, 1862

Clement of Alexandria, *Oeuvres*, trans. de Genoude, Paris, 1839

Eusebius, *Eusebius' Werke*, Leipzig, 1902–26

Harnack, Adolf von, *Die Mission und Ausbreitung des Christentums*, Leipzig, 1915

Lactantius, *The Works of Lactantius*, trans. Wm. Fletcher, Edinburgh, 1871

Macrobius, *Oeuvre de Macrobe*, trans. Ch. de Rosoy, Paris, 1827

Misson, J., *Recherches sur le paganisme de Libanios*, Louvain, 1914

ALCHEMY

Albertus Magnus, *Libellus de Alchymia*, in *Theatrum Chemicum*, vol. 2, Strassburg, 1613

Arnaldo da Villanova, *Speculum Alchimiae*, Frankfurt, 1602

Bacon, Roger, *Opus Tertium*, London, 1859

Berthelot, Marcellin, *Les Origines de l'alchimie*, Paris, 1885

Conti di Macerata, L., *Clara Fidelisque Disceptatio . . . de Liquore Alcahest . . .*, Frankfurt, 1644

Crollius, Oswald, *La Royalle chymie*, Lyon, 1627

Figuier, Louis, *L'Alchimie et les alchimistes*, Paris, 1854

Flamel, Nicolas, *His Exposition of the Hieroglyphical Figures . . .* (reprint), London, 1898

Helvetius (Johann Friedrich Schweitzer), *Vitulus Aureus*, Frankfurt, 1726

Hermes Trismegistus, *Mercurio Trismegisto, Il Pimandro*, trans. Tommaso Benci, Florence, 1548

Hitchcock, E. A., *Remarks upon Alchemy and the Alchemists*, New York, 1865

Jung, C. G., *Psychologie und Alchemie*, Zurich, 1944

Khunrath, Heinrich, *Amphitheatrum Sapientiae Aeternae*, Hanau, 1609

Lenglet-Dufresnoy, Nicolas, *Histoire de la philosophie hermétique*, Paris, 1742

Lullus, Raymundus, *De Secretis Naturae Sive Quinta Essentia*, Venice, 1542

Majer, Michel, *Scrutinium Chymicum* . . . , Frankfurt, 1687

Musaeum Hermeticum . . . Reformatum et Amplificatum, Frankfurt and Leipzig, 1749

Mylius, Johannes Daniel, *Philosophia Reformata*, Frankfurt, 1622

Nazari, Giovanni Battista, *Della tramutatione metallica*, Brescia, 1599

Norton, Samuel, *Mercurius Redivivus*, Frankfurt, 1630

Paracelsus, *Traité des trois essences premières*, trans. from the Latin by Grillot de Givry, Paris, 1903

Sendivogius, Michel, *Traicté du soulphre, second principe de la nature*, The Hague, 1639

Silberer, Herbert, *Probleme der Mystik und ihrer Symbolik*, Vienna, 1914

Trismosin, Salomon, *La toyson d'or ou la fleur des thrésors* . . . , Paris, 1616

Ulstadius, Philippus, *Coelum Philosophorum*, Paris, 1544

Valentinus, Basilius, *Azoth, ou le moyen de faire l'or caché des philosophes; les douze clefs de la philosophie*, Paris, 1660

Vaughan, Thomas, *Chymica Vannus* . . . , Amsterdam, 1666

Vigenère, Blaise de, *Traicté du feu et du sel*, Paris, 1618

Waite, Arthur E., *Lives of Alchemistical Philosophers*, London, 1888

Wilson, William Jerome, 'The Background of Chinese Alchemy; Leading Ideas of Early Chinese Alchemists', *Ciba Symposia*, vol. 2, no. 7, Summit, New Jersey, 1940

- 'Historical Background of Greco-Egyptian Alchemy' and 'The Greek Alchemical Papyri', *Ciba Symposia*, vol. 3, no. 5, Summit, New Jersey, 1941

MIDDLE AGES AND ARABS

Albertus Magnus, Latin edition by Anton Zimara, containing: *De Physico Auditu, De Coelo et Mundo, De Generatione et Corruptione, De Methauris, De Mineralibus, De Anima, De Intellectu, De Metaphysica*, Venice, 1517–18

Albumazar, *De Magnis Conjunctionibus*, Venice, 1515
- *Flores Astrologiae* . . . , Venice, 1484

Arnaldo da Villanova, *Regimen Sanitatis*, trans. into English by Thomas Paynell, London, 1577

Bacon, Roger, *The Opus Majus*, trans. Robert Belle Burke, Philadelphia, 1928

Belot, Jean, *L'Art de mémoire de Raymond Lulle; les sciences stéganographiques, Paulines, Armadelles, Lullistes*; in: *Les Œuvres de Jean Belot* . . . , Lyon, 1649

Boethius, *La Consolation philosophique*, trans. Octave Cottreau, Paris, 1898

Bréhier, Louis, and René Aigrian, *Grégoire le Grand, les états barbares, et la conquête arabe*, Paris, 1938

Brown, James Wood, *An Inquiry into the Life of Michael Scot*, Edinburgh, 1897

Charles, Emil, *Roger Bacon, sa vie, ses ouvrages, ses doctrines, thèse par E. Ch.*, Bordeaux, 1861

Diepgen, Paul, *Arnald da Villanova als Politiker und Laientheologe*, Freiburg i/Br., 1908

Ferguson, John, *Bibliographical Notes on the Works of Michael Scot*, Glasgow, 1931

Keicher, Otto, *Raymundus Lullus und die Grundzüge seines philosophischen Systems* . . . , Münster, 1908

Lilly, William, *The Astrologer's Guide Containing 146 Considerations of the Famous Astrologer Guido Bonatus*, San Diego, Calif., 1918

Pietro d'Abano, *Conciliator Differentiarum Philosophorum*, Venice, 1520

Schreiber, Heinrich, *Beda Venerabilis und die mittelalterliche Bildung*, Munich, 1937

Scot, Michael, *The Texts of Michael Scot's Ars Alchemia*, ed. by S. Harrison Thomson, Bruges, 1938

Thorndike, Lynn, *The Writings of Peter of Abano*, Baltimore, 1944

DEVILS, SPIRITS, POSSESSIONS

Anania, Johannes Laurentius, *De Natura Daemonum Libri IIII*, Venetia, 1581

Barett, Francis, *The Magus or Celestial Intelligencer*, London, 1801

Boaistuau, Pierre, *Histoires prodigieuses*, Paris, 1561

Bosroger, Esprit du, *La Piété affligée, ou discours historique et théologique de la possession des religieuses dictes de St Élisabeth de Louviers*, Rouen, 1652

Caesarius of Heisterbach, *The Dialogue of Miracles*, trans. H. von E. Scott and C. C. Swinton Bland, London, 1929

Carus, Paul, *The History of the Devil and the Idea of Evil*, Chicago, 1900

Collin de Plancy, *Le Diable peint par lui-même*, Paris, 1825

Crespet, Célestin, *Deux livres de la hoyne de sathan*, Paris, 1590

Defoe, Daniel, *The History of the Devil, Ancient and Modern*, Durham, 1822

Grosius, Henningus, *Magica de Spectris*, Leyden, 1656

Lavater, Lewis, *Of Ghosts and Spirits Walking by Night*, intr. note by J. Dover and Mary Yardley, Oxford, 1921

le Loyer, Pierre, *Discours et histoires des spectres* . . . , Paris, 1605

Mengus, Hieronymus, *Flagellum Daemonum, Exorcismos Terribiles* . . . , Venice, 1697

Michaelis, Sébastien, *Pneumalogie ou discours des esprits* . . . , Paris, 1582

Perreaud, Fr., *Démonologie ou traité des démons* . . . , Geneva, 1653

Psellus, Michael, *Traicté par dialogue de l'énergie ou opération des diables*, Paris, 1577

Rosskoff, Gustav, *Geschichte des Teufels*, Leipzig, 1869

Schott, Caspar, *Physica Curiosa, Sive Mirabilia Naturae*, Würzburg, 1697

Sinistrari d'Ameno, L. M., *De la démonalité et des animaux incubes et succubes* . . . , trans, Isidor Liseux, Paris, 1876

Swinden, Tobias, *An Inquiry into the Nature and Place of Hell*, London, 1714

Taillepied, F. N., *Traicté de l'apparition des esprits* . . . , Lyon, 1582

Torquemade, Antoine de, *Héxameron, ou six journées*, Lyon, 1582

WITCHES, THEIR JUDGES AND DEFENDERS

Binsfeld, Peter, *Tractatus de Confessionibus Maleficorum et Sagarum* . . . , Trier, 1589

Bodin, Jean, *De la démonialité des sorciers*, Paris, 1582

Boguet, Henri, *Discours des sorciers* . . . , Lyon, 1603

Danaeus, Lambertus, *De Veneficiis* . . . , Paris, 1574

de Lancre, Pierre, *Tableau de l'inconstance des mauvais anges et démons* . . . , Paris, 1612

Delrio, Martin, *Disquisitionum Magicarum Libri sex* . . . , Louvain, 1599

Erastus, Thomas, *Deux dialogues de Th. E.* . . . *touchant le pouvoir des sorcières: et de la punition qu'elles méritent* . . . , Geneva, 1579
Godelmann, Johann Georg, *Bericht von den Zauberern, Hexen und Unholden* . . . , Frankfurt, 1592
Guaccius, Fr. Maria, *Compendium Maleficarum*, Milan, 1608
James I of England, *Daemonologie in Form of a Dialogue* . . . , London, 1603
Masini, Eliseo, *Sacro arsenale* . . . , Genova-Perugia, 1651
Molitor, Ulrich, *Von den Unholden oder Hexen* . . . , Constanz, 1498
Prierias, Sylvester, *De Strimigarum, Daemonumque* . . . , Rome, 1521
Remigius, Nicolas, *Demonolatry*, trans. E. A. Ashwin, London, 1930
Scot, Reginald, *The Discoverie of Witchcraft* . . . , London, 1665
Spee, Friedrich von, *Cautio Criminalis Seu de Processibus Contra Sagas* . . . , Cologne and Frankfurt, 1632
Sprenger, Jacob, and Kramer, Heinrich, *Malleus Maleficarum*, trans. Montague Summers, London, 1928
Wierus, Ioannes, *Histoires, disputes et discours des illusions et impostures des diables* . . . , Geneva, 1579

ASTROLOGY

Boll, Franz J., *Sternglaube und Sterndeutung*, Leipzig, 1926
Gauric, Luc, *Tractatus Astrologiae*, Venice, 1522
Junctin of Florence, *Accesserunt Etiam Commentaria* . . . , Lyon, 1583
Lilly, William, *Christian Astrology Modestly Treated of in Three Books* . . . , London, 1647
Morin de Villefranche, J. B., *Ad Australes et Boreales Astrologos, pro Restituenda Astrologia Epistolae*, Paris, 1628

MAGI

Adelung, G. Ch., *Geschichte der menschlichen Narrheit*, Leipzig, 1885–9, contains articles on Guido Bonatti, Guillaume Postel, Michel Nostradamus, etc.
Agrippa von Nettesheim, Cornelius, *The Vanity of Arts and Sciences* . . . , London, 1694
 – *Three Books of Occult Philosophy*, London, 1651
 – *Fourth Book of Occult Philosophy*, London, 1755
 – *Sur la noblesse et excellence du sexe féminin, de sa prééminence sur l'autre sexe, et du sacrement du mariage*, Leyden, 1726
Hartmann, Franz, *Theophrastus Paracelsus als Mystiker*, Leipzig (n.d.)
Morley, Henri, *Agrippa, Doctor and Knight* . . . , London, 1856
Paracelsus, *Opera Omnia*, Geneva, 1658
 – *Astronomia Magna oder die gantze Philosophia Sagax der grossen und der kleinen Welt* . . . , Frankfurt, 1571
Pelletier, A. le, *Les Oracles de Michel de Nostradamus*, Paris, 1867
Pico della Mirandola, Article by Lynn Thorndike, in *History of Magic and Experimental Science* (*q.v.*), vol. 3
Porta, Giovanbattista, *Della celeste fisonomia*, Padova, 1616
 – *De Humana Physiognomia Libri IV*, Rouen, 1650
 – *Phytognomonica Octo Libris Contenta* . . . , Rouen, 1650
 – *Natural Magic in XX Books*, London, 1658
Postel, Guillaume, *Absconditorum Clavis, ou la clef des choses cachées* . . . , Paris, 1899
 – *De Universitate Libri Duo*, Leyden, 1633

Spunda, Franz, *Paracelsus*, Vienna and Leipzig, 1925

Trithemius, Johannes, *Traité des causes secondes, précédé d'une vie de l'auteur, d'une bibliographie et d'une préface*, Paris, 1897
  – *Polygraphie et universelle escriture caballistique*, Paris, 1651

CABALA

Blau, Joseph, 'The Diffusion of the Christian Interpretation of the Cabala in English Literature', *The Review of Religion*, vol. 6, no. 2, New York, 1942

Fludd, Robert, *Mosaicall Philosophy Grounded upon the Essential Truth*, London, 1659

Franck, Ad., *La Kabbale ou la philosophie réligieuse des Hébreux*, Paris, 1892

Grillot de Givry, *Adumbratio Kabbalae Christianae* (in *Kabbala denudata*, 1677), trans. from the Latin, Paris, 1899

Knorr von Rosenroth, Christian, *Kabbala Denudata*, Sulzbach, 1677, and Frankfurt, 1684

Pistorius, Ioannes, *Artis Cabalisticae . . . , tomus primus . . .* , Basel, 1587

MAGICAL ARTS

Albertus Magnus, *Les Secrets merveilleux de la magie naturelle*, Lyon, 1786

Cardano, Girolamo, *Metoposcopia*, Paris, 1658

Cocles, Barthélémy, *Physiognomiae et Chiromantiae Compendium*, Strassburg, 1551

Etteilla, *Manière de se recréer avec le jeu de carte nommé les tarots*, Paris, 1783

Fludd, Robert, *Utriusque Cosmi Historia . . .* , Oppenheim, 1617–19

Indagine, Joannes de, *The Book of Palmistry*, London, 1676
  – *Chiromantia*, Strassburg, 1531

Peruchio, le Sieur, *La Chiromance*, Paris, 1657

Phinella, Philip, *De Metoposcopia*, Antwerp, 1648

Ronphyle, *La Chiromantie naturelle*, Paris, 1665

Saunders, Richard, *Physiognomie and Chiromancie . . .* , London, 1671

Schott, Kaspar, *Thaumaturgus Physicus*, Würzburg, 1659

Spontini, Ciro, *La metoposcopia*, Venetia, 1637

Taisner, Joh., *Opus Mathematicum*, Cologne, 1679

Tricassius, P., *Enumeratio Pulcherrima Principium Chiromantiae*, Nuremberg, 1560

Weckerus, Ioan. Jacobus, *De Secretis Libri VIII*, Basel, 1613

Wirth, Oswald, *Le Tarot des imagiers du moyen âge . . .* , Paris, 1927

REFORMERS

Andreae, Johann Valentin, *Chymische Hochzeit*, Strassburg, 1616
  – *Christianopolis Descriptio*, Strassburg, 1619

Baader, Franz von, *Les Enseignements secrets de Martines de Pasqually*, Paris, 1900

Fama Fraternitatis, beneben der Confession oder Bekanntnuss derselben Fraternität, Frankfurt, 1615

Fama Remissa ad Fratres Roseae Crucis . . . (n.p.), 1616

Fludd, Robert, *Summum Bonum* (n.p.), 1629

Hartmann, Franz, *The Secret Symbols of the Rosicrucians* (n.p., n.d.)

Libavius, Andreas, *Wohlmeinendes Bedencken von der Fama und Confession der Bruderschafft des Rosen Creutzes . . .* , Erfurt, 1616

Matter, Jacques, *Saint-Martin, le philosophe inconnu, sa vie et ses écrits*, Paris, 1862

Pernéty, Dom Antoine Joseph, *Les Fables égyptiennes et grecques dévoilées*, Paris, 1786

Saint-Martin, Claude Louis, *Tableau naturel des rapports qui existent entre Dieu, l'homme et l'univers*, 'Edimbourg', 1782

Swedenborg, Emmanuel, *Abrégé du traité des merveilles du ciel et de l'enfer, publié et annoté par J. H. Cahagnet*, Argenteuil, 1855

Villars, Montfaucon de, *The Count of Gabalis . . .* , London, 1680

Waite, Arthur E., *The Real History of the Rosicrucians*, New York, 1888

THE EIGHTEENTH CENTURY

Bila, Constantin, *La Croyance à la magie au XVIIIe siècle en France*, Paris, 1925

Boissier, A., *Recueil de lettres au sujet des maléfices et du sortilège . . .* , Paris, 1731

Bordelon, l'Abbé, *Voyages imaginaires*, including *Histoire de monsieur Oufle*, Paris, 1789

Calmet, Dom Augustin, *Traité historique et dogmatique sur les apparitions, les visions et les révélations particulières*, Paris, 1751

– *Traité sur les apparitions des esprits et sur les vampires . . .* , Sénones, 1759

Carré de Montgeron, *La Vérité des miracles opérés par l'intercession de M. de Pâris*, Utrecht, 1737

d'Alméras, Henri, *Cagliostro, la franc-maçonnerie et l'occultisme au XVIIIe siècle*, Paris, 1904

de Saint-André, M., *Lettres . . . au sujet de la magie, des maléfices et des sorciers . . .* , Paris, 1725

Delaulnay, F. H. S., *Thuileur des trente-trois degrés de l'écossisme . . .* , Paris, 1813

Descremps, M., *La Magie blanche dévoilée*, Paris, 1789

Fabre d'Olivet, *Un Médecin d'autrefois . . .* , Paris, 1836

Fiard, l'Abbé, *La France trompée par les magiciens et les démonolâtres*, Paris, 1803

Franck, Ad., *La Philosophie mystique en France au XVIIIe siècle*, Paris, 1866

Fritsche, Johann, *Mutmassliche Gedanken von den Vampyren oder blutsaugenden Toten*, Leipzig, 1732

Gouriet, J. B., *Les Charlatans célèbres . . .* , Paris, 1819

Lenglet-Dufresnoy, Nicolas, *Recueil de dissertations anciennes et nouvelles sur les apparitions, les visions et les songes*, Paris, 1751

Lenormand, Mademoiselle, *Souvenirs prophétiques d'une sibylle . . .* , Paris, 1814

Maine, Laroche du, *Mémoires authentiques pour servir à l'histoire du comte Cagliostro*, Hamburg, 1786

Mesmer, Friedrich Anton, *Précis historique des faits relatifs au magnétisme animal . . .* , London, 1781

Nerval, Gérard de, *Les Illuminés*, Paris, 1841

Ranfft, M. Michel, *Tractat von dem Kauen und Schmatzen der Toten in den Gräbern*, Leipzig, 1734

Restif de la Bretonne, Nicolas Edmé, *Suite du vade-mecum maçonnique*, Paris, 1841

Thiers, l'Abbé Jean-Baptiste, *Traité des superstitions . . .* , Paris, 1779

Vallemont, L. L. de, *La Physique occulte ou traité de la baguette divinatoire . . .* , Amsterdam, 1693

Zwinger, Th., *Dissertatio de Morbis a Fascino et Fascino Contra Morbos*, Basel, 1723

Index